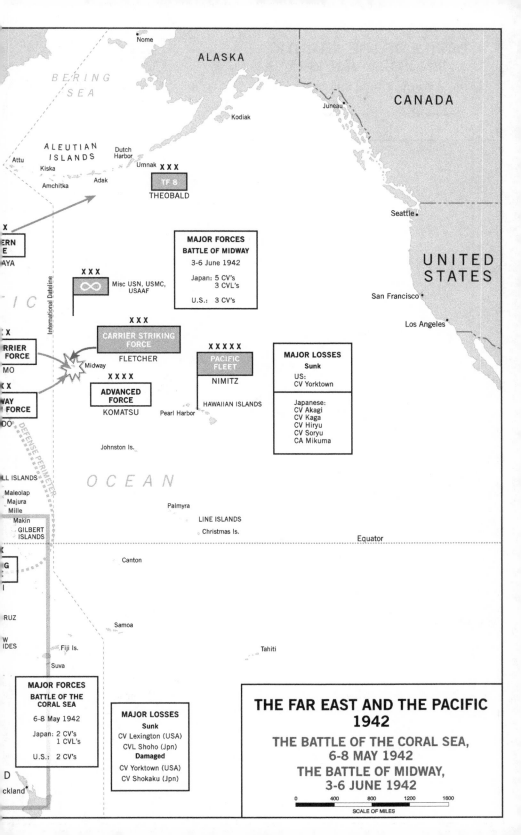

THE FAR EAST AND THE PACIFIC 1942

THE BATTLE OF THE CORAL SEA, 6-8 MAY 1942

THE BATTLE OF MIDWAY, 3-6 JUNE 1942

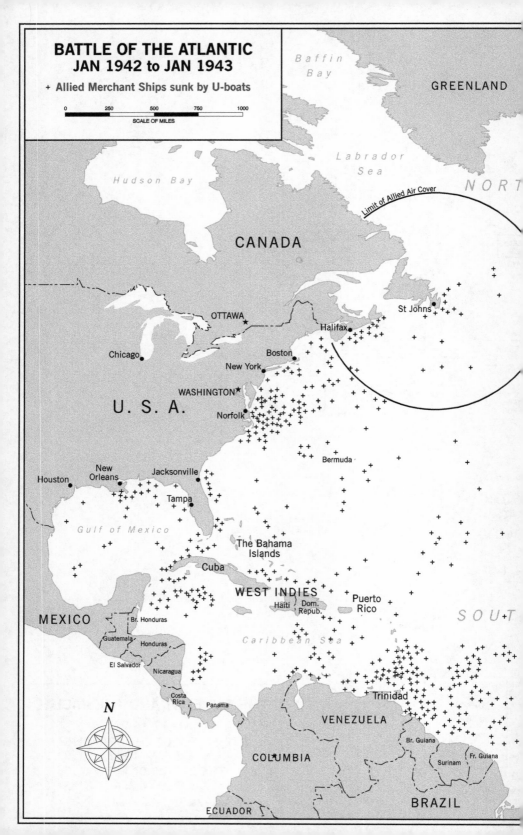

BATTLE OF THE ATLANTIC
JAN 1942 to JAN 1943

+ Allied Merchant Ships sunk by U-boats

0   250   500   750   1000
SCALE OF MILES

Baffin Bay

GREENLAND

Labrador Sea

Hudson Bay

NORT

Limit of Allied Air Cover

CANADA

St Johns

OTTAWA

Halifax

Chicago

Boston

New York

WASHINGTON

U. S. A.

Norfolk

Bermuda

Houston

New Orleans

Jacksonville

Tampa

Gulf of Mexico

The Bahama Islands

Cuba

WEST INDIES

Haiti   Dom. Repub.

Puerto Rico

SOUT

MEXICO

Br. Honduras

Caribbean Sea

Guatemala

Honduras

El Salvador

Nicaragua

Costa Rica

Panama

Trinidad

VENEZUELA

N

Br. Guiana

COLUMBIA

Surinam

Fr. Guiana

ECUADOR

BRAZIL

Also by Winston Groom

Better Times Than These
As Summers Die
Only
Conversations with the Enemy
  (with Duncan Spencer)
Forrest Gump
Shrouds of Glory
Gone the Sun
Gumpisms
Gump & Co.
Such a Pretty, Pretty Girl
The Crimson Tide
A Storm in Flanders

1942 ★

The Year that Tried Men's Souls

Winston Groom

Grove Press
New York

Published simultaneously in Canada
Printed in the United States of America

Library of Congress Cataloging-in-Publication Data
Groom, Winston, 1944–
   1942 : the year that tried men's souls / Winston Groom.
      p. cm.
   ISBN 978-0-8021-4250-4
   eISBN 978-1-55584-778-4
   1. World War, 1939–1945.   I. Title.
   D755.4.G76 2005
   940.53—dc22   2004062779

Grove Press
an imprint of Grove Atlantic
154 West 14th Street
New York, NY 10011

Distributed by Publishers Group West

groveatlantic.com

In memory of my parents, both of whom did their part
when their nation called

"The Axis knew that they must win the war in 1942 or lose everything."
  —Franklin Delano Roosevelt, State of the Union speech, January 6, 1943

"Now, this is not the end, it is not even the beginning of the end. But it is, perhaps, the end of the beginning."
  —Winston Churchill, November 10, 1942

Foreword

To the generation of Americans who lived through it, the Second World War was the defining event of the twentieth century, much as the Civil War had been eighty years earlier. Those born in the first part of the century who came of age in the 1930s and '40s routinely began to describe almost every event and memory of their lives as having occurred "before the war," "during the war," or "after the war."

It was the most dangerous and deadly conflict ever inflicted on the planet. At stake was the fate of the world. If the war had been lost to the Axis powers, modern civilization would have fallen under the sway of cruel tyrants and the world perhaps subjected to another forty generations of darkness, as it was after the barbarians conquered the Roman empire. No nation was safe from the evil, whether it chose to be neutral or not; it was spreading like a cancer across the world.

Twenty years earlier a savage four-year-long war had been fought in Europe, Africa, and the Middle East between the Western democracies, Russia, and the German–Austria-Hungarian empires over control of those same areas. The Germans lost and were subjected to a harsh peace. This was the Great War, and, in the hopeful eyes of many, the War to End all Wars. Later it became known as the world war but, finally, just the First World War, to distinguish it from what came later.

The truce of 1918, followed by the peace of 1919, did not last long. Whereas the rulers of Germany in 1914 and her allies who provoked World War I were—to use the term in its most generous sense—at least "gentlemen," the leaders of the Axis powers in 1941 were thugs. They were, most of them, amoral murderers and brutish torturers who gained power through assassination and corruption, and more than sixty years after the fact this remains a stubborn truth.

That is not to say that America, Great Britain, and the other Allied nations were always on the side of the angels. Joseph Stalin in his totalitarian Soviet Union was certainly a great monster, as the Russian people finally now can, and will, freely admit. But war often makes strange bedfellows, and the Western democracies' alliance with the Soviet communists, however expedient or necessary, was among the strangest.

If the Second World War defined the twentieth century, then the year 1942 can be understood as having defined the war itself. It was the most perilous of times; for the United States and its allies, the first six months of that year saw a relentless flood of military disasters with the Axis almost everywhere victorious—especially in the Pacific, where Imperial Japan conquered territory after territory, despite the most strenuous efforts to stop them. In the minds of many Americans the final outcome of the war was in doubt.

Into this roiling, fearful, fateful year I was conceived, as were many others of the so-called war-babies generation. I was not born into a family of warriors, although practically every generation of it has served in one American war or another, from the War of Independence and the War of 1812, to the Creek Indian wars and the Civil War, to the Spanish-American War and the First World War.

Now came my father's turn. Like many young men of his day he was a member of the National Guard, an institution that each of the states maintains under federal guidance and law to keep the peace and, more important, provide the structure for a responsive army in case of a national emergency. This emergency soon came as war clouds gathered over Europe and the Pacific, and practically all national guardsmen found themselves on the front lines during the first year of the war.

The National Guard was both a social and a military organization in most southern states, and in my home state of Alabama this was certainly the case. Fine dinners and balls were held in the Fort Whiting National Guard Armory, an imposing three-story white stone structure alongside Mobile Bay. In faded photograph albums there are pictures of my father, escorting my mother, soon to be his fiancée, in his dress uniform, complete with sword and formal military regalia. But of course there was also the serious side, and as war broke out with the Japanese attack on Pearl Harbor, my father was ordered to Fort Riley, Kansas, with, of all things, a regiment of horse cavalry.

These "horse soldiers" were already an anachronism, but in the military services traditions die hard, and so my father, then thirty-six years old, found himself at the reins of a large animal on the plains of Kansas, practicing tactics and maneuvers long rendered archaic by the evolution of modern warfare. Not long afterward his bemusement was relieved when somebody at headquarters discovered that he was, by trade, an attorney, and as the U.S. War Department had almost completed an enormous structure in Arlington, Virginia, known as the Pentagon* he was requested to report there and assume lawyerly duties as a captain in the U.S. Army Judge Advocate General's Corps.

It was in the little military chapel at nearby Fort Myer, Virginia, that my parents were wed, in 1942, and there, at Garfield Hospital across the Potomac River in Washington, D.C., that I was born the following year. My father's side of the family was American by many generations but my mother's was first-generation Norwegian. Her father, Mathias Knudsen, my grandfather, came here in 1899 as a ship's captain with the United Fruit Company. While in Washington my mother worked tirelessly with the Norwegian embassy (then in exile) raising funds for that beleaguered country of her parent's heritage. Today on a wall in my study is an elaborate thank-you proclamation in her honor from the King of Norway, whose son, King

*At that point, in fact, the Pentagon was the largest building in the world.

Olaf IV, once paid a personal visit to our family twenty-odd years later. The note begins: "Dear Mrs. Knudsen Groom, His Majesty the King of Norway wishes to thank you . . ." And so that complex mix of Americans served however they could.

As the years passed and the war ended and I grew older I clearly remember sitting at large family dinners where my father, mother, aunts, uncles, grandparents, and guests spoke the far-off language of adults, the sentences of which were almost always preceded by "Before the war . . . ," "During the war . . . ," and "After the war . . ." But to me and to my cousins and friends, in truth, the war was something that had happened long ago, to a different generation, *their* generation, in different, distant times.*

Later, at school, we got a smattering of the war's history and import. Since mine was a military school, we probably got more of a smattering than most, but it was covered generally in the courses on United States history, and probably more was discussed about the American Civil War than World War II. Still later, in college, I had my most meaningful acquaintance with the magnitude of the world war. I had decided to take a summer correspondence course after my junior year in order to be less fettered with academic concerns during my final year, which I had intended to spend in splendid debauchery. To that end I selected a subject called "United States Naval History," which I thought would be both easy and fun. It was neither. It was without qualification the hardest course I ever took in college and, despite the fact that one could use any text available and write from it, I almost failed the thing. (In the end I pulled out a low "B.")

The professor at the university who taught this intellectually demanding (I could use the word "cruel") subject had been a naval officer in the Pacific during the war. His texts were *Sea Power* by Alfred Thayer

*A great story, apocryphal or not, was once told by Mark Twain, recounting how he went down the Mississippi River just after the Civil War had ended and arrived at a fashionable party on a plantation near New Orleans as a full silver moon came rising up against the live oaks and magnolias. Twain remarked, offhand, to one of the black serving women on how lovely and full the moon was that night. Her response, handing him a mint julep, was, "Oh yessir it shore is, but you ought to have seen that moon befo' de war!"

Mahan, *The Two-Ocean War* by Samuel Eliot Morison, and *The Great Sea War* by Admiral Chester Nimitz and E. B. Potter. It was then that I began to understand the enormity and perils of the war, especially in the Pacific during 1942, and the suffering and sacrifices that attended it. I learned in detail of the disaster at Pearl Harbor, December 7, 1941, a sneak attack on America by a band of fanatically religious emperor-worshipers who became the first to practice suicide airplane attacks.* I was astonished by the fantastic lack of preparedness and foresight that caused the loss of the Philippines along with General Douglas MacArthur's entire 120,000-man army, by the wreckage of the American Pacific and Far East fleets and the week-by-week Japanese conquests of nearly all of the Pacific Ocean territory from the Aleutian Islands in Alaska to the Australian continent in the South Seas.

Born when I was, it was my luck good or bad to come of military age just as the Vietnam War reached its most pitiless intensity and, having served there, I began to take an interest in wars and warfare for it seemed to me even at that younger age that this would be, regrettably, a permanent condition of mankind, at least in my time, and, more or less, I have been writing about war ever since. Over the years this has led to an evident conclusion: that most wars, like all great dramas, have a single, seminal act that defines the future course of events. During the Second World War, that act was played out in the menacing year of 1942.

After the barbarous attacks on the World Trade Center and the Pentagon on September 11, 2001, it was easy to recollect that the tale of America in 1942 also began as one of shock, uncertainty, and fear, beginning with Pearl Harbor. Even though 1942 ended in triumph over Axis expansion, to most people that triumph was only partially clear at the time; anyone with a brain knew there was a long, bitter, and uncertain fight ahead, until these powerful enemies were contracted back from whence they had come.

One expects this will be so, too, with the present war against international terrorism—a world war in every sense of the word—and one point

*As many have recently remarked, Pearl Harbor has eerie parallels to the events of September 11, 2001.

of this story is to recall for the reader what Americans can do when they get mad and set their minds to something. Terrorist organizations have been in existence at least since the mid-1800s, no doubt even earlier, throwing bombs and gunning down symbols of the power they have resented, mainly European royalty, aristocracy, and its representatives. In those days they were called anarchists, and they even bombed Wall Street and the New York Stock Exchange; for that matter, a terrorist act actually touched off World War I. The important difference in present times is the firepower modern terrorists can bring to bear, their relentless religious fervor, and their callous disregard for innocent civilians and even their own lives.

While I have tried to bring as much fresh material as possible to this tale of tragedy and triumph in the year 1942, some of the stories will be familiar, perhaps even old hat to those who devour every scrap of detail about the Second World War. While I hope they will enjoy it too, it is not for them that I write but to the average American reader, in hopes that he or she will take renewed pride in what our forefathers dealt with, and determined to accomplish, when faced with danger of the utmost severity. The focus of this story is on the American ordeal during 1942, its tragedy and triumph, and those of the ally it fought with so closely then, Great Britain; I have not gone into extensive detail to catalogue the heroic fight of the Soviet Union during this time because it would require a separate book to do it justice.

Following the Pearl Harbor disaster, America was in grave military danger. Most of our Pacific fleet and air force no longer existed and the Japanese were running amok all over that ocean and in the Far East, banging at the very gates of Australia and India and even invading U.S. territory in Alaska. America was almost totally unprepared for war and would not be fully equipped for another year. By a wide margin she was losing the battle of the Atlantic to German submarines, and the U.S. fighting forces were nowhere near to being properly trained and ready to fight. That they did so anyway—so that by the end of 1942 the worldwide Axis onrush was blunted for good—should be considered nothing less than awe-inspiring.

Chapter One ★

World War II descended on planet earth as swift and deadly as a desert whirlwind, but the forces that unleashed its terrible power had been building beyond the horizon for years. Whole libraries exist to house only the books that grapple with the roots and causes but, as most wars do, it boils down to three simple things: pride, property, and power—and two more complicated things: prejudice and persecution. With this in mind I believe it is useful for readers of this story to have an appreciation, however abbreviated, of the events leading up to the critical year of 1942, and in that spirit a concise narration is offered.

Germany's role of instigating the conflict is better understood than that of the Japanese. The Nazi militarists had arisen bitter and venomous from the bones and ashes of the First World War, convinced that they had been stabbed in the back by their own cowardly politicians and the Jews—these latter perceived as either communists (the poorer ones) or war profiteers (the rich). Added to that was the loathing that practically all Germans felt over the terms of the Treaty of Versailles, which the Allied Powers, principally France and England, imposed upon Germany following the armistice of 1918. Among other things, this document stripped the Germans of 25,000 square miles of their territory, which included vast amounts of its raw materials such as coal, ores, and oil, as well as all of its overseas colonies and practically all of its military armaments. Most gallingly, it required the German people to pay "war reparations" to the victors to the tune of many billions of dollars. Germany struggled under these conditions, plagued by labor strikes (ultimately, so they claimed, forced on them by the Jews) and other internal strife, for the next ten years.

Then in 1929 the American stock market crashed, setting into motion a worldwide economic depression. In Germany, monetary inflation at one point reached such stupendous proportions that a mere loaf of bread cost a *million* or more German marks! At the normal ratio of four marks to the dollar, this was devastating, and many Germans saw their life's savings wiped out almost overnight.*

Finally there was the matter of German honor. Up until the very moment in 1918 when the Germans sought an armistice, that nation's people were persuaded by its leaders and the press to believe that they were only a few footsteps away from total victory. News of their defeat came as an unbelievable shock. This was where the stabbed-in-the-back theory came into play. The American army had arrived on the scene in force just six months before the cease-fire was requested by Germany, but the American commander in chief, General John J. Pershing, was all for marching into Berlin anyway, herding the German army before him with all of its soldiers' hands in the air.[1]

This was the only way, Pershing declared, that the German people would believe they had been beaten. But France and Britain, exhausted by four years of slaughter in the trenches of the Western Front, disagreed about further military action, and their view prevailed. Thus the Germans increasingly came to think that they had not been beaten at all, but had been betrayed by dishonorable politicians (backed by Jews) who gave up the fight before victory could be won. Humiliation is a stern taskmaster,

*It has been argued, though not conclusively proven, that the German government intentionally printed money to devalue its own mark and thus avoid paying the hated war reparations. In other words, if the German mark became almost valueless, then the amount previously designated to be paid to the victors under the Versailles Treaty would be nearly valueless also.

and the Germans had long memories. Thus some historians, and many others, are of the opinion that the Second World War was merely an extension of the First World War, with a twenty-year "rest period" in between.

Into this combustible mix entered Adolf Hitler, a cranky aspiring Austrian artist who had served as a corporal in the German army from 1914 to 1918. Having been decorated with the Iron Cross, Hitler emerged from the First World War even more bitter than most of the rest of his adopted countrymen. By 1922 he had assembled about him a clique of like-minded people who called themselves Nazis (National Socialist Party) and who distributed pamphlets such as *Bolshevism from Moses to Lenin,* which attempted to prove that "Judaism was the great destructive force which had ruined Western Civilization."[2] Psychiatrists have diagnosed Hitler's case history as that of a "psychopathic escapist type with a complex effecting megalomania." Historians smugly described him as someone who had "escaped from his *case* history into *world* history, before the psychiatrists got him."[3]

The Nazis were a disturbing grab bag of thugs, criminals, zealots, and dupes aided by not a few misguided aristocrats and otherwise intelligent people such as General Erich Ludendorff, who had masterminded the German army in World War I and nearly engineered a German victory in 1918. In 1923 Hitler felt strong enough to challenge the new Weimar government but only got himself thrown in jail, where he penned his grimly prophetic *Mein Kampf* (my struggle). This seven-hundred-page screed, published in 1925, was the blueprint for Nazi dictatorship (with Hitler himself, of course, as dictator), advocating ethnic cleansing and aggressive territorial expansion, and has been described as "a satanic Bible."[4] It remains a great curse that so few people in positions of power have ever read it, or understood its sordid implications.

Thereafter, Hitler and his cronies organized themselves into a kind of paramilitary party, goose-stepping up and down the streets in brown shirts and displaying the swastika* as their national emblem. Yearly their

*The swastika consists of two interlocking Greek crosses, thought by the ancient Germans to bring good luck.

power grew, feeding off hatred, intimidation, resentment over the Versailles Treaty, staggering unemployment, leftist labor strikes, and the seeming inability of the new democratic Weimar government to solve the nation's problems.

By 1933 the Nazi party had gained not only enough votes to make itself a formidable force in the German Reichstag (parliament) but also enough power to force the eighty-six-year-old president, Paul von Hindenburg, to appoint Hitler chancellor, from which position he quickly consolidated his strength and seized total control of the German government, setting it up as a brutal police state. Calling himself "Der Führer" (the leader), Hitler then set about pacifying the seething German nation, building the vast autobahns, housing projects, and industrial plants, and, of course, repudiating payment of any more war reparations.

Also, from that point on, Hitler and his Nazis began a stealthy but deliberate program to rearm Germany with the most modern weapons, converting otherwise peaceful businesses into war-making enterprises. Even though the Treaty of Versailles forbade the Germans from having a naval fleet, tanks, heavy artillery, and an air force, the Nazis brazenly defied the Allied nations and the new League of Nations—forerunner to the United Nations, set up in 1919 to maintain world peace—and continued creating what would become one of the most powerful military forces in history.*

Still horrified by the slaughter of the 1914–1918 war, as well as financially devastated by it, and caught up like everyone else in the worldwide depression, France and England did nothing to head off Hitler's warlike machinations. The great pity is that they easily could have, at least at the beginning; France's army alone outnumbered Hitler's infantry divisions by more than ten to one. But the mood in the so-called Great Democracies was quiescent, perhaps, more accurately, ostrichlike, while Hitler fulminated from the speaking platforms of huge outdoor stadiums and the German people became true believers, eagerly and delectably cheering every violation of the Treaty of Versailles.

*For instance, in order to avoid international reaction to the building of a formal air force, the Germans organized presumably harmless civilian "flying clubs" in which young men were secretly taught by World War I flying veterans all the techniques of aerial combat.

Not only that but the Nazis began to fulfill their grisly prophecy of ridding the nation of all but their own concept of a pure Aryan (Nordic) race. Millions of Jews, Gypsies, Slavs, and anyone else unlucky and un-Aryan enough to be caught in Germany from the mid-1930s onward were subjected to almost unendurable hardships and indignities and, in many cases, death. First, Nazi victims were stripped of their citizenship, then their property, then the right to practice their trades and professions. Finally, they were herded into concentration camps, which, beginning in 1942, became death camps. Those who had been unable to emigrate or escape were worked or starved to death, and many were murdered by firing squad and, later, more efficiently, in gas chambers.

In Italy, meanwhile, a similar though somewhat lesser evil had been at work. Benito Mussolini, like Hitler, had fought in World War I and, also like Hitler, appeared to be promising material for psychiatric study. The child of socialist parents, Mussolini was editing a socialist newspaper in 1914 when the war broke out and quickly became a draft dodger until the authorities caught up with him in 1916 and marched him into the army. At war's end, great labor strikes paralyzed Italy, many organized by Italian communists. Mussolini, who has been described variously as a crude bully, an atheist (in Catholic Italy!), and a womanizer, soon abandoned his socialism and in 1922 he became the leader of what was called the Fascist party, a group consisting primarily of former soldiers who had by a decade presaged Hitler's Nazi "brownshirts" by adopting their own "blackshirts" and strutting around town beating up anyone who disagreed with them.

Many of the early Italian fascists simply wanted jobs or for the government to halt the chaos and run the country effectively, but Mussolini had a far greater plan: he envisioned an Italy returned to the glory days of the Roman empire (with himself, naturally, as a Caesar). Like Hitler, Mussolini could legitimately be described as a comical character, right down to his dress and the hands-on-hips posturing—like something out of Laurel and Hardy pictures—were it not for the fact that he was a brutal dictator who murdered people at the drop of a hat.

He called himself "Il Duce" (the leader), "a superman, in the words of Nietzsche, with whom of course he agreed," and became a much-celebrated windbag among disaffected Italians.[5] It was said that "he made the trains run on time," and this was true enough, but at dear cost to any tardy train-man. In 1922, four years after the armistice to end World War I, Mussolini and his fascists—now comprised of a huge throng of gangsters as well as the ex-soldiers and other well-wishers—marched on Rome, and for their efforts the hapless king of Italy anointed Mussolini prime minister. As Hitler was to do later, Mussolini quickly consolidated his power, abolished parliament, and became a totalitarian ruler. In a move that Hitler would also emulate, Mussolini forthwith outlawed all political parties except his own fascists and set about turning Italy into his personal vision of a great empire. First, though, he made certain improvements on the domestic scene, as Hitler was to do later, building much-needed housing and roads and getting industries operating again, mainly the armaments industry. For this he was publicly admired by such diverse personalities as Thomas A. Edison, the playwright George Bernard Shaw, and Mohandas Gandhi.

Then, perceiving correctly that one cannot have an empire without colonies, Mussolini decided to acquire more of these for himself. In 1935 he mandated that every male between the ages of eighteen and thirty-five be subjected to military service. As a victim of colonial conquest Mussolini selected the peaceful and undeveloped African nation of Abyssinia (Ethiopia), just down the Red Sea from the Mediterranean. It was one of the few African countries not yet colonized by other powers and, besides, the Italians had lost an important and humiliating battle there at the end of the previous century, and this still rankled. Ruled for years by its hereditary emperor Haile Selassie, who sat on a throne draped in leopard skins, this poor tribal land was hardly a match for Mussolini's new army of tanks, artillery, and air force bombs. Testing every weapon in the Italian arsenal, including poison gas, which had been outlawed by worldwide treaty, Mussolini's army slaughtered an estimated 500,000 Ethiopian natives and subjugated the rest. The League of Nations condemned Italy but took no action, thus paving the way for mid-twentieth-century dictators to flout the international democracies' efforts to contain them.

In 1937 Mussolini met Hitler for the first time and was suspicious of him (the feeling was mutual) but, dictators being dictators, Mussolini agreed as a sop to Der Führer to strip Italian Jews of all their civil rights and, for some odd reason as well, to adopt the German "goose step" as the official Italian army marching cadence. Two years later, on the eve of World War II, he and Hitler signed their names to what was called the Pact of Steel, a fateful decision for everyone concerned, which created the first two of what would soon become known as the Axis powers.

With the Nazi rise the Germans, particularly the warlike Prussians, were becoming more belligerent by the moment. The whole nation seemed to be on some kind of war footing, including teenage German "youth groups," who paraded around in khaki short-pant uniforms shouting *Heil Hitler!* at everyone they passed on the streets. The "stabbed-in-the-back" theory assumed renewed national importance, spurred on by state-sponsored propagandists who had begun shortly after the end of the 1914–1918 war to distribute all sorts of material aiming to prove that Germany was not responsible for starting World War I.

This disinformation soon reached foreign shores, including Great Britain and America, where revisionist scholars began publishing books and articles denouncing German "war guilt" and laying blame for the great conflict on France, England, Russia, and even the United States.* Hitler's ranting diatribes merely fueled the flames of this fiery new nationalism, born of the humiliation of defeat and the urge to avenge its perceived dishonor.

One of the main grievances the Germans had was the dismemberment of part of what it considered its own territory by the Allied victors who in 1919 had created the independent states of Poland, Austria, and Czechoslovakia and returned to France the Alsace-Lorraine provinces, which had been seized by Germany in 1871. These separate entities contained some seven million German-speaking citizens, and the Fatherland,

*Led by German-American academics and writers, and their associates, this soon resulted in what became known in scholarly politics as the "textbook wars."

as defined by Hitler and his associates, wanted them back. Here lay the immediate bones of contention that would eventually rattle and herald World War II.

There was something else in Hitler's mind, too, more momentous than merely occupying or reoccupying such small-potato territories as Poland, Austria, and Czechoslovakia. This was his doctrine of *lebensraum* (living space), in which he hoped to relocate into huge areas of Europe Germany's overpopulation of millions of peasants. And where was he to find this immense *lebensraum*? In Hitler's own words, taken from his *Secret Book,* a sort of sequel to *Mein Kampf:* "The only area in Europe that could be considered for such a territorial policy therefore was Russia."[6]

One of the first statesmen to read true danger in the Hitler regime was the British parliamentarian Winston Churchill, and he remained a lone voice in the wilderness until it was far too late to halt the German juggernaut. The policy of both his country and France, the only two European states then powerful enough when combined to have stopped Hitler, was one of "appeasement." But the victors of World War I had lost their stomach for war, or even the prospect of it. The year that Hitler came into power the prestigious Oxford Union, a student debating society, overwhelmingly approved a motion stating that "this House will in no circumstances fight for its King and Country," and within a short period similar resolutions were adopted by most of England's other colleges and universities. When in 1934 it became apparent that the Germans were swiftly rearming, the leader of the British Labour Party vowed "to close every recruiting station, disband the Army and disarm the Air Force," and he got his candidate elected by saying so.[7] The Peace Ballot, a national survey of public opinion, was distributed throughout Great Britain in 1935 and a majority of those polled stated that while they supported collective national security, they did so only "by all means short of war."

At a time when Hitler was openly flouting the Versailles Treaty by building up his army strength to exceed that of England and France combined, those two nations were cutting their military budgets to the bone, and Britain's new Labour Party leader, Clement Attlee, was declaring:

"We on our side are for total disarmament because we are realists." Antiwar literature inspired by the World War I generation, such as Robert Graves's *Goodbye to All That,* the poetic works of Siegfried Sassoon and Edmund Blunden, Erich Maria Remarque's *All Quiet on the Western Front,* as well as stage plays such as R. C. Sherriff's passionately convincing *Journey's End,* had become extremely popular and added to the growing notion that all war was a stupid, wasteful, unacceptable enterprise. This was not a bad notion at all, except that Adolf Hitler had no such innocent visions and kept a careful eye on what he perceived as the pacific mood of the "decadent democracies," which he gleefully realized were playing right into his hands.

The only other European power remotely capable of dealing with Hitler at the time was the communist behemoth of the Soviet Union, which, since its inception in 1917, had been cloaked in a dark veil of secrecy. Its leader, Joseph Stalin, had succeeded Lenin and was as tyrannical a brute as Hitler and Mussolini ever hoped to be. During the 1930s Stalin purged his vast army of almost all its useful officers—as if the word *purge,* with its ironically sanitary connotation, could do justice to the wholesale murder this tyrant inflicted on his victims. Despite Hitler's and Mussolini's constant and fanatical ravings against the evils of communism, Stalin seemed blithely unaware of Hitler's designs on his country. He therefore kept quiet and inscrutable in Moscow and adopted a wait-and-see attitude, concentrating his considerable energies on converting Soviet Russia from an agrarian peasantry into an industrial giant. Thus the Nazis, and their cohorts the Italian fascists, were left with practically a free hand to work their aggressive machinations against their weaker neighbors.

Only one other force existed that might have stopped Hitler and the Axis powers during the dark days when the war clouds began to loom over Europe. This was the United States of America, comfortably safe (or so it was generally thought) on the other side of the Atlantic with even less inclination than France and England to get itself embroiled in another European conflict. Since the days of George Washington's presidency, Americans had taken heed of the warning to "avoid all foreign entanglements."

Their mood by and large had become one of disillusionment and disappointment that the Europeans after World War I seemed to have learned nothing from that hideous slaughter and appeared headed for another senseless and savage contest. And who could blame them?

A large part of the American constituency felt that they had seen all this before. After promising in 1916—in order to get reelected—that "American boys will not be sent to war overseas," President Woodrow Wilson soon realized the dangers posed by the great conflagration in Europe and by 1917 had asked Congress for a declaration of war against Germany and its allies. When he got it, American soldiers began pouring into France, and the weight of their numbers is generally credited with Germany's ultimate suit for peace. Wilson, however, had a greater plan in mind. After trying for two years to mediate between the warring nations, he produced his Fourteen Points, which included the slogan "Peace Without Victory," the notion of self-determination for all nations, and a plan for a League of Nations that would somehow provide collective security throughout the world and prevent any reoccurrence of the "War to End All Wars." Most of Wilson's scheme was quickly blown apart at the Versailles Peace Conference, and though the League of Nations was indeed established it was so, to Wilson's great chagrin, without the support of America, whose Congress wanted no part of any "world government."

Throughout the 1920s and 1930s America's post–World War I military might was virtually dismantled in favor of domestic programs—especially after the Great Depression deepened. Its army and navy were not only neglected but almost forgotten. The American attitude became again one of "Europe's problems are Europe's problems," and a wave of isolationism began to take hold in the country, especially in the Midwest, where the mostly right-wing newspapers (with their many Germanic subscribers) inveighed heavily and often against American involvement in European and Far Eastern troubles. This was due in part to the aforementioned wave of so-called revisionist scholars and historians during the 1930s who had removed the blame for the First World War from Germany and placed it upon France and England. In addition, there was an all-out effort by American leftists, pacifists, isolationists, and socialists to publicly denounce munitions makers and war financiers such as

J. P. Morgan as being largely responsible for all the misery caused by that war, or any war. And there was the fact of the Kellogg-Briand peace pact of 1928, signed into international law by the U.S. Congress, Britain, France, and other nations, including Germany, which actually *outlawed* war, but which, in fact, had no more validity than the passing of laws against invention of perpetual motion machines.

The American left still clung to the notion of the League of Nations, even though the U.S. Senate had refused to ratify the agreement.* After all, the League was perhaps the penultimate experiment in idealism, as typified by Harold Nicolson in a passage from his book *Peacemaking 1919* where he describes his emotions upon attending the first conference of the Treaty of Versailles in 1919 as a young British diplomat: "We were journeying to Paris, not merely to liquidate the war, but to found a new order in Europe. We were preparing not Peace only, but Eternal Peace. There was about us the halo of some divine mission. We must be alert, stern, righteous and ascetic. For we were bent on doing great, permanent and noble things." Much irony attaches to these stirring words, since Nicolson did not write them until years later, in 1933, when the world had again begun marching down the tragic path of war.

In any event, Hitler loved it: cowardly decadent idealistic democracies, forever arguing among themselves and letting their people vote on everything!

And so the kettle heated with no one, so to speak, minding the stove, except perhaps for Winston Churchill, whose increasingly shrill but prophetic warnings fell on mostly deaf ears. Churchill, who turned sixty years old in 1934, was by then a humpty-dumpty-looking man, in stark contrast with his dashing appearance as a young British officer who had captured his nation's fancy with a series of on-the-spot newspaper and magazine pieces

---

*If in fact the U.S. Congress had ratified the League of Nations treaty and put its considerable teeth behind it, things could have turned out differently. But by then the United States, in the throes of the Great Depression, had dismantled its "considerable teeth," like most of the Allied nations, and its armed forces by the early 1930s ranked behind even the country of Portugal.

on British army exploits before World War I. As a member of government during that war he ran the Admiralty until his insistence on the disastrous Gallipoli campaign forced him to resign and he joined his old regiment in the terrible trenches in Flanders. Always controversial, Churchill floundered between the wars, and except for a brief stint as chancellor of the Exchequer and colonial secretary in the 1920s, he held on on to his parliamentary office but did not receive another major appointment to government. As Hitler came to power, Churchill reached the height of his oratorical powers, and his alarms against both the Nazi menace and England's unpreparedness to meet it if heeded might well have saved the nation some of the wretched ordeal it was soon to undergo.

In 1936 Hitler made his move. He marched troops into the Rhineland, a direct violation of the Versailles Treaty, which had set up that area along the French-German border as a demilitarized zone. The French and British squawked but did nothing. Hitler, for his part, made a series of false promises such as: "We have no territorial intentions in Europe. . . . Germany will never break the peace." Thus was the pattern Hitler repeated until the outbreak of total war, and it very often worked. He even tricked old Arnold Toynbee, best known among British historians, who returned from a visit with Hitler convinced of "the Fuhrer's sincerity in desiring peace in Europe and close friendship with England."[8]

True to form, Hitler next marched on Austria and annexed it to the Nazi empire; again the Western democracies did nothing. It was true that the Austrians did not resist and many even welcomed Hitler's storm troopers with flowers and cheering, but it was another flagrant violation of the Treaty of Versailles. Next it was Czechoslovakia's turn, and both England and France were finally and thoroughly alarmed. Czechoslovakia had been carved out of the old Austro-Hungarian empire in accordance with the Versailles settlement. Hitler had been making threatening gestures toward this peaceful neighbor ever since the *Anschluss* (the annexing of Austria), and France was actually sworn by treaty to protect it, but was unwilling to do so without British support. The British now began to feel they were being slowly sucked into a war on the continent that they did not want, and during the month of September 1938, there was a sort of collective foot stomping and hand wringing throughout the United Kingdom.

Der Führer's pretext this time was that there were some three million German-speaking citizens living in Sudaten Czechoslovakia who were unhappy at being separated from their Fatherland. Meantime, the British government was desperately seeking some way to placate Hitler. Prime Minister Neville Chamberlain, who not only had suffered the abomination of the First World War but had lost two close relatives in it, went on a last-minute journey to Munich to dissuade Hitler from dismantling Czechoslovakia. He failed miserably. Hitler wound up persuading Chamberlain to agree that Germany could control all Czech areas in which German-speakers were a majority. Here was a perfect example of the old Arab proverb about never allowing a camel to get its nose into your tent lest the rest of the camel soon be inside as well. In any case, the Czechs themselves were not consulted in this betrayal.

The tall, bowler-hatted, wing-collared, umbrella-carrying Chamberlain arrived back in London waving the agreement with Hitler and declaring "peace in our time."* For the most part the British and the French held their noses but also managed to breathe a sigh of relief. One of those who did not sigh with relief was Churchill, who declared, "We have passed an awful milestone in our history . . . the whole equilibrium of Europe has been disarranged."[9] He denounced the Munich agreement as cowardly, and in a towering prophetic rage he roared, "The government had to choose between shame and war. They have chosen shame, and now they will get war."

As if on cue six months later, in March 1939, Hitler's storm troopers moved in and annexed all of Czechoslovakia, including its vast armament factories at Skoda and elsewhere. Again the British and the French governments did nothing, but it was becoming painfully clear, in places high and low, that Hitler had to be stopped. Then, in August 1939, Hitler pulled off one of the most breathtaking diplomatic coups of all time. Nazi foreign minister Joachim von Ribbentrop concluded with the Soviet government a ten-year "nonaggression" treaty, thus making Hitler's rabid anticommunist regime an ally of the world's most powerful communist power. This news shocked the world and more than befuddled leftists and fellow travelers. In the United States, for example, the Communist organ *The Daily*

*After Chamberlain left Munich, Hitler privately referred to him as "a worm."

Worker, which for years had been preaching of the dangers Hitler posed, fell suddenly silent, but then quickly took up the Soviet line that Nazi Germany was now a good friend and no action should be taken to restrain Hitler.

For his part Chamberlain, who had consistently blocked all attempts to rearm Great Britain in the face of Hitler's threats, now warned that the British armed forces were "not strong enough" to take on the Germans. Nevertheless, he agreed to a treaty with France pledging that if Hitler should attack Poland, both countries would come to her aid. In September 1939 Hitler did exactly that—overrunning Poland in a matter of weeks—but Britain and France did not come to Poland's aid at all. Instead they declared war on Germany, then squatted along their own lines of defense to await developments, which were not long in coming. Meanwhile, Germany's new ally Communist Russia also maliciously marched into Poland and took about half the country as spoils of its own, at the same time making a grab for the small Baltic Sea nations on its border, Lithuania, Latvia, and Estonia.*

For the next seven months the action between the Allies (Britain and France) and their German antagonists took place mostly at sea, with each side losing a battleship. This came to be known as the Phony War, because correspondents who knew of the mayhem of the Western Front in the 1914–1918 war naturally expected more of the same. Meantime, Germany set about gobbling up the small Scandinavian countries Denmark and Norway.

Then on May 10, 1940, with a stunning swiftness that would startle the world as *Blitzkrieg* (lightning war), Nazi tanks and infantry smashed through neutral Holland and Belgium and headed for France. Chamberlain

*The attack on Poland opened with a typical Hitler sneak. Earlier, he had sent a battleship, the *Schleswig-Holstein,* on a "courtesy visit" to the city of Danzig, which Germany had lost under the Versailles Treaty following World War I. Without warning or a declaration of war, on the morning of September 1, 1939, this great naval behemoth opened a devastating barrage on Danzig, which was also the signal for thousands of German soldiers who had entered Poland dressed as tourists to go into action.

was forced to resign, with the words "peace in our time" still warm on his lips. He had embraced the shame of Munich and could not be trusted to fight the war Winston Churchill had predicted. The British Parliament named Churchill prime minister that same day. It took Hitler just over a month to crush France, which surrendered under the absurd understanding that the French could continue governing a small part of the nation, as well as its foreign colonies, from the inconsequential town of Vichy. This so-called Vichy government became internationally recognized as merely a puppet regime of the Nazis, who could abolish it at any time (and eventually did so). Nominally, Vichy was headed by the ancient field marshal Henri-Philippe Pétain, the so-called Hero of Verdun during World War I, who was then in his dotage and dusted out of retirement as a figurehead. It was actually run by a right-wing lawyer and media mogul named Pierre Laval, whose cooperation with the Nazis spilled over into collaboration; after the war he was stood up to the firing squad.

Mussolini, meantime, promptly declared war on France and England in order to get in on the plunder. A British army of 300,000 that had gone to France to help out was isolated by the German onslaught and narrowly escaped destruction by a miraculous evacuation from the cross-Channel port of Dunkirk.

With France securely in his grasp, Hitler then contemplated his invasion of England, which thankfully never came off. Knowing that no invasion could succeed without knocking out the British will to fight, Hitler launched the Battle of Britain with mammoth air strikes against England's cities and ports, especially against the mostly working class of London's East End. He had concluded that the common British people, whom he had scornfully lumped among those in the category of "weak and decadent democracies," would soon rise up against their government in the face of massive bombing attacks. Fortunately for the British, their military had been able to establish powerful air defenses, built around a new English invention called radar, as well as fast, maneuverable, and high-flying fighter planes, the Hurricane and the Spitfire. Churchill later described this as the "wizard war," because technology and new arms helped the British shoot the Germans out of the skies by the hundreds.

Less than a year after razing thousands of buildings and killing tens of thousands of British civilians, Hitler sourly abandoned (at least temporarily) his plan to conquer England by invasion and turned without warning upon his erstwhile partner in crime, Stalin's Soviet Union, with a monstrous assault along a two-thousand-mile front. Although he did not yet realize it, Hitler had become like the sorcerer's apprentice, who had set the broom to hauling water and then forgot the spell to turn it off.

Chapter Two ★

Until Commodore Matthew C. Perry sailed his sleek black-hulled United States naval squadron into Tokyo Bay on July 8, 1853, and anchored under the looming eminence of Mount Fujiyama, the island kingdom of Japan had remained the most remote civilized nation on earth. In the nearly six hundred years since the great *Kamikaze* (divine wind) had blown up across the Sea of Japan to sink and scatter the ships of an invading Mongol army, its shogun rulers had decreed that no foreigners would ever touch the sacred shores of Japan.

Commodore Perry changed that in a hurry by running out his big cannons and firing off a thirteen-gun salute over the heads of the startled Japanese on shore, followed by his unheard-of demand to see the *mikado*. Menaced by U.S. military might, the illustrious sovereign shogun agreed to accept in the name of his emperor a letter from President Millard Fillmore that offered the mysterious and medieval Japanese ruler "friendship and commerce" with the American people. Perry then sailed off, only to return some months later with a full fleet of twenty-four warships bearing gifts of whiskey, champagne, women's velvet fashions of the day, modern tools, guns, a telegraph, a steam engine, pictures of New York City, and an English-language dictionary. Thus Perry was able to "sail triumphantly home, having brought 'a mighty empire into the family of nations without bloodshed.'"*[1]

*At this point in Japan's history the emperor was merely a figurehead. The shogun, a military governor, actually ruled the country.

Perry's feat launched a chain of events that, in some fifty years, would change the world and then, in less than fifty years more, would change it again, and not for the better. The opening of Japan to international trade had a profound effect on its leaders and, consequently, on all its citizens. The old feudal system was replaced with a national monarchy under the "boy emperor" Meiji, who began incorporating Western science, customs, and military technology into the Japanese culture at such an astounding rate that by the turn of the century Japan had become a powerful modern state, which was likewise astounding to the rest of the modern world. Unfortunately, her role model would be the Prussian government (from eastern Germany's warlike province), which inspired her new constitution and government administration.[2] Tens of thousands of silk farmers harvested their cocoons for the looms of the many new silk factories, which shipped this valued staple to nations far and wide. Railroad and telegraph systems soon connected the country; a modern banking system made the economy boom; and their diplomats were dispatched to capitals throughout the world. The Japanese purchased large warships from the British and were trained to use them by British officers. Their new Imperial army was modernized with the latest in weaponry and was trained by German officers.[3]

The Americans provided teachers and missionaries to improve the Japanese school system, and Japanese students were soon attending prestigious colleges and universities in the United States. The Japanese took to copying eagerly and shamelessly whatever they thought useful from the modern Western nations. A perfect example: In the late 1930s an American engineer named Stanton wanted to bring two gigantic electric generators to Japan. In mid-Pacific the ship was threatened by a typhoon and Stanton ordered that the generators, which had two huge holes bored into each leg to bolt them down, immediately have two more holes bored and bolted to better secure the generators from breaking loose in the rough seas. He and the generators arrived in Japan intact. When Stanton returned to Japan ten years after the Second World War he visited a number of electrical generating plants throughout Japan. At each site he was amazed to see that every generator was an exact copy of the two he had originally brought over, right down to having *four* holes bored in each of its legs.[4]

The Japanese also began copying the principles of imperialistic expansion so much in vogue among the Western powers in the second half of the nineteenth century. In the words of her own foreign minister at the time of the Pearl Harbor attack, "Japan saw that success, not to say survival, meant empire, and forthwith she set about attaining one."[5] Beginning in 1894 she sent her armies to Korea, as well as to the vast Chinese island of Formosa and the southern part of Manchuria. Alarmed, the Russians, with a country a hundred times the size of Japan, forced the Japanese to retreat from Manchuria, then took the entire country for themselves. But the Japanese were not to be denied. In a chilling parallel to the Pearl Harbor raid thirty-seven years later, Japan in 1904 launched a sneak naval torpedo attack that annihilated the Russian Oriental Fleet, including two of the czar's largest battleships, which had been lying at anchor at Port Arthur. Only afterward did the Japanese bother to declare war. Fighting broke out immediately in Manchuria between the Japanese and Russian armies, and the Japanese quickly got the better of it, laying siege to Port Arthur and causing a hundred thousand Russian casualties at the Battle of Mukden.

One year later the Japanese defiantly faced the much larger Russian Baltic Fleet, which had steamed halfway around the world to suppress the upstart Orientals. It was the worst naval defeat in modern history. Twenty-two Russian warships were surprised by the Japanese fleet and were sent to the bottom during the Battle of the Tsushima Straits, including four new Russian battleships. Seven other Russian battleships struck their colors and were captured. In a blazing barrage of two thousand shells per minute at least four thousand Russian sailors were killed (some say six thousand), at a cost to the Japanese of a few patrol boats. Thus was the world awakened to the fact that Japan was now a military power to be reckoned with.

The Russo-Japanese War also marked the first stirrings of anti-American sentiment in the new and prideful Japanese empire. American victory in the Spanish-American war of 1898 had ceded to the United States the vast Philippine Island archipelago, as well as outposts in such remote places as Guam and Wake Island, all of which were in East Asian waters uncomfortably close to the Japanese homeland. President Theodore Roosevelt was one such person "awakened" to the dangers of the growing conflict in

East Asia. Japanese armies were driving the Russians fiercely in Manchuria but, after fifteen months of total war, Japan was at the end of her resources. Russia, on the other hand, at the losing end of a humiliating series of defeats, was also anxious to end the war.

Into this diplomatic tangle stepped TR to mediate between the two warring powers. Japanese and Russian diplomats met with the president first at Sagamore Hill, his home in Long Island's Oyster Bay, and then, curiously, were taken by (separate) U.S. Navy cruisers all the way up to the small town of Portsmouth, New Hampshire, to get down to business. The Japanese, holding the winning hand, at least so far as military victory went, were hard bargainers. They issued a long list of "nonnegotiable" demands, including a really sticky one calling for war reparations. Russia said it would not pay and Japan insisted it pay or fight. They haggled for weeks, but at long last Roosevelt persuaded the Japanese to drop the demand for a war indemnity and a treaty was signed between the two combatants.

Roosevelt was hailed as a peacemaker and a master diplomat by everybody in the world—except the Japanese. In Tokyo people rioted in the streets and Japanese newspapers shrieked that even though Japan had won the war she had been cunningly swindled out of her just deserts by the president of the United States. Even the president's daughter Alice was treated with coolness when she traveled there for a visit.

Worse to come were Japanese accusations of racism by the United States. The Japanese had been immigrating to America—many of them illegally—in increasing numbers until by the early 1900s they were arriving at the rate of a thousand per month in California alone. West coast newspapers began shouting warnings about the "yellow peril." This prompted the San Francisco Board of Education in 1906 to issue an order segregating all Japanese schoolchildren from the white student population. Moreover, the California legislature had passed a resolution that branded Japanese immigrants as "immoral, intemperate [and] quarrelsome."[6] Not only that but workers in California began rioting and beating immigrant Japanese who, they claimed, were willing to work for "coolie" wages, thus putting them out of their jobs.

Roosevelt was aghast and sent emissaries from Washington out to California to ameliorate the situation, but little was accomplished. In the

Japanese Diet (parliament) there was loud and angry talk of declaring war on the United States, fueled further by reactionary newspapers in Tokyo. Moreover, Japan began to order new warships from Europe, including one of the new dreadnought-class battleships from England. Diplomatic relations between the two countries chilled considerably and Admiral George Dewey, hero of the Spanish-American War, warned that Japan, at present, could capture with impunity the Philippines, Hawaii, and all other U.S. possessions in the Pacific.

Roosevelt, whose motto, "Speak softly and carry a big stick," had become a slogan in the American lexicon, now decided to wield his stick. He ordered all sixteen of the U.S. Navy's battleships freshly painted white and sent around the world on a "goodwill" cruise. What he was aiming at was to demonstrate to the Japanese, in the most highly visible way, that the United States was no pushover—the supreme example of gunboat diplomacy.

On December 16, 1907, the Great White Fleet, as it soon came to be known, set sail from the Chesapeake Bay in the wake of a 336-gun salute* to the president, who was on hand for its departure, headed south for Cape Horn and thence into the Pacific Ocean. Even before the Great White Fleet arrived in Japan, it had created a change in attitude among those in the Tokyo government. In what was diplomatically called a "gentleman's agreement," Japan at last agreed to sharply curtail the immigration of its citizens to the United States. As if by magic the recent animosities seemed to melt away and by the time the Great White Fleet reached Yokohama its sailors were greeted by throngs of cheering Japanese and showered with gifts.

One of those sailors who felt suspicious of this outpouring of friendship was a young American naval ensign and recent Annapolis graduate named William F. Halsey aboard the battleship *Kansas*. "Bull" Halsey, destined for fame as a U.S. Pacific Fleet commander during World War II, recalled, "I felt that the Japanese meant none of their welcome; that they actually disliked us," he wrote afterward. "Nor was I any more convinced of their sincerity when they presented us with medals confirming the 'good will' between our two governments."[7]

---

*Each of the sixteen Great White Fleet battleships fired a twenty-one-gun salute.

* * *

With the outbreak of the First World War, Japan weighed her options and sided with the Allies, but her role in the fighting was limited to the comparatively easy task of ejecting the Germans from their mid-Pacific colonial possessions in the Marshall and Gilbert Island chains. At the Versailles Peace Conference of 1919 Japan was rewarded by being given a "mandate" over these former German territories, which would prove to be terribly costly for the American armed forces during the Second World War.

Following the end of World War I the major Allied powers, principally the United States, had become distressed over the expensive and threatening race by nations to build ever more and ever larger naval warships. This resulted in the 1921–22 Naval Armament Limitation Conference, held in Washington, D.C. As there were only three major navies left in the world, it was agreed between the United States, Great Britain, and Japan that the ratio of "capital ships" (battleships and later aircraft carriers) should henceforth be 5:5:3, with the Japanese begrudgingly accepting the smaller number. In exchange, the United States agreed to halt further fortifications of its Pacific island possessions the Philippines and Wake, Guam, and Midway Islands.* As well, the three parties agreed to take a ten-year-long "naval holiday" on new warship construction, after which a second treaty conference was to be held.

Not only that but other international agreements arising from the conference led to treaties between Japan and those Western democracies that had possessions or interests in the Far East, pledging mutual respect of each other's rights and territories, principally in turbulent but resource-rich China, which was even then on the verge of civil war. From this point on events moved rapidly and relentlessly toward the deterioration of relations between Japan and the Western democracies—mainly the United States.

First, beginning in the mid-1920s, there was a rise in militarism in Japan. The militarists, often influential and with access to the press, pro-

---

*This last part of the treaty—the American concession not to build up its naval bases in the Pacific—is now seen by many military strategists as the equivalent of allowing Japan to build a dozen or more unsinkable aircraft carriers, since the many islands it inherited following World War I as mandates would soon be developed with airstrips from which Japanese warplanes swarmed by the thousands.

tested that the naval arms-limitation treaties had placed Japan in second-class status and jeopardized her national security. They also objected to Japan's signing of the treaties pledging mutual respect for Western interests in Asia. The way the Japanese militarists saw it Asia, in particular China with its lucrative markets, was in Japan's sphere of influence, and Westerners had no legitimate business there.

Then, in 1924, the Japanese were insulted yet again by the old "yellow peril" specter. Until then the United States was taking in just about everybody on earth to fuel its voracious need for labor and settlement. But by 1924 the hordes of immigrants from central Europe, Soviet Russia, and other poverty-stricken nations had led many Americans to conclude that they were being swamped by foreigners. Congress responded by enacting an immigration law that set quotas on U.S. immigration from the various countries of the world—all except Japan. Under the Exclusion Act, Japanese—who were by then becoming the most numerous of the Asian immigrants—were forbidden entirely from settling in the United States. Naturally, the Japanese saw this as new evidence of anti-Oriental racism and "a gratuitous affront."[8] Again riots erupted in Tokyo, and "Westerners were refused rooms in some hotels, publicly insulted and occasionally beaten in sight of police."[9]

In 1930 the second Naval Armament Limitation conference convened in London. Japan demanded a more equitable parity of ships but was rebuffed, further fueling the militarists' charges that she was being treated with scorn.* Meantime, in Manchuria, the so-called Japanese Kwantung Army, stationed there ostensibly to guard the Japanese-owned railroad, in 1931 created an "incident" that set off Japan's fatal gamble for Asian domination. "This military establishment," wrote foreign minister Shigenori Togo from his jail cell after the Second World War, "had come to regard itself as the chosen instrument of Japan's manifest destiny . . . and had developed a certain impatience with civilian governments which failed to evince sufficient concern for Japan's prestige as a continental power."[10]

*Japan was not being treated with scorn but with suspicion. Her actions in the Far East had alarmed the other members of the conference, the Western powers of France, England, and the United States, who saw a rising militarism and no concomitant interest in joining in their own mutual interests.

Acting without approval from anyone in Tokyo, Kwantung Army officers manufactured a story that a Chinese bomb had blown up a railroad track and they forthwith set about seizing strategic positions all over Manchuria. Despite orders from Tokyo to cease their aggression, the army commanders proceeded apace, and within three months the Japanese occupied all of Manchuria. Presented with a fait accompli the Japanese government collectively shrugged its shoulders and welcomed Manchuria into the new Japanese empire, renaming it Manchukuo.

The "Manchurian incident," as the Japanese officially chose to call it (there would be other "incidents" as well, which led to war and Japanese occupation of her neighbors), demonstrated a peculiar quirk in the Japanese national persona. In any other country a military commander who flagrantly disobeyed orders from his civilian superiors would have been sacked and punished. But in Japan, often as not, this wasn't the case and would lead to much trouble and suffering down the road. The League of Nations deplored the "incident" and its consequences, and dispatched a commission to Manchuria to investigate the affair. When the commission returned in 1932 with its report, the League voted 42 to 1 (all but Japan herself) to condemn Japan for its aggression. As in the upcoming cases of Hitler and Mussolini, however, no punitive action was taken. Nevertheless, her pride wounded, Japan walked out of the League, branded with the international mark of Cain.

From that point on Japan seemed content with having become a pariah to most of the world. For the next five years, through the good offices of the Kwantung Army, she created almost countless "incidents" against the Chinese, after which demands were made and ultimatums issued, until it became obvious to even the remotest Chinese peasant that his country was being relentlessly gobbled up by the empire of Japan. The Japanese dilemma was described thusly by the Australian prime minister, who, upon his return from the 1921 naval conference, had seen the handwriting on the wall. "For us, the Pacific problem is for all practical purposes the problem of Japan. Here is a nation of 70 millions of people, crowded together in narrow islands, its population increasing rapidly, and is already pressing on the margin of subsistence. Japan then, is faced with the great problem which has bred wars since time began. For when the tribes and nations of the past outgrew the resources of their own territory they moved on and on, hacking their way to the fertile pastures of their neighbors. This is the problem of the Pacific—the modern Riddle of the Sphinx."*[11]

Be that as it may, the increasingly disastrous Japanese foreign policy was made possible by what was then a time-honored Japanese tradition: government by assassination. In the period between the wars no less than three Japanese premiers and a wide assortment of other high government officials met their deaths at the hands of the militarists. Toward the end of the 1930s multiple conspiracies within the officer ranks of the army and navy resulted in a perfect orgy of assassinations and assassination attempts, most of which, according to Japanese custom, went unpunished. Voices of moderation were silenced by murder or other means and by 1937 the army effectively ran the government.

Worse, Japan's status as an outcast nation drew her into collaboration with the two other international outcasts, Germany and Italy. In 1936 Japan signed an anticommunist pact with Hitler—and later with Mussolini—dedicated to suppressing the spread of communism but obviously aimed at Soviet Russia, then the world's only communist power.

All the while, Japanese editorialists and writers were fanning the flames of racial hatred of the Americans and Europeans. In particular, they justified their attempt to take over China and create an "Asia for Asians" sphere in the East on the grounds that the Americans, British, French, and Dutch had taken over, respectively, the Philippines, India-Burma-Malaya–Hong Kong, French Indo-China, and the countries now comprising Indonesia. Thus, the argument went, why should Japan, now the major power

---

*The Japanese islands are approximately the size of California but the population density—340 people to the square mile—was ten times greater. The average Japanese farm just prior to the war was a mere one-quarter acre. Not only that, but in the twenty years between the Australian prime minister's remarks and the beginning of World War II the Japanese population had grown by another ten million people.

in the Orient, stand by while white Christians controlled large parts of Asia and they themselves were being vilified for trying to grab China?

These Japanese writers and opinion makers cited as particularly odious American expansionism over Mexican territory in 1848, including California and the Southwest, as well as the usurpation of American Indian lands. What they failed to emphasize, however, was that all of these imperialistic endeavors, including American occupation of the Philippines, had occurred primarily in the previous century, and that British, French, and Dutch colonial conquests went back much further than that; and that with the dawn of the new century and the enlightenment that followed the tragedy of World War I, these Western powers had actually begun agreeing to return many (but of course not all) of their overseas possessions to the native inhabitants. (There is a rather small school of thought even today that agrees with this Japanese logic and its rationale for the Japanization of all Asia, and their point might be well taken but for the horrific brutality that the Japanese demonstrated toward those benighted peoples once they had conquered their countries.)

In the summer of 1937 the Kwantung Army, or so it is generally believed, precipitated its most ambitious "incident" of all, which would lead ultimately to world war in the Far East. Japanese troops on a night-training maneuver near the ancient bridge named for the Italian explorer Marco Polo claimed they had been shot at by Chinese soldiers in the area. The Japanese army general staff ordered a retaliation, seizing the Chinese capital Peking (Beijing). Fighting soon broke out all over China and the Japanese used the opportunity to initiate a full-scale war. They captured one major Chinese city after the next, including Soochow, Shanghai, Hankow, and Canton, as the nationalist government of General Chiang Kai-shek fled into the vast Chinese interior, ultimately setting up the capital at Chungking, far to the west.

The Japanese were not benevolent rulers. They rounded up thousands of Chinese, tied them to poles, and used them as live guinea pigs for bayonet practice and to refine their swordsmanship; a Japanese soldier was expected to be able to chop off a human head cleanly, in a single stroke.

One Japanese described the experience: "I personally severed more than forty heads. Today I no longer remember each of them well. It might sound extreme, but I can almost say that if more than two weeks went by without my taking a head, I didn't feel right. But even I sometimes botched the job. Their bodies tended to move. They swayed. Sometimes I'd hit the shoulder. Once a lung popped out, almost like a balloon. Most of the officers did this. If they didn't, their authority was weakened."[12] The Japanese army also operated so-called comfort stations for their soldiers in China, Manchuria, and Korea. Some 200,000 "illiterate rural women" were told they were being sent to high-paying factory jobs. In reality, they were placed in barracks and required "to sexually service up to fifty Japanese soldiers a day." The soldiers called these women "public toilets."[13]

Frustrated by lack of quick victory, the Japanese singled out for particular attention the peaceful Chinese metropolis of Nanking, exacting upon it an almost unimaginable savagery, which would come to distinguish the new breed of Japanese soldier. During the Russo-Japanese War of 1904–05, it was remarked worldwide how the Japanese treated prisoners and civilians alike with unusual courtesy and respect. But these new type of soldiers, conscripted from the illiterate peasant class, were too often brutish creatures, drunk on notions of power, superiority, and invincibility imbibed from their superiors and, worse, far worse, unrestrained by their officers. In what the international newspapers and newsreels recorded as the Rape of Nanking, the Japanese murdered some 300,000 helpless civilians of that city. More than 80,000 women were raped, some of them seventy and eighty years old; children were speared on bayonets; looting was the order of the day and much of the city was burned to the ground; and citizens were roasted alive in a reign of cruelty so abominable that people still writhe at the telling of it.

Despite world outrage and condemnation, the Japanese claimed the reports were exaggerated, though subsequent investigation proved they were not. Soon Japan had an army of more than a million men fighting on Chinese soil but, in spite of holding almost all of coastal China, the Japanese army, then some two million strong, had overextended itself in the immensity of that huge country, where a bleak and murderous stalemate ensued until the outbreak of World War II.

★ Chapter Three

By 1940 thoughtful Americans perceived the unfolding world events with almost breathless consternation. Across the Atlantic, England was fighting alone for her life against the ever expanding Axis powers; across the Pacific, the Japanese appeared to have a death grip on China. Anyone with a grasp of history and geography realized that if both the British empire and China fell, the fascist dictators and their communist allies would soon seize and control most of the world and its resources and that America would be squeezed to death between them; that with modern armaments the great oceans no longer provided the security they once had; that international trade, upon which much of the American economy depended, would be strangled until the Great Democracy became, of necessity, a vassal state to wicked and rapacious empires.

These were no idle fears. Allied counterintelligence had intercepted an astonishingly detailed Nazi scheme for dividing up South America and Central America for the new German empire. A Nazi courier from the German embassy in Argentina was shanghaied by British agents and in his pouch was found a top-secret map showing how South America—then composed of fourteen separate nations—was to be consolidated into five huge Nazi puppet states, one of which included Panama and the Panama Canal. The American public was not much comforted when President

Franklin D. Roosevelt revealed news of this plot, declaring, "The geographical experts in Berlin have ruthlessly obliterated all the existing boundary lines to bring the whole [South American] continent under their domination."[1] Accordingly, Roosevelt commissioned some gunboat diplomacy of his own, ordering a number of large American warships to cruise offshore of Brazil and other South American countries where Nazi-inspired movements seemed to be making inroads.

Furthermore, Roosevelt himself was privy to a Japanese plan divulged to him years earlier when he was assistant secretary of the navy by a Japanese who informed him "in confidence" of his government's intention to annex the American Pacific possessions as well as Mexico and Peru.[2] By 1940 U.S. intelligence had revealed a renewed Japanese interest in these areas.

Much as Roosevelt recognized the mounting peril, he knew that politically his hands were nearly tied. National polls showed that up to 70 percent of the American population wanted no part of war, and in Congress powerful isolationist forces had him hamstrung. Additionally, surely his mind was on the fact that he was up for reelection in 1940, for he was already—like Woodrow Wilson before him—publicly promising not to "send American boys to fight in foreign wars." But with the fall of France and continued Nazi conquests in Europe, Roosevelt did manage to persuade Congress in September 1940 to pass the Selective Service Act, which called for a draft of 900,000 men, but whose terms of service would expire in one year without renewed congressional approval.*

Worse for Roosevelt was the U.S. Neutrality Act of 1936, sardonically described by the playwright Robert Sherwood, who worked in the White House during the war years: "It was born of the belief that we could legislate ourselves out of war, as we had once legislated ourselves out of the saloons (and into the speakeasies). Like Prohibition, it was an experiment 'noble in motive' but disastrous in result."[3]

---

*A perfect example of the isolationist mood in America; when the issue came up a year later of whether or not to extend the draft, it passed by just a single vote.

The Neutrality Act forbade the United States from aiding or trading with any warring power, but Roosevelt managed to get around it at least once—in order to help stave off the German invasion of England in late 1940—by trading fifty World War I–vintage U.S. destroyers for long-term American leases on British naval bases in the western Atlantic and Caribbean. This transaction ignited such an uproar from the isolationists that it convinced the politician in Roosevelt yet again that he had best move very carefully.

One thing he could do, and it was one of the most important things he *did* do in all the war, was set science into motion in October 1939, when the president received a letter from the famous mathematics and physics professor Albert Einstein, who had escaped Nazi Germany and was then teaching at Princeton. Einstein informed the president that he and other distinguished scientists had calculated that "splitting the atom" was theoretically possible and, more ominously, that the Germans were actually well along in the process. "This new phenomenon," Einstein told Roosevelt, "would also lead to the construction of bombs, and it is conceivable—though much less certain—that extremely powerful bombs of a new type may thus be constructed."

Roosevelt, whose mind was undoubtedly on many things beyond any theoretical exploration of the tiny atom, scrawled a note on Einstein's letter: "We ought to do something about this." He might easily have tossed the letter in the trash or simply had his secretary dictate a thank-you note to the old mathematical genius.[4]

This coincided with another great stroke of fortune. Atomic fission was not possible without uranium ore and the only viable source of uranium ore at that time lay in a gold mine deep in the Belgian Congo. When seven months later the Germans overran Belgium, one M. Edgar Sengier, director of Union Miniere, the vast Belgian mining complex in the Congo, fled to America. Once in the United States, however, Sengier became aghast that the world's largest cache of uranium ore was still stored in one of his mines. Forewarned a year earlier of the dark and bizarre significance of this material, Sengier took it upon himself to order his agents in Africa "to ship discreetly to New York, under whatever ruse was practicable, this

very large supply of uranium ore."* Thus, for better or worse, some two
and a half million pounds of uranium found its way to a warehouse on Staten
Island, safe from the Germans and available for American use in one of
the greatest and most menacing scientific enterprises of all time.[5]

Roosevelt fully understood that if war was to come it would be a
thoroughly modern war and that it would be won in large part by the
side that could develop the most efficient and massive production of war
materials and the most powerful and innovative technologies. He therefore called upon the leading scientists and businessmen in the country
to serve on special boards toward achieving these ends, and had he not
done so America's position after it was finally drawn into the war on
December 7, 1941, would have been far worse than it already was.

The problem over what to do about Japan was becoming ever more vexing.
Recognizing correctly that if Japan gained control of China she would soon
exercise hegemony over all East Asia, the Roosevelt administration had
begun, in 1938, to extend large loans to the Chinese government to aid
Chinese defense. For its part, Japan proclaimed its Greater East Asian Co-
Prosperity Sphere, which was nothing more than a flimsy excuse for taking
over nearly half of the world. By then nearly 70 percent of the entire Japanese
national budget was going to its military and the whole country was on a
war footing. While the United States army was languishing with fewer than
250,000 undertrained and underequipped men (plus the incoming draftees)[†]

*The person who enlightened Sengier to the dire possibilities of uranium was none
other than the noted British scientist Sir Henry Tizard, who told him five months before
war broke out that the British government would like to buy his entire supply of this radio-
active element. The deal did not get done, but Sengier remembered the conversation, which
ended with these parting words by Tizard: "Be careful, and never forget that you have in
your hands something which may mean a catastrophe to your country and mine if it were
to fall in the hands of a possible enemy."

†There were not many volunteer enlistees in those days. The salary of a private in
the U.S. Army was $31 per month. In the months that contained thirty-one days, he was
making a dollar a day.

the Japanese Imperial army now contained more than six million, including reserves. Her navy had built up so rapidly that the Japanese Imperial Fleet had become more powerful than the Pacific fleets of the United States and Great Britain combined.[6]

Roosevelt cautiously put an unofficial "moral embargo" on certain items such as selling aircraft and aircraft equipment to Japan, but the two things Japan needed most to fuel its war machine were oil and scrap metal, which since the 1930s she had been importing from the United States in immense quantities. These, for the time being, still moved across the Pacific from West Coast ports, but in nowhere near the amounts needed to keep up with Japan's huge military expansion. Oil in particular was a problem. Japan produced virtually no oil, and had been able to stockpile enough for only two years under the most favorable conditions. In case of full-scale war with the United States and the Western Allies, those reserves would possibly not last a year. Fear of an oil shortage had become so rampant that Japan's military government banished almost all civilian motorcars and trucks except those that ran on charcoal or wood-burning engines, and the people either walked or rode bicycles. So far as scrap metal and steel went, Japan was down to her last few months' supply.

In order to pressure Japan to get out of China, the U.S. embargo was stepped up the following year. Official American sanctions now forbade shipping to Japan such things as high-octane aviation fuel, arms and ammunition, and strategic materials such as aluminum. By the end of September 1940, with Hitler's Axis powers rolling over Europe and Africa, Japan for all practical purposes removed the last pretense of diplomacy when its government joined with Hitler and Mussolini in the Axis alliance. The United States reacted by adding scrap metal and steel to the list of materials embargoed to the Japanese.

In March 1941, just after he was sworn in for an unprecedented third term, Roosevelt boldly led the United States a step closer to war by manipulating Congress to get his Lend-Lease Act signed into law. This measure, which effectively obliterated the Neutrality Act, provided that America would grant England and China "all possible aid short of war." The Axis now faced the prospect of America's industrial might being turned against it while the United States, in Roosevelt's words, became the great "arsenal of democracy."

The furor with which this deed was received by the American isolationist movement was expressed by Senator Burton K. Wheeler, a Montana Democrat and former socialist, who prompted an outrage by declaring that Lend-Lease would mean "ploughing under every fourth American boy for the sake of British imperialism." Wheeler and like-minded colleagues in Congress had labored long and hard to restrain Roosevelt from what they saw as "dragging" the United States into a European war, or, perhaps more accurately, allowing England to drag America into such a war. By 1940 the wave of isolationism that had been spreading across the United States was reaching its apogee and it was all too true that, for one reason or another, the majority of Americans opposed getting into the war.

In the summer of 1940 the America First Committee, headquartered in Chicago, declared its existence. Its board of directors included some of the most well known and respected people in the country, including a former U.S. Army general in command of the American Legion, a Chicago meatpacking baron, automaker Henry Ford,* the famous World War I flier Eddie Rickenbacker, various Nobel Prize winners, and the president of Sears and Roebuck.[7] Its chief spokesman would turn out to be the most notable American hero of the period, Colonel Charles A. Lindbergh, who had made history by being the first to fly solo over the Atlantic Ocean.

After the kidnap-murder of his infant son, Lindbergh and his wife moved to Europe. He had made visits to Germany and was highly impressed by what he had seen of the Nazi military machine, in particular its airpower; he was so impressed, in fact, that he became convinced no European nation could stand up to it, especially not the decadent and foolish British or French. Not only that but the famed pilot of *The Spirit of St. Louis* publicly declared that the only people who favored war with Germany were "the Roosevelt family, the British and the Jews." His America First movement claimed a membership of nearly one million

*Ford had also been America's best-known pacifist during the First World War.

and held frequent mass rallies at such places as Madison Square Garden to preach against the war.[8]*

The isolationists were a mixed bag of pacifists, Anglophobic Irishmen who wished to see England destroyed at any cost, anti-Semites, Roosevelt haters of all stripes, conservatives with investments abroad, liberals such as Kingman Brewster Jr., who would go on to become president of Yale and rail against the Vietnam War, nervous parents, anxious students, much of the organized labor movement under one of its Roosevelt-hating leaders, John L. Lewis, and a host of pro-German and pro-Italian immigrants who made up such organizations as the German American Bund, the American Nazi Party, and the American Fascist Party. And as soon as the Soviet Union threw in its lot with the Nazis, the Communist party too came on board—an interesting mix, since the German-Italian fascists were dedicated to the eradication of communists and vice versa. Nevertheless, each faction ground its own ax and put Roosevelt and his people in a difficult, even precarious way.

Among those who stood out prominently as spokesmen for these diverse bedfellows was one Father Charles E. Coughlin, a renegade Catholic priest from Detroit, who rallied both British-hating Irish Catholics and chauvinistic Italian-American Catholics to the cause through his rabid nationally broadcast radio show and syndicated newsletter. Transcripts of Father Coughlin's radio program make today's conservative talk show hosts seem mild by comparison. Of the so-called interventionists (read the Roosevelt administration) Father Coughlin had this to say: "Like thieves who operate under the cover of night, there are in our midst those who operate beneath the cloak of protected auspices to steal our liberty, our peace and our autonomy. . . . Sneakingly, subversively, and un-Americanly hiding behind a sanctimonious stuffed shirt . . . these men form the most dangerous fifth column that ever set foot upon neutral soil. They are the

*Many people subsequently interpreted Lindbergh's remarks as demonstrating that he was an arch anti-Semite. In fact, he was probably no more so than most people of his time. He felt genuinely for the plight of Jews in Germany and voiced concerned predictions that if America entered the war the Jews would suffer even more horribly than they had already—a forecast that proved all too true.

Quislings* of America. They are the Judas Iscariots within the apostolic college of our nation."⁹

In an America still mired in the throes of the Great Depression, with millions still wondering where their next meal would come from, and with images of the slaughter of World War I still fresh in their minds, the appeals of Father Coughlin and his cohorts struck a resonant note. Roosevelt accordingly continued to move with caution and circumspection.

In the meantime all sorts of clandestine spying, sabotage, and propaganda schemes were being acted out across America, most notably in New York, Washington, and on the West Coast. Agents from the warring nations, or those soon to be at war, sought secret information and technology and conspired to influence members of Congress and other important American citizens to pronounce themselves on one side or the other in the growing conflict. The FBI and the armed services intelligence branches were responsible for uncovering treacherous activity, which was growing ever more frantic. Some of these incidents deserve attention for the purposes of illuminating the lengths to which people are driven in tempestuous times.

At the center of many intriguing activities was an extraordinary man named William Stephenson, a wealthy forty-four-year-old Canadian who had been a champion Olympic boxer and an ace fighter pilot during World War I. Afterward he settled in England where he became famous as the inventor of modern wireless photography, which also made him a millionaire and set him up as the owner of many large and diverse companies. When war broke out Stephenson was sent by none other than Winston Churchill himself to run the British intelligence service in America where, working out of an office in New York City, his code name became "Intrepid."

With Great Britain fighting for her life and the United States nowhere near entering the war, Stephenson, with Roosevelt's blessing, set about to counter pro-German and pro-Italian propaganda that was being financed

*Vidkun Quisling (1887–1945) was a Norwegian fascist who set up a puppet Nazi government in his native country after Hitler invaded it. After the war the Norwegians hanged him.

by the Axis powers. One of the first things Stephenson noticed was that isolationist groups had gotten to various members of Congress and, using the congressmen's free franking or postal privileges, were able to send out millions of antiwar and pro-German newsletters throughout the country. By cultivating friendships with members of the press, Stephenson exposed this abuse and was instrumental in bringing down the virulent isolationist New York congressman Hamilton Fish.

He then set about exposing an important German agent named Dr. Gerhard Westrick who, through his friendship with the president of the Texas Oil Company (Texaco), had succeeded in getting that corporation to violate the British blockade and supply oil to the Axis powers. After Stephenson passed along this information to the *New York Herald Tribune,* Dr. Westrick found himself deported back to Germany on a Japanese ship.

Next Stephenson dedicated himself to unraveling the immensely complex relationships between the German industrial giant IG Farben and its dummy subsidiaries in the United States. IG Farben has been described as "probably the largest corporation of its kind in the world," and was an octopustic monopoly that would make any antitrust lawyer drool. Stephenson and his people waded through the labyrinths of agglomerations and cartels that made up the American operation of this Nazi-controlled behemoth and succeeded in getting the U.S. Department of Justice to indict and put out of business a number of its American subsidiaries on grounds of restraint of trade.[10]

One of Stephenson's juicier and most successful operations, however, lay in the field of true espionage and is worthy of any spy novel. This was his use of an attractive American divorcée named Amy Elizabeth Thorpe, the thirty-year-old daughter of a Marine Corps officer, whose code name was "Cynthia." Tall, blond, and possessed of "explosive sexual charms," Cynthia went about her tasks apparently "not for money, but for thrills."[11]

In the winter of 1940–41 the Italian fleet vastly outnumbered the British Mediterranean fleet and posed a direct threat to the British convoys presently bringing troops and supplies to the fighting in North Africa. Cynthia's first assignment was to try to procure the Italian navy's code ciphers, a daunting task to say the least. Nevertheless, she somehow got herself introduced to the Italian naval attaché serving with the Italian embassy in Washington, Admiral Alberto Lais, who, though married with a wife and children, fell promptly in love with her.

Whatever "explosive sexual charms" Cynthia used must have been wildly effective, because this otherwise respected senior officer ordered his cipher clerk to hand over a copy of the Italian codes to her, and she in turn gave them to Stephenson, who immediately dispatched them to the British Admiralty in London. Two months later they were put to good use when the British Mediterranean fleet ambushed the Italian navy in the Battle of Cape Matapan and put it out of action for nearly a year. Churchill proudly declared that this victory "disposed of all challenge to British naval mastery of the Eastern Mediterranean at this critical time."[12]

A month later the love-struck admiral stupidly disclosed to Cynthia that he had ordered the sabotage of all Italian ships then in U.S. ports in order to keep them from being seized by the Americans in case war broke out between the United States and the Axis. Cynthia reported this news to Stephenson, who gave it to the U.S. Office of Naval Intelligence, which saw to it that the sabotage was arrested, that the ships were seized anyway, and that Admiral Lais was deported back to Italy as an "undesirable" person. At the dockside before his departure the admiral devoted all his attentions to Cynthia, who had come to see him off, and ignored entirely his weeping wife and children. Cynthia then turned to her next assignment, which would be even more difficult and which will be reported here further along.

While all this was going on in the East, U.S. intelligence gatherers began to observe an alarming flow of unfriendly messages from Tokyo to its Japanese consulates on the Pacific coast. There were at that time some 112,000 Japanese-born noncitizens (issei) and American-born Japanese (nisei) located mostly from the state of Washington down to the southern tip of California. Many were small businessmen and vegetable farmers and many others were fishermen, whose proximity to U.S. naval bases, shipyards, and ports disturbed American security officers. This was because all Japanese, whatever their origins, were thought to be loyal and obedient to their emperor, who was considered to be divine.

By late 1940 the Japanese Foreign Ministry in Tokyo was sending secret messages to its U.S. embassy and various consulates requesting "uti-
lization of our 'Second Generations' and resident nationals" to commit acts
of espionage and to stir up antiwar feelings among "Negroes, communists,
anti-Semites and labor union members." The U.S. Office of Naval Intelligence reported that "a number of second-generation Japanese have been
placed in airplane plants for intelligence purposes" and "will observe closely
all shipments of airplanes and other war materials [from the West Coast]
and report the amounts and destinations of such shipments." The Japanese
consulates were soon sending a series of detailed responses to the Tokyo
authorities outlining almost every aspect of U.S. warplane production on
the Pacific coast, as well as which warships were in harbor and which ones
had sailed.[13]

What made U.S. interception of these sinister communiqués possible
is one of the greatest success stories of World War II: the American intelligence establishment broke the Japanese diplomatic code, which was called
PURPLE. This mind-boggling feat was largely the work of one exceptional
man, William F. Friedman, chief of the U.S. Army Signal Intelligence Service, but to understand just how remarkable his accomplishments were
we must first go back to the way Americans approached such subjects as
code breaking, and eavesdropping in general.

Modern code breaking by the United States had its beginnings in
World War I with the establishment of the cryptologic section of the Military Intelligence Division, headed by Herbert O. Yardley, a $17.50-a-week
telegraphic clerk in the State Department, who created a near hysteria
when, for fun, he managed to break all its top-secret diplomatic codes,
which the embassies used to communicate with headquarters and vice
versa. When America entered World War I Yardley was put in charge of
all cryptological intelligence, but the Americans were far behind the British and French in such skullduggery and were not particularly successful.
When the war ended the Departments of War and State decided to continue their code-breaking efforts and Yardley was put in charge of this highly
clandestine enterprise. Operating out of a converted town house off Fifth
Avenue in New York City's Murray Hill neighborhood, it became known
as the Black Chamber.

All sorts of methods were used to obtain the codes: intercepting them from radio waves, burglary, bribery, and inducing or coercing the telegraph companies to give them up. During the Naval Armament Limitation Conference of 1921–22 Yardley was able to break the Japanese code, providing the Americans with Japan's rock-bottom position for negotiations. During the 1920s, the Black Chamber solved the diplomatic codes of some forty nations, an amazing achievement, but when Henry L. Stimson, an old-fashioned Wall Street lawyer, became secretary of state upon the election of Herbert Hoover, he was appalled to learn of Yardley's black-bag operations and disbanded the Black Chamber with the observation, "Gentlemen do not read each other's mail."

Enraged at being canned, Yardley decided to wreak his revenge by publishing a book, *The American Black Chamber* (1931), which sold briskly and was serialized in the widely popular *Saturday Evening Post*. In it he told all, destroying the Black Chamber's work of a decade. It especially created a furor of outrage in Japan with the revelation that the U.S. State Department had been intercepting Japanese cables to their delegation at the Washington Naval Conference. The Japanese promptly scrapped their code-cryptology system and in its place substituted what would become known as PURPLE, the most difficult encryption process the United States had ever encountered.*

When the Black Chamber was abolished, code breaking by the Americans did not stop but was simply relocated to the U.S. Army Signal Corps where, presumably, it could be more properly controlled. The branch was called the Signal Intelligence Service and was staffed with a host of extremely talented personnel, including professional cryptanalysts, mathematicians, electromechanics, crossword puzzle nuts, statisticians, philologists, and people learned in Oriental and classical languages. It was headed by the aforementioned William Friedman, a Romanian-born Jew whose family had immigrated to the United States when he was a year old and who had subsequently aspired to become a plant geneticist. While working at

---

*Two years after publishing *The American Black Chamber* Yardley decided again to capitalize on his inside knowledge of U.S. code breaking with a new book, *Japanese Diplomatic Secrets,* but this time he was stopped, literally, by an act of Congress, which hastily made it a criminal offense to reveal cryptology secrets.

a sort of commune of agricultural geneticists, Friedman became interested in unraveling the mysteries of alleged Shakespearean authorship by Francis Bacon, posed by an eccentric English teacher, and which evolved into reading cryptographs supposedly embedded in Shakespeare's plays.

From there Friedman, like Yardley, served with the U.S. Army in France as a cryptologist and upon his return remained with the Signal Corps. When the Black Chamber was disbanded, Friedman, at the age of thirty-nine, was made chief of the Signal Intelligence Service, where he would become the greatest code breaker of all time. As it became clear that Japan and the United States were on a collision course of some kind, the importance of successfully attacking the Japanese codes was obvious and in 1939 Friedman dropped everything else and went to work on the problem.

By this time the Japanese had devised an electrical encoding machine of their own that improved vastly (they thought) on one they had purchased from the Germans. By using a system of rotors keyed to specific letters the PURPLE machine could generate a code with millions of possible solutions. And to make matters even more difficult, its language was, of course, Japanese, which with its ideographs is, in itself, one of the hardest to translate into English. Moreover, "telegraphic Japanese," David Kahn in *The Code Breakers* tells us, is "virtually a language within a language." . . . These things come out in the form of syllables, and it is how you group your syllables that you make your words. There is no punctuation." For instance, according to another senior cryptologist at the time, "[the syllable] 'ba' may mean horses or fields or old woman or my hand, all depending on the ideographs with which it is written." To complicate things even further, there were only a handful of people in the United States with the ability to translate the Japanese code language precisely, since Japanese Americans were not considered to be trustworthy of this splendid secret.[14]

Listen again to David Kahn, whose book on code breaking is a masterpiece of its kind: "A cryptanalyst, brooding sphinxlike over the cross-ruled paper on his desk, would glimpse the skeleton of a pattern in a few scattered letters; he tried fitting a fragment from another recovery into it; he tested the new values that resulted and found that they produced acceptable plaintext; he incorporated his essay into the over-all solution and pressed on. Experts in Japanese filled in missing letters; mathematicians tied in one cycle with another and both to the tables. Every weapon of cryptanalytic science—which in the stratospheric realm of this solution drew heavily upon mathematics, using group theory, congruences, Poisson distributions—was thrown into the fray."[15]

Yet the Americans under Friedman's supervision, and with his active assistance, did it. They cracked Japan's diplomatic codes and built themselves their own PURPLE machine, cobbled together from spare parts and stuff purchased at local electronics shops. When they finally turned it on the thing sometimes hissed and shook and occasionally threw out a startling shower of sparks on its operator—but it worked. After eighteen solid months of toil and sweat and mental anguish the Americans began reading Japan's most secret diplomatic communications, and the name they chose for what they had done was MAGIC. No sooner was it working, and a handful of U.S. government officials became suddenly privy to the machinations of the empire of Japan,* than William Friedman (by then a colonel) had a nervous breakdown and was put into the psychiatric ward of Washington's Walter Reed Hospital. It is a wonderful irony that one of those high government officials who was most grateful for the MAGIC code breaking was none other than the new secretary of war, Henry Stimson, who, as secretary of state, had disbanded the Black Chamber a decade earlier.[16]

Meantime, the militarists in Tokyo frantically sought a way to solve their oil crisis. First they began to pressure and threaten the Dutch who, even though their home country had been overrun by Hitler, still controlled the oil-rich Dutch East Indies, including Sumatra, Java, Borneo, and countless thousands of islands in between. The Dutch, however, declined politely but firmly to meet Japan's oil quotas, having experienced firsthand how Axis powers behaved. Japan, true to Axis form, then began planning an attack to seize the Dutch possessions, and threw in the British colonies as well, principally Malaya, with its immense rubber plantations and tin mines, and Burma, next-door neighbor to the jewel in England's Crown, India.

---

*Including the intercepts of the Japanese civilian espionage activities on the West Coast.

To facilitate this "southward movement," as the Japanese military euphemistically phrased it, Japan needed to establish prepared bases thousands of miles farther south as jumping-off points for her attacks. Thus she cast an acquisitive eye on rice-rich French Indochina (Vietnam, Laos, and Cambodia), which had fallen from the legitimate government of France to the puppet Vichy French regime after the surrender of the French nation. It didn't take long for the Germans to convince the craven Vichyists that it would be in their best interests to allow Japan to occupy that part of their Far Eastern empire.

The Roosevelt administration responded furiously to this blatant and ominous aggression. On July 26, 1941, the day after Japanese troops marched into Saigon, America froze all Japanese assets in the United States, effectively and completely shutting Japan off not only from her major source of oil but from her cash as well, since much of it was stored in banks and Japanese-held companies in America. Both sides realized this was the last straw and would lead to trouble one way or the other. When Japan weighed her options, the way she saw it, it boiled down to this: unless she could persuade the United States to reinstate her shipments of oil and other vital military materials, the only choice was to attack and possess the resource-rich South Seas colonies of Great Britain, France, and the Netherlands. In other words, if Japan could not get what she wanted by negotiations, she would take it by force. Japan also knew that by doing so, she risked war with the United States, whose formidable Pacific fleet at Pearl Harbor, on Oahu, Hawaii, was the only possible obstacle standing in the way.

Japan justified aggression upon its neighbors with the same rationale that Germany had been using in its wars since Frederick the Great—including the present one—which was the complaint of encirclement by her enemies. Unlike the Germans, Japan's encirclement was mainly economic rather than geographical; nevertheless she felt just as strongly about it.

For years, the Japanese had sent emissaries throughout East Asia preaching "Asia for the Asians." For the most part the tactic was a success, and not without good reason. Carlos Romulo was a Philippine native and a young and prosperous editor/publisher of a chain of newspapers when, before the outbreak of war in 1941, he decided to travel throughout that part of the world to survey just how Asians felt vis-à-vis Japan and the Western colonial powers. His findings were both interesting and disturbing.

In the prosperous Dutch colony of Java he met a "beautiful and cultured Indonesian girl, world traveled, a graduate of Barnard College, who would have graced any gathering in the world. I invited her to dine with me at the Hotel des Indes. I shall never forget her bitterness. 'We are not welcome there!' She was pro-Japanese. 'Anything is better for us,' she said, 'than life under the Dutch.'" She introduced Romulo to an underground organization with identical leanings.* Romulo had similar experiences in the British colony of Burma where he was told by a group of newspaper editors, "Any situation is better than to be under the British." He also noticed that many of the Buddhist monks in Burma were recently arrived Japanese and "the spearheads of Japanese propaganda." Moving on to Thailand, Romulo was flabbergasted to find that the premier himself "was openly pro-Japanese."

Little did these people know. It was in the countries that were Japanese held—Indochina—or under Japanese attack—China—that Romulo got another eye opening, and here is where the "prejudice and persecution" part of the war equation comes into play, just as it had in the Rape of Nanking. In China he saw firsthand the sort of brutality the Japanese were capable of inflicting on the civilian population, and was warned by Chinese officials, "You had better prepare in the Philippines. You are going to be the next victims of Japan."

At Chungking, where the Chiang Kai-shek government had been driven, Romulo received a whiff of what the Japanese version of "the China incident" was actually like. In between the daily aerial bombings by Japanese planes he found time to interview a Chinese boy missing an arm and

---

*Indonesian hostility toward the Dutch and other European colonists was touched off by a cataclysmic event nearly sixty years earlier. In 1883 the giant volcano Krakatoa, in the straits between Java and Sumatra, exploded with such force that it was felt worldwide and killed some 30,000 natives in the islands. Islamic mullahs who had migrated from the Arabian peninsula years earlier used the tragedy to persuade their converts that Allah was against Western infidels and had blown up the volcano to show his displeasure. This prompted a wave of radical Islam, which to this day remains vexatious in what has since become the nation of Indonesia.

a leg. The Japanese had slaughtered the boy's family on their farm, then chopped off his limbs with swords. Later, traveling to Saigon, Romulo got a good look at the so-called Greater East Asian Co-Prosperity Sphere in operation, noting that "the police records listed from fifty to one hundred and fifty cases a day of assault on women by Japanese soldiers." Like the Germans in Europe, the Japanese considered themselves the Asian master race, and other Asians were treated accordingly—that is, with prejudice and persecution. Romulo's dispatches were published in newspapers worldwide and for his efforts he received the 1942 Pulitzer Prize.[17]

Meanwhile, in early August 1941, just a week after he had imposed the oil embargo on Japan, Roosevelt announced myteriously to the press that he was going "on a fishing trip" off the coast of New England. He even had the presidential yacht *Potomac* brought up from Washington for the occasion. In fact, he was doing no such thing. Soon as the *Potomac* got out of sight of land the cruiser U.S.S. *Augusta* showed up and transferred him and a number of top aides, including the U.S. army and navy commanders, aboard and set steam for remotest Newfoundland, where she dropped anchor in bleak Placentia Bay. Presently an even larger warship appeared, the new British battleship *Prince of Wales,* which had just taken part in the celebrated sinking of the German battleship *Bismarck.* This day she was carrying precious cargo: British prime minister Winston Churchill, come to meet President Roosevelt for the second time.*

The two leaders enjoyed themselves immensely. They had been corresponding in secret for nearly two years and Churchill was especially delighted, since he hoped the meeting would draw Roosevelt and the Americans closer to declaring war on the Axis. It did not have the desired effect; Roosevelt was still concerned about isolationist feelings among the voters at home. However, it did produce one tangible result, the Atlantic Charter, which proclaimed, among other things, that the United States and Great Britain

*The two had met briefly in 1918 at a banquet in England when Roosevelt was a young assistant secretary of the navy and Churchill was Great Britain's minister of munitions. Churchill did not remember the encounter.

were pledged to defend "freedom of the seas." It was also agreed secretly that in the event of the United States entering the war, a policy of "Germany first" would be adhered to; that if war broke out in the Pacific as well, it would be best to remain on the defensive there and put all available resources into defeating Hitler, after which Japan could be dealt with in detail.

It was also revealed to the British at this time that America's twenty-year-old strategy for the Pacific had been altered. The old War Plan 5, which assumed that the Philippines could not be held, had been scrapped. Months earlier Roosevelt had appointed General Douglas MacArthur as commander of U.S. forces in the Far East, and the planners in Washington were shipping him a vast fleet of the new B-17 strategic bombers; in addition, MacArthur was raising a powerful army of 200,000 Filipinos, which, he declared, by the following spring would be trained, equipped, and ready for anything the Japanese could throw at them. What MacArthur or anyone else did not know was that the sands of time were running out.

For decades Japanese military strategists had been contemplating how best to deal with the Americans in the event of a Pacific war. The military consensus had been to create an "incident" that would lure the U.S. fleet across the Pacific where, cut off from its bases* and harassed for thousands of miles by Japanese submarines and warplanes based on mandated Pacific island possessions, it would finally be destroyed by the navy in Japanese home waters.† Into this now volatile state of mind, however, stepped a remarkable man, with a novel and daring approach.

Admiral Isoroku Yamamoto at fifty-seven years old was commander in chief of the Japanese Combined Fleet. He was also dead set against any war with the United States. Having served as a naval attaché in Washington and, later, attended Harvard University, Yamamoto correctly perceived

*The main U.S. Pacific bases were the Hawaiian Islands, Midway and Wake Islands, Guam, and the Philippines. The Japanese controlled the Marshall and Gilbert Island chains, which they obtained control over following Germany's surrender in World War I.

†Interestingly, this was also in fact the strategic plan of the U.S. Navy, not including of course the part about being sunk by the Japanese.

the vast industrial power of the Americans. "Anyone who has seen the auto factories in Detroit and the oil fields in Texas," he cautioned Japanese hot-heads, "knows that Japan lacks the national power for a naval race with America."[18] Not only that, Yamamoto went on record to the Japanese premier with an astonishing declaration: "If I am told to fight regardless of consequence, I shall run wild for the first six months or a year, but I have utterly no confidence for the second and third years."[19]*

This notwithstanding, Admiral Yamamoto was a realist and knew there was little he could do to prevent the army militarists from their so-called Southward Movement into the resource-rich countries on the China Sea and below the equator. And if that was to be, Yamamoto did not wish to leave on his flank and rear the powerful U.S. Pacific Fleet, recently moved to Pearl Harbor from the West Coast. From his time as attaché in the Japanese embassy in Washington, Yamamoto had become well known to a good many U.S. Navy officers, who knew him as an excellent poker and bridge player as well as a master of chess. In short, he was a gambler and a calculator, and what he contemplated gambling on now was for the highest stakes imaginable—the fate of his nation and its empire.

Yamamoto's plan called for superseding the decades-old strategy of luring the American navy into Japanese waters and instead conceived its annihilation in one gigantic stroke: a surprise attack from Japanese carrier-based aircraft on Pearl Harbor while the U.S. Pacific Fleet lay at anchor. The diminutive (five-foot-three) admiral was well aware of the virtues of surprise attacks. As a young ensign during the Russo-Japanese War in 1904 he had rejoiced at the Japanese sneak attack on Port Arthur—with no declaration of war—in which the Russian fleet was devastated and, as a further reminder, he had lost two fingers of his left hand the following year when the Japanese ambushed and destroyed the cream of the Russian navy at the Battle of the Tsushima Straits.[20] Most recently, Yamamoto was made fully aware of the devastation wrought on the Italian fleet at Taranto, in November 1940, when carrier-based British airplanes had attacked it with aerial torpedoes as it lay at anchor.

---

*There are numerous versions and translations of this remark, but the one given in Dr. Morison's *The Rising Sun in the Pacific* seems to hold up as well as any.

No one can say Yamamoto was not inventive—suicide, like assassination, was an old and honorable custom in Japan. Yamamoto's original concept of the attack on Hawaii, believe it or not, was a one-way lightning strike in which his carriers would launch their torpedo- and dive-bombers about five hundred miles from Pearl Harbor, well out of range of American retaliation. The carriers would then immediately turn for home, leaving the pilots to crash into the ocean after the bombing, their fate sealed, since this distance would be twice beyond their airplanes' fuel capacity to return to the ships. It was certainly an audacious and (except for the three hundred Japanese pilots) safe plan and, to Yamamoto's mind, would have the additional value of convincing the Americans that it would be pointless to go to war against any nation that would resort to such a diabolical and fearless blow.[21]

With all this in mind, Yamamoto gathered about him a handful of trusted officers and instructed them to draw up a plan in utmost secrecy. Many problems remained to be solved: what route should the Japanese armada take across the Pacific to avoid early detection; how must aerial torpedoes be altered to run in the shallow waters of Pearl Harbor; what intelligence would be required to ensure that the American fleet would be at its anchorage when the attack commenced? All this they undertook while the civilian government tried frantically and with some earnestness to restore relations with the United States and resume the vital flow of oil to Japan.

For months the negotiations between Japan's amiable ambassador Admiral Kichisaburo Nomura and U.S. Secretary of State Cordell Hull, a brusque-spoken* Tennessean who had described Japan's foreign minister as being "crooked as a bundle of fish hooks," had floundered. Hull's position was doubtless reinforced by his adviser on Far Eastern affairs Dr. Stanley Hornbeck, who counseled his boss that the Japanese were not to be trusted and that the only way to handle them was by the hardest line possible. At the same time, General George C. Marshall, the U.S. Army chief of staff, and Admiral Harold R. "Betty" Stark, chief of naval operations, were stewing themselves sick that some ill fluke of diplomacy would plunge America

---

*Hull actually had a lisp, but it made him no less brusque.

into a Pacific war when she was not yet prepared for it. The referee in this contest was, of course, President Franklin Roosevelt, who tended to side with the military men and "baby along" the Japanese for as many months as possible in order to strengthen U.S. positions in that vast part of the world.

Japan's position was pure and simple: she wanted a resumption of oil and petroleum trade from the United States, the freeing of her frozen assets, and the end of U.S. financial and military aid to China. The American position was pure and simple too: she wanted Japan out of China and Indochina and a promise to respect the rights of her neighbors, as well as for Japan to denounce the Axis pact with Germany and Italy. Put simply, both the United States and Japan were playing for time—the Americans for as long as they could to further strengthen their Pacific bases and the Japanese for as short a time as possible since every day their oil supply was dwindling and, most secretly of all, by early December 1941, the winter weather window for attacking Pearl Harbor would nearly be shut. The North Pacific in winter could be a very rough customer.

In point of fact, American diplomats were negotiating with the Japanese with none of the gullibility of England's Neville Chamberlain, who had actually *believed* Hitler at Munich. They suspected Japan of treachery, and not a few of their suspicions came directly from MAGIC intercepts of Tokyo's instructions to its Washington embassy. Roosevelt, however, still held out the hope that Japan's dire situation vis-à-vis its oil supply might just well persuade its government to concede the U.S. demands in order to restore their oil trade. This of course was unrealistic; Japanese pride, another of the bugaboos of war, would never have allowed them to pull out of Indochina, let alone China itself, after so many years of bitter fighting. It would also have meant an ignominious collapse of the much-vaunted Greater East Asian Co-Prosperity Sphere, which the Japanese government and press had convinced the people was their national destiny.

The negotiations stalled in September 1941 when the Japanese war minister General Hideki Tojo refused to consider even a token withdrawal from China and called for a council of war. When two weeks later the Japanese ambassador Admiral Nomura informed Tokyo that the Americans were adamant on the China issue, Japan's prime minister Prince Fumimaro Konoe and his government fell and in its place came the fateful and fanatically chauvinistic and expansionist government of General Tojo. Now the militarists were in total control.

Tojo was somewhat different from the other fascist dictators of the Axis. He was born into a military family, his father had been a general, and he attended military schools and rose rapidly in rank commensurate with his abilities. He was a militarist and pro-expansionist and it was under his reign that the war was made and the subsequent heinous Japanese behavior was conducted, and which in the end left him twisting from the hangman's rope. He was fifty-seven years old when he took charge, a slight, humorless, bald, and bespectacled man with a "brushy" mustache. His face, according to one magazine writer, "has a parched look, as though he had caught his head in an oven." He has been described thusly by one historian: "Tojo was not the stuff of which dictators or great leaders are made. He had none of Churchill's magnificence, Roosevelt's political acumen, Hitler's evil genius, Mussolini's extravagant dash, or Stalin's peasant shrewdness. But he was rigidly disciplined, honest, and had a team of draft horses for work. He had a sharp but narrow mind and was quite simply a successful general in an organization which discouraged flair and personality, the perfect instrument of Japan's collective dictator—the Army."[22]

Japanese militarism had been sparked by the spectacular victories over Russia in 1904. The idea that the Asian no longer had to fear the European and the American began to take on new meaning: expansion. Spurred in some measure by Japanese newspaper editorialists, Japan's leaders realized they needed ever-increasing natural resources if they were to compete as a world power, and it became apparent to certain hard-line military and civilian leaders that the easiest way to obtain these resources was simply to take them, thus the expansion into Korea, Manchuria, and China, which were all precipitated by so-called incidents.

Slowly, over the first part of the twentieth century, the military gained greater and greater influence over the emperor and the prime minister's cabinet, while at the same time building up Japan's military might. By the 1930s, the Japanese had amassed a great army and navy and, in the minds of the militarists, what good was it to have these powerful forces just sitting in Japanese ports or languishing in training camps? Like a boxer who has trained for years to fight, and with the newspapers goading them on daily, the Japanese were bursting to prove how tough they were. Racism played its hand, too. Still smarting from American slights of bygone years (the "yellow peril") they began to indulge in racism of their own, in which Americans, British, and other Westerners came to be described as "devils."

With Tojo in charge, the handwriting was on the wall and one man who could read it clearly was the longtime American ambassador to Japan, Joseph Grew. He believed, correctly, that the U.S. State Department was not taking the Japanese threat seriously enough and warned anyone who would listen against "any possible misunderstanding of the ability or readiness of Japan to plunge into a suicidal war." He foretold that Japan was prepared "to commit national hara-kiri," and that the fall of the Konoe government would "probably lead to unbridled acts," which could come with "dangerous suddenness." Hull did not quite think so, though, based on the hard-line views of his adviser Dr. Hornbeck, who had been raised in China and despised Japan and refused to believe that even the militarists would be so stupid as to go to war with the United States.

Diplomacy was not quite dead, although it was on its last legs. Since the entire responsibility now rested on his own shoulders, Tojo seemed to get cold feet—with a little help from the emperor, Hirohito, who told him to "go back to blank paper."

The emperor himself was an odd sort of duck and certainly occupied a unique place among leaders of developed nations, for he was venerated as a god by the Japanese people. Anyone passing near the Imperial Palace was expected to take off his hat and taxi drivers often stopped so that their passengers could get out and bow at the walls. Children were warned they would be "struck blind" if they ever looked into his face. He was grandson to Meiji, the first emperor of modern Japan, but had adopted all the proper Western customs such as wearing a striped-pants morning suit to official functions. As war approached, he began dressing in European-style military garb and carrying a samurai sword, and he was usually depicted riding a white horse, complete with English saddle.* A

---

*When the U.S. Eighth Army occupied Japan after the war, its commander, Lieutenant General Robert L. Eichelberger, went looking all over Tokyo for the emperor's white horse so he could give it to MacArthur as a present. He never found it.

mild-mannered man who had just turned forty, the emperor had acquired a taste for jazz music, scotch whisky, golf, and in his private hours devoted himself to the study of marine biology. Yet Hirohito was obviously anxious over the prospect of fighting the United States, and so told his military advisers, who were shocked by his admission. This was because, god or not, under Japanese custom the emperor wasn't expected to interfere in national affairs.[23]

Accordingly, as a result of the emperor's "go back to blank paper" remark, in early November 1941 Tojo sent to the United States a "special emissary" he thought could help the beleaguered Nomura with negotiations. Saburo Kurusu was a former Japanese consul in Chicago, a short, bespectacled man who often wore a morning suit, complete with top hat and cane, and who had married his American secretary and spoke perfect idiomatic English, which Nomura did not.

For his part, Secretary of State Cordell Hull quickly concluded that this new Japanese emissary was "deceitful," an assessment that was not without foundation. Six years earlier, in 1935, when Kurusu had been a minor official with the Japanese Foreign Office, he had remarked during a conversation with one of the undersecretaries at the U.S. embassy in Tokyo that "Japan is destined to be the leader of the Oriental civilization and will in the course of time be the 'boss' of a group comprising China, India, the Netherlands East Indies."[24] This engaging comment had been duly relayed through channels back to the State Department in Washington and Hull no doubt had it before him as he formed his appreciation of Japan's latest addition to its diplomatic team.

Kurusu came bringing two plans: Proposal A, which called for a limited withdrawal of Japanese troops from China as well as a "comprehensive peace plan" that, in effect, was no more than a promise that "peace" would come to China just as soon as the Japanese had conquered it. Hull, who had already seen Proposal A through MAGIC intercepts, stalled for a few days, then rejected it, calling once more for Japan to get out of China. Nomura and Kurusu, on November 20, then presented Proposal B, which Hull had also seen, compliments of MAGIC. It stated that Japan would temporarily stop further aggression in Asia—while still leaving its troops in place—only if the United States would immediately ship it one million gallons of high-octane aviation gasoline. This Hull regarded as an ultimatum but stalled for time on his reply.

Tokyo received this news poorly and told Nomura that he had until November 29 to get the Americans to change their minds or, "after that, things are automatically going to happen." MAGIC intercepts picked this up too and it was viewed darkly by U.S. officials. On November 25 the president and the secretary of state, holding their noses, agreed to a modified version of Proposal B, which would have restored to Japan a limited supply of oil, "on a monthly basis for civilian purposes," in return for Japan's promise of no further aggression for the next three months. This would have given the U.S. military precious time to rush men, guns, planes, and ships to its vital Pacific outposts.* Next day, however, before the counterproposal could be communicated to the Japanese ambassador, it was dropped after intelligence discovered that a large Japanese attack force had put to sea and was apparently sailing for Indochina or Malaya. Roosevelt, when he received this news, was beside himself and, according to his aide Harry Hopkins, "nearly jumped out of his seat." Hull, likewise infuriated, instead handed Ambassadors Nomura and Kurusu a blunt document informing the Japanese yet again that no U.S. oil would be forthcoming until they got out of China and Indochina and reneged on their Axis obligations—in other words, the original American negotiating positions.

By then even Hull had concluded that the situation was hopeless, telling Secretary of War Henry Stimson, "Now it's in the hands of you and [Secretary of the Navy Frank] Knox," that is, he was handing over responsibility to the War Department. That same day, Admiral Yamamoto's huge carrier strike force set sail from its bleak anchorage rendezvous in the remote islands north of Japan, destined for Pearl Harbor.

*For example, there were at that time some 20,000 U.S. troops, including artillery and tanks, waiting on the docks at San Francisco for ship transportation to the Philippines.

Chapter Four ★

By late autumn 1941, tensions between the United States and Japan had become taut as an overused violin string, but most Americans were still blissfully unaware that the thing could snap at any moment. True, public opinion polls showed that two-thirds of the population believed that war with Japan was *inevitable* but most did not believe it was *imminent*. Even as the Japanese armada was sailing inexorably toward its rendezvous with Pearl Harbor, the *New York Times* was reporting hopefully, "An impression prevailed in diplomatic circles that something approaching a status quo may have been reached temporarily that might permit the exploratory conversations between the United States and Japanese emissaries to continue with less disturbance."[1]

Ever since the shocking German victories in Europe eighteen months earlier, America had gone on a modified war footing, beginning with the institution of the first peacetime draft in U.S. history and enormous appropriations of military funding. Aircraft plants and shipyards had expanded their production of warplanes and warships manyfold and automobile manufacturers had begun making tanks, jeeps, trucks, and other military vehicles. The big firearm companies such as Colt and Winchester had retooled to produce military weapons and electronics giants like RCA and Motorola were turning out everything from top-secret radar to commonplace walkie-talkies.

Furthermore, under the emergency War Powers Act granted to the president, the Washington bureaucracy began multiplying itself into a bewildering array of preparedness and administrative agencies that would include such acronymic organizations as the NDAC, OEM, OPM, WPB, OPACS, OES, and, before it was all over, between fifty and sixty other war agencies, "empowered to lay down rules and regulations affecting nearly every sector of the economy, from General Motors to the corner grocer. They were told what they could produce, buy, or sell, the prices they could charge, and the profits they could make. Their performance was dictated by a deluge of orders and printed forms—often confusing and contradictory—and policed by an army of bureaucrats and citizen busybodies."[2]

America was certainly trying, but nothing seemed to go smoothly. There was precious little equipment as yet available for the million or so soldiers recently drafted into the army. Men were training with broomsticks for rifles, chicken eggs for hand grenades, trucks for tanks, and the old "soup plate" helmets left over from the First World War. Modern warplanes were scarce; warships were obsolete. Labor strikes frequently slowed or stopped production of vital war materials. The automobile industry continued to produce cars as fast as it could because the profits from these were higher than for those in their weapons and arms production plants, which were subject to government price controls. Some civilian industries were put out of business entirely because of a shortage of raw goods, which were mandated for war production. So many marginal workers such as farmhands, domestic servants, cooks, and day laborers were rushing to grab the higher-paying defense jobs that it threw some parts of the economy into an uproar.

Still, on the eve of war there were some four million Americans out of work (down from more than twice that number a decade earlier), but even though most economic indicators had picked up considerably the vestiges of the Great Depression lingered sourly. Nevertheless, even as the Japanese battle fleet steamed remorselessly across the Pacific many, if not most, of the 134 million Americans had reason to believe that hard times were fading, despite the fact that a terrible war might be lurking in the near future.

About two-thirds of all Americans were in some form of the middle class, earning from $1,000 to $3,000 a year (about $15,000 to $40,000 today). But lunch was 50 cents and a couple could dine out at most good restaurants for well under $5; a decent suit could be had for under $50, bread was anywhere from 5 to 8 cents a loaf, and a glass of beer cost a dime. Women could buy a pair of nylons for $1.75 (expensive but traditional silk stockings had become unavailable due to the trade embargo against Japan). Fewer than 50,000 American citizens earned more than $25,000 a year (about $325,000 in today's dollars).

At the movies people were watching the critically acclaimed *Citizen Kane* or still going to see the popular, long-playing *Gone With the Wind,* or else they stayed home and listened to the Jack Benny or Edgar Bergen and Charlie McCarthy shows on the radio—or to Edward R. Murrow's riveting transatlantic news broadcasts during the London aerial blitz. There was no home air-conditioning. They sang anyway, or listened to music on the radio or record player, perhaps such wistfully haunting wartime tunes as "The Last Time I Saw Paris," or "There'll Be Bluebirds Over the White Cliffs of Dover," or rousing numbers such as "Deep in the Heart of Texas"; they danced to the swing bands such as Benny Goodman's and Glenn Miller's, and did the boogie-woogie. "Chattanooga Choo Choo" was a popular favorite. For vacation people traveled to the mountains or the shore where rates at good resorts were about $10 per day, including meals. A six-day cruise to Havana cost $75, third class. Tourists wishing to go to Hawaii were informed that they would "scarcely notice the Army pillboxes, they were so well concealed." Naturally, nobody talked anymore about vacationing in Europe.[3]

America's attitude vis-à-vis the war was difficult to read. Except for the diehard isolationists, the majority disliked Hitler and hoped England would win but were still not ready to leap into the fray. So far as Japan went, the sentiment was harsher. Americans had seen the newsreels of the Rape of Nanking, with Chinese citizens lined up by Japanese soldiers and shot in the back of the head into their own graves.* They had read the best-selling

---

*The Germans were far more circumspect and hid their atrocities; the world would not see extensive pictures of them until after the war.

novel *The Good Earth* by Pearl Buck, which described the pitiless Japanese oppression in that forlorn land. All in all, Japan got bad press in the United States, the lone exception being the popular *Mr. Moto* movies, based on a fictional Japanese-American detective of that name created by John P. Marquand and played by the actor Peter Lorre. Even so, most people considered Mr. Moto to be "tricky," unlike his equally popular movie counterpart, the Chinese detective Charlie Chan.

The American view of the Japanese was such as to give some credence to Japanese complaints of racial stereotyping. The typical Japanese soldier was depicted in newspaper cartoons as a short, bandy-legged, buck-toothed, nearsighted, chattering ape.* That aside, the Japanese remained a weird enigma to average Americans. The historian John Toland gave this description in perfect candor: "To most Westerners, the Japanese was utterly inscrutable. The way he handled his tools was all wrong; he squatted at the anvil; he pulled rather than pushed a saw; he built his house from the roof down. To open a lock, he turned his key to the left, the wrong direction. Everything the Japanese did was backwards. He spoke backwards, read backwards, wrote backwards. He sat on the floor instead of in chairs, ate fish raw, and live, wriggling shrimp. He would tell of the most tragic personal events and then laugh; fall in the mud in his best suit and come up with a grin. . . . [He would] discuss matters in a devious, tortuous manner, treat you with exaggerated politeness in his home and then rudely shove you aside in a train—even murder a man and then apologize to his servants for messing up the house."[4]

The popular American humorist-poet Ogden Nash added to the caricature with this piece of doggerel, depicting Japanese international behavior:

> *How courteous is the Japanese;*
> *He always says, "Excuse it, please."*
> *He climbs into his neighbor's garden,*

---

*Even General Douglas MacArthur, commanding the U.S. Far East forces during the fall of the Philippines, subscribed to this notion. After witnessing the skill of Japanese fighter pilots during the Battle of Manila, he concluded that the planes must have been flown by Germans or other Europeans—not ignorant, nearsighted Japanese. Interestingly, Winston Churchill agreed with this assessment.

And smiles, and says, "I beg your pardon";
He bows and grins a friendly grin,
And calls his hungry family in;
He grins, and bows a friendly bow;
"So sorry, this my garden now."[5]

How such a people could pose a serious threat to the United States of America was not clear to most Americans, but it wouldn't be long before they found out.

The Japanese war plan was based on the somewhat logical but faulty assumption that a "lightning strike" against all of East Asia and the mid-Pacific, followed by rapid fortification of the conquered lands, would cause the United States, Great Britain, and the Dutch to sue for peace on the notion that it simply would not be worth their efforts and expense in lives and treasure to try to drive the Japanese out of countries thousands of miles distant that were peopled by Asians anyway. Thus, having acquired all the oil, raw materials, and rice they needed, Japan would then proceed to finish off what they had started in China, and the empire would then extend and expand from the far northern Kuril Islands near the U.S.-owned Aleutians, southward nearly the length of the Pacific to New Guinea off the coast of Australia, thence westward for five thousand miles, encompassing the rich island countries on the China and Philippine Seas, and all the way to the border with British colonial India—and maybe into that, too. Although most of it would be ocean, twenty-five million square miles of new territory, land and sea, would nevertheless fall under the permanent domination of the empire of Japan—and after the war began, as we shall see, this was to be just the beginning.

In order to accomplish the lightning strike that had been assigned to him, Admiral Yamamoto, as discussed, had concluded that he must first destroy the U.S. fleet based in Hawaii, as well as eliminate the American forces in the Philippine Islands. Other countries and colonies would fall in short order: Hong Kong, Thailand, Burma, Indochina, Malaya, Singapore, Borneo, Sumatra, Java, Celebes, and New Guinea, and including scores of small islands spread out across the Pacific, which would soon bristle with Japanese guns, troops, warplanes, warships, and fortifications ready to repel any attempt to retake the conquered region,* which would then contain half of the human population on earth. It was estimated by Japanese military planners that it would take four to six months to over-run all the desired objectives and consolidate the gains, and that this could be done before the United States and her allies could recover from Pearl Harbor and other disasters that the Japanese had in store for them.

The Pearl Harbor operation, however, was the key to the whole busi-ness. The U.S. Pacific Fleet and air force had to be put out of business, lest they interfere with the Southern Movement. As Yamamoto himself put it, "If we fail, we might as well give up the war."

The man chosen to train and lead the air strike itself was Commander Minoru Genda, a thirty-six-year-old ace fighter pilot who had distinguished himself in aerial strategy and by planning mass bombing raids during the long war with China. A lean, handsome man with "piercing eyes," Genda has been described as brilliant, and certainly was a man before his time in the Japa-nese navy. He has also been described as the Japanese Billy Mitchell,† being the first in Japan to advocate eliminating the idea of a navy built around battleships, instead organizing the navy around a fleet of fast aircraft car-riers, which, concentrated in task forces of six or more, could carry the offensive thousands of miles from the Japanese homeland.[6]

After determining that the strike on Hawaii was risky, but that it "had a reasonable chance of success," Genda set about persuading Yamamoto that his maniacal one-way strike was nothing more than wasteful suicide since it would deprive the navy thereafter of the services of its best and most expe-rienced pilots. Yamamoto conceded Genda's arguments, leaving the young commander to begin tackling the problems he foresaw. Among them were

---

*These small islands would soon enough become all too well known to U.S. sol-diers, sailors, and marines. Among them: Guadalcanal, Tarawa, Bougainville, Peleliu, New Georgia, Saipan, Iwo Jima, and Okinawa, to name a few.

†Mitchell was a flamboyant U.S. Army Air Corps brigadier general and airpower advocate who in the 1920s, after sinking a leftover German World War I battleship in a demonstration of what aerial bombing could accomplish, got himself court-martialed for being too vociferous on the matter.

how to keep the aerial torpedoes from diving into the shallow mud bottom of Pearl Harbor and how to prevent the level bombers' ordnance from exploding on contact with the heavily armored decks of the American battleships instead of plowing through and exploding below where they would do the most damage. Genda solved the first problem by installing wooden fins on the torpedoes, which somewhat controlled their running depth, and the second by the ingenious idea of converting big sixteen-inch battleship shells as bombs with reinforced noses to allow them to crash through the armor plating to the belowdecks before exploding.[7]

In September 1941 training began in earnest. Japanese pilots practiced daily on the Inland Sea with astonishingly low-level torpedo runs—in the process, frightening the daylights out of sampan fishermen—and dive-bombers perfected their craft by pulling up at the last possible moment to ensure accurate hits. Certain rocks sticking out of the sea were selected as practice targets for the high-level bombers because they approximated the size of the American ships. But at that time neither the pilots nor even the ships' captains knew what all this training was about; the ultimate mission was still privy to only a handful of trusted staff officers.

Meantime, Genda had concluded that merely to destroy the U.S. Pacific Fleet was not good enough. His fertile mind conceived an even bolder stroke—landing troops and occupying Hawaii itself, for with it would come Japanese control of the entire Central Pacific. After all, he reasoned, what was America going to do about it, with its fleet at the bottom of the ocean? But Genda's superiors shot down his idea on grounds that what with the war still going on in China and their huge Southern Movement on the horizon, there were simply not enough troops or transports, they told him, to support such a vast expansion of the original plan.[8] It is clear that Genda's proposal had much to recommend it. If the Japanese had occupied Hawaii it would have created almost unimaginable problems for the Allies in the Pacific war. Hawaii was and would become the great American staging area for the future operations against Japan, and if the U.S. fleet had been forced to operate from the West Coast or even Australia, this could have prolonged the war by years. Even the use of the atomic bomb would probably have been set back because the Americans would have had trouble getting in close enough range of Japan to drop it.

Not everyone in Japanese military circles was as sanguine as Yamamoto about success in eliminating the U.S. Pacific Fleet in the manner prescribed. Naval war games had indicated that the Americans might be able to sink at least two of the carriers, and there was also the ever tricky question of achieving surprise, without which the raid might become a disaster. Then there was the thorny possibility that the U.S. fleet might be somewhere other than Pearl Harbor when the Japanese attackers arrived. For his part Yamamoto clung to his plan like a bat to a cliff; when pressed against the advisability of the attack by the navy's general staff the much revered commander threatened to resign, effectively ending any opposition.

In order to forestall the obnoxious possibility that the U.S. fleet would not be lying at anchor in Pearl Harbor when the Japanese struck, the Imperial Navy general staff had installed itself a spy to operate out of the Japanese consulate in Honolulu. Takeo Yoshikawa, a twenty-nine-year-old graduate of the Japanese naval academy, had been dropped from the service because of a stomach ailment caused by heavy drinking but was later reinstated and sent to intelligence school. Using the alias Tadashi Morimura, Yoshikawa arrived in Honolulu harbor aboard a Japanese ocean liner in March 1941, looking like a tourist complete with a lei around his neck, and went to business under the phony cover of being an employee of the Japanese consulate.

He soon set up operations in a Japanese teahouse overlooking Pearl Harbor, where he used a telescope to count the number and location of American ships and track their movements to and from the ocean on fleet maneuvers. Yoshikawa used various ploys and disguises to get the information requested of him by his controllers back in Tokyo. A few times he disguised himself as a laborer in a sugarcane field to get a better look at the Pearl Harbor defenses. Mostly he just wore one of his garish Hawaiian shirts and cruised around the area either in a taxi or in a car provided by a sympathetic Japanese immigrant. Often he took with him a geisha girl from one of the several teahouses he favored; on one occasion he chartered a small single-engine plane to get a better view of the U.S. military installations. As well as the ship dispositions at Pearl Harbor, Yoshikawa noted on his aerial excursion the number and types of warplanes and runways at

Wheeler and Hickam Fields and the Kaneohe Naval Air Station, in the process becoming, in essence, the proverbial fly on the wall. Once, when asked by his superiors to find out if the U.S. Navy used an antisubmarine net at the entrance to Pearl Harbor, Yoshikawa dressed up as a fisherman complete with cane pole and after dark slipped into the murky waters to try to find the net. He was unsuccessful, apparently due to nervousness.

However, flush with an expense account from his Tokyo handlers, Yoshikawa's old habits of drinking and womanizing soon returned and before long he found himself in bitter arguments with the senior consular staff, who were concerned that his behavior would create suspicion by American counterintelligence agents, which it did; at one point he was arrested by Hawaiian police for public drunkenness. In fact Yoshikawa had been under surveillance by U.S. authorities from the moment he stepped off his ship; the Office of Naval Intelligence and the FBI had noticed that even though he was listed as a diplomatic "chancellor," there was no record of him ever having served in any Japanese diplomatic post. He was tailed and his phone wiretapped, but nothing extraordinary turned up. The U.S. agents certainly suspected Yoshikawa of spying, but there was little they could do about it since he was shrewd enough not to break any U.S. laws such as taking photographs or actually entering any military facility. Besides that, he was with the consulate and it was "sacrosanct," according to an FBI agent assigned to the case. And finally, according to the State Department, any move to deport Yoshikawa might have revealed to the Japanese that the United States had broken into their top-secret diplomatic message system.[9]

Then, as luck would have it, barely two months before the Pearl Harbor attack, Tokyo sent a message ordering Yoshikawa to draw up a specific plotting grid for every U.S. warship in Pearl Harbor, dividing the anchorage into five subareas known as A-B-C-D-E, and wanting to know such things as whether two or more ships were moored side by side at the docks (vital information for Genda and his planners because the inboard ship or ships would be impervious to the aerial torpedoes).

This message was, naturally, intercepted via MAGIC and in due time it was decoded and translated and wound up on the desk of Colonel Rufus Bratton, chief of the Far East division of army intelligence in Washington, D.C. It especially attracted Bratton's attention because for the first time in his experience the Japanese were showing curiosity as to the precise loca-tion of U.S. ships at Pearl Harbor, and not just when they came and went. Unfortunately, Bratton's superiors did not share his interest in this obvi-ously noteworthy request from Tokyo and before it was all over the "bomb plot message," as it came to be called, would later trigger a firestorm of maledictions during the various hearings in Congress and elsewhere look-ing to assign blame for the intelligence failure at Pearl Harbor. [10]

Meantime, U.S. intelligence was doing some spying of its own, though perhaps not in as exotic a manner as the ubiquitous Japanese agent Yoshikawa. Six months before the Japanese attack the U.S. Navy had detached Commander Joseph John Rochefort from his duties as intelli-gence officer of the U.S.S. *Indianapolis* and told him to take charge of what he would rename the Combat Intelligence Unit at Pearl Harbor, which was responsible for snatching Japanese radio waves and decoding them. The forty-three-year-old Rochefort was a wise and obvious choice for the navy, since he was the only man in the entire service who was an expert in radio, cryptology, and the Japanese language.

As we know, the MAGIC system had already broken the Japanese dip-lomatic code, but breaking the Japanese naval code was a different problem entirely. Still, Rochefort set at it with a vengeance because he understood that he now had perhaps the most crucial single job in the Pacific: keeping track of the Japanese navy. Rochefort employed about a hundred people—most experts in one field of radio intelligence or another, some headquar-tered in a windowless, airless basement of an office building. He himself was something of an eccentric; he lived almost exclusively in this dank chamber and his working uniform consisted of a red satin smoking jacket and carpet slippers.

Rochefort's section worked around the clock trying to crack the Imperial Navy's code but with little success; up until the end of Novem-ber 1941, they had managed to decipher only about 10 percent of it. But there are other ways to skin a cat; for instance, they were often able to identify the regular telegrapher aboard certain Japanese warships by his particular touch on the telegraph key. For example, the radio telegrapher aboard the Japanese carrier *Akagi,* according to the U.S. fleet intelligence officer, "played that key as if he were sitting on it." Thus armed with the identity of a particular ship, Rochefort's section was then often able to locate its position by radio direction finding. This was an intelligence-gathering system in which stations of specialists were set up across the far reaches of the Pacific, from Hawaii to the Aleutians to the Philippines to the Dutch East Indies, to intercept radio traffic from the Japanese fleet. They would home in on a signal until it was at its loudest and then take a bearing. If two or more direction finders were able to home in on the same signal, they could fix the exact position of that ship and, in fact, track its course and speed by continual interceptions. It wasn't as good as being able to decipher the message itself but, at least so far, Rochefort was able to keep track of where the Japanese navy was, if not what it was up to.[11]

Then at the end of November 1941, an ominous development took place; the Japanese navy suddenly changed all of its call signals. Until then, Rochefort and his section had reliably placed the fleet—especially the carriers—in Japanese home waters, primarily in the Inland Sea. Even more ominously there was a noticeable drop in radio traffic. Now Rochefort was in the dark and promptly reported this to his boss, U.S. Pacific Fleet intelligence officer Edwin T. Layton, who promptly reported it to *his* boss, Admiral Husband E. Kimmel, commander in chief of the Pacific Fleet.

Kimmel immediately ordered Layton to prepare a paper on what currently was known about the disposition of the Japanese navy. When Layton delivered it next day, Kimmel was shocked to read that there was no information whatever on two full Japanese carrier divisions.

"What!" he demanded. "You do not know where they are?"

Layton replied that Rochefort's intelligence people still thought they were in home waters, but could no longer be sure.

"Do you mean to say," the admiral asked incredulously, "that they could be rounding Diamond Head and you wouldn't know it?"

That was about the size of it, but Layton managed a lame reply: "I would hope," he told the Pearl Harbor commander, "that they would be sighted by now."[12]

All through the autumn of 1941 the negotiations between Tokyo and Washington had continued at an agonizing snail's pace. Part of the problem was the translations provided to Secretary of State Hull by the MAGIC people who, of course, were reading Japan's top-secret messages to its Washington ambassador. The difficulties of precise translations from Japanese to English have been noted in the previous chapter, but here are some concrete examples. The Japanese foreign minister cabled Ambassador Nomura that he must persuade Hull and Roosevelt to accept Japan's A or B proposals because "THE SECURITY OF THE EMPIRE DEPENDS ON IT." The people over at the MAGIC shop, however, translated the intercept as saying: "IN FACT WE GAMBLED THE FATE OF OUR LAND ON THE THROW OF THIS DICE." Further, Tokyo informed Nomura that "THIS IS OUR PROPOSAL SETTING FORTH WHAT ARE VIRTUALLY OUR FINAL CONCESSIONS." But what Hull read in translation was: "THIS PROPOSAL IS OUR REVISED ULTIMATUM."[13]

True, the general sense in both these examples—and there are many others—is essentially the same, but given the delicacy of the ongoing crisis, every nuance had added meaning, and it too often appears that the American translators went for the more "interesting" and direct version. In the end, the result would probably have been the same, but it is perhaps unfortunate that Hull seemed to be getting the more strident renditions of Japan's political stances.

By the end of November 1941, matters were fast coming to a head. It had become obvious to the U.S. military commanders, General Marshall and Admiral Stark, that war with Japan was simply a matter of time, and that the U.S. Pacific possessions might be struck with terrible suddenness. Secretary of War Stimson recorded in his diary that President Roosevelt had decided (for political reasons peculiar to the American voting population) that if war did come, it was desirable that Japan fire the first shot, so to speak. In other words, that the United States should be the one attacked, not the other way around. This was never to suggest that American commanders in the Pacific leave themselves open and defenseless for a crushing blow, but many of the so-called revisionist historians have interpreted it as such in the race to blame Roosevelt and others for deviously plotting the disaster at Pearl Harbor.

Mistakes were made, to be sure, and afterward heads rolled, though perhaps not the right ones. For more than a week as autumn turned to winter, a high drama began to unfold between Washington and its outposts in the far Pacific. On November 27, 1941, after Secretary of State Hull's peremptory reply to Japan's peremptory response to his previous note, the Japanese concluded that negotiations were over and, in any case, they already had their carrier fleet skulking toward Pearl Harbor. And so on that date Admiral Stark issued his now famous "war warning" message to naval commanders in the Pacific, and Stimson issued a similar one to the army commanders, suggesting that the Japanese might break out hostilities "within a few days" and reiterating the business about not attacking the Japanese first.

Unfortunately, neither of these messages even hinted that an attack might be imminent on Pearl Harbor itself. Instead they suggested—reasonably—that Japanese movements would probably be against the far-off Philippines or targets farther south such as Malaya. In Hawaii the senior U.S. Army commander, General Walter Short, was warned by officials in Washington that sabotage seemed his greatest danger because of the large number of Japanese, both native and American-born, living in the islands. General Short reacted by ordering that all military aircraft at the major bases be lined up wingtip to wingtip on the runways to make guarding them easier against saboteurs. It also, of course, made them perfect targets if an attack came from the air rather than from the ground.

After much last-minute internal squabbling as to whether or not to actually provoke war with the United States, the dictator Tojo, the emperor, and various other high functionaries decided to let war plans go ahead. Accordingly, they proposed a response to Secretary of State Hull's last note to them. It was basically a long screed that ticked off everything they didn't like about the United States of America. It was ordered sent to the Japanese ambassador in Washington in fourteen parts, the first thirteen to arrive on Saturday, December 6, and the final part to arrive on Sunday, December 7. Tokyo further instructed its ambassador that after the full message was received, he was to see to it that all major codes and code machines in the embassy were destroyed.

This message was of course snatched out of the air via MAGIC and arrived translated on the desks of the pertinent intelligence officers in

Washington, who then began to distribute it to higher authorities. The Japanese ambassadors had not even read it yet. Navy lieutenant commander Alvin D. Kramer was alarmed when he read the first thirteen parts and, using his wife as a driver, he began delivering copies to appropriate high-ranking naval authorities, as well as to the White House. Kramer's opposite number in army intelligence, Colonel Rufus Bratton—who had become disturbed when he saw the earlier MAGIC intercept asking for information on ships in Pearl Harbor—was told by his boss, General Sherman Miles, that this latest Japanese message was of "little military significance" and ordered him not to disturb General of the Army Marshall with its contents.[14]

When the message reached the White House about nine P.M., however, there was quite a different reaction. Roosevelt was seated in his study talking with his aide Harry Hopkins, who was pacing the floor, when a naval assistant brought it in. Roosevelt read the thing and handed it to Hopkins, and when Hopkins had finished it Roosevelt said to him, "This means war."

Hopkins agreed and suggested that if that were so, then it might be best to attack the Japanese first. "No, we can't do that," Roosevelt replied. "We are a democracy and a peaceful people." Then he added something strange: "But we have a good record."

What was meant by this odd remark has never been fully explained. Roosevelt did try to reach his chief of naval operations, Admiral Harold Stark, but Stark had gone to the theater to see *The Student Prince* and Roosevelt decided not to disturb him. Nor did he call General Marshall.[15]

What followed remain a lot of what-ifs.

Next morning, December 7, Marshall, still unaware of the Japanese message, went out for his usual long Sunday morning horseback ride in the fields near Arlington, Virginia. When somebody finally found him about eleven-thirty A.M. he had gotten to his office and was slowly reading the first thirteen parts of the message. Colonel Bratton held in his hand the final (fourteenth) part, as well as something that had alarmed Bratton even more: the final instruction to the Japanese ambassador indicating that Tokyo had ordered him to deliver the message to the U.S. secretary of state at precisely one P.M. Washington time. To Bratton, this meant that something was probably going to happen in the Pacific at that time, he just didn't know where; he never suspected Pearl Harbor because, as he explained later, "After the original 'War Warning' the week earlier, everyone in Washington naturally assumed the fleet would be at sea."

Commander Kramer, who had delivered copies of the message the night before, was equally alarmed. He had calculated that at one P.M. in Washington it would be dark in the Philippines, but it would be just after sunrise in Hawaii. The full import of this reckoning did not immediately strike him, but he did communicate it to Admiral Stark.

Bratton stood fidgeting in Marshall's office while the general perused the first thirteen parts of the message with excruciating slowness. Bratton tried several times to interrupt him to show him the last part and the one P.M. deadline message, but the chief of staff waved him off.

Finally Marshall accepted Bratton's remaining documents and at last recognized the significance of the whole message, especially the one P.M. time frame. Though the message contained no actual declaration of war,*[16] it did state that the Japanese were breaking off negotiations and Marshall assumed they were certainly up to something.

He conferred over the phone with Stark, who had by then also read the message. Stark was at first reluctant to send out another "war warning" to his Pacific commanders. He assumed the one he had sent a week earlier had been sufficient, and did not want to appear to be crying wolf. After all, if he sent out another, and nothing happened, and then after that something else arose, and he sent out another, and so forth, the commanders were almost sure to relax their guard. It is almost impossible to keep a large military force on a constant alert status, to the detriment of all else.

However, after further consultation with Marshall, Stark agreed that whatever message Marshall was going to send should be communicated by the various army commanders to their navy counterparts in the Philippines, Panama, the West Coast, and, belatedly, Pearl Harbor. It read: "Japanese are presenting at one P.M. eastern standard time today what

*The Japanese foreign minister later declared that "breaking off negotiations was clearly a cessation of peace, that is to say, a resort to war." A formal declaration of war in this note, he said, "would merely reiterate the obvious." The Americans, however, did not see it quite that way.

amounts to an ultimatum, also they are under orders to destroy their code machine immediately. Just what significance the hour set may have we do not know but be on alert accordingly. Inform naval authorities of this communication. Marshall."

In Washington, it was now nearly noon. People were returning from church services or preparing for Sunday dinner. The D.C. football stadium (Griffith Field; now demolished) was filling up with fans for the Redskins–Philadelphia Eagles game. Stark had offered Marshall the use of the navy communication services, but Marshall declined and Bratton was given the assignment to get the warning to the Pacific commanders by the highest priority. As historian Gordon Prange has pointed out, "No one seriously considered using the telephone, even with its scrambler, because it was still considered insecure—and, given the wording of Marshall's message, it would be obvious to anyone listening in that the U.S. was reading Japan's secret communications."[17]

Bratton anxiously rushed Marshall's handscribbled warning to the army communications center, where it would have to be typed out, encoded, and sent, then decoded and delivered. There was still nearly a precious hour left to alert the Pacific to the coming danger, but then a new glitch appeared. A big solar storm had brewed up overnight and the army's radio communications with Hawaii became impossible. The signal officer on duty decided on the spot that civilian commercial services would be the next-best way to get Marshall's warning out. So he had it teletyped from his office directly to Western Union, which sent it on to San Francisco, which sent it to the RCA office there, which cabled it to Honolulu, which would deliver it by messenger to the army message center at Pearl Harbor, which, after decoding it, would give it to the commanding general, Walter Short, who would pass it along to somebody who would give it to the navy admiral commanding the fleet, Husband Kimmel. By the time it finally got there, neither General Short nor Admiral Kimmel would have need of it.

Chapter Five ✯

As General Marshall's warning message was wending its tortuous path across the Pacific, the sailors and soldiers at and near Pearl Harbor were only beginning to wake up. Sunday was generally a lazy day in the prewar military; men were sitting around in mess halls enjoying coffee and cigarettes. Some were preparing for Sunday morning services or recreational activities, perhaps planning to spend the day at the beach; some were sleeping it off from Saturday night on the town. All in all it looked to be another beautiful Hawaiian tropic day.

Two hundred miles north of Pearl, just as the first rosy glow of dawn began to spread over those desolate reaches of the ocean, a hair-raising tableau would have appeared to anyone who came across it unsuspecting. There in the roiling misty sea was a mighty gray battlefleet flying the flag of the Rising Sun—twenty-four fast warships: battleships, cruisers, destroyers, supply vessels—and standing out against these in stark relief, dwarfing them even, were six enormous aircraft carriers, launching hundreds of planes.*

---

*The carriers were *Akagi* (Red Castle), *Hiryu* (Flying Dragon), *Kaga* (Increased Joy), *Soryu* (Green Dragon), *Shokaku* (Soaring Crane), and *Zuikaku* (Happy Crane). Before the war ended, all would lie at the bottom of the ocean—the first four within the next six months—as would all but one of their escort fleet, a lone destroyer.

Here was the zenith of Yamamoto's scheme, and it had so far gone perfectly. They had made their way across the deserted and freezing North Pacific in December completely undetected; the spy Yoshikawa in Honolulu had just made his final report, indicating that the U.S. battleship fleet was in, the weather was clear, and there seemed to be no undue alarm. Just another Sunday at Pearl Harbor.*

One person who was not particularly pleased was the Japanese air commander Minoru Genda because the U.S. aircraft carriers were missing from Pearl Harbor, and he did not know why or where they were. As an airpower advocate the American Pacific carriers had been Genda's ultimate target, for they were the main force capable of striking back at Japan itself or, for that matter, at his own carriers. In fact the U.S.S. *Enterprise* and *Lexington* were off to the West, delivering fighter planes to Wake and Midway Islands, and the *Saratoga* was just arriving in Seattle for an overhaul. *Yorktown* and *Hornet* had recently been sent to the Atlantic.

Despite the original qualms of Admiral Chuichi Nagumo, commanding the Japanese armada, the First Air Fleet was finally entering into the riskiest and, up to then, most crucial mission of its existence. Nagumo, a fifty-four-year-old veteran of the old "gun navy"—battleships and cruisers—was inexperienced with airpower and he had fretted and stewed all across the far reaches of the North Pacific about the success of the attack. Fierce winter storms were encountered with mountainous seas. During refueling operations sailors had vanished overboard after being swept from the carrier decks by hoses used for fueling at sea, which often snapped in the

---

*The Hawaiian Islands had been discovered in 1778 by the English explorer Captain James Cook, who named them the Sandwich Islands after a patron, the Earl of Sandwich. Cook returned the following year but, while ashore, the Hawaiians clubbed and stabbed him to death in plain view of his ship, and later dismembered him and returned some of his body parts to his crew. America annexed the islands in 1898 and in 1906 established the Pearl Harbor naval base. In 1940, with the rising tensions between Japan and the United States, President Roosevelt ordered the U.S. Pacific Fleet moved from its West Coast base and permanently stationed at Pearl as a "deterrent" to Japanese aggression. The then fleet commander, Admiral James O. Richardson, objected because of logistics and morale ("too few white women; shopkeepers gypped the sailors"), but when he complained to the president he was fired and replaced by Admiral Husband E. Kimmel.

storms and whipped across deck like giant writhing snakes. Still the fleet sailed on, observing strict radio silence, communicating by signal lamps, and flags if weather permitted. The ships could receive messages from Japan, however, without giving up their positions, and seven days out the fleet received from Tokyo the word everyone had been anticipating: "Climb Mount Niitaka." This was the code phrase telling them that the negotiations with America had failed; that the Pearl Harbor attack was to proceed; that there would be no turning back.

Almost everyone had been up since the late midnight hours. The pilots dressed in their newly pressed uniforms and some put on the white *hashamaki* headband of the Japanese samurai warrior. The night before, many had written farewell letters to their families. They were treated to a special ceremonial breakfast of red beans and rice and sake. The man who was actually to lead the air attack forces was Lieutenant Commander Mitsuo Fuchida, a classmate and friend of Genda's from their days together at the Japanese Naval Academy. As he walked into the officers' mess Fuchida was greeted by a fellow officer who said to him, "Good morning, commander, Honolulu sleeps."[1]

Of course not everybody in Honolulu was sleeping. There was for instance the overtime-paid disc jockey at station KGMB, who had, at the request of the U.S. Army, played Hawaiian music all night so that a flight of B-17 heavy bombers en route from the West Coast would have a signal to home in on before they landed around eight A.M. Also there had been some strange doings around Pearl Harbor itself that morning, which caused some consternation.

The destroyer *Ward* was on antisubmarine duty near the entrance channel to Pearl when a lookout spotted something strange in the water. The *Ward,* a World War I–vintage ship, had been instructed to sink on sight any submarine it saw, because no U.S. subs were supposed to be in the area. At first in the thin light of dawn they believed the strange object might be a buoy, but then it seemed to be following a supply ship, which was heading into Pearl through the opened antisubmarine nets. A closer look through binoculars revealed that the strange object appeared to be a conning tower of a submarine—except that it did not look like the conning tower of any submarine they were familiar with. The skipper of the *Ward,* Lieutenant William W. Outerbridge, was summoned. He immediately called general quarters.

In fact what the *Ward* had sighted was one of five Japanese midget subs launched from five mother ships—regular submarines to which the midgets had been bolted on deck and ferried all the way across the Pacific to sneak into Pearl Harbor and, carrying two torpedoes each, do as much damage as possible in concert with the massive air attack. Basically, it was a suicide mission, since there was no way to recover the mini-subs, but their two-man crews were enthusiastic to sink American ships and die for their emperor.

Lieutenant Outerbridge ordered the *Ward* to open fire on the sub when it was one hundred yards away, dead ahead. The first shot missed, but the second hit the conning tower and the sub wallowed. The *Ward* pressed on until the sub was "right alongside, almost sucked against the ship,"[2] then it spun off in the *Ward*'s wake. Outerbridge ordered depth charges fired, and soon the ocean astern erupted in gigantic undersea blasts no submarine that close could have withstood. Outerbridge then sent a radio message to his headquarters at Pearl: "Attacked, fired on, depth bombed, and sunk, submarine operating in defensive sea area." It was 6:53 A.M., barely an hour before the first wave of 183 Japanese warplanes were due to strike Pearl Harbor.

Receipt of the *Ward*'s message was only the first of many snafus* that morning, which might otherwise have put Pearl Harbor on alert. The office that received it was manned only by an old navy reserve officer and a Hawaiian enlisted man "who understood little English and nothing about the teletype."[3] It took nearly twenty minutes to decode and comprehend the message, and even longer to reach the proper authorities. Even when this was done, Admiral Claude C. Bloch, commanding the Fourteenth Naval District, spent nearly ten more minutes trying to decide if the report was true. In the past there had been many such reports, which turned

---

Snafu was a naval term that came into use during the war. It stood for "Situation normal, all fouled up."

out to be attacks on whales or giant blackfish or just plain old flotsam. So Admiral Bloch turned to a time-honored navy custom: he told the duty officer to have the *Ward* verify its message and, in the meantime, to "await further developments." These were not long in coming.

Commander Fuchida was flight leader of the 183 planes in the first strike: 49 high-altitude level bombers, each carrying one of the big sixteen-inch navy gun shells converted into armor-piercing bombs; 40 torpedo planes with one torpedo slung under the fuselage; 51 dive-bombers; and 43 Zeros—escort fighter planes. Navigation was not difficult; after all, just like the flight of incoming American B-17s, they had the Honolulu radio station music to home in on.

One hour and forty minutes after leaving their carriers the Japanese attack force was flying at about 10,000 feet, above a thick layer of clouds, when, Fuchida recalled, "Suddenly, through an opening in the clouds, a long white line of breaking surf appeared directly beneath my plane. It was the northern shore of Oahu." Fuchida veered southwest and Pearl Harbor came into view, veiled in a light morning mist. The American ships were lying peacefully at anchor; nothing below seemed to stir, not even a breeze. They had not been discovered (or so Fuchida thought) and he tapped out on his radio the message that everyone back on the carriers had been praying for: "*Tora, Tora, Tora*" (Tiger, Tiger, Tiger); this meant that Japan had achieved complete surprise.

In fact, they *had* been discovered. Out on a hillside at the northernmost point of Oahu was the Opana mobile radar station, manned by two U.S. Army privates. At seven A.M. they were about to shut down after their three-hour duty stint when "suddenly the oscilloscope picked up an image so peculiar that Lockhart [one of the privates] thought something must be wrong with the set."[4] Radar was fairly new to the U.S. military; these mobile radar stations were only a few months old and many of the crews were still in training. But a check of the set indicated it was working properly and what it was looking at was unmistakably an enormous flight of planes—at least fifty, maybe more—coming in from the north.

The radar operators—even though they were technically now off-duty—decided to telephone in this discovery to the Fort Shafter information center, about thirty miles south, which was responsible for plotting and tracking aircraft movements. Here another glitch developed. The duty officer that morning was one Lieutenant Kermit Tyler, a rookie fighter pilot who had pulled this duty only one time previously. Not only that, but when the mobile radar station was presumed to be shut down at seven A.M. all the plotters promptly left and went to breakfast, effectively leaving Lieutenant Tyler alone.

He digested the information from the Opana station privates and considered several things. First, that what they were looking at might be a flight of planes from a U.S. carrier (the *Enterprise* was headed back to Pearl that day). Then he also recalled that the flight of B-17s—the one the Honolulu radio station was playing Hawaiian music for—was due in the area about this time. So, without further explanation to the radar privates, Tyler told them, "Well, don't worry about it." They kept on watching, however, fascinated, as the blips drew nearer and nearer until they were finally blocked out by the shadow of a mountain just as Fuchida made his veer to the southwest toward Pearl Harbor.

Fuchida's attack plan was efficient and sensible. First the torpedo planes would glide in low and drop their deadly cargo; then the dive-bombers would swoop down at breakneck speed and deliver their explosives; next the level bombers with their big armor-piercing naval shells would unload—all while some of the covering Zero fighters hovered above, waiting for any sign of American aircraft, and others flew down on the deck to strafe the airfields themselves. And just when they thought it might be over, the second wave of 153 planes would arrive to finish the job. Fuchida, his canopy open, fired a flare from his rocket pistol, the signal to commence the attack.

Fuchida's dive-bombers had already climbed high in the sky for altitude while his torpedo bombers had descended and circled so as to come in low from the southwest, that is, the ocean side of Pearl Harbor. The American battleships were moored in line two by two alongside Ford Island, which is in the center of the harbor. It was almost eight A.M., time for morning colors, and aboard the U.S.S. *Nevada* bandleader Oden McMillan had just raised his baton to begin playing "The Star-Spangled Banner." Some of the bandsmen were puzzled to see large flights of planes diving down toward the battleships at the opposite end of the island, but McMillan concluded it must be some kind of army air corps drill and with a wave of his baton the band struck up the national anthem. Almost in the same moment he heard explosions at the far end of Battleship Row.

One of Fuchida's torpedo bombers skimmed across the harbor and launched its torpedo at the *Arizona,* just astern of the *Nevada,* as McMillan's band was finishing the first stanza, then swooped up right over the *Nevada*'s fantail, where the American flag was being raised. The Japanese tail gunner let loose a burst of machine-gun fire on the musicians, who continued to play the anthem. No band members were hit, but the American flag was suddenly shredded. Other sailors on deck, momentarily confused, stood at attention, their right arms still raised in salute.[5]

According to author Walter Lord's account of the attack, "McMillan knew now, but kept on conducting. The years of training had taken over—it never occurred to him that once he had begun playing the National Anthem, he could possibly stop. Another strafer flashed by. This time McMillan unconsciously paused as the deck splintered around him, but he quickly picked up the beat again. The entire band stopped and started again with him, as though they had rehearsed it for weeks. Not a man broke formation until the final note died. Then everyone ran wildly for cover."[6]

As the first torpedo bombers came in, some Pearl Harbor personnel waved at them before they realized who they were. Seeing the red rising sun "meatball" on the wingtips, some even concluded that they were Russian planes, perhaps come from a visiting Russian carrier. Most still assumed at first it was some sort of drill being conducted by the army. Even when the bombs and torpedoes began to fall and explode, some believed it was a U.S. pilot "gone crazy," or that "a wheel had just fallen off an airplane." Recreational fliers in small light planes out for an early Sunday spin were bewildered, then terrified, as they realized what these huge flights of foreign warplanes meant. Great geysers of water shot into the air as Fuchida's torpedoes splashed into the harbor on their way toward the U.S.

battleships. Meantime, at Wheeler and Hickam Fields and other U.S. air bases, the American airplanes—lined up in rows per the antisabotage instructions of General Walter Short—were being systematically wrecked and turned into burning infernos on the runways.

All of this took only a few minutes. In his home in the hills overlooking Pearl Harbor, Admiral Husband Kimmel, commander in chief of Pacific Fleet, had been in the process of dressing for a golf game with his army counterpart, General Short. But by then the duty officer had phoned with news of the destroyer *Ward*'s attack on the Japanese sub. Kimmel canceled the game and began redressing in his navy whites to attend to the situation from his office when the phone rang again with frantic news that Pearl Harbor had just come under Japanese air attack. The admiral rushed outside, his uniform jacket still unbuttoned and flapping, just in time to see the first explosions. He dashed next door onto a neighbor's lawn, which had a better view of Battleship Row. There he encountered Mrs. John B. Earle, wife of the Fourteenth Naval District commander's chief of staff. The two of them gaped appalled at the unfolding spectacle. The sky was completely filled with Japanese planes and Kimmel instantly recognized this as no casual raid but a full-scale assault. The booms from the torpedo and bomb explosions began to reach their ears. Suddenly the battleship *Oklahoma* seemed to shudder and then slowly roll over in the shallow harbor until only its bottom was visible.*[7]

"It looks like they've got the *Oklahoma*," Mrs. Earle remarked, awestruck.

"Yes, I can see they have," Kimmel told her, his face now a blanched mask of horror.[8] He was experiencing a naval commander's worst nightmare, as his fleet was being destroyed before his very eyes.

Then the battleship *Arizona* seemed actually to lift out of the water and an enormous flash of fire and smoke mushroomed above her forward decks; slowly she began to list and settle, and kept on settling. In that instant

---

*American battleships were named for U.S. states, cruisers for U.S. cities; destroyers were named for influential or heroic people. In those days U.S. aircraft carriers were named for Revolutionary War battles—*Lexington, Saratoga, Yorktown*—or stinging insects—*Hornet, Wasp*—and there were also the *Enterprise* and the *Ranger*.

eleven hundred U.S. sailors perished. One of the big Japanese sixteen-inch naval shell bombs had hit the *Arizona*'s deck forward of the turrets and penetrated four decks below into the powder magazine. The ship blew up. The concussion was so stupendous that it blew sailors off of other nearby ships into the water; it sucked up all the air in the area, actually stopping the engines of cars and military vehicles onshore rushing to or away from the scene; it blew people down inside of their own homes and offices, and even Fuchida, the Japanese air leader circling high above, felt his plane rock and roll. Battleship division commander Admiral Isaac C. Kidd and the *Arizona*'s skipper, Captain Franklin Van Valkenburg, had been standing on the bridge and were incinerated by the blast.[9]

Kimmel's staff car roared up from nowhere and the stricken admiral jumped in and set off for his Pacific Fleet headquarters. By the time he got there the first wave of attack was reaching its most pitiless crescendo: bombs, torpedoes, and machine-gun fire from dive-bombers and fighters filled the air; great billows of smoke from burning fuel oil obscured much of the harbor; and added to this was the constant roar of American anti-aircraft guns, which had finally begun coming to life.

Kimmel stood watching from the window of his War Plans office calm but grim-faced, with teeth clenched. Like the O*klahoma,* the *Arizona* had gone down. The explosion had broken her in half. The battleships *California* and *West Virginia* had also begun to settle to the bottom. Another battleship, the *Utah,* had sunk too, but the Japanese had basically wasted their bombs and torpedoes on her: *Utah* was old and being used only as a target-practice ship. For the moment there was little Kimmel could do. The now famous message had already been dispatched to Washington and other naval commands: "Enemy Air Raid Pearl Harbor. This Is Not a Drill," and Kimmel had quickly ordered all flyable navy planes to begin searching for the Japanese carriers. (By this time, there were precious few of these aircraft left.) Suddenly a spent .30-caliber machine-gun bullet smashed through the window and hit Kimmel on the chest before dropping to the floor. The admiral looked at it, picked it up, and said to one of his staff members, "It would have been merciful if it had killed me."[10] At that point Kimmel was feeling so low that he would probably have accepted crucifixion as his punishment, and in the end that is what he got, although it was a long and slow crucifixion.

Out in the harbor the hundreds of men ordered to abandon ship, or who had been blown off their ships, floundered in oily goo several inches thick, much of it on fire. The torpedoes had loosed millions of gallons of fuel from the stricken battleships. An odd assortment of boats scurried about plucking as many as possible from the treacherous blazing waters— admiral's gigs, launches, yard tenders, workboats, even a "honey barge" (garbage scow) joined in the rescues—all while the skies continued to rain down Japanese bombs and bullets.

Oil-coated men, many seriously burned or otherwise injured, hauled themselves up on nearby Ford Island. Hundreds of wounded were laid in improvised medical areas such as tennis courts and mess halls. In one instance, sixteen-year-old Mary Ann Ramsey, daughter of Lieutenant Commander Logan C. Ramsey at the Ford Island command center, went from wounded man to wounded man, writing down their names and comforting the dying, of which there were many.

Aboard the sinking West Virginia, which had taken six or seven torpedoes in her port side, Captain Mervyn Bennion had been disemboweled by a shard from the Arizona when it exploded. He lay on the bridge perfectly conscious as his ship was gradually engulfed in fire, inquiring how the fight was going. At some point his officers decided to move him to a safer spot and for this agonizing task they recruited a large black cook, third class, named Doris Miller, who was the West Virginia's heavyweight boxing champion. Captain Bennion died a short while later and Doris Miller, who knew nothing about weapons or weaponry, went out to a machine-gun station and in no time was "blazing away as though he had fired one all his life."*[11]

---

*In May 1942, Miller was awarded the Navy Cross for heroism by Admiral Chester Nimitz in a ceremony aboard the Enterprise. After the West Virginia was wrecked, Miller served briefly aboard the ill-fated cruiser Indianapolis, then was assigned to the U.S.S. escort carrier Liscome Bay, on which he was killed less than a year after the Pearl Harbor attack.

Lieutenant General Walter Short, the army commander on Hawaii who had just missed his golf game with Admiral Kimmel, heard the racket at home and stepped out on his porch to see what he could see, which was not much more than smoke since he lived near Honolulu. He was soon informed and rushed to his headquarters. Arriving, he encountered an intelligence officer on his staff and asked, "What's going on out there?"

The officer, Lieutenant Colonel George W. Bicknell, replied, "I'm not sure, General, but I just saw two battleships sunk."

Short looked at him like he was crazy. "That's ridiculous!" he snorted, and stalked off.[12]

Meantime, the U.S. military was fighting back as best it could. Short had immediately ordered army troops to the antiaircraft guns, which was hardly necessary, but many guns did not have ready ammunition and much of what they did have was old World War I stuff with many duds. They tried their best. At one point a Japanese bomb blew out the side of the prison stockade at Schofield Barracks and the suddenly freed prisoners rushed to help where they could.

Two young army fighter pilots, Lieutenants Kenneth Taylor and George Welch, had planned to spend their Sunday at the beach. When they saw the runway wreckage at Wheeler Field they jumped into a car and rushed off to a little grass landing strip about ten miles away where there were a few P40 fighters parked. Soon they were in the air and loaded for bear. Before it was over they racked up seven of the eleven Japanese planes shot down that day by the U.S. Army Air Corps.

Among the most startled people that morning—and that included everyone—were the pilots and crews of the big four-engine B-17 bombers who arrived at Pearl Harbor at the height of the attack. The twelve planes had flown fourteen hours straight from the West Coast with skeleton crews, their machine guns still packed in Cosmoline, listening to the soothing Hawaiian music on the radio guiding them in. They had just about enough gas to make land when they arrived on the scene of the carnage. Japanese fighters, whom the crews first thought were U.S. Army planes, suddenly attacked them. Hickam Field, their designated landing spot, was mostly ablaze with burning aircraft. One B-17 somehow made a landing with three Japanese Zeros on his tail, blazing away at him. Others followed but the rest scattered for the other airfields on Oahu. One managed to land on a golf course, another on a twelve-hundred-foot grass strip half the size of what it took to safely land a B-17. Amazingly, only one bomber was lost when a Japanese fighter bullet set off a box of flares in the tail section; the pilots managed to land the plane, but the rear half broke in two and burned. The difficulty of shooting down these lumbering "Flying Fortresses" impressed at least one Japanese pilot, who predicted to his superiors that they would have much trouble in the future from such heavily armored flying machines. In this he was correct.

At 8:40, half an hour after the attack had begun, there was a fifteen-minute lull, and then the second wave of 153 Japanese planes arrived. Pearl Harbor was so enshrouded in smoke by then that it was difficult to find targets, so many Japanese amused themselves by shooting up anything and everything. They strafed private homes, churches, hospitals, mess halls, groups of men, and, for target practice, speeding automobiles and trucks. One army ambulance received fifty-two bullet holes. What the Japanese did not do—and in hindsight this was one of the few blessings of the Pearl Harbor raid—was to destroy the huge fuel-storage tanks containing millions of gallons of precious fuel oil; nor did they destroy the vast naval repair shops and facilities. This oversight allowed the United States military to go on the offensive almost immediately after the attack.

By this time military wives living near the base were taking all sorts of refuge against the attack to protect themselves and their children: some hid under mattresses;* others huddled in bathtubs or crawled under houses. The Japanese planes seemed to be everywhere, swooping and darting at treetop level and firing at anything that moved. One woman even hid under the lid of a galvanized-tin garbage can, as if that would have done any good. Another stuck her head into a bush, "literally like an ostrich."[13]

In the middle of all this a stirring spectacle unfolded. The U.S.S. *Nevada*, whose crew at the beginning of the attack had stood at attention while "The Star-Spangled Banner" was played and they were being bombed

---

*The expression "taking to the mattresses" was a time-honored tradition in Sicily, lower Manhattan, Chicago, and other regions with large Italian populations where gang warfare was prevalent.

and machine-gunned, had somehow raised enough steam to get under way—the only big ship that did so. Her senior officers were all ashore but there was an experienced reserve officer aboard, Lieutenant Commander Francis Thomas, who took charge. He knew next to nothing about handling anything as big as a battleship but Chief Quartermaster Robert Sedberry did and by some miracle, or a series of them (it normally took four tugboats to free a battleship from a mooring and set her straight in the channel), the *Nevada* came on, so as not to remain a sitting duck for the Japanese. She was seriously afire amidships and had a hole blown into her bow the size of a house, but out of the smoke and flames and crash and gloom of the battle she emerged into the bright morning sun full speed ahead, her American flag snapping in the breeze. Men onshore stopped whatever they were doing and gaped at this sight to behold. Many wept tears down their grimy, oil-stained cheeks and a great cheer arose all along Battleship Row, for to see the *Nevada* headed for the open sea, all her guns blazing at the Japanese planes, meant there was still a fighting U.S. Navy left in the Pacific.

By ten A.M. it was over, except for the horrid mess that remained to clean up, and the dead to be buried and the dying to die and the wounded to be cared for. The *Nevada,* bold as her dash for freedom had been, quickly became the target of practically every Japanese warplane over Pearl Harbor and, after taking six huge bomb hits, she beached herself to keep from blocking the narrow channel. Ships burned far into the night and the next day and the next. Many men were still trapped in the bowels of the sunken ships and heroic efforts would be made to extract them. Not all were successful. Some tapped on the insides of the hulls for more than two weeks, until Christmas Eve, when their tapping finally stopped.

Grim scenes abounded all over the area. There had been ninety-four U.S. Navy warships in Pearl Harbor before the attack. Now eighteen of them, most importantly the great battleships, were either sunk or wrecked and on fire. Two thousand three hundred and forty American sailors, soldiers, and marines had been killed, and about sixty civilians, most killed by errant U.S. antiaircraft fire, which landed in or near Honolulu. Most of the U.S. airplanes had been wiped out on their runways—347 of them. But as historian John Toland put it, "It was a disaster, but it could have been a catastrophe." Quite true, as we shall see later on. The Japanese had not gotten the American carriers, which were at sea, nor as mentioned did they seriously damage the oil storage and naval shops or the submarines.[14]

Back in Washington it was early afternoon and the news was just getting around. Roosevelt was finishing lunch with his chief adviser Harry Hopkins at the White House, eating an apple, when, at 1:40, Secretary of the Navy Knox called to report the attack. Hopkins "expressed the belief that there must be some kind of mistake,"* but Roosevelt "thought it was just the kind of unexpected thing the Japanese would do, and that at the very time they were discussing peace in the Pacific they were plotting to overthrow it."[15]

Unfortunately for the Japanese ambassadorial delegation of Nomura and Kurusu (who were even then ignorant of the attack), there had been delays in decoding and typing up the final reply from Tokyo, which they had been instructed to deliver to Secretary of State Hull at one P.M. Sunday, December 7, while the Japanese warplanes were already winging their way from the carriers toward Pearl. Accordingly, they had to postpone their date with Hull for an hour. When they arrived at his office at two o'clock Hull had by then not only learned of the attack but of course already read the contents of their diplomatic note thanks to MAGIC. His was not a warm reception; the two Japanese were not even invited to sit down, but stood there, hats in hand, while Hull gave a cursory glance to the reply they had brought him.

"I must say that in all my conversations with you over the last nine months I have never uttered a word of untruth," said Hull, interspersing this with what Roosevelt historian Robert Sherwood described as "some pretty strong Tennessee mountain language."

"This is borne out absolutely in the record," Hull seethed. "In all my fifty years of public service I have never seen a document that was more crowded with infamous falsehoods and distortions—infamous falsehoods

---

*That was what Knox had initially thought too, that "they must mean the Philippines," and others involved had similar reactions.

and distortions on a scale so huge that I never imagined until today that any government on this planet was capable of uttering them." He then dismissed the two mortified emissaries without even a good-bye and, characteristically, referred to them immediately afterward as "piss-ants."[16]

In Japan, which had installed a nationwide system of radio hookups plugged into loudspeakers on power polls in the streets of the major cities and towns, news of the attack was broadcast. Japanese citizens stopped and digested the information, then began cheering "and clapping as if it had been a ball game," and dancing in the streets. Then martial music began playing over the loudspeakers and the broadcast included a General Tojo speech about "annihilating" the West, "which was trying to dominate the world." One of the songs they played, "Umi Yukaba," was a sort of Japanese version of "God Bless America." It went this way:

> Across the sea, corpses in the waters;
> Across the mountains, corpses in the fields,
> I shall die only for the Emperor,
> I shall never look back.[17]

Meantime, the jubilant and victorious Japanese pilots had returned to their mother ships to a chorus of great cheering and backslapping. Commander Fuchida, the flight leader, immediately stormed onto the bridge of Admiral Nagumo's flagship *Akagi* and buttonholed his friend Commander Genda, who had organized the mission. Fuchida urged Genda to let the pilots refuel and then go after the missing American carriers, which he assumed to be south of Oahu. (In fact, they were to the west, but still not far away.) Genda became enthusiastic too, and recommended this change of plan to Admiral Nagumo. But there was a hitch; the Japanese tanker train, which was already headed for a prearranged refueling point, could not possibly catch up with the fast carriers if they headed south, and the scheme had to be ditched for fear of running out of fuel.

Not to be dissuaded, Fuchida then argued for continuing the strikes on Pearl Harbor to destroy the oil-storage tanks and machine shops missed in the first two attacks. After all, he reasoned, the Japanese attack force had lost only twenty-nine planes over Pearl that morning, leaving them with more than three hundred yet, and complete control of the air. Why not punish the Americans more while they were here and while they could—to finish the job, so to speak.

Nagumo was already persuaded. He had been anxious about the entire operation from the start and now that his main mission had been accomplished he wished to take no further chances. At midday, December 7, 1941, the Japanese fleet came about and sailed for home.[18]

Chapter Six ★

By midafternoon radios had begun to break the news all across America; people were of course shocked and horrified but, more significantly, they were furious, and their fury would not cease until the empire of Japan was crushed. This was not the reaction anticipated by the Tokyo militarists who, like Hitler, thought that Americans, with their ridiculous argument-plagued democracy, were a weak and divided people who had no stomach for a bloody and prolonged war—especially one in the far distant reaches of the Pacific Ocean.

To read contemporary accounts, one would almost have to assume that the majority of American citizens that Sunday afternoon were either attending professional football games, or listening to them on the radio, or were enjoying classical music concerts broadcast by the networks. In Washington, for instance, by halftime of the Redskins–Eagles football game, nearly a third of the fans had gone, called away by loudspeaker.

It was the same all over the country, north, south, midwest, and Pacific coast. In St. Louis, Missouri, for example, one man who wasn't dealing with ball games or music was John R. Shepley, a physician who had been born in 1860 and had had his share of war, even as a child. When the radio broadcast the news he said to himself, "Here we go again." West Coast citizens were more immediately alarmed because they feared they would be next. The young movie star Evelyn Keyes (*Gone With the Wind,* *Here Comes Mr. Jordan*) was at the Hollywood home of director King Vidor when they got word. "We were on the West Coast," she said, "and we thought surely they [the Japanese] would be along here. Shock! Horror!"[1] Perplexed and angry crowds filled the streets of Los Angeles, creating huge traffic jams. A blackout had been ordered by the mayor and people began throwing rocks and other objects at anything lit up. Some antiaircraft batteries opened up around dark, firing at suspicious objects in the sky— including stars and planets—adding to the fear and confusion. Japanese residents caught on the streets were chased and beaten, while others were rounded up by the FBI using a prearranged list of suspected enemy agents. Many people immediately fired their Japanese gardeners and kitchen help.

Meanwhile, by midafternoon on the day of the attack a massive America First rally was getting under way in Pittsburgh. The featured speaker was North Dakota senator Gerald P. Nye, perhaps the most fervent of all the isolationists. Also on the ticket was the famous dancer Irene Castle, whose husband, Vernon, the other half of the dance team, had been killed in the First World War. Before he went to the podium, Nye was handed a wire-service teletype report about the Pearl Harbor attack. He refused to believe it and proceeded to open the rally by branding President Roosevelt a warmonger. Thousands in the crowd roared their approval. An army colonel arrived in the hall to try to tell the Firsters what had happened, but he was accused of being a warmonger too and was thrown out of the building.

Nye was still carrying on when a newspaper reporter who had just spoken to his editor was told that Japan had formally declared war on the United States. The newsman got the word to Nye by writing it on a piece of paper and placing it in front of the senator on the rostrum. But even after Nye read it, he continued with his harangue, working his audience up into a fever pitch until they were shouting that Roosevelt was a "traitor," and should be impeached.

Finally, after about an hour, the dramatic news sitting before him on the rostrum must have begun to sink in. Nye stopped his prepared bombast and declared, "I have before me the worst news that I have encountered in the last twenty years." Breaking into a sweat, he then read from the newsman's message about the Japanese declaration of war. Later a reporter asked Nye what the country should do now. "We have been maneuvered into this by the President," the senator replied, "but the only thing to do now is to declare war and jump into it with everything we have and bring it to a victorious conclusion." Thus the final America First meeting was concluded.[2]

Governors from Boston to Seattle began calling up National Guard units to protect railways, bridges, and other strategic sites. In Washington, near the Jefferson Memorial, somebody chopped down a number of the cherry trees that had been a gift of friendship from the citizens of Tokyo back in 1912. Mysterious flights of planes (most nonexistent) were reported on both coasts. An angry crowd gathered at the Japanese embassy in Washington; the police held them at bay while smoke rose from its backyard and roof, where the Japanese were burning documents.

At Pearl Harbor the drama continued. A Japanese invasion was anticipated by everyone. Army soldiers manned the shorelines, digging trenches and setting up guns, assuming that a huge fleet of Japanese troop transports would appear above the horizon at any moment. Civilians pitched in, including Edgar Rice Burroughs, author of the popular *Tarzan* books, who was vacationing at the time. In military hospitals army and navy wives and local women, including prostitutes, helped roll bandages and perform other helpful duties. Boy Scout troops signed up as messengers, served coffee, and did whatever else they could. The football team from San Jose College scheduled to play in a benefit game that week stayed over and volunteered for guard duty.[3]

About three that afternoon General Marshall's warning to the Pacific commanders finally arrived, handed over by an RCA courier of Japanese ancestry who had dodged bombs and bullets all day to make his delivery. When it reached Admiral Kimmel he glanced at it and angrily threw it in the trash.

Rumors flew everywhere: the Japanese were landing paratroops north of Pearl; they had sunk the *Enterprise* on the high seas; they had invaded San Francisco. Shots from nervous sentries rang out all over Oahu and not a few innocent people were injured or killed. Into this state of quasi-panic flew a squadron of U.S. Navy fighters from the *Enterprise,* which had been searching for the enemy carriers. It was too dark to try a landing on the ship, so they headed for Pearl. As they approached Ford Island runway they were instructed by the control tower to turn on their lights before landing. Soon as they did, practically every ship in the harbor opened up on them and five of the six U.S. planes were shot down.

Simultaneous with the Pearl Harbor raid, the Japanese attacked the other American possessions in the Pacific, most importantly the Philippines, where General MacArthur waited with his army of 120,000. They also invaded Thailand in order to seize British Malaya with its vast natural resources and its fortress city of Singapore, as well as British Hong Kong.

Before turning to these fascinating battles let us first deal in summary with the matter of American blame for the tragedy at Pearl Harbor. For more than fifty years an entire cottage industry of book publishing has grown up around the subject of who was culpable for allowing the Japanese to surprise us so completely. Some are written by cranks, some even by crackpots; many are thoughtful and reasoned. As is often said, hindsight is twenty-twenty. Further, there were half a dozen public investigations of the thing, some political, others less so.

Once the initial shock of the attack wore off, Americans high and low—politicians, the press, the Roosevelt administration, and of course the military—began searching for somebody to condemn for the disaster. How, they asked, could the U.S. Pacific Fleet let itself be caught napping? The most obvious suspects were Admiral Kimmel and General Short, U.S. Navy and Army commanders in Hawaii, and indeed they held their share of culpability. Yet there was still blame enough to go around for all. From the best this author can tell, the reason for the Pearl Harbor calamity lies mostly in a lack of coordination and communication between Washington and Hawaii, as well as a misreading and misinterpretation at various levels of the vast quantity of intelligence available at the time from MAGIC and other sources. As well, the American people themselves deserve a good part of the blame, for the leaders they elected to Congress were, for too long, loath to vote money for adequate defenses, especially long-range patrol planes, to their Pacific outposts.

First, this sort of raid was not entirely unexpected. Ever since 1936 the Pacific Fleet had practiced at-sea war-game maneuvers based on a theoretical Japanese carrier attack on Pearl Harbor delivered from north of Oahu. Studies had been conducted at Pearl Harbor itself indicating it was certainly a possibility, though nobody ever suggested that the Japanese would come with as many as *six* aircraft carriers. It was a classic example of one of the most common military intelligence failures seen throughout human history: calculating what an enemy *would* do, instead of what he *could* do.

All MAGIC intercepts were sent directly to Washington to the army and navy intelligence sections, where they were to be decoded, translated, and interpreted and their information passed along to the highest authorities. Then, a digest of this intelligence was passed along to the Pacific theater commanders. This digest of the intelligence, instead of the raw intelligence itself, was what both Kimmel and Short complained of afterward because they said they felt handicapped by not being able to collate the raw intercepts themselves; that if they had, they would have somehow caught indications that the Japanese were about to attack them.

A prime example cited by Kimmel was the so-called bomb-plot message, which was intercepted from the Japanese spy Yoshikawa in Honolulu. In it Tokyo wanted to know all grid coordinates for the positions of Kimmel's ships while in Pearl Harbor, and Kimmel, understandably angry, testified later that if he had received this intelligence it would have made an important impression on him. But the navy high command in Washington, while admitting that they, too, were "impressed" with the bomb-plot message, chose not to send it to Kimmel.*

Nevertheless, as Pearl Harbor historian Roberta Wohlstetter put it, "If anything emerges clearly from a study [of the attack] it is the soundness of having a center for evaluating a mass of conflicting signals. It would have

---

*Admiral Stark, chief of naval operations, testified later that he thought Kimmel *was* getting MAGIC raw material, though he never explained the basis for this assumption.

created endless confusion if Washington had tried to relay all available signals to the overseas commands."[4] But both Admiral Kimmel and General Short still wondered, and wondered loudly and publicly in years to come, why the Hawaiian command did not have a MAGIC machine of its own. (The reason was that the one scheduled to be sent to them had been sent to the British instead, in exchange for one of the Ultra machines used to read the German codes.)

The principal facts during the weeks and months leading up to the attack are these:

• Washington knew after putting the embargo on oil sales to the Japanese that war with Japan might ensue though, as in all intricate assessments of this kind, some high-level officials did not agree. The most notable among those who believed the Japanese would declare war against the United States were Roosevelt and Cordell Hull. But the military—Admiral Stark, General Marshall, as well as both of their intelligence staffs—seriously doubted it, and said so many times.

• Washington sent numerous messages and warnings to the Pacific area indicating that war might be imminent, but instructed the Pacific commanders that they were to let the Japanese strike first (i.e., let *them* be the bad guys).

• Nobody in high authority believed—even if Japan did declare war—that an attack on Pearl Harbor was a strong possibility; instead their warnings foretold of a Japanese attack against the Philippines, Russia, or the British and Dutch possessions in the southern Pacific.

• Both Kimmel and Short were aware of the possibility of an attack on Pearl Harbor, but neither thought it likely, owing to the information they were getting from Washington.

• There had been discussion of placing torpedo nets to protect the big ships in Pearl against aerial attacks but they came to nothing. Earlier in the year Stark had assured Kimmel that Pearl Harbor did not have enough water depth to permit an aerial torpedo attack and Kimmel was glad to get the news; he felt that antitorpedo nets would further congest a harbor in which it was already difficult to maneuver.[5]

• There had also been discussion about installation of barrage balloons around the harbor. In the event of an imminent attack this would have been a great aid to the fleet at anchor. Several hundred barrage balloons suspended from cables all over Pearl would have made enemy plane maneuvers infinitely more difficult since the aircraft would have to dodge all those cables while at the same time keep a steady course on their torpedo and bombing runs. Unfortunately, it was again the story of too little, too late. Army troops were at the time of the attack training on the installation and operation of barrage balloons for Pearl back in the States, but none had yet been delivered to Hawaii.

• Both Kimmel and Short were concerned that they did not have enough patrol planes to perform the necessary daily 360-degree long-distance reconnaissance around Pearl. In fact, Kimmel had informed Washington that in order to do this, he would need an additional 180 B-17 long-distance planes, when there weren't even that many in existence in the United States (many of the B-17s were going to England straight from the production lines).[6]

• The few existing B-17s in Hawaii were in fact destined for the Philippines and their crews were in training for that mission. Though they were bombers and not patrol planes, the B-17s had exceptional long-range capabilities. The navy had only a limited number of PBY "flying boat" planes in Hawaii that were suitable for long-range patrols. Of only sixty-nine available, most were badly handicapped by a shortage of both spare parts and relief crews.[7] These shortages were so critical that if twenty-four-hour, 360-degree patrols covering half a million square miles of ocean had been instituted, in less than two weeks all the planes and their crews would be worn out and grounded for rest, maintenance, and spare parts.

This was a crucial issue because Kimmel, as Pacific Fleet commander, could not afford to have his reconnaissance "eyes" grounded if some sudden further intelligence showed that an attack on his ships was imminent. Since the messages from Washington indicated an attack most likely would come thousands of miles farther west, he decided to hold off on flying all-out long-range patrols and, in time-honored naval tradition, "to await further developments." Kimmel guessed wrong and paid the price.

*   *   *

The principal facts during the last days and hours leading directly to the attack itself are these:

Admiral Stark's "war warning" message to Kimmel of November 27, ten days before the attack, indicated that any Japanese action against America would likely fall on the Philippines or some of the outlying U.S. islands such as Guam, Wake, or Midway. It did not put any special emphasis on Pearl Harbor or, for that matter, even mention it.

General Short's decision to go on the lowest army alert instead of the highest was based on his interpretation of the message similar to Kimmel's, which he received from Washington. In a further clarification Marshall had instructed Short to guard especially against sabotage and not to "alarm the local population." Short accordingly went into his sabotage alert level—the lowest—and when he informed Marshall of what he had done, he received no instructions to the contrary from his boss in Washington.

As to the final day before the attack and the morning of it, there seems to have been a rather casual attitude in Washington.

When Colonel Bratton interrupted the chief of military intelligence General Miles's dinner party to show him the first thirteen parts of the MAGIC-intercepted final Japanese reply to the United States, Miles did not consider it important enough to disturb the chief of staff at home. Thus, next morning, Marshall went on his usual Sunday horseback ride blithely unaware that the Japanese might be about to immediately declare war. If there had been cell phones in those days, Marshall might have found himself at his desk reading the fourteenth and most important part several hours earlier than he in fact did. In the event, it was nearly noon Washington time when he finally got off his latest warning to the Pacific command, and by then the Japanese bombers were already in the air.

Admiral Stark seemed even more cavalier about the impending crisis that morning. When it was suggested to him that the fourteen-part message meant war, he declined at first even to notify his Pacific commanders, saying that he had already told them to be on lookout. Later in testimony he cited an earlier warning he had sent Kimmel on November 24, saying that "a surprise aggressive movement *in any direction* [emphasis added] including attack on Philippines or Guam is a possibility," and used this to defend against suggestions that he had not properly warned Pearl Harbor. As historian Roberta Wohlstetter points out, "How Stark could have believed that the phrase 'in any direction' could have carried over from a sentence in a less urgent message [thirteen days before the attack] . . . is incomprehensible."[8] In fact, Stark's testimony *was* comprehensible: he was making an excuse, grasping at straws.

Then there is the matter of the actual transmission of Marshall's (and, by proxy, Stark's) final warning message (indicating Japan's one P.M. suspense deadline for delivery of Tokyo's reply), which was sent to Pearl Harbor the morning of the attack. How it somehow got shifted from an urgent top-priority radio transmission, which because of solar flares became a low-priority Western Union via undersea cablegram that did not reach the Hawaiian commanders until long after the attack was over, remains something of a mystery.

This is yet another example of the ubiquitous fog of war, in which somewhere between "I told him to do it" and "I ordered it done," the thing got screwed up. Nevertheless, some blame attaches to Marshall for, first, not accepting Stark's offer to transmit the message through his navy channels and, second, for not personally—or not having one of his people personally—follow up the matter in detail. Even fifteen or twenty minutes' warning might have made some difference in the severity of the attack.

Having noted this, it is also quite possible that nothing would have become of it anyway, even if the message had arrived hours before the Japanese warplanes. All that Marshall's message told the Hawaiian commanders was that the Japanese were breaking off relations and that the Japanese ambassador had been instructed to deliver this news to the U.S. State Department at one P.M. Washington time. They were told to make of that time frame what they would.

It did not, of course, say anything like: "The War and Navy Departments have reliable information that six aircraft carriers of the Japanese fleet are planning to launch a surprise attack with 350 planes from 200 miles due north of Oahu on the U.S. ships and airfields in and around Pearl Harbor at 8 A.M., your time. Be prepared." If it had, and if such a message had been received in a timely fashion, things undoubtedly would have turned out somewhat differently. But of course it could not have, because nobody in the U.S. government knew these terrible things.

Furthermore, Marshall could simply have picked up the telephone in his office and said to Short something cryptic, such as, "I hope you and Admiral Kimmel are on full alert now." The fact that army security officials did not consider the telephone a secure form of communication, even if equipped with a scrambler, probably discouraged Marshall from doing this. It is a pity that he didn't.

Finally, of course, there was the warning of the two army privates manning the mobile radar station at the northern tip of Oahu that morning. Their duty consisted of plotting aerial movements from four A.M. until seven A.M. Radar was a new technology then, and not well understood, but somebody should have figured out that if the Japanese launched planes from carriers two hundred miles away at dawn, they would not reach the outward span of northern Oahu's radar until *after* seven A.M.

Nevertheless, by a fluke the two privates did in fact pick up the Japanese inbound flight and they reported it. The radar plotters back at the army base, however, had all gone to breakfast by that time, leaving only the unfortunate and inexperienced lieutenant on duty, who assumed that what the radar was seeing was the expected flight of B-17s from the West Coast and told them to "forget about it." More unfortunately, the two privates did not specify to the lieutenant just how many planes they were seeing, only "a big flight" of them. If they had said they were picking up fifty or more, it might have given the lieutenant pause, for he likely would have known that there were only twelve of the B-17s scheduled to arrive. In the event, they did not specify, and we will never know what might have happened if an alert had been sounded at that time.

There has been a school of thought almost from the beginning—which in fact continues today—that holds President Franklin D. Roosevelt, in varying degrees, culpable for the disaster at Pearl Harbor. This theory invariably begins with the notion that Roosevelt wanted war with Japan in order also to draw the United States into a war with Germany. The theory goes on to cite Roosevelt's provocative embargo on U.S. oil sales to Japan, which forced them into attacking the United States.

From there it proceeds to the strained conclusion that Roosevelt had, through U.S. intelligence sources, gained positive knowledge that the Japanese were going to attack Pearl Harbor, the Philippines, and other U.S. territories in the Pacific. Some even assert that Roosevelt knew the date and time of the attack, but had ordered this critical information withheld from the Pacific commands. This was because he wanted Japan to strike the first blow, so as to enrage the American people to such a vengeful frenzy that there would be no question of isolationists or America Firsters raising any opposition to entering the war.

Among those who subscribed to this theory, in greater or lesser degrees, were a few admirals, captains, and other high-ranking naval officers, as well as the distinguished historian John Toland, who reached this conclusion late in his career. Others have published similar books over the years, painstakingly parsing bits of information from documents long moldering in the bowels of World War II records centers and from other sources, some dubious, some valid.

Superficially, a case might be made for some of their hypotheses. It is certainly true that Roosevelt believed the United States should enter the war. The Axis was both despicable and a real menace and, if victorious, would certainly pose a great peril to the United States and the Western Hemisphere. That Roosevelt actually wanted war is a different thing; no president in his right mind *wants* war, but seeing the inevitable hazards of a world ruled by dictators the likes of Hitler, Mussolini, and Tojo, Roosevelt was keenly aware that America's best interests—indeed, her very survival—lay in defeating these malignant and bloodthirsty despots. In possessing this awareness he can hardly be faulted.

Almost all of what professor Gordon Prange, a preeminent Pearl Harbor historian, called "revisionist" histories cite Roosevelt's instructions to "let Japan strike the first blow" as proof that he in fact wanted the Japanese to achieve a surprise attack on the U.S. fleet at Pearl Harbor. But any sensible reading of the context of Roosevelt's order reveals that what the president was trying to convey to his Pacific commanders was that the

United States should not attack the Japanese first, before war was declared by either side. The notion that America should let Japan strike first indicates to the revisionists that Roosevelt knew the Japanese would attack without a declaration of war. He did not know this (as the evidence suggests) but of course he suspected it, given the nation's behavior ever since the Russo-Japanese War of 1904–05, and so did the Washington military command, evidenced by the various warnings they sent out all over the Pacific.

In short, to follow all the arguments suggesting that Roosevelt conspired to let the Pacific command be surreptitiously attacked by the empire of Japan is exceedingly tedious and in the end wasteful of effort because it defies simple logic.* First, such a conspiracy would have to involve not only Roosevelt but his two top military commanders, Marshall and Stark, as well as their intelligence and planning staffs, plus probably the secretary of war, Henry Stimson, and Secretary of State Hull, all of whom were receiving daily intelligence materials from MAGIC. Anybody who has worked the political game in Washington knows that such a shocking and widspread conspiracy would be absolutely impossible to keep secret for very long.

Second, Roosevelt, himself a former assistant secretary of the navy during World War I, was perhaps the nation's foremost champion of the sailors and great ships that constitute the United States Navy. He was then, and has been since, accused of many devious things—and many of the accusations stick—but the idea that Roosevelt would willfully allow all those ships to be sunk and all those sailors, soldiers, and marines to be killed is a notion too monstrous to entertain seriously.

Finally, along the same line, even assuming that Roosevelt *had* somehow known about a pending Japanese attack on Pearl Harbor, it flies in the face of reason that he would have singly "let it happen," and permitted

---

*Whenever a calamity strikes, the conspiracy people go into business. After President Lincoln's assassination, it was suggested that his secretary of war Edwin Stanton and abolitionist members of the administration conspired to have Lincoln killed because they thought he would go too easy on the defeated South. The assassination of President Kennedy still abounds in conspiracies today: e.g., the Mafia, Fidel Castro, the CIA did it. Since the attack on the World Trade Center and Pentagon on September 11, 2001, there are those who insist that President Bush knew of the plot in advance and "let it happen" in order to somehow raise his poll numbers.

his main naval battle force to be destroyed just as war was breaking out. At the very least he would have made absolutely sure that the Pacific commanders were alerted in such a fashion that they would be ready and waiting for the Japanese when they arrived, and shot down *their* planes and sunk *their* ships. Clearly, anything otherwise would have been, simply, idiotic. The American public would have been just as outraged and eager for revenge upon learning that the Japanese had *attempted* and *failed* at a sneak attack as they were when they learned it had been successful.

December 8, 1941, broke dark and blustery in Washington, and the mood of the American people matched the weather. Military recruiting stations had long lines out in front almost from the crack of dawn. The young men who signed up all over the country were treated to speeches similar to this one from a marine recruiting sergeant in New York: "Where you are going it will not be easy. When you get to Parris Island you will find things plenty different from civilian life. You won't like it! You'll think they're overdoing things. You'll think they're stupid! You'll think they're the cruelest, rottenest bunch of men you ever ran into! I'm going to tell you one thing. You'll be wrong! If you want to save yourself plenty of heartache, you'll listen to me right now: you'll do everything they tell you and you'll keep your big mouths shut!"[9]

That same morning Archibald MacLeish, the Librarian of Congress, ordered the originals of the U.S. Constitution, Declaration of Independence, Bill of Rights, Magna Carta, and the Gutenberg Bible packaged up and sent by armed guard railroad to the underground safes at Fort Knox, Kentucky, where the U.S. gold reserve was stored. At 12:30 President Roosevelt entered the House chamber for a joint session of Congress.* Wearing a black armband, he shuffled slowly and deliberately to the rostrum on the arm of his son Jimmy, a marine officer.†

*Roosevelt had arrived in style. The Treasury Department, at the request of the Secret Service, had turned over Al Capone's bulletproof limousine to chauffeur the president to the Capitol.

†Roosevelt, who suffered from polio, rarely walked, and the press in those days, out of courtesy, rarely photographed him in his wheelchair.

The galleries upstairs were packed with dignitaries, including Mrs. Woodrow Wilson, wife of the previous wartime president. Then into the chamber filed the justices of the Supreme Court, wearing their robes with black armbands also affixed. The silence was absolute when Roosevelt began to speak. Millions heard him over the radio.

> Yesterday, December 7, 1941—a date which will live in infamy—the United States of America was suddenly and deliberately attacked by naval and air forces of the Empire of Japan.
>
> The United States was at peace with that nation, and, at the solicitation of Japan, was still in conversations with its government and its Emperor looking toward the maintenance of peace in the Pacific.

The president pointed out that given the distance from Japan to Hawaii and the magnitude of the assault it was obvious the Japanese had been planning it for a long while, and he went on to tell of the many lives lost and ships damaged. Then he gave the American people further news, which had come in overnight.

> Yesterday, the Japanese government also launched an attack against Malaya.
>
> Last night Japanese forces attacked Hong Kong.
>
> Last night Japanese forces attacked Guam.
>
> Last night Japanese forces attacked the Philippine Islands.
>
> Last night Japanese forces attacked Wake Island.
>
> Last night Japanese forces attacked Midway Island.

Roosevelt proceeded to describe the "great danger" emanating from the attacks but expressed confidence in ultimate victory, then concluded:

> I ask that the Congress declare that since the unprovoked and dastardly attack by Japan on Sunday, December 7, a state of war has existed between the United States and the Japanese Empire.

The speech took less than five minutes and when the president had finished the House chamber erupted with applause, shouting, foot stamping, and fist shaking. It was done. Both House and Senate voted unanimously for the declaration of war, with one dissent.*

Next day Adolf Hitler foolishly declared war on the United States, followed by his stooge Mussolini.† Isolationism and the America Firsters vanished overnight. To show their solidarity, isolationist congressmen and senators walked about the Capitol corridors arm in arm with their interventionist counterparts, while the people of the city, and elsewhere, went around in a kind of daze, the conflagration enveloping the entire globe now reeling in their minds. For nearly a year they had known the thing was there and had groped to make out its form and nature and to comprehend how it came to be and have so much power. Now they saw it clearly for the first time. It was a true world war now, and America was in it to the hilt.

Back in Hawaii, General Short and Admiral Kimmel had been fired, with Roosevelt's approval, by the secretaries of the army and the navy, respectively, and accusations of dereliction of duty were hurled at them. As an interim commander of the fleet for the next couple of weeks Vice Admiral William S. Pye was selected. Pye's title had been commander of battleships, Pacific Fleet, but after the attack he suddenly found himself to be a man without a job. It was a fateful choice because Pye, as a battleship man with little understanding of aircraft carrier warfare, would be hard put to make strong, decisive choices in the immediate days to come.

*The dissenting vote was cast by Montana Republican congresswoman Jeanette Rankin, a die-hard pacifist who had also voted against American entry into World War I. It was reported that she hid in a telephone booth afterward to avoid newsmen.

† Hitler was not obligated to do this under the Axis agreement with Japan, but did so anyway because he was angry about the United States supplying weapons to the British. With most of his armies now tied up in Russia, it probably would have made better sense to let the German-American question linger until the Russian situation clarified itself, instead of declaring full-scale war simultaneously against a nation so powerful as the United States.

After he left Hawaii, General Short simply retired to Texas where he spent his time growing roses in the backyard of his surburban home in Houston, but Admiral Kimmel, until his dying day, went around like the Ancient Mariner, telling his story to anyone who would listen. As a permanant replacement for Kimmel as commander of the U.S. Pacific Fleet—or what was left of it—Roosevelt selected fifty-six-year-old Admiral Chester W. Nimitz, who was presently chief of the navy's Bureau of Navigation. Nimitz had graduated from the Naval Academy in 1905 and served aboard submarines and cruisers, but his staffing and organizational abilities soon became paramount to his career.

Nimitz arrived in Hawaii on Christmas Day while the bodies of sailors were still being fished from the oil-soiled waters of Pearl Harbor, on his way to becoming "the most accessible, considerate and beloved of fleet commanders." A man of "cheerful yesterdays and confident tomorrows," was how his Naval Academy yearbook had pictured him. A native of Fredericksburg, Texas, Nimitz was a trim, medium-sized man with piercing blue eyes and a shock of blond hair going white, who endeared himself to Kimmel's shattered staff when he told them upon arrival that he had confidence in them, and intended to make no changes. According to Dr. Samuel Eliot Morison, official U.S. Navy historian of the war, Nimitz had "an almost impeccable judgment of men, and a genius for making prompt, firm decisions." This was fortunate, too, for in the days ahead many strained decisions would fall upon him.[10]

After he was told of his appointment, Nimitz was congratulated by his wife for "getting the fleet," to which he is said to have replied, "The fleet, dear, is at the bottom of the ocean."

Chapter Seven ★

Pleasant surprises would not overtake the American and Allied forces in the weeks and months to come. From the moment of the Pearl Harbor attack, dramas great and small began being played out as the Japanese swarmed across the Pacific and Far East like a biblical plague of locusts. Each conquest went according to plan, except one: a nasty little episode that arose on the Japanese fleet's homeward journey from Hawaii, and which also inspired the American people with a short-lived glimmer of exhilaration. Admiral Nagumo had dispatched two of his carriers and a cruiser division from the Pearl strike force to fall upon tiny Wake Island, which the United States was busily fortifying as a mid-ocean aviation outpost.

Wake had been discovered by the Spanish explorer Alvaro de Mendana in 1568, by accident, while he was desperately searching for any island that contained water. Wake, the Spaniards found, was "destitute of water and bare of every living thing except sea-birds and a few stunted shrubs." They christened it San Francisco and sailed away "in bitter disappointment,"[1] and Wake remained a speck on the lonely ocean, literally a thousand miles from nowhere.

Two hundred and twenty-odd years later a British exploration came across the island and didn't even bother to stop, but renamed it on their maps Wake, after their captain. All they could see was a low bleak atoll, the remnant of a sunken volcano, about five miles long and four wide with a big lagoon in the middle. In all, Wake has only about two square miles of usable land. Another hundred years passed before an American naval officer happened on it in 1899, rowed ashore, ran up an American flag, and claimed it as a U.S. possession on the theory that someday it might become useful. This proved to be so when it was decreed a bird sanctuary by Teddy Roosevelt. Some years later, in 1935, Pan American Airways established an overnight refueling station on Wake Island for its famous weekly China Clippers, the big flying boats, which could land in the lagoon. They even built a small modern hotel and dining hall for passengers as well as a hospital.*[2]

By the autumn of 1941 the picture at Wake had changed dramatically. In addition to Pan Am, there were now some twelve hundred civilians on the island, building an airstrip and other facilities for the U.S. military. In addition there was a 449-man detachment from the First Marine Defense Battalion. These defense battalions were a new animal in the Marine Corps. They were designed for just the sort of duty they were getting—defending the small, isolated military outposts scattered across the Pacific and the Panama Canal. Unfortunately, the First Battalion had left nearly half of its 850-man strength behind in Pearl Harbor with orders to catch up later. But the 449-man detachment brought with it several batteries of modern three-inch antiaircraft guns as well as several batteries of World War I–era five-inch cannons, which had been stripped from obsolete battleships to be turned into shore defenses against surface ship attacks.

The plan was that once the large runways were finished, Wake would be an early warning outpost at the edge of America's Pacific Sea Frontier, with patrol planes fanning out in all directions to keep an eye on the Japanese. But until then the only U.S. planes at Wake were a marine squadron of twelve F4F Grumman Wildcat fighter planes, which had been delivered only four days before the attack on Pearl Harbor by carriers from Admiral Halsey's carrier fleet. (Incidentally, this was the reason the U.S.

*Because of its sanctuary status, no cats or dogs were allowed on Wake and a vast population of a large and odd kind of rat, big as a prairie dog, had infested the place by the time Americans began to arrive in numbers. They were shot, poisoned, and electrocuted but it made no difference; the rats flourished, and threatened to prevail.

carriers were not at Pearl when the Japanese attacked, one of the few strokes of American good luck on that black day.)[3]

The marines were under the command of (then) Major James P. S. Devereux and he worked them fiercely day and night setting up defenses. During the time leading up to the outbreak of war all sorts of people passed through on the Pan Am Clippers: generals, ambassadors, a family of Jews trying to escape the Germans and get to America, even the Japanese "special envoy," Saburo Kurusu, stopped at Wake on his way to the fateful show-down with Secretary of State Cordell Hull. He bought Major Devereux drinks and informed him, "I am just going to Washington to see what I can do. I hope I can straighten out affairs and avoid trouble."[4]

Devereux did his best to prepare for the defense of Wake but was handicapped by the usual difficulties that attended all U.S. military services in those days: lack of supplies and trained personnel and, most of all, time. Parts for some of the big guns were missing; radar had been promised but not delivered; and there were not even enough rifles and helmets to go around. At Pearl Harbor, before he'd left for Wake, Devereux had been told that his mission was to defend against a "raid"—a sort of small-scale hit-and-run—not a full-scale attack, which is what he got.

The instant word flashed from Pearl Harbor that the Japanese had begun the war (it was then Monday, December 8, on Wake, since it was across the international date line), Devereux knew pretty much what to expect next. He sounded general quarters and within half an hour all his gun positions up and down the island were manned. A China Clipper that had taken off at sunrise for Guam got word and returned to Wake, and since the marine fighters were only short-range planes, the captain of the Clipper agreed to fly a hundred-mile-distant patrol for 360 degrees around Wake. Then, within two hours, the unexpected happened. Since there was no radar, the defenders of Wake had to rely on sight and sound to detect approaching enemy aircraft, which failed them. The crash of surf on the coral rocks and a fast-moving rain squall conspired to allow the Japanese to swoop down with three squadrons of thirty-six medium-range bombers from their mandates in the Marshall Islands, about six hundred miles to the south. The bombers came in so low and so fast that the Americans were taken completely by surprise.

Seven of the twelve Grummans of Marine Fighter Squadron 211 were destroyed in a matter of seconds as they waited on the runway for takeoff or service. Others were damaged. Several marine pilots were killed rushing to their planes. The Japanese bombed the hospital and the Pan Am hotel, killing eleven civilians. Before leaving they shot up the big China Clipper that was floating in the lagoon; then, to the mortification of every American, civilian or military—they could actually see them, they were flying so low—the Japanese pilots waved and grinned out of their open cockpits and wagged their wings in triumph before heading home. The whole thing had taken less than ten minutes and Wake was a shambles. No Japanese planes were lost. Twenty-three marines on the airstrip, plus the eleven civilians, lay dead or dying, with others injured.[5] The only good news was that the riddled China Clipper was able to load up with civilians and make it to Midway, a thousand miles back toward Pearl.

Next morning the Japanese returned to finish the job. Fifty-five civilians were killed and seven military personnel. This time, however, two of the remaining three marine fighters were in the air and shot down one of the bombers, while fire from Devereux's antiaircraft batteries shot down another. Wisely, Devereux had calculated that the Japanese on the raid the day before would have located the positions of his batteries and be gunning for them, so he had all of them moved to different places, some as far as six hundred yards away—a stupendous task, considering that the guns weighed eight tons each. Next day, the tenth, the Japanese came back but, aside from blowing up several "dummy guns" (big pieces of timber) that Devereux had cagily contrived to leave in the place of his real ones, exploding a dynamite dump, and killing one marine, little damage was done. Two more Japanese bombers were shot down by the three remaining U.S. fighters.

Most of the civilian construction workers ran off into the bushes when the first bomb fell, not to return until it was over. But others stayed and helped, most notably a big former football star from the University of Washington, Dan Teters, who was the supervisor of construction on Wake. He organized the remaining civilians into groups and work parties, digging air-raid shelters, helping man the coast guns, filling sandbags, and hauling ammunition, food, and hot coffee to the marines at their posts around the Island.[6]

At three A.M. on December 11, Devereux was awakened in his command post dugout by a phone call reporting movement offshore. He got up and, with one of his runners, walked to the beach. He studied the seemingly empty sea through his wide night-vision binoculars and was about to return to the CP when his heart caught up.

"Well," he said, "there they are." A line of ships stretched across the horizon from south to east. "We knew there was no American task force anywhere near Wake Island."[7]

Devereux ordered everyone to prepare to repel an invasion and added, very wisely, "Hold your fire until I give the word."

Two hours passed before the first faint glow of dawn appeared in the east. The Japanese invasion fleet consisted of three light cruisers, six destroyers, and a number of troop transports for the landing force. At five A.M. the Japanese cruisers opened fire but did little damage. Devereux realized that the cruisers, with their six-inch guns, outmatched in range the five-inch guns he had in his batteries and could, if they wished, simply stand offshore and pound the Wake defenses into rubble without risking damage to themselves.

The Japanese did not do this, however. After the first salvos, the Japanese cruisers hauled along with the destroyers and transport ships toward shore, evidently thinking, as Devereux hoped they would, that the previous days' aerial bombing had knocked out all his guns. The men manning the American artillery were itching to fire, but Devereux repeated his order to wait until he said so. The Japanese force was within a mile of shore when Devereux gave the order at 6:10 A.M.

The American batteries opened up. The first salvo missed but the second caught the *Yubari*—which was the Japanese commanding admiral's flagship—amidships and it began to belch smoke and steam. The cruiser slowed and began to veer "crazily" as the marines furiously fed shells into their five-inch guns. Two more salvos struck home before the ship managed to "limp over the horizon," according to Devereux, carrying the Japanese admiral with her. Meanwhile, U.S. fire blasted one of the destroyers accompanying the troop transports. It simply exploded, broke in half, and sank with all hands in less than two minutes.

All the Japanese warships were now firing wildly when the shore batteries turned their attention to another destroyer and blew her stern off; in addition they blasted one of the troop transports and it sank without a trace. Another one followed her down in short order. Some of the civilian construction workers made themselves useful by hauling ammunition from the magazines to the guns, freeing the marines to man the batteries.

Another cruiser was hit and wobbled off out of range in a smoke screen it had laid. Now all four remaining Grumman Wildcats got into the act. (Marine mechanics had managed to patch up two more of the Wildcats that had been damaged in the first day's air attack.) They had gotten off the ground when the battle began and one of them, flown by Captain "Hammering Hank" Elrod, put a bomb in another Japanese destroyer before his plane was totally riddled by antiaircraft fire from the stricken ship. Right behind him, a second pilot came in for a run when, as he reported later, "As I prepared to bomb this ship, it blew up and sank."

Captain Elrod somehow managed to crash-land his plane on the beach, but it was a total loss, and he kept apologizing, as if it were his fault, for not bringing it in safely. Meanwhile, the Japanese decided to retire and try again when conditions were more favorable. More than five hundred Japanese had been lost.

It was a fine day for the United States Marines and they were justifiably proud. When Devereux reported the action to Pearl Harbor the people there were elated. Finally there was some kind of victory. It was also reported that when Devereux was asked if there was anything he needed, he replied, "Send us more Japs." It was a great line, and it was broadcast and printed all over America and gave the American people a lift they sorely needed. Problem was, it wasn't true, as Devereux himself said after the war: "I would not have been damned fool enough to send such an idiotic message."

Nevertheless, Americans ate it up. They tuned in breathlessly each evening as broadcasters began referring to the defenders of Wake as "the gallant little band" or "the heroic band," and "Send us more Japs" was played up prominently—all of which was received via shortwave radio by the men on Wake, who generally hooted at it; they knew the Japanese weren't finished with them. One of the network commentators described Wake Island as the Alamo of the Pacific. This, according to Devereux, "caused the marines to use bad language . . . Even Private Joe Blow knew enough history to know what happened at the Alamo, and he didn't like the idea."*[8]

Meanwhile, back at Pearl Harbor there was much teeth-gnashing about what, if anything, could be done to relieve Wake Island. Admiral Kimmel, who was still in charge during the first Wake attack, had immediately organized a relief force and set it into motion. Then word came that Navy Secretary Knox, with Roosevelt's approval, had fired Kimmel and that effective immediately Admiral Pye would take his place. Pye went ahead with Kimmel's relief expedition for Wake, built around the carrier *Saratoga,* which had raced back across the Pacific from the West Coast at the first news of war. Task Force 14 would consist of *Sara,* as well as a cruiser division commanded by Admiral Frank Jack Fletcher, who would direct the operation. An accompanying transport contained a reinforcement battalion of marines and replacement supplies. This force sailed from Pearl on December 16.

On Wake the situation was becoming desperate. Following the marines' successful defense of the Wake beaches, the island was nevertheless bombed almost daily from the Japanese Marshall Islands, slowly demolishing the fortifications and even the inroads of civilization itself: Devereux's artillery was destroyed; his repair shops were put out of action; and his men were being worn down by the constant strain. On December 21 the two carriers that had peeled off from Nagumo's Pearl Harbor strike force on its way home to Japan had arrived off Wake to add their power to the fray. They shot down the two remaining Grumman

---

*The origin of the "Send us more Japs" remark has never been successfully explained. Some have ventured that it was the work of a public relations officer at Pearl or elsewhere, or the creation of an overenthusiastic journalist. Historian John Toland believes it was created by the wire room on Wake as "padding," the sort of nonsense telegraphers put at the end of messages to confuse anyone trying to break their code.

Wildcats. What was left of the marine aviation section joined Devereux as combat infantrymen.

Late at night on December 22 Devereux and others who had been anxiously watching out to sea for the relief expedition saw flashes of light in the northwest. They did not know what to make of this, but assumed it must be their salvation. It was not. It was the Japanese, come to invade them yet again and with a much larger force; Fletcher's Task Force 14 was still some five hundred miles away, owing to difficulties of refueling at sea, as well as conflicting orders from Pye's headquarters in Hawaii. Back in Washington Admiral Stark had concluded that Wake could not be held and it might be best to let Task Force 14 simply evacuate everybody there. Pye, still shaken from the disaster at Pearl Harbor, was reluctant to risk his force, especially since nobody knew the whereabouts of Nagumo's colossal fleet following its attack on Pearl Harbor. He radioed Fletcher to detach a seaplane tender to Wake, unescorted, to evacuate the civilians and marines. No sooner had Fletcher received this perplexing message than Pye countermanded his own order. Whatever information they had back at Pearl Harbor, they didn't seem very decisive about acting on it, was Fletcher's reaction.

Just past midnight, now December 23, the Japanese began landing troops on beaches all over the island, outnumbering the marines three to one. From Japan, Radio Tokyo aired a broadcast from Tokyo Rose that lamented, "Where, oh where, is the United States Navy?" The people on Wake were wondering the same thing.*

Devereux was now in a bad fix. It was still dark and most of his searchlights had been destroyed by Japanese bombing. He knew the enemy was landing because of various reports from his batteries and strong points, but not exactly where. He would have to wait until sunrise for the situation to clarify itself.

*"Tokyo Rose" was an American citizen of Japanese ancestry who made propaganda broadcasts for the Japanese. There were actually several Tokyo Roses but the American one was imprisoned after the war. Likewise, an American actress named Mildred Gillers broadcast propaganda for the Germans under the name "Axis Sally." She got twelve years. An Englishman who broadcast from Berlin was dubbed "Lord Haw Haw," and so obnoxious was his palaver that after the war the British government hanged him.

All through the early hours the Japanese relentlessly staged night attacks against the American positions. At one point a civilian worker lurched into Devereux's headquarters and shrieked, "They're killing them all!" He said he had seen the Japanese taking the airstrip and that they were bayoneting the marines who had manned the machine guns. This sort of thing went on until dawn—desperate radio reports of Japanese crawling up on marine positions, and then the radio would go dead.[9]

Commander Winfield Scott Cunningham was the senior officer present on Wake, but he commanded nothing but a headquarters office—Devereux had the marine force under his own control. Nevertheless, Cunningham was ostensibly in charge. It was just after sunrise when, acting on reports from Devereux, Cunningham composed a message to Pearl Harbor: "Enemy on Island—Issue in Doubt."

This news was received with dismay by Admiral Pye and his staff. Fletcher's task force was still nearly a day away to the east. They all agreed it was probably too late either to save Wake or to evacuate it. The question then became whether or not they should tell Fletcher to keep steaming and try to engage the Japanese fleet. In the end, Pye decided no; he was unwilling to risk one of his only three carriers and her supporting force against an enemy of undetermined strength.

When this word was received aboard *Saratoga* there was fierce consternation and anger. Fletcher's staff argued that he should just ignore the orders and keep on going. The marine pilots were especially distressed, since they well knew what would happen to their fellow marines on Wake if it was abandoned to the Japanese. Many cursed, some wept, but Fletcher ordered Task Force 14 to come about and retire to Pearl Harbor, a bitter pill to swallow.[10]

Meanwhile on the island, despite fierce marine opposition and many individual acts of bravery, it was becoming apparent that organized resistance would not be possible much longer. Sunrise had revealed Japanese flags flapping in the breeze all over the island, marking Japanese positions for their own inevitable air strikes. Offshore lay a fleet of twenty-one Japanese ships. About seven-thirty A.M. Cunningham sent out word that Task Force 14 would not be coming after all and Devereux replied that he was going to try to consolidate his troops for one last stand. Cunningham, however, had concluded that surrender was the only option lest they all be killed, and as island commander he was responsible for all the civilians.

Devereux was both furious and heartbroken but he understood. He gave orders for his men to destroy their weapons and raise white flags. Commander Cunningham suddenly appeared, having changed into his formal blue navy uniform, and the two of them began walking toward the Japanese positions with a sergeant carrying a white rag tied to the tip of a mop. The first Japanese they encountered was a very junior officer who as luck would have it spoke broken English. When Devereux told him they were surrendering, the Japanese officer gave him a cigarette and cheerfully informed the Americans that he had attended the San Francisco World's Fair in 1939.

For the next several hours Devereux and Cunningham walked around Wake under Japanese escort shouting out for the marines to surrender, in case they hadn't already gotten the word. Unnerving incidents occurred, one in particular when the surrender party approached the main headquarters and saw a Japanese soldier hauling down the big American flag. In some bushes nearby was a marine sergeant who did not know of the surrender and had drawn a bead on the Japanese with a machine gun. He was just about to pull the trigger when he heard Devereux's shouting. If he had fired, no telling what would have happened.[11]

When the surrender was complete Devereux and Cunningham were taken to the Japanese commander's headquarters. One of the first things the commander demanded to know was, "Where are the women's quarters!" Told that there were no women on Wake, he refused to believe it and threw Cunningham, Devereux, and the other officers into a cramped prison building. For the next two and a half weeks the marines and navy personnel as well as the civilians were subjected to unpleasant but tolerable treatment by their captors. The enlisted men had been stripped to their underwear, trussed up tightly with telephone wire, and marched into a dark, sweltering blockhouse. On January 12 the Japanese began shipping out the Americans, civilians and military alike, to various prison camps, where their treatment grew progressively worse: beatings, starvation, neglect.*

Devereux and Cunningham and most of the marines were sent to a prison camp near the Japanese occupied city of Shanghai, China. There they met up with a U.S. Navy commander named Columbus Darwin Smith, who had been captain of the navy gunboat *Wake* on the old Yangtze River patrol before the Japanese seized it and made him a prisoner. The Wake Island prisoners and the former skipper of the *Wake* decided on the spot that "Wake" must be an unlucky name.

Smith was an unusual character in a war filled with unusual characters. To begin with, he had the dubious distinction of being the first American taken prisoner by the Japanese, since they had seized him on the Shanghai docks within minutes of the Pearl Harbor attack. How he came to Shanghai and got to be a commander in the U.S. Navy was also unusual. The son of a prominent Atlanta physician, Smith had run away at age sixteen to become a merchant seaman and in 1906 found himself running a watermelon schooner from Tampa to Key West. He was still making the run eleven years later when America entered the First World War. He was commissioned a naval lieutenant and assigned to a sub chaser fighting the Austrian navy in the Mediterranean, where he became a convert of steam over sail and for the next ten years captained ships of various shapes and sizes. In 1929 he heard about a high-paying job skippering river boats on the Yangtze and made a decision that would land him smack in the beginning of World War II.

At age fifty-one Smith had become an old China hand. He knew the Yangtze upstream and down for thousands of miles and had become a fixture around Shanghai, which was home to a number of American and British corporations doing business in China. In 1937, following the Rape

*By 1943 there were still nearly a hundred American civilians left on Wake, ordered to remain and work for the Japanese. On October 7, the Japanese, using a pretext that they were operating a secret radio, marched the civilians out to the beach and to a man machine-gunned them to death. After the war, the Japanese commander of Wake and eleven of his officers were sentenced to death by hanging by an Allied tribunal.

of Nanking, the war between the Japanese and Chinese had spread to Shang-hai, and the Japanese were bombing the helpless city. Smith was there for the sinking of the *Panay* but managed to maintain friendships with many Japanese army and navy officers.*

In March of 1941, nine months before Pearl Harbor, Smith was asked to accept a new commission in the U.S. Navy and skipper the *Wake,* which he did, making him the ranking U.S. Navy officer in China. Actually, the *Wake* was less a gunboat than a clandestine floating radio spy ship, used to keep track of Japanese movements. The day before the Pearl Harbor attack a Japanese officer of Smith's acquaintance phoned Smith to inquire where he would be next morning. Smith replied that he would be on the *Wake,* whereupon the Japanese informed Smith that he had several turkeys with which he wished to make Smith and his crew a gift, and that he would have them delivered next morning. Before this kindness could be trans-acted, however, Smith received news from his quartermaster on the radio-ladened *Wake* telling him of the Pearl Harbor attack. Smith rushed to his ship to find it under Japanese guard.†

Presently a Japanese naval officer appeared and told Smith to surren-der himself and he would be treated like an officer and a gentleman. Smith did as he was told and while he was under supervision of the Japanese navy that promise was kept. But as soon as the army took him over he was promptly and roughly thrown into a filthy prison, along with sixteen hun-

---

*The *Panay* was a U.S. gunboat on the Yangtze River patrol that was attacked and sunk by yet another rogue Japanese army commander and nearly precipitated war between Japan and the United States four years early. The two-hundred-foot warship carrying American consular officials escaping from the Nanking horror was first fired upon from shore by Japanese batteries, then relentlessly bombed by Japanese planes flying high and low, even though she had American flags plastered all over her as well as her own U.S. ensign flying. The Japanese government avoided a confrontation by hastily apologizing—insincerely, it turned out—and paying a large indemnity.

†Apparently the Japanese in Shanghai had offered similar largesse to other U.S. of-ficers and officials so as to determine where they would be when the planned Pearl Harbor attack occurred.

dred other Americans, which included the personnel from Wake Island. In the face of tortures, beatings, and starvation Smith became legendary for his fabulous escape attempts. Finally successful, his great escape involved an odyssey of more than seven hundred miles, on foot, through Japanese-held territory. From time to time in this narrative we will revisit Commander Smith in his travails to reach freedom.

✯ Chapter Eight

The Japanese had opened World War II in Asia ahead of schedule, by mistake, about an hour before Pearl Harbor was attacked. This seemed to be the work of a fanatical militarist, Colonel Masanobu Tsuji, who a few years earlier had plotted to assassinate the Japanese prime minister on grounds he was trying to keep peace with the Americans. For his punishment Tsuji was banished to a war plans office on Formosa, where he quickly began assembling around him a clique of like-minded army officers to draw up the scheme for the Japanese Southward Movement.

Tsuji's fanciful scheme to defeat the British in Malaya began with a trick, similar to Hitler's tacky artifice in having one of his battleships on a so-called goodwill visit to Poland suddenly open fire at the unsuspecting citizens of Danzig. Tsuji's trick was ingenious, to say the least. In the dark of night while the Japanese carriers were launching their planes at Pearl Harbor, Tsuji's men would land in a troop convoy on the Thailand side of the Kra isthmus, just north of the border with Malaya. There, more than one thousand armed Japanese dressed in bogus Thai army uniforms would enter the Thai city of Singora, sweep through saloons grabbing up Thai dance hall girls, expropriate several dozen Thai buses, and, singing and shouting with the girls, drive the buses to the Malay border crossing and claim that the Japanese had landed in Thailand and they were trying to escape. When they were let through, the Japanese would then drive on to Kota Bora, a Malay town where the British kept an air base, and capture it, thus eliminating a major air threat to the main invasion force. "A modern version of the Trojan Horse," was the way historian John Toland described the adventure.

It might have worked, except the Japanese agent who was supposed to have arranged things ashore with the dance hall girls, buses, Thai police, etc., had fallen asleep in the Japanese consulate and, consequently, Tsuji's scheme unraveled. It didn't much matter. The Japanese landed their army anyway, some 26,000 battle-hardened troops from the China war, while Japanese bombers from the newly acquired airfields at Saigon rudely awakened the citizens of Singapore, five hundred miles to the south, killing sixty-three civilians.[1]

At first the Singaporeans were not terribly alarmed. After all, Singapore was touted as the impregnable fortress of the Pacific, formidable as the Rock of Gibraltar. But this was illusory. Even though the British had been fortifying Singapore for years, they had done so against an attack from the sea, not from a land attack through what they believed were the impassable jungles of Malaya. Consequently, when the British began laying in the enormous fifteen-inch guns all around the fortress itself, they pointed them out to sea, set in concrete. Further, the British had no tanks in Malaya for the same reason—they assumed tanks could not operate in the jungle. Nor were their aircraft adequate: many were American-made Brewster Buffaloes, which were obsolete and considered death traps even by American pilots and had an inadequate flying range.

By mid-morning of the attack a fateful decision was made by the general staff to thwart the Japanese landings in northern Malaya. A few weeks earlier a mighty but unbalanced British fleet had arrived at Singapore, built around the fast new battleship *Prince of Wales* and the powerful battle cruiser *Repulse*. The British carrier *Indomitable* was supposed to have rendezvoused with this fleet to provide air cover but, most unfortunately, had run aground in Bermuda and was still undergoing repairs. Nevertheless, it was decided to send the two big ships north to attack and repel the Japanese invasion force, which was reported to be still unloading men and equipment.

The commander of this armada was Vice Admiral Sir Tom S. V. "Tom Thumb" Phillips, who was so short he needed to stand on a crate to see over his bridge. Two days earlier he had flown to the Philippines to beg Admiral Thomas Hart, commander of the U.S. Asiatic Fleet, to lend him some American destroyers to reinforce his Malayan operations. (Hart agreed to lend him four.) When he was asked by Hart when he intended to return to Singapore, Phillips answered, "First thing in the morning."

Hart told him, "If you want to be there when the war starts, I'd get on your plane right now."[2]

And so, as the great red ball of a setting sun dipped slowly into the shimmering horizon, Phillips's fleet steamed majestically out of Singapore harbor and headed north along the Malay coast, "Off to look for trouble," as the captain of the *Repulse* put it. Trouble was not long in coming. Tom Thumb Phillips was pugnacious and a "big gun" man all the way; he refused to believe battleships could be sunk by airplanes on the open sea, where they had room to maneuver. There was something to be said for his thinking, too: it had never been done. Certainly battleships could be sunk by bombs—Billy Mitchell had proved that back in the 1920s, as had the British again just the year before when they wrecked the Italian fleet at Taranto. But those ships had been at anchor, sitting ducks with no place to run. It would be different when a battleship was out on the open ocean, able to reach speeds approaching forty miles per hour, twisting and turning and firing all her vast weapons at a puny airplane trying to drop a bomb from high altitude on a ship wheeling around faster than many a speedboat.

Still, Phillips was given pause. The situation was not clear as to what he might run into five hundred miles north, within reach of the Japanese airfields in Indochina. At the last minute he requested of the British air commander in Malaya some air cover but was turned down because the Japanese had already knocked out the airfields in northern Malaya and many of the planes at Singapore did not have the range to reach north Malaya. "Well," said Tom Thumb, "we must get on with it."[3]

Phillips obviously knew he was sailing into danger, but his sense was that it would have been too great an embarrassment for his powerful warships, about which so much ballyhoo had been brandished, to retire in the face of the enemy, and he also knew it would be suicide to just let them sit in the harbor, waiting for the Japanese planes. His plan was to race north as quickly as possible to ambush the unloading Japanese transports on the beaches but to retire if his force was spotted by reconnaissance planes, since the element of surprise would have been lost and the Japanese transports would have put to sea.

By December 9 (Far East time), the day after Pearl Harbor, everything seemed to be going well. Heavy rainstorms shrouded Phillips's fleet and allowed it to go undetected until the ships were within less than a day of the Japanese landing point at Kota Bora. Then the first piece of luck ran out; a lookout on the *Prince of Wales* spotted a Japanese reconnaissance plane, which had obviously also spotted them. Phillips reluctantly came about and headed he knew not where. Then came a report of Japanese landings farther south, not far from his position. They turned out to be false, but Phillips now encountered his second piece of bad luck—a Japanese submarine had spotted them also.[4]

Before first light on December 10 Japanese bombers and torpedo planes—eighty-eight of them in all—were scrambled from fields in Indochina and sent south looking for the British warships. They found nothing and were flying dispiritedly home when, at eleven A.M., one of the pilots looked through a hole in the clouds and saw the big ships, fifty miles from the Malay coast. The Japanese air fleet immediately attacked. *Repulse* suffered a direct hit almost immediately from a high-level bomber. *Prince of Wales* received two torpedoes, which jammed her rudder and reduced her speed to fifteen knots, making her easy prey. For two more hours the Japanese tormented the helpless behemoths; Phillips's third and final piece of luck had run out.

Aboard the *Repulse* was a thirty-four-year-old American CBS radio correspondent named Cecil Brown, who kept a diary of the battle. What he saw first was nine Japanese twin-engine bombers strung out in a line above the ship at 10,000 feet. One of the bombs penetrated into the bowels of the *Repulse*, setting off uncontrollable fires. The loudspeaker ordered, "Stand by for barrage!" Brown wrote, and, "We are twisting and turning violently to avoid torpedoes."

The attack had been going on half an hour as more Japanese planes showed up. "The guns are deafening. The smell of cordite is almost suffocating and the explosions are ear shattering and the flashes blinding. An officer beside me yells, 'Here comes a tin fish!'" All the torpedoes missed, despite the fact that the Japanese pilots had come in so low as to be seen in their cockpits by the British sailors, and many of them were shot out of the sky. More Japanese planes approached. They were now an hour into the battle. Brown found time to look over at the *Prince of Wales* and found her "definitely stopped. Her guns are firing constantly and we are twisting [so that] one moment the *Wales* is on our starboard, the next it's on our port. The calmness of the crew is amazing. The cool precision of all hands seems unreal and unnatural.

"A watcher shouts, 'Stand by for torpedo!' Someone says, 'This one got us.' The torpedo struck the side where I was standing. It felt like the ship had crashed into a well-rooted dock. It threw me four feet across the deck. Almost immediately it seemed we began to list and less than a minute later there was another jar. The communication system coolly announced, 'Blow up your life belts. Prepare to abandon ship. May God be with you.' It was most difficult to realize I must leave the ship. It seemed incredible that the *Repulse* could go down."

The ship was now heeling dangerously and correspondent Brown scrambled across a deck littered with the bodies of dead sailors, lying around their guns. As he went over the side, Brown got a look at the *Prince of Wales,* half a mile away, burning furiously but with all her guns still blazing—the perfect picture of an enraged and mortally wounded beast swatting at her tormentors. When Brown hit the water his watch was smashed. It stopped at 12:25. Eight minutes later the big battle cruiser rolled and vanished beneath the ocean. The *Wales* had begun to list also, which made many of her guns unusable, but she managed to stay afloat another forty minutes. Then, with the hundreds of men from the *Repulse* treading water and watching in awe, at 1:19 P.M. the *Prince of Wales* slowly rolled and settled by the stern; her bow rose up into the air "like a church steeple," and she slid to the depths of the South China Sea. Only four months earlier she had been resting peacefully at anchor in Placentia Bay, Newfoundland, where, upon her broad deck, Winston Churchill and Franklin D. Roosevelt had signed the Atlantic Charter.[5]

The escorting destroyers, which were not damaged by the attack, had already begun picking up oil-covered survivors. Of the nearly 3,000 sailors aboard both ships, most were fished out and lived to fight another day, but 840 were killed, including Admiral Tom Thumb Phillips, who went down with his ship. As the rescue operation was in progress, a flight of the slow and obsolete Brewster Buffaloes arrived from an inland airfield to see what they could do, but it was too late; the Japanese planes had headed home. One pilot looked down at the carnage and afterward wrote, "Never have I seen anything comparable with what I saw yesterday. I had seen many men in dire danger waving, cheering and joking as if they were holiday-makers at Brighton. It shook me, for here was something beyond human nature."[6]

A Japanese pilot told his commander afterward, "As we dived for the ship, I didn't want to launch my torpedo. It was such a beautiful ship, such a beautiful ship." Next day the commander and his men flew back over the site, now just empty sea, and flung a wreath of flowers out over the shimmering oil slick.[7]

The Japanese attack had lasted just under two hours, but it forever changed the way navies would view their primary fighting strategy. Two incredibly expensive capital ships, free to maneuver in the open ocean, had been sunk by a handful of cheap airplanes. Even the Japanese senior naval officers in Tokyo found it difficult to believe. Overnight came the painful revelation that if battleships were to play any major role in the war, they would require massive protection by carrier-based fighters, and that the carrier itself had now become the principal instrument of sea war.

Winston Churchill, who only a few days earlier upon getting news of the Pearl Harbor attack had declared to himself, "So we had won after all," received word of the sinkings within the hour, early in the morning. "I writhed and twisted in the bed as the full horror of the news sank in," Churchill wrote later. "In all the war I never received such a direct shock."[8]

Simultaneous with the Pearl Harbor raid the Japanese attacked Guam, a small American possession that the United States had liberated from Spain after the Spanish-American War. The island had been under Spanish rule for more than two hundred years and its population of about twenty thousand consisted of rather tall, lighter-skinned natives with long straight black hair, whom the Spaniards had converted to Roman Catholicism. Being a Pacific way station en route to the Philippines, Guam for centuries had been the stopping-off point for Spanish galleons but now housed a U.S. naval base, which Congress had recently decided not to fortify, as they had Wake Island. Consequently, when the Japanese attacked they found only five hundred or so sailors and marines whose only weapons consisted of small arms. After killing seventeen Americans and Guamanian citizens, the Japanese took possession of the Island.[9]

Also, a week after Pearl Harbor, the Japanese attacked the British colony of Hong Kong, where the British made a heroic stand. There were about 11,000 Scottish, Indian, and Canadian troops defending Hong Kong, as well as a 1,700-man local militia known as the Gin Drinkers, who were not highly regarded by the regular troops. After driving the British force from the China mainland, the Japanese commander crossed the narrow bay in a launch under a truce flag and demanded that the British governor surrender the colony of some two million residents. He refused and two days later the Japanese, in a fleet of commandeered rafts, junks, and rubber boats, crossed the bay for invasion. They were blown out of the water. Three days later a terrific Japanese bombardment from the Chinese shore opened on the north part of Hong Kong, followed by a much larger invasion force, which shoved off in launches and rubber boats. This time the invasion succeeded and by next day, December 20, the Japanese occupied half of Hong Kong and split the British forces in two.

The only hope for the defenders rested on a communication from the Chinese army that it had some 60,000 troops ready to attack the Japanese from the rear. This proved illusory; a subsequent communication from the Chinese reported that they could not begin their attack until New Year's Day, which, as most realized, would be far too late. The British forces were down to half their strength, exhausted and low on ammunition, food, and water. The only thing they were not low on was courage, and some of most courageous fighting was being done by the Gin Drinkers volunteer militia. By Christmas Eve there was no electrical power on Hong Kong and the Japanese had taken the waterworks as well and shut off the water supply. Food for everyone was running out.

In the dark hours of Christmas morning a party of Japanese soldiers entered an emergency hospital where some sixty wounded defenders lay on cots. They immediately began bayoneting them beneath their blankets. A doctor who tried to stop it was shot. Eleven nurses were carried off to an adjoining room and gang-raped, then seven of them were murdered by the wild-eyed Japanese. By midafternoon of Christmas Day the British authorities knew there was no course but surrender. At last the shooting stopped, but next day a Scottish soldier whose wife was a nurse at the hospital, having heard rumors of the rape, somehow made his way there to find British prisoners under Japanese guard piling the bodies of the bayoneted soldiers into a huge outdoor funeral pyre. A Japanese officer conducted the Scotsman to a heap covered by a coat that he immediately recognized. He gently pulled it back to reveal the bodies of three women. One of them was his wife.[10]

It was not a very merry Christmas on Singapore either. Since their landings on Pearl Harbor, the Japanese had made fantastic headway down the Malay peninsula. This action pitted some 86,000 troops of the British army against a 26,000-man Japanese force under the command of Lieutenant General Tomoyuki Yamashita, who would soon gain the sobriquet the Tiger of Malaya. The difference was that contrary to British expectations, Yamashita had come equipped with a regiment of fifty-seven tanks. Ironically, another, less modern difference was that the Japanese had also come equipped with thousands of bicycles. A third difference was that many of the British troops consisted of regiments of the Indian army, who were probably less than enthusiastic about defending a colonial outpost of the nation that was occupying their own country. A fourth, major difference was that because of the terrain—thick jungle and impenetrable swamps, with no good roads and few poor ones—the British could not bring their full force to bear against the much smaller Japanese army.

The tactics used by the Japanese troops were those that had been successful in so many of their military operations. First they would infiltrate a relatively small force around the British flank, usually under cover of darkness. Often they used the bicycles as their transport and sometimes along the coast they would get around the defenders in rubber boats. When this surreptitious force was in place behind the unsuspecting enemy, it would open fire with mortars and small arms, alarming the defending troops and creating mass confusion; then the tanks would come into play along the front, firing rapidly and moving fast, convincing the defenders— especially the Indian soldiers, who had never seen a tank before—that they were trapped. Time and again the Japanese used this tactic against the disconcerted Indian troops until, by Christmas Day, they were only two hundred and fifty miles from Singapore itself.

In the meantime, Winston Churchill was paying his second visit to American shores. The week after Pearl Harbor he boarded the battleship *Duke of York*—a sad reminder, perhaps, that the *Prince of Wales,* his original transatlantic crossing vessel, now rested at the bottom of the sea—to meet Roosevelt in Washington to firm up strategy and boost spirits. It was a rough trip, taking nine days. The winter weather was atrocious; the ship had to be battened down most of the time and a number of sailors suffered broken bones from falls. Churchill, cooped up, restless and irritated, spent his time watching Rita Hayworth movies and reading C. S. Forester seafaring stories.[11]

The prime minister had been invited to stay at the White House, alarming the army's and navy's chiefs of staff, who were concerned that such close proximity to Roosevelt might sway the American president to agree with some of what they considered Churchill's screwy ideas.* What was actually agreed upon at this so-called Arcadia conference was that the United States would commit 90,000 troops to invade German-occupied North Africa in an operation that would be called Torch. In addition, some thousands of American soldiers would immediately be sent to keep the

*Among these included a wish by Churchill to send some kind of U.S. naval fleet into the Mediterranean to cooperate with the British—this when half the fleet was at the bottom of Pearl Harbor and the other half fighting for its life against German submarines in the Atlantic. Another was a plea to divert thousands of the U.S. troops earmarked for the Philippines to help defend Malaya.

peace in rebellious Ireland, freeing up British troops there to go to the fighting fronts. Also, the Americans promised to increase their output of warplanes to 60,000 in 1942 and 125,000 in 1943, with commensurate increases in tanks, merchant marine transports, artillery, and so forth. The prime minister was much pleased.[12]

On Christmas Day Churchill and Roosevelt attended services at the Foundry Methodist Church, where the Briton was greatly moved by a song he had never heard before, "O Little Town of Bethlehem." The next day at noon he strode into the U.S. Capitol to address the second joint session of Congress since America had entered the war. Churchill perfectly charmed his audience, opening with this remark: "I cannot help reflecting that if my father had been American and my mother British, instead of the other way around, I might have got here on my own."* Time and again he was interrupted by applause and foot stamping, but none more enthusiastic than when he alluded to the Japanese attack on Pearl Harbor and snarled, "What kind of people do they think we are!" At the end of this stirring oration, his eyes flashing and glistening with tears, Churchill strode off the platform to the roar of a standing ovation, flashing his famous V for victory sign.[13]

This goodwill visit by Churchill was crucial to the entire war effort. It must be remembered that Great Britain, at that time, was not well liked or trusted by many Americans, and had not been for a long while. The rupture of cordial relations between the two countries began before the American Revolution of 1776, and it took that war to throw off the oppressive yoke of King George III. Next came the War of 1812 during which the British set fire to the U.S. Capitol and the White House in addition to other reprehensible things on American soil. During the Civil War England tacitly sided with the Southern Confederacy, buying their cotton, selling them arms, and building them fast blockade-running ships. In the late nineteenth and early twentieth centuries came the great waves of German and Irish immigrants, who despised England to the core, and they

*Churchill's mother, Jenny Jerome, was the daughter of a New York speculator and racetrack owner, Leonard Jerome. She married Churchill's father, Randolph, a son of the sixth duke of Marlborough, in 1874.

and their descendants had embedded their notions into the fabric of society. When, in 1917, America finally entered World War I on the side of the British and French, there were much publicized disagreements over troop deployments; then after the war the British refused to pay the colossal debts owed the United States for war loans. Many Americans considered the British ingrates and pikers and, until just a few days earlier, believed they were trying to drag the United States into war only in order to save their far-flung empire.

Now all had changed; if the Axis was to be defeated, Great Britain would by necessity play a critical role and cooperation with them was paramount. With the wildly favorable press and radio coverage of Churchill's speech, his remarks went a long way in bringing the two nations together, a state of affairs that exists to this day.

The situation in Singapore in the opening month of 1942 was grave. By January 5 a fresh division of Australians had arrived and Singapore breathed a sigh of relief: these men were no mere native colonials but a tough fighting bunch who could stop the Japanese. It did not happen; the Japanese pulled their same crablike flanking tactics on the Aussies and within two weeks General Arthur Percival, commander of the British Malay army, was forced to order a final retreat onto Singapore island itself.

There disaster waited. As General Yamashita scanned the northern approaches to Singapore atop the watchtower of the great palace of the sultan of Johor, what he saw across the straits must have warmed his heart. No big guns were visible to oppose his invasion. Several days earlier, on January 31, the last of the British army had crossed over the causeway linking the island to the Malayan mainland, accompanied by the mournful tunes of a bagpiper. Then the causeway was blown up, but another blunder had been made. Not enough explosives were used and the resulting debris had settled to the bottom, lowering the water depth by several feet, so that at low tide even a short Japanese could wade across it.[14]

In Singapore City itself a sort of panicky carnival atmosphere took hold. Singapore had been anglified for nearly a century and a half and was replete with cricket and rugby pitches, golf courses, racetracks, and such institutions as the famous Raffles Hotel. Many European families lived there, but who were now desperately trying to flee on any available ship or boat. Most did not make it; the liner *Empress of Asia* was sunk in the channel and the Japanese continued to bomb and strafe the capital every day. Casualties mounted and there was little for anyone to do but drink gin and hide from the attacking bombers. The streets were jammed with wild-eyed and drunken deserters and frenzied civilians struggling to get out. The Japanese warplanes seemed to particularly enjoy picking off small boats filled with people trying to make it south across the Strait of Malacca to the Dutch island of Sumatra. Fifty of these were sunk in a single day.

In the midst of all this, General Sir Archibald Wavell arrived on the scene. He had just been placed in command of all British forces in the Far East and, in Singapore, was appalled by what he saw. Upon inspection of the north side of the fortress, where the Japanese army waited just half a mile across the strait, he found practically no artillery at all and not even a serious plan to repel an invasion. When he learned that the great fifteen-inch guns that faced the sea were set in concrete and could not be turned around, Wavell was both shocked and furious. He wired the news to Churchill, who became positively apoplectic and berated his chiefs of staff: "How is it that not one of you pointed this out to me at any time when these matters have been under discussion? This will produce the greatest scandal." He went on to order, "The city of Singapore must be converted into a citadel and defended to the death. No surrender can be contemplated."[15]

These were hollow words. "Defeat-itis" had set in during all those bitter retreats down the long Malay Peninsula. Wavell got into shouting matches with his army commander, General Percival, and issued a stern directive: "Commanders and senior officers must lead their troops and if necessary die with them. Every unit must fight it out to the end and in close contact with the enemy."

Meantime, General Yamashita's army was crossing the strait in hundreds of rubber boats. After a feint the previous day east of the causeway, on February 8 the Japanese opened up with a terrific barrage from four hundred artillery pieces on the opposite shore, setting fire to the oil-storage tanks at the naval base to keep the British from leaking the oil into the strait and setting it on fire. Then they began to land by the thousands in the mangrove swamps west of the causeway, which were only lightly defended by the exhausted Australians. The British seemed powerless to stop them and by midday the Japanese controlled nearly half of the twenty-seven-mile-wide island. Artillery and tanks were ferried over and more troops arrived.

By late morning Yamashita himself arrived and sent to Percival what by any standard was a polite and reasoned appeal for him to give up: "In the spirit of chivalry we have the honor of advising your surrender." It went on to catalog all the reasons why Percival should agree: army isolated and surrounded . . . resistance futile . . . fate of Singapore sealed . . . danger to civilians. After complimenting Percival on "raising the fame of Great Britain by the utmost exertions and heroic feelings," Yamashita closed by informing his opponent: "We do not feel you will increase the fame of the British Army by further resistance." Percival turned him down.

Five days later, while the British army consolidated itself into a tight little perimeter on the outskirts of Singapore City, a weird sort of calm imposed itself over the embattled citizens. Many stood in line at the cinema to see *The Philadelphia Story*. Others lined the bar at Raffles or other watering holes until the governor uncharitably ordered all liquor stocks destroyed to keep them from falling into Japanese hands. Chinese merchants cut off all credit to Europeans. The prevailing mood was expressed by some scrawled graffiti: "England for the English, Australia for the Australians, but Malaya for any Son of a Bitch who wants it."[16]

On Friday the thirteenth, a black day indeed, the Japanese pressed ever closer, at one point reprising their barbarity in Hong Kong by breaking into the military hospital at the edge of town and bayoneting the wounded in their beds. They even burst into an operating room, shoved the surgeons aside, and beat to death with rifle butts a solider undergoing an operation. Also as in Hong Kong the Japanese took the waterworks and shut off supply to Singapore's nearly two million inhabitants. The end was clearly near.[17]

Two days later Percival called a council of war and told his officers that he intended to ask for a truce. He had done all he could. Wavell, on nearby Java, reluctantly agreed, telegraphing him, "Whatever happens I thank you and all troops for your gallant efforts of the last few days."

Percival himself carried the big white flag of truce into the Ford Motor Company factory on the outskirts of the city, where the surrender ceremony had been arranged. Japanese reporters, photographers, and newsreel cameramen flooded the building. When Yamashita finally arrived his greeting was a far cry from the niceties of the note he had sent Percival a week earlier. "The Japanese army will consider nothing but surrender!" he told the British commander. Percival hedged; he wanted to construct a surrender document that would give his men and the citizens of Singapore the best possible terms. He asked for more time.

Yamashita was unmoved and threatened to resume firing if Percival did not surrender immediately and unconditionally. Between the various poor translations by interpreters, Yamashita grew increasingly impatient. "There is no need for all this talk! I want a simple answer," he screamed. "We want to hear 'Yes' or 'No' from you. Surrender or fight!"*

Percival, red-faced and bloodshot on the worst day of his life, could barely speak, but finally he managed a weak, "Yes, I agree," and signed the surrender document that was put in front of him. First, however, he asked Yamashita if he would guarantee protection of the women and children and British civilians on Singapore. The Japanese general so promised, but shortly afterward he went back on his word and allowed his troops to murder many thousands of Chinese living on the island.

Thus ended the largest and most humiliating surrender in British history: some 130,000 soldiers, including recent reinforcements, became Japanese prisoners of war. Many of them were sent to prison camps in Burma and set to work building a Japanese railroad through the steaming, pestilent jungles, where they died by the thousands. Their story was told two decades later in a book, which was made into the Academy Award–winning David Lean film *The Bridge on the River Kwai*.

---

*The historian John Toland tells us that Yamashita's impatience was caused by the fact that he had suddenly realized the British army outnumbered his own four to one and that he actually feared the Japanese army could lose the fight. After the war Toland says Yamashita described his strategy as "a bluff, a bluff that worked."

★ Chapter Nine

If the ordeal of Malaya and its fortress of Singapore was a British disaster, the Philippines proved to be an American calamity. Following Pearl Harbor the war had been rushed upon the Philippine command, and they were still months away from even basic preparedness. Naturally the Japanese did not wait for this. But unlike Pearl the Philippines had ample warning. A little past three A.M., December 8, 1941 (December 7 in Hawaii), the harsh words flashed out from Admiral Kimmel's Pacific Fleet headquarters: "Enemy Air Raid Pearl Harbor. This Is Not a Drill."

The first authority to receive this shocking news was Admiral Thomas Hart, commander of the small U.S. Asiatic Fleet, which had been recently gathered in Manila from stations far and wide in anticipation of the outbreak of war. Hart, however, did not immediately share his information with General Douglas MacArthur, overall commander of the U.S. Far East forces, apparently on the assumption that the army had its own ways of finding out.

It did. An alert army radioman with a shortwave tuner had been listening to music on a San Francisco commercial radio station when the announcer broke in with a wire service bulletin. He went screaming into the night to tell his boss, who soon got the news to MacArthur who, with his wife Jean and three-year-old son Arthur MacArthur IV, was sleeping in his luxurious penthouse atop the Manila Hotel. After dressing, the general asked his wife to bring him his Bible, which he read for a while before going off to his headquarters.[1]

Admiral Hart was waiting for him there and after a lengthy conference he received MacArthur's blessing to steam his fleet south toward Australia to save it from Japanese bombers. While this conversation was going on Lieutenant General Lewis Brereton, commander of the Far East Air Force, rushed in wanting to see MacArthur. Told by the chief of staff, General Richard Sutherland, that MacArthur was in conference, Brereton informed Sutherland that he wanted permission to send his thirty-five B-17 heavy bombers to attack the Japanese airfields on the island of Formosa (now Taiwan) some five hundred miles to the north. He said they could be ready to go at first light. Sutherland entered MacArthur's office and when he returned a few minutes later it was with news that has caused controversy and finger-pointing ever since. MacArthur, Sutherland said, would not give permission to bomb Formosa because of the directive from Washington the previous week about the president wanting to "let Japan strike the first blow."

Well, wondered Brereton, hadn't they just done so at Pearl Harbor? Good soldier that he was, however, Brereton went out to his headquarters and ordered his long-range bombers and fighters into the air to scout for any approaching Japanese invasion force and, also, to keep them off the ground in case of a surprise enemy attack. Brereton soon received word that radar had picked up flights of enemy planes approaching Luzon, the principal Philippine island, where Manila was located. At 9:15 he phoned Sutherland and again asked for MacArthur's permission to attack Formosa. Again it was denied. Nearly an hour went by before Sutherland called again and said MacArthur had authorized a "reconnaissance mission" over Formosa to take pictures and locate enemy airfields. In another hour Sutherland called back saying MacArthur had finally authorized the Formosa bombing attack itself. Brereton recalled all his B-17s from patrol and ordered them to Clark Field, about sixty miles north of Manila, to refuel and load up with bombs.*

*There are conflicting versions of the sequence of these events: Brereton's, Sutherland's, and MacArthur's. Brereton's seems to this author the most convincing, but the true story may never be known.

Scarcely had these lumbering aerial behemoths landed than the Japanese arrived in force.* All thirty-six of the modern P-40 fighters, which had been aloft to scout for Japanese planes, had been recalled for fueling as well and were now sitting on the runway. Shortly after noon, while many pilots were in the mess hall having lunch, fifty-four Japanese high-level bombers attacked Clark Field, followed by seventy dive-bombers and fighters, which bombed and strafed everything on the field. The Japanese attack had been delayed by heavy fog on Formosa, otherwise the P-40s would have been in the air to greet them and the B-17s flying high and far away. It was an incredible stroke of bad luck for the U.S. Air Force, compounded by confusion, indecision, and blundering by a variety of military operatives, high and low. No less than three direct warnings of the incoming flight of Japanese planes had been sent to Clark Field; none got through. A teletype sent to Clark by coast watchers who had spotted the Japanese flight failed because the teletype operator, like the pilots, was having his lunch. A frantic phone call from a radar operator was taken by an unnamed lieutenant who promised he would get the word out but never did; a radio message was jammed by static. The astonished Americans could plainly see the hundreds of Japanese bombs "glistening in the sunlight" as they hurdled toward them. Most of their ten-year-old antiaircraft ammunition failed to explode and when it did it was several thousand feet below the flying height of the bombers.[2]

General Jonathan Wainwright had gone to his house near Clark air base to begin packing some personal items in anticipation of being moved out into the field. When the first bombs began falling he went out on the porch to see what was happening and reported that "The very air rattled with concussion." In the midst of all this his Filipino houseboy came rushing out of the house, "his eyes as big as black marbles. In his frenzy," Wainwright recalled, "he had put on my steel helmet."

---

*The B-17 was truly the workhorse of the war. Dubbed the Flying Fortress because of its heavy armor and eleven .50-caliber machine guns bristling in every direction, it was extremely hard to bring down, as the Japanese learned at Pearl Harbor. It carried a crew of nine or ten, could fly at 317 mph at 25,000 feet, and deliver a 5,000-bomb load at targets a thousand miles distant. It cost $236,000 to build. When war broke out there were 150 B-17s in the U.S. Air Force; by war's end there were 12,700.

"Mother of God, General, what shall I do?" the houseboy shouted.

"Go and get me a bottle of beer," Wainwright told him. "It seemed to help him," the general said later. "I know it helped me."[3]

When it was over an hour later, most of Brereton's Far East Air Force had been wiped out and several hundred airmen lay dead. Of the thirty-six P-40s, only four managed to get off the ground; the rest were blown to bits. The B-17s became gigantic infernos of aviation fuel where they sat. All the hangars and shops and stores and the headquarters were wrecked. Another Japanese attack on the airfield at Iba, forty miles to the east, was similarly surprised and another sixteen P-40s were destroyed, as well as the radio set and its operator. Brereton later called it "one of the blackest days in U.S. military history."[4]

The smoke had not yet cleared when Brereton's phone rang. It was General Henry "Hap" Arnold in Washington, chief of the U.S. Army Air Force, who was hopping mad.

"How in hell could an experienced airman like you get caught with your planes on the ground! That's what we sent you there for, to avoid just what happened!"

Brereton was trying to explain the situation to his boss when a fresh flight of Japanese fighters roared over and began strafing the base anew.

"What in the hell is going on there!" Arnold shouted.

"We are having visitors," Brereton replied sourly.[5]

For the next week the Japanese continued to bomb and strafe airfields and other military facilities all over Luzon while American pilots made heroic but futile efforts to contain them. One B-17 pilot whose plane had been jumped by eighteen Japanese Zero fighters counted a thousand to fifteen hundred bullet holes in his fuselage, testimony at least to the durability of the big bombers. The massive navy base at Cavite, in sight of downtown Manila, was totally destroyed by an afternoon-long Japanese bombing attack as Admiral Hart "looked on in helpless rage." Like Kimmel before him at Pearl Harbor, Hart was experiencing a fleet commander's worst nightmare. Although most of the larger ships had already departed, submarines, oilers, seaplane tenders, tugs, barges, and other useful craft were ruined or damaged and the base itself with all its shops, stores, and warehouses was a complete loss. Most unfortunate was the destruction of several hundred torpedoes crated on the docks, almost the entire supply for the Far East command.[6]

After seven days of losses it had become painfully apparent that the Japanese had gained almost total control of the air above Luzon. Brereton had to keep his remaining bombers in the air during daylight hours just to prevent them from being wrecked on the ground by the Japanese. "It was a game of hide-and-seek that wore out men as well as planes," was the way the agonized Brereton put it. Besides, there were simply no spare parts for any of the planes and no way to get any. It was finally decided to move most of the big planes to Darwin, Australia, fifteen hundred miles to the south, where at least they could be maintained.[7]

Thus MacArthur was left with no navy and no air force to contend with the rapacious Japanese, who were certainly preparing for an invasion. This was perhaps all the more galling because of MacArthur's tight affiliations and genuine love for the Philippines and its people. His father, Arthur MacArthur, who had won the Congressional Medal of Honor in the Civil War, had been named military governor of the Philippines in 1900, when Douglas was still a West Point cadet. After graduation the young MacArthur quickly distinguished himself as a junior officer, serving in the Philippines and on the Veracruz, Mexico, expedition; when World War I rolled around he found himself commanding a brigade in France. After that his rise was meteoric; he became commandant of West Point and, later, the youngest chief of staff in U.S. Army history. Yet the Far East still called. In 1935 he accepted the position of commander of U.S. forces in the Philippines and later resigned his commission to accept the role of field marshal of the Philippine army, in the pay of the Philippine government. The uniform he wore in this exalted position had more gold braid than a French admiral's and was of his own flamboyant design.

MacArthur's biographer William Manchester suggests that during these early days of the Japanese attack on the Philippines MacArthur seemed to be in a kind of "daze" similar to that which momentarily afflicted Napoleon, George Washington, and even Stonewall Jackson at crucial moments in their military careers. Perhaps this was so; MacArthur was then sixty-one years old, an age when most people are looking forward to retirement, when suddenly upon his shoulders was thrust a stupendous responsibility.

Since his appointment to the Far East command a few months earlier MacArthur had convinced the planners in Washington to reverse their long-standing notion that in any major attack on the Philippines the defenders should hole up on the Bataan Peninsula until the Pearl Harbor fleet could fight its way across the Pacific to relieve them. Static defense was never MacArthur's style; he was an aggressive fighter and it was his intention never to let the enemy land in the first place, but to throw them off the beaches as soon as they arrived. "His optimism was contagious and infected the highest officials in the War Department and the government," is how the official army historian put it. "By the fall of 1941 there was a firm conviction in Washington and in the Philippines that, given sufficient time, a Japanese attack could be successfully resisted."[8]

To that end MacArthur had assembled an army of 31,000 U.S. Army regulars, including 11,000 crack Philippine scouts and more than 100,000 Filipino reservists who had been in training for only several months, who were underequipped, unskilled as fighters, and spoke eight different languages with approximately sixty-five different dialects. But with Roosevelt "babying along" the Japanese in the months prior to Pearl Harbor, MacArthur was looking forward to the arrival of the additional 21,000 regular army troops then waiting to board ships in San Francisco. In addition, Washington had promised MacArthur all sorts of modern equipment: hundreds of artillery pieces, tanks, antiaircraft guns, radar, some 300 of the new B-17 long-range bombers, and 260 of the most modern P-40 fighters. By April 1942, about as long as most in the know thought Roosevelt could baby the Japanese, MacArthur hoped to have all of this in his possession as well as have completed the training of the raw Filipino troops, giving him a formidable army of 150,000 well-trained men equipped with the latest weaponry. Unfortunately, the Japanese were operating on their own timetable.

After blasting the U.S. Army Air Force out of the skies and wrecking what remained of the U.S. Navy's presence in the Philippines, the Japanese air force turned its attention to the city of Manila. In those days Manila was a lovely, thriving metropolis with broad boulevards framed by tall swaying palms and scented by tropical flowers and the fragrant breezes of

Manila Bay. The country of the Philippines itself consists of two major land-masses, Luzon in the north and Mindanao in the south, and in the thousand miles in between lie some seven thousand islands of various shapes and sizes. By 1941 the population numbered seventeen million, mostly of Malayan stock.

The Philippines had been occupied by the Spanish since its earliest explorations and the population—except for primitives in the far outreaching islands—had been converted to Catholicism. Its main exports were sugar, copper, mahogany, and yo-yos and, since Spain coughed it up after the Spanish-American War, the Philippines' main trading partner was the United States.* By act of Congress, the Philippines had been promised its independence in 1946 but this, too, was not in the Japanese timetable.

At present loomed the destruction of Manila, where the Japanese assumed U.S. forces would make their stand. Slowly but deliberately the city was blown apart by bombs. The Old City, which had been designed by the Spanish, was enclosed inside a thick stone wall, while outside were the more modern buildings of steel and glass. Carlos Romulo, the Manila editor and publisher, arrived at his office at the *Manila Herald* to find that it did not exist anymore. His life's work, "rotary presses, roto-gravure, linotypes, Ludlows, all the machinery of a carefully built publishing plant, was red-hot slag that would shortly be carted away as scrap metal by the thrifty Japanese. The building itself was a diminishing pillar of flame."[9]

Wandering the streets in a sort of stunned astonishment, Romulo encountered dreadful and pathetic sights, "stepping aside to avoid the bodies of three little schoolgirls laying on the pavement. They had been skipping along holding hands . . . evidently they had been hit by pieces of flying shrapnel. They were bathed in blood and their hands were still clasped." Later, Romulo recognized a man who was a former classmate of his at Manila High School. The man was glassy-eyed and raving. His wife came up and took her husband by the arm. "Please understand," she said. "Our two children were killed yesterday when our house was bombed."

*Then still visible from shore were the rusted, blackened masts of the Spanish fleet, which was sunk in Manila Bay in 1898 by the U.S. Pacific Fleet of Admiral George Dewey.

Romulo came to a river: "The saddest thing I saw that day was a house-boat of the type that some poor Filipino families use as homes. When I saw it the muddy water around was purple with blood. There had been a family of seven living aboard. Now only the mother and father and two of the boys were left. They kept diving into the river in a desperate effort to find a trace of the other three children who had been lost when the house-boat was split by a bomb. When I left the riverbank the police were force-fully restraining the mother. She knelt there, wailing in her dripping clothes, while the father and two boys kept diving—diving."[10]

Just as at Pearl Harbor, all kinds of rumors abounded: the Japanese were landing paratroops; local Japanese were shooting off flares and rockets to guide in their planes; a Japanese invasion fleet was landing troops north of the city. Many innocent people were shot by nervous sentries and guards. The Japanese had in fact landed in the Philippines, but only in small force on the remote islands far to the north where they hoped to use established air bases to bomb the rest of the country. MacArthur did not try to repel these invaders; he knew the main landing would come in a different fash-ion and was saving his army for that inevitability. Not only that, but by now he had recovered from his malaise, or whatever it was, during the initial attacks and was increasingly defiant of the Japanese. At one point one of his aides pointed out that the American flag flying over his head-quarters made a perfect target for the Japanese planes that swooped over Manila with impunity all day. "Take every precaution," MacArthur told him, "but let's keep the flag flying."[11]

In the early darkness of December 22, the inevitable finally arrived: the Japanese Fourteenth Army, at first 43,000 strong, under command of Lieutenant General Masaharu Homma, was lying offshore in the Lingayen Gulf on the west coast of Luzon, about 150 miles north of Manila, while a second force of 7,000 was preparing to land at Lamon Bay, on Luzon's east coast, about 150 miles south of Manila. Homma's plan was to march his Lingayen force southward toward Manila while the Lamon Bay force con-verged on the city from the southeast. The idea was that once the capital city fell, an American surrender would necessarily follow. In this he was wrong.

General Homma seemed a strange choice to lead the invading force. He was an amateur playwright who had been outspoken against the war, couldn't stand Tojo, and, moreover, was something of an Anglophile and Ameriphile. He got the job anyway and was ordered by Imperial General Headquarters to get it done in precisely fifty days.

Opposing Homma's main landing force at Lingayen was General Jonathan (Skinny) Wainwright, a gaunt, hard-drinking West Pointer and cavalryman with 28,000 Philippine troops, many commanded by American officers, but woefully undertrained and underequipped. They were described by one observer as being at the "kindergarten level" of military training. At dawn on December 22 the sun rose over eighty-four Japanese transport ships lying off the Lingayen beach—sitting ducks—except there was no American air force left to sink them. The Japanese managed to land their troops on a fifteen-mile stretch of beach that was largely undefended except for some scattered Filipino units who had only small arms. Their .50-caliber machine guns killed a number of Japanese but their .30-caliber weapons jammed because of faulty ammunition and they soon headed for the hills. Wainwright scrambled desperately to pour his troops into the area but it was too late; the Japanese had their beachhead or, as Wainwright put it, "The rat was in the house." This is an excellent, if disagreeable, example of how difficult it is to defend a large stretch of coastline, even with superior forces, when you do not know where the enemy intends to land.

By next morning the Japanese were pushing Wainwright's inferior forces before them. Wainwright even threw in a regiment of American horse cavalry, the last such large-scale attack ever made in modern warfare, but Japanese planes mowed them down. "We lost more of our few first class fighting men that day," Wainwright lamented, "and a number of fine horses—including my Little Boy, who took a bullet through the head." There were scattered successes, and "a thousand acts of valor," as Wainwright remembered, but by nightfall on December 23, Wainwright received a call from MacArthur's headquarters informing him that they had dusted off War Plan Orange, which was now in effect.[12]

This was disappointing news for everyone, but Wainwright knew it was probably the proper decision. His army of 28,000 men—25,000 of them raw and underequipped Filipino recruits—was scattered all over north Luzon, trying to contain Homma's 43,000 well-trained and well-equipped troops. War Plan Orange dated from 1921, when it had been concluded by the military that there were not powerful enough forces in the Philippines to forestall a determined Japanese attack and that the defenders should retreat into the vast mountainous jungles of the Bataan Peninsula and hold off the enemy until help arrived from across the Pacific.

On the surface the scheme had much to recommend it. Bataan was about fifty miles across Manila Bay from the capital city. It was approximately twenty-five miles long, north to south, and twenty miles wide. MacArthur knew it well; when he had been a young lieutenant in 1903 he had surveyed the place as assistant to the chief engineer and understood its excellence for tactical defense. There were only two ways an enemy could get at it: push down from the north through the jungles and mountains—a costly proposition by any standard—or try to land an invading force from the sea, a much harder endeavor. It had been predetermined in War Plan Orange that the defending forces could hold out on the peninsula for at least six months, by which time American forces, fighting their way across ocean, would have destroyed the Japanese fleet and, with following troopships, could retake the Philippines.[13]

But War Plan Orange had been abandoned with MacArthur's somewhat grandiose strategy of forming his mighty 150,000-man American-Filipino army to hurl the Japanese back into the sea at the beaches. In fairness, both MacArthur and the highest staff officers in Washington assumed it would be April before war broke out and that in the intervening five months the Filipino army would be trained and all necessary armaments and equipment arrived from the States. For this misjudgment they all now paid dearly.

War Plan Orange assumed that when the U.S. forces entered Bataan there would be sufficient food, ammunition, equipment, and spare parts to last six months, but when MacArthur had persuaded his superiors to scrap the plan he likewise did not take the necessary early steps to ensure that Bataan was adequately stocked with all these required provisions. Consequently, with all of the U.S. and Filipino forces now rushing to Bataan just ahead of the Japanese army, there was much confusion and many foul-ups. Thus, while this massive and hasty withdrawal got under way, somebody forgot the food.

Major Ernest Miller, a recently activated officer of the Minnesota National Guard, was commanding a battalion of tanks guarding the crucial bridge at Calumpit, over which the entire South Luzon Force would have to cross. He was standing there beside one of his tanks when a young tanker cried out, "Hell—they're *empty*!" To Miller's dismay, he saw that the young tankman was right: there were U.S. Army trucks passing, hundreds of them, crossing the bridge and entering Bataan completely empty. Miller would remember this episode with legitimate bitterness. In the months to come the Bataan defenders, Miller among them, would be slowly starved to death or submission. It was all the more galling because of the vast stores of canned goods and rice that remained in the warehouses in Manila and elsewhere that had been earmarked under War Plan Orange for just this eventuality. In the nearby town of Cabanatuan,* for instance, there was a depot containing fifty million bushels of rice, enough to feed the defenders for two years or more. But none of it found its way into Bataan, despite the fact that from the first Japanese landings until Bataan was sealed off, there were twenty-three days in which this transfer easily could have been made.[14]

Two days before Christmas, on the day the Japanese landed, MacArthur and his wife, Jean, decided to hold an early Christmas party for little Arthur. A Christmas tree had been decorated in the penthouse and a new tricycle and other toys were wrapped, as well as clothes for Jean, which MacArthur had thoughtfully sent his aide to purchase at a Manila department store. All things considered this was not a very merry Christmas, but MacArthur wasn't ready to give up—not by a long shot. Since he was never let in on the decisions between Roosevelt and Churchill at Arcadia to "defeat Germany first," MacArthur naturally assumed that the planners in Washington were busy organizing a great relief force to come to his rescue. He assumed that U.S. aircraft carriers were already in the process of ferrying over fighter planes, and to that end he optimistically ordered his engineers to construct no less than thirteen new airstrips in remote regions of central Luzon and Mindanao to house them. He wired General Marshall: IF THE WESTERN PACIFIC IS TO BE SAVED IT WILL HAVE TO BE SAVED HERE AND

*Cabanatuan would soon become known for another reason besides its rice stores. It was the site of the most infamous Japanese prison camp in the Pacific.

NOW. By then General Marshall had come to agree with Admiral Stark that the western Pacific was not going to be saved, at least not for now, but he was reluctant to impart this unpleasant conclusion to MacArthur. For his part, Secretary of War Stimson wrote bitterly in his diary: "There are times when brave men have to die."

With the Japanese marching relentlessly toward Manila from two directions, MacArthur desperately cabled Marshall that he needed a goodly number of P-40 fighter planes, adding, almost pathetically, CAN I EXPECT ANYTHING ALONG THAT LINE? Marshall told him no, that the navy said it was impossible. Not only that, but the large convoy that had left San Francisco with the 21,000 U.S. Army troops and mountains of artillery, tanks, and other vital equipment had been turned back after the disaster at Pearl Harbor. It was rerouted to Australia, fifteen hundred miles south of the Philippines, but any chance of getting it through the Japanese blockade were remote, according to a conversation MacArthur had with Admiral Hart. MacArthur charged later that the navy had been "terrified" by Pearl Harbor, which was probably true to some extent. But a simple look at the facts should have told MacArthur how bad a predicament he was in. After Pearl Harbor the Japanese still had their full complement of sixteen battleships plus eleven aircraft carriers. The U.S. Pacific Fleet had no battleships and only three carriers. If the American navy was terrified it was not without good reason.[15]

Next day, MacArthur sat at his desk seeing to the enormous problem of destroying any supplies that might be useful to the enemy. These included all of the vast supply depots, warehouses, and oil-storage facilities located in and around Manila. In the midst of this chore his chief of staff, General Sutherland, informed MacArthur that one of the warehouses contained the library of MacArthur's father, former governor-general of the Philippines—four thousand books. The general thought for a moment, then said, "Blow it."*[16]

---

*Manchester cites the source of this vignette as Major General Courtney Whitney's book *MacArthur: His Rendezvous with History*. However, the page cited in Whitney's book by Manchester for the "Blow it" quote alludes to an order given by General Wainwright about the dynamiting of the Calumpit Bridge, not the library warehouse. I therefore cite Manchester's book as the secondary source, on the assumption that he had supporting material other than Whitney.

*   *   *

On Christmas Eve MacArthur, his wife and son, and a number of staff members boarded a small steamer for his retreat to the fortress of Corregidor, a pollywog-shaped island ten miles long and a mile wide at its widest point, known familiarly as the Rock. Corregidor lay at the entrance to the bay two miles off the tip of Bataan and—like Singapore—was touted as one of the most heavily fortified bastions on earth. For twenty years it had been prepared under War Plan Orange as the headquarters of American forces defending the Bataan positions. The trip across the bay that night was a strange one for the Americans, upon whom it was just dawning that the Manila they had all known would soon be in enemy hands. A moon was beaming and the air was tropic and gentle. Somebody began singing "Silent Night" but there was little enthusiasm to join in; everyone understood the seriousness of the situation. MacArthur had already decided to declare Manila an "open city," to spare its civilians from further Japanese bombings. This meant that Manila would no longer defend itself; antiaircraft guns would be removed and the blackout lifted. The Japanese continued to bomb it anyway, though, apparently just for the hell of it.

One hundred miles to the north, Wainwright's army fought valiantly to hold the Japanese, who were pressing fiercely on the roads leading to Manila. The American plan was to fall back slowly from one defensive position to the next until all troops were safely in the Bataan perimeter. That this was accomplished is testament to the skill, fortitude, and devotion of both the U.S. regulars and the Philippine recruits. In all there were five defensive lines, some as many as thirty miles across, beginning about ten miles south of the Japanese landing sites on Lingayen Gulf. On Christmas Day Wainwright's men held for two days, then withdrew another ten miles to a second defensive line. The lines were hastily prepicked on bridge crossings of the many east-west rivers that mark the geography of northern Luzon. This tactic repeated itself for the next five days until an orderly movement into Bataan was completed.

Here is one good example of the kind of fighting that took place: the battle at Zaragoza Bridge. It occurred December 28, the third day of Wainwright's withdrawal, at a spot where the river Dalagot impeded the Japanese advance. One of the recently arrived U.S. National Guard tank platoons and a battalion of Filipino infantry were told to hold up the onrushing Japanese, lest they cross the bridge and outflank Wainwright's defenses.

One of the tankers, hidden in foliage, saw a column of Japanese infantry approaching the bridge on bicycles. He waited until they were well in range then opened up on them point-blank with his cannon and machine guns, leaving about eighty of them lying dead or wounded in the road. A preset dynamite charge then blew the bridge to smithereens, the tanks withdrew, and the Filipinos went into action. Although they were bombarded by Japanese artillery, they crossed the river and attacked the Japanese from the jungle, throwing them back for an entire day. Only 156 of the 550 Filipinos in the battalion returned to form the next defense line, but this kind of action, and scores more like it, was what allowed MacArthur to move his entire Luzon force into Bataan. "Again and again these tactics would be repeated," MacArthur wrote afterward. "Stand and fight, slip back and dynamite. It was savage and bloody but it won time."*[17]

Military historians have lauded the Bataan withdrawal as one of the classic retrograde maneuvers in the history of warfare. Even the Japanese general staff concluded that MacArthur's successful "sideslip" into Bataan was a fine strategic move, probably because they never expected it. General Homma was convinced the Americans would make their stand at Manila, and consequently he did not bomb out the crucial bridges over the wide and impassable Pampanga River, which would have left MacArthur's entire South Luzon Force stranded.†[18]

The Americans were going to blow it up themselves, however, as soon as the last soldier was across. To that end the high command had assigned Major Miller's tank battalion (he who had witnessed the empty trucks crossing over) with orders to kill anyone, friend or foe, who tried

---

*The success of the tank attack against the Japanese column was all the more remarkable because all they had was armor-piercing shells—good for antitank work but practically useless against personnel. There was not a round of high-explosive tank ammo in the Philippines. Some U.S. tankers, if they happened to be located on a road, would depress their guns and fire ahead of the enemy so as to blow deadly chunks of stone or concrete into their faces.

†It also, of course, would have denied use of these same bridges to the Japanese themselves, who were pushing for Manila.

to blow the bridge prematurely. On New Year's Eve Wainwright himself arrived on the scene. The last of the straggling American forces were moving across, or so it seemed. They trudged all night and into the dawn of the new year, when it was reported to Wainwright that the Japanese were near at hand. Wainwright adjusted his field glasses "and in the light of early dawn I could see the tip of the Japanese Advanced Guard, coming at us." He turned to his engineering officer and said, "Blow it." The engineer hesitated, telling Wainwright that a platoon of fellow demolition engineers was still not across. Wainwright "looked again at the approaching Japs and had to choose. 'Blow it now,' I repeated." It was just past 6:15 A.M.

The bridge collapsed into the river below with a "deafening roar." Now Wainwright ordered the remainder of his battered force to go into Bataan and it wheeled and closed like a ten-mile-long swinging door, buttoning up the peninsula. Of Wainwright's original 28,000-man army only 16,000 remained.[19]

There was frenzy and desperation as the U.S. and Filipino troops poured into Bataan; strong (and, it was hoped, permanent) defensive lines had to be hastily constructed, units had to be reconsolidated, hospitals, food, ammunition, and supply depots had to be organized. The original War Plan Orange had envisioned 43,000 troops having to retreat to Bataan. When the final tally was taken, no less than 80,000 troops were on the peninsula, as well as more than 20,000 frightened civilians who had come along too.

The food situation quickly became critical. After a hurried inspection by the quartermaster, it was determined that only one month's supply was available. MacArthur immediately put the troops on half-rations—two thousand calories a day—about half of what active young men, often in combat for twenty hours at a stretch, needed. A sergeant, an old-timer in one of the antiaircraft batteries, predicted, "They'll eventually get us, but they'll pay dearly for their efforts." He was written off as a pessimist by most of the troops; they were fully confident that a massive U.S. naval convoy was on the way to rescue them.[20]

New Year's Eve in Manila was surreal. The citizens, not knowing what else to do, began to dress for the traditional celebrations. Nightclubs,

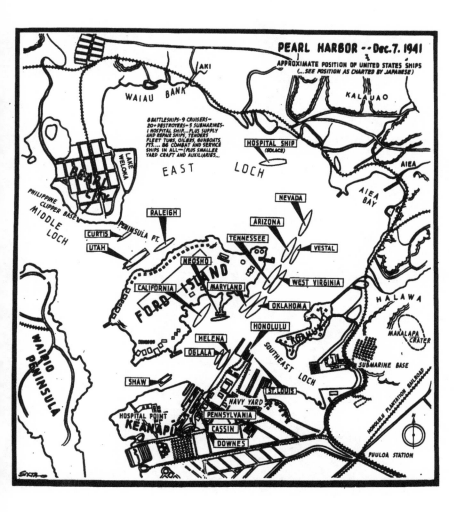

PEARL HARBOR -- Dec. 7. 1941

APPROXIMATE POSITION OF UNITED STATES SHIPS
(...SEE POSITION AS CHARTED BY JAPANESE)

AKI

WAIAU BANK

KALAUAO

8 BATTLESHIPS-9 CRUISERS-
20+ DESTROYERS-5 SUBMARINES-
1 HOSPITAL SHIP...PLUS SUPPLY
AND REPAIR SHIPS, TENDERS
FLEET TUGS, OILERS, GUNBOATS
PTS.... 86 COMBAT AND SERVICE
SHIPS IN ALL—(PLUS SMALLER
YARD CRAFT AND AUXILIARIES...

HOSPITAL SHIP
(SOLACE)

EAST   LOCH

AIEA

LAKE WELOMA

AIEA BAY

PHILIPPINE CLIPPER BASE

MIDDLE LOCH

RALEIGH

NEVADA

PENINSULA PT.

ARIZONA

CURTIS

TENNESSEE

VESTAL

UTAH

NEOSHO

FORD ISLAND

CALIFORNIA

MARYLAND

WEST VIRGINIA

OKLAHOMA

HALAWA

WAIPIO PENINSULA

HONOLULU

MAKALAPA CRATER

HELENA

OGLALA

SUBMARINE BASE

SOUTHEAST LOCH

SHAW

ST. LOUIS

NAVY YARD

HOSPITAL POINT

PENNSYLVANIA

KEANAPU

CASSIN

HONOULIULI PLANTATION RAILROAD

DOWNES

PUULOA STATION

SKTR

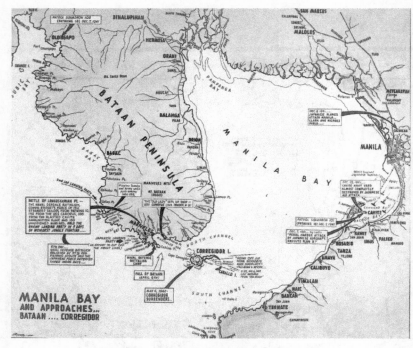

MANILA BAY
AND APPROACHES...
BATAAN .... CORREGIDOR

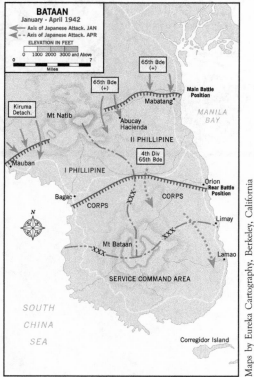

BATAAN
January - April 1942

→ Axis of Japanese Attack. JAN
⇢ Axis of Japanese Attack. APR

ELEVATION IN FEET
0   1000 2000 3000 and Above

Miles
0   7

Kiruma
Detach.

Mt Natib

65th Bde
(+)

65th Bde
(+)

Mabatang

Main Battle
Position

MANILA
BAY

Abucay
Hacienda

II PHILLIPINE

4th Div
65th Bde

Mauban

I PHILLIPINE

CORPS

CORPS

Bagac

Orion
Rear Battle
Position

Limay

Mt Bataan

Lamao

SERVICE COMMAND AREA

SOUTH
CHINA
SEA

Corregidor Island

Maps by Eureka Cartography, Berkeley, California

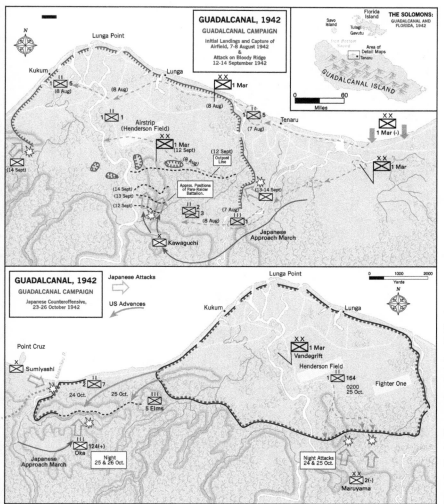

GUADALCANAL, 1942

GUADALCANAL CAMPAIGN

Initial Landings and Capture of
Airfield, 7-8 August 1942
&
Attack on Bloody Ridge
12-14 September 1942

THE SOLOMONS:
GUADALCANAL AND
FLORIDA, 1942

Florida Island
Savo Island
Tulagi
Gavutu
Iron Bottom Sound
Area of Detail Maps
Tenaru
GUADALCANAL ISLAND

0   60
Miles

N

Lunga Point

Kukum

Lunga

1 | 5 (8 Aug)

(8 Aug)

XX 1 Mar

(8 Aug)

1 | 1

Airstrip (Henderson Field)

(8 Aug)

XX 1 Mar (12 Sept)

(12 Sept) Outpost Line

1 | 5 (7 Aug)

Tenaru

XX 1 Mar (-)

XX 1 Mar

(14 Sept)

(14 Sept)
(13 Sept)
(12 Sept)

Approx. Positions of Para-Raider Battalion.

(13-14 Sept)

2 | 3 (7 Aug)

X Kawaguchi

(8 Aug)

1 | 1

Japanese Approach March

GUADALCANAL, 1942

GUADALCANAL CAMPAIGN

Japanese Counteroffensive,
23-26 October 1942

Japanese Attacks ⇨

US Advances ⬅

Lunga Point

Kukum

Lunga

0   1000   2000
Yards

N

Point Cruz

X Sumiyashi

Matanikau R.

2 | 7

24 Oct.   25 Oct.

III 5 Elms

III 124(+) Oka

Night 25 & 26 Oct.

Japanese Approach March

XX 1 Mar
Vandegrift

Henderson Field

1 | 164
0200 25 Oct.

Fighter One

Night Attacks 24 & 25 Oct.

XX 2 (-) Maruyama

Maps by Eureka Cartography, Berkeley, California

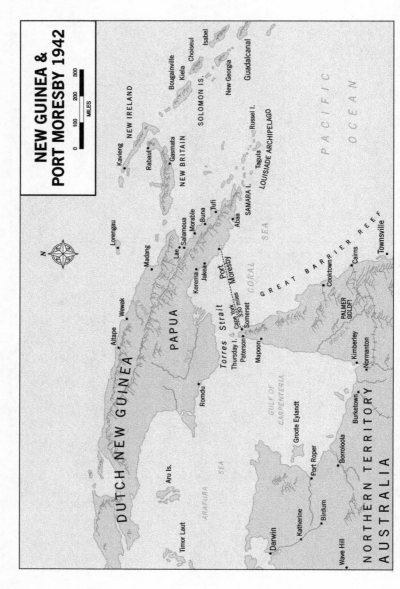

NEW GUINEA &
PORT MORESBY 1942

0   100   200   300
MILES

N

DUTCH NEW GUINEA

PAPUA

Timor Laut

Aru Is.

Aitape

Wewak

Lorengau

Madang

Lae

Salamoua

Morable

Buna

Tufi

Kerema

Jakea

Port
Moresby

Torres Strait

Cape York
330 miles

Thursday I.

Paterson

Somerset

Mapoon

Romdu

GULF OF
CARPENTERIA

Groote Eylandt

Port Roper

Borroloola

Kimberley

Normanton

Burketown

PALMER
GOLDF'

Cooktown

Cairns

Townsville

GREAT BARRIER REEF

CORAL
SEA

Abaa

SAMARA I.

Tagula

LOUISIADE ARCHIPELAGO

Russel I.

SOLOMON IS.

New Georgia

Guadalcanal

Kiela

Bougainville

Choiseul

Isabel

NEW IRELAND

Kavieng

Rabaul

Gasmata

NEW BRITAIN

PACIFIC

OCEAN

ARAFURA
SEA

Darwin

Katherine

Birdum

Wave Hill

NORTHERN TERRITORY
AUSTRALIA

Map by Eureka Cartography, Berkeley, California

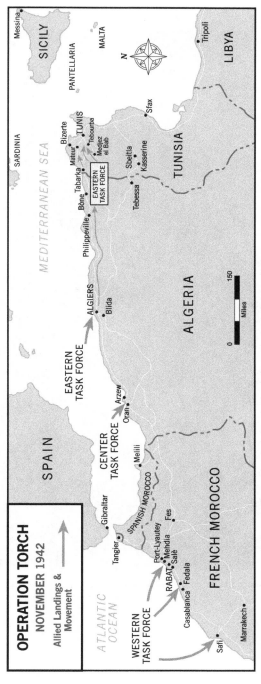

Map by Eureka Cartography, Berkeley, California

Franklin D. Roosevelt and Winston Churchill relax in a viewing tower in Marrakech, Morocco, during the Casablanca Conference in January 1943, to decide the future course of the war in Europe.

General Douglas MacArthur and Admiral Chester Nimitz, the two main architects of the Pacific War against Japan.

General George Marshall, army chief of staff, confers with Secretary of War Henry Stimson, 1942.

Axis partners Benito Mussolini and Adolf Hitler on parade in Rome.

Japanese envoys Kichisaburo Nomura and Saburo Kurusu leave the U.S. State Department smiling after conducting peace talks with Secretary of State Cordell Hull. At this very moment Japanese warships were making their way toward Pearl Harbor for the infamous sneak attack of December 7, 1941. After the attack Hull dismissed the envoys as "pissants."

The Japanese emperor Hirohito on his famous white horse. He liked golf, jazz music, and scotch whisky, but was unable to control the militarism in his government.

eneral Hideki Tojo, the Japanese dictator many re-
rd as responsible for starting the war. In 1948 he
as hanged by an Allied tribunal.

Admiral Isoroku Yamamoto, who instigated the Pearl
Harbor attack.

Japanese crewmen on the carrier *Shokaku* cheer the Pearl Harbor raiders on their way to Hawaii,
December 7, 1941.

Admiral Husband Kimmel and General Walter Short, commanders, respectively, of the navy and the army in Hawaii, received much of the blame for being caught off guard by the Japanese attack.

A Japanese attacker took this picture of Ford Island at Pearl Harbor during the raid. U.S. battleships can be seen at anchorage on the far side of the island, amid geysers of water thrown up by the bombs.

Burning U.S. battleships at Pearl Harbor during the Japanese raid. A few Japanese planes can be seen among the bursts of flak from American antiaircraft guns.

The spectacular explosion of the U.S.S. *Shaw* during the Pearl Harbor attack.

The thrilling breakout of the burning battleship *Nevada* brought tears to the eyes of sailors who watched her steam out of the smoke and flames toward the entrance of Pearl Harbor at the height of the attack, all her guns blazing upward at the Japanese planes.

The sinking of the U.S.S. *Lexington* during the Battle of the Coral Sea, May 8, 1942. Crewmen stood calmly on the flight deck, some of them eating ice cream from the ship's canteen, waiting to go overboard.

An explosion on the *Lexington* during the Battle of the Coral Sea.

An American torpedo bomber in action.

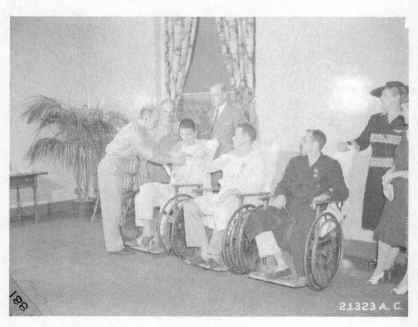

Walter Reed Hospital, 1942. General Jimmy Doolittle pins medals on three of his crew members injured in the Tokyo Raid.

A captured American aviator led from a plane by two Jap soldiers

Sergeant Robert Hite, one of Doolittle's fliers, led through the streets after the Tokyo Raid. He and two other captured airmen were later executed by firing squad.

Chinese soldiers carry Doolittle's fliers to safety, April 1942.

above: The U.S.S. *Yorktown* sank after she was bombed by the Japanese during the Battle of Midway, June 7, 1942. *right:* U.S. Navy Avenger torpedo bombers.

hotels, and restaurants were reopened, and of course under the open city policy the blackout had been lifted for a week now. "A dance was held at the Fiesta Pavilion of the Manila Hotel and women donned evening gowns for the first time since the start of the war." Still the festivities were understandably subdued. Many fine buildings and homes had been wrecked by the bombing and two weeks of garbage had piled up in the streets. The air was foul and rank with the stench of burning oil, for before the U.S. military evacuated it had ordered the destruction of all the oil-storage facilities around Manila—commercial and military—enough, if it had fallen into Japanese hands, to fuel the entire Japanese navy for a year or more.*[21]

On January 2 Japanese troops arrived in Manila proper and hauled down the American flag from the residence of the U.S. high commissioner. A Japanese soldier stomped it into the dirt before hoisting up the Rising Sun while a band played the Japanese national anthem. Unlike Nanking, Hong Kong, and Singapore, there was no rape or looting by the Japanese. Tens of thousands of Japanese nationals living in the Philippines greeted their fellow countrymen as conquering heroes. After the war, Carlos Romulo discovered that his longtime Japanese gardener was actually a major in the Japanese army, doing a little early reconnaissance. General Homma moved himself into the MacArthurs' sumptuous penthouse apartment in the Manila Hotel and installed on its balcony an enormous Rising Sun flag, which could be seen, with great aggravation, with field glasses on clear days by the Americans on Corregidor.

Soon as General Homma discovered that he had been tricked he became furious. The day the Japanese hauled down the Stars and Stripes from the U.S. high commissioner's residence, Homma triumphantly cabled his bosses in Tokyo that the Philippines had fallen. No sooner had he done this than he discovered MacArthur was bristling in the Bataan peninsula

---

*The man sent to accomplish this task was Lieutenant, j.g., Malcolm Champlin, a former FBI agent. Champlin sneaked back into the city and contacted the representative of Standard Oil, whom he found in the bar of the University Club. This man agreed to the torching, but representatives of British-owned Shell Oil said they could not cooperate without instructions from their superiors. Champlin bought the men drinks as the Standard Oil man went to a phone. Suddenly huge explosions reached their ears. "Gentlemen," Champlin said to the astonished Englishmen, "your oil is now in flames."

with almost his entire army, an army nearly twice the size of Homma's own. His fury and frustration were compounded by Tokyo's response to the news of his capture of Manila—it ordered Homma's best infantry division to be detached and sent south to join in the great Southward Movement. Homma had already used up nearly half of his fifty-day deadline for securing the Philippines and now he was faced with trying to root out a large, well-entrenched, and dangerous force from one of the most difficult pieces of terrain in the Philippines. It was maddening, and it would become more so as the weeks and months marched by—a face-losing proposition in the making.

At first glance MacArthur's position was extremely strong. His troops were dug in all across the north end of the peninsula in jungle terrain divided only by a range of seemingly impassable mountains. This was known as the Abucay Line. At the opposite end was Corregidor with its massive artillery guarding the south. As the official army historian wrote, "No better place than Bataan could have been chosen for a final stand." But there was more to it than just "first glance." The food shortage was dangerous. And even though MacArthur had superior numbers, his Filipino troops remained untrained; in the days to come, however, they would get a great deal of on-the-job training. Nevertheless, morale was high. Now the troops were dug in and there were to be no more of the frantic retreats of the past few weeks. "The general feeling," wrote MacArthur's assistant operations officer, "seemed to be that we have run far enough; we'll stand now and take 'em on."[22]

Homma was correspondingly weak, too, on the face of it. With his best division gone he had to rely on far less satisfactory troops to confront MacArthur. These were a brigade of mostly older and lesser-trained men who had been included in the invasion to serve principally as occupation forces, under the command of Lieutenant General Akira Nara. But the Japanese were much stronger than the Americans in artillery and had total control of the air and seas. That was a big difference.

The First Battle of Bataan began in the afternoon of January 9, 1942, when a great artillery barrage roared from the Japanese lines and their infantry moved forward. This did not produce the desired effect. The American artillery responded in kind ("particularly ferociously," according to Japanese official records) and mangled many Japanese soldiers. Worse, Nara was victim to bad intelligence concerning the location of the American lines, which were actually several miles south of where he thought they were. Consequently he reported encouragingly to Homma that his infantry was penetrating the American positions and that the Americans and Filipinos had "fled into the jungle without putting up a fight." In this he was wrong.[23]

Ironically, the day General Homma had selected for the Japanese to attack MacArthur was the same day MacArthur selected to pay an inspection visit to his front lines. Leaving his headquarters on Corregidor, he traveled by PT boat* and crossed over into Bataan. He first paid a visit to General Wainwright, commanding the First Corps, which was holding down the left flank of the U.S. position. As the Japanese opened the battle, MacArthur inquired of Wainwright, "Where are your 155mm guns?" Wainwright offered to show him, but MacArthur told him: "Johnathan, I don't want to *see* them, I want to *hear* them!"

Homma also used the occasion to demand a surrender, dropping thousands of leaflets over American positions, forecasting the usual doom and gloom: you are surrounded . . . no chance of relief . . . avoid needless bloodshed . . . etc. The reply the Japanese received was a huge barrage from Wainwright's heavy artillery.[24]

For the Americans and Filipinos, this was the first time they experienced fighting the Japanese from prepared and solid defensive positions; previously, they had tried merely to hold them back before retreating. And here for the first time Americans experienced the famous Japanese banzai charge.[†] In a large standing sugarcane field the night after the main attack began an entire battalion of Japanese sneaked in between the stalks and lay

*The PT boat was the brainchild of MacArthur. Designed as a very fast (50 to 60 mph) motor torpedo boat, these craft were lightly constructed of wood and armed only with .50-caliber machine guns. Equipped with huge Rolls-Royce engines, as MacArthur envisioned it, there was to be a fleet of hundreds of these boats able to dash in and out of any Japanese convoy and sink ships with torpedoes. As it turned out, like the troop reinforcements, tanks, and massive airplane reserves, there was not time enough to build the PT boats and at war's outbreak there were only half a dozen in the Philippines.

[†]*Banzai* stood for, more or less, "May the emperor live a thousand years!"

waiting near the barbed-wire entanglements of a U.S. infantry regiment. As a midnight moon bathed the surroundings in ghostly light, the Japanese suddenly rushed out of the cane toward the American lines, screaming "*Banzai!*" As the first wave reached the barbed wire, they threw themselves upon it, like human bridges, to make way for the second wave, which ran up their backs and into the U.S. positions. They continued this most of the night, "despite the appalling effects of the point blank fire" from 75mm field guns. At first light, the Americans still held their line and counted some two hundred to three hundred Japanese bodies in front of them. People who would do that, most agreed, were an enemy to be reckoned with.[25]

Soon the Americans also got to know another device of the Japanese: the dead or wounded soldier gambit. After the cane-field fight, a company commander had instructed his men to give first aid to any wounded Japanese, and when one of these was located they began bandaging him up. Suddenly a "dead" Japanese nearby snatched a rifle and killed one of the U.S. soldiers. It was a bitter learning experience for the young American commander, who decreed that the enemy henceforth—wounded and dead alike—would be bayoneted. This harsh philosophy became a common practice through the rest of the war.

Nonetheless, the Japanese were making progress. The great fault of the American position on the Abucay Line was that it was split in two by forty-five-hundred-foot Mount Natib and several other mountains of similar altitude. The Americans did not believe the Japanese could scale these precipitous, heavily jungled heights, but they were wrong. A regiment of Japanese dove into the jungle and when they emerged ten days later they were behind U.S. lines. This and other infiltration tactics—the same as those that flummoxed the British during the Malay campaign—had caused MacArthur to decide to pull back to his second—and last—defensive position five miles farther south. This, on January 23, became the Bagac Line.

Moreover, the Japanese had all sorts of tricks up their sleeves. To rattle and wear down the Americans, the Japanese developed a catapult device that hurled strings of firecrackers toward U.S. lines at all hours of the night, putting everybody on edge. They used powerful loudspeakers to blare irritating music and surrender pleas through the jungle. They employed large numbers of suicidal snipers who tied themselves in treetops and picked people off until they themselves were killed. It was not the kind of warfare the Americans and their Filipino friends had trained for but, as with the supposedly dead Japanese soldier, they learned it anyway—the hard way.

Both sides by now were exhausted, like two panting, bloodied beasts who lay glaring at each other, gathering strength so they could go at it again. The problem was that the American forces were not gathering strength; they were losing it. The food shortage, which had been critical, was now acute. The Twenty-sixth Cavalry, which recently conducted the last cavalry charge in modern history, tearfully killed the rest of their horses and ate them. The horses had consumed the last of the grain and shucks on Bataan and were themselves starving. Men shot monkeys from the trees and ate them. One officer bitterly complained that some joker had secretly put a "hairy monkey paw" into a pot of monkey soup they were cooking. By then they had killed all the carabao (a sort of water buffalo) on the peninsula. General Wainwright reported: "We would soak the tough old meat in salt water overnight and beat it for extended periods, but even then it was a test for the strongest teeth." The quartermaster reported: "One Filipino caught a snake and ate it one day to die unpleasantly the next. There were always plenty of experimenters ready to try any kind of native flora or fauna, although the experimenting individual frequently paid a high price."[26]

Food became an obsession with almost everyone. Americans who weighed 170 to 200 pounds were down to around 150 within the month. The Filipinos did not suffer as much, since they were smaller and required less food. Soon everyone's clothes hung off them like a scarecrow, that is, what was not already in tatters or rotten from the harsh jungle fighting. As they were slowly starving, Americans and Filipinos alike fell prey to an assortment of disgusting tropical diseases: malaria, dengue fever, scurvy, beriberi, hookworm, amebic dysentery, edema, and night blindness. At any given time there were ten thousand patients in Bataan's two military hospitals. Both of these institutions were marked with large red crosses on their roofs. Japanese planes bombed them anyway and soon the crosses were removed; they were just being used for target practice. Another frightening problem was gas gangrene. Although in the period between the wars medical science had developed antitoxins for this dread complication, many wounded men had to have limbs amputated because the antitoxins were unavailable on Bataan.

Probably half the soldiers on the front lines were unfit for duty, but they stayed there anyway. At first morale had been high, but constant hunger was making its inevitable inroads. A week after he and his troops had arrived on Bataan MacArthur sent out a message to all troops: "Help is on the way from the United States. Thousands of troops and hundreds of planes are being dispatched." MacArthur's proclamation was at the least disingenuous; he was in contact with Washington and knew what the score was. He saved himself from being branded a liar by not revealing the timetable for this great relief expedition. (It did not arrive until three years later.) Wainwright put it this way: "When we first heard that, some of the men wept for joy. The joy did not last long." A war correspondent composed this darkly popular tune:

> We're the battling bastards of Bataan:
> No momma, no poppa, no Uncle Sam,
> No aunts, no uncles, no nephews, no nieces,
> No rifles, no guns or artillery pieces.
> And nobody gives a damn.

It wasn't that the military authorities in Washington weren't trying; it was just that there wasn't much they could do. But to this end it was decided by General Marshall, who received daily, depressing reports from the Philippines that the soldiers were starving, that at least *something* had to be done. Though it was apparent that the navy could or would not try to break through the Japanese blockade, toward the end of January a seat-of-the-pants scheme was hatched. Small ships procured in Australia or the Netherlands East Indies would be loaded with food and ammunition and run the fifteen-hundred-mile-long gamut of Japanese warships and planes. The notion was to get three million rations to Bataan—a two-month supply —within three weeks.

Organizers of this bold and hazardous attempt immediately ran into trouble. First, there were few steamers in Australia and the Dutch Indies with enough speed and fuel capacity to reach the Philippines. Still, about a dozen were rounded up and their crews offered fantastic bonuses and life insurance policies for making the dangerous trip. Five days after the first two of these ships sailed, the Japanese discovered and sank them. Three others actually made it to the lower Philippines while two more were taken over and returned by mutineers when they reached Japanese-controlled waters. Another three never left port in Australia and one that did was never heard from again.

Then there was the tricky problem of getting to the cargoes of the three ships that made it through the fifteen hundred miles of Philippine Islands that separated the southern Philippines from Bataan. Smaller, faster inter-island boats were used for this and the cargoes were unloaded, then reloaded upon them. They traveled only at night, hiding during the day wherever they could. Ten of the cargo boats were discovered and sunk by the Japanese, who were flying overhead night and day, and in the end only about a thousand tons (a four-day supply) ever reached the starving men on Bataan. One of those that made it was described this way by an army captain: "Part of its bow was blown away. Its decks and sides were riddled with shell fragments. Its captain and half the crew were dead. Ninety per-cent of its rice was floating in sea water."[27] Official army historian Louis Morton labeled the blockade-running scheme "a dismal failure."[28]

Within a month further Japanese conquests in the southwest Pacific had rendered Australia unsuitable for blockade running, so it was decided to try the long cross-ocean route from the U.S. West Coast. Six old World War I destroyers were converted to carry cargo but none got any farther than Pearl Harbor. Submarines were also used for cargo but they could not carry much. On one trip the U.S.S. *Spearfish* returned from Corregidor with a dozen American army nurses whom they'd gotten safely off the Rock. (This feat later became an inspiration for the 1959 Cary Grant movie *Operation Petticoat*.)

Meantime, Corregidor itself was taking a tremendous beating from aerial bombing. Before the war the nearly two-thousand-acre Rock had been an almost idyllic place where wealthy Filipino families vacationed for the summer. There was a golf course and a large army barracks and parade ground. Fruit trees, flowering plants—orchids and hibiscus among them—and coconut palm trees abounded. An electric funicular railway ran from the five-hundred-foot-high northern heights (topside) down to loading docks on the shore (bottomside). At that point, Corregidor contained nearly 10,000 U.S. troops and civilians.

The nerve center for Corregidor lay within the labyrinthine confines of the Malinta Tunnel, completed in the 1920s. This bomb-impervious structure carved through the stone and dirt that composed Malinta Hill was nearly a quarter mile long with about fifty laterals, or branches, some of which were as long as four football fields. In this complex reposed such varied operations as headquarters, a hospital, food service and stores, a radio station, a barber shop, gasoline and ammunition storage, repair shops, and sleeping quarters for officers and selected noncoms.

MacArthur and his people had been there less than a week when Japanese planes attacked Corregidor in force. Day after day hundreds of twin-engine bombers (called Sallys by the Americans) dropped thousands of bombs ranging from 100 to 500 pounds, hoping to re-create another Pearl Harbor, Cavite, or Clark Field and bring the Americans to their knees. In this they were bitterly disappointed. Though the raids made the inhabitants plenty uncomfortable, the tunnel was bomb-proof. One day MacArthur, who spurned the tunnel as shelter, went out during an air raid and began counting the number of Japanese planes dropping bombs. Members of his staff were horrified, though they themselves were pressed nose to ground in nearby slit trenches. As the bombs began falling closer MacArthur's orderly, a Filipino sergeant named Adversario, tried to shield MacArthur with his body. When MacArthur refused to put on a steel helmet Adversario held his own helmet over the general's head until a bomb fragment wounded him in the hand. When the raid was over MacArthur, in disgust, ordered his headquarters and his wife and son into the tunnel. He was brave, but not stupid.

As the raids continued day after day the island quickly began to lose its charm. The golf course was ruined and the trees and bushes stripped of their vegetation. The barracks and other buildings were blown up, the parade grounds ruined, and the electric train cut up. Life in the tunnel was miserable. Clouds of dust from exploding bombs choked those inside; the electricity went out, leaving everyone in the dark. Air in the tunnel was fetid and nurses from the hospital regularly brought less seriously wounded men outside the tunnel entrance for a little fresh air. Flies swarmed over them but they chose to remain until the next Japanese attack, when they were dragged back inside. People who sought shelter in the tunnel began to wonder about its safety. Some saw places in the ceiling where the stone had cracked and foul-smelling water drained down. The entrance to the hospital lateral was drenched in the blood of wounded soldiers, sailors, and marines. Often ambulances would wait to pick up blanket-covered corpses, which would be buried between attacks.

Newspaperman Carlos Romulo had by now joined MacArthur at Corregidor as a press aide and was given the rank of major. He had just emerged from the tunnel after the latest bombing attack when he came upon an American soldier he knew, a Private Hamby, who was crying. Romulo asked what was wrong. "He had a lot of trouble telling me. It seems he had just been out on hospital detail and had pulled a man's leg out of a rubbish heap that ten minutes before had been an anti-aircraft battery. It came away in his hand—a flesh and blood human leg. He was standing staring at it when something moved under the rubble. He dug up the rest of the man. It was his best friend, who Hamby had enlisted with back in the states. What was left of the boy grasped Hamby's hand, then he died."[29]

About the only bright spot in the tunnel was when MacArthur's four-year-old son Arthur, dressed in a sailor's suit, would respond to the siren by rushing up and down the tunnel shouting, "Air raid! Air raid!" At least it made some people chuckle.

Romulo remembered MacArthur's canny analysis at the time of the Japanese theory of warfare. "It is a reckless method," the general said. "The Japanese don't care how many thousands die, if only they can win quickly. They can't win a war of attrition and they know it. That is why for insignificant skirmishes where I would not want to lose a single life, they will sacrifice thousands of lives."[30]

It was all too true. With the U.S. establishment of the last-ditch Bagac Line, MacArthur knew he was trapped and faced annihilation. He wired Marshall in Washington: "With its [the Bagac Line] occupation, all maneuver

possibilities will cease. I intend to fight it out to complete destruction."
Marshall obviously was not pleased, but neither was he totally distraught,
because he kept telling MacArthur that the longer he could keep the Japanese in the Philippines at bay, the longer it would be for them to be able
to send those troops to conquer something else.

By now Homma's fifty-day deadline to capture the Philippines was
drawing to a close, so he resorted to a bold flanking tactic, similar to those
employed by Yamashita in Malaya. On January 24 he sent some hundreds
of soldiers in landing barges all way around the American positions to land
at four or five points on the southwest of Bataan. These were fingers of
land that jutted out into the China Sea, and if the plan had succeeded U.S.
forces would have a large force of Japanese behind them as well as in front.
But the Battle of the Points did not succeed. As the Japanese came ashore
they ran into a fierce defense by a single battalion of American infantry,
and after twelve blood-drenched days the Japanese force was annihilated.
This did not come without a price. The American battalion had gone into
battle full strength, with six hundred officers and men. It came out with
only 212 men, commanded by a lieutenant because all the other officers
were killed or wounded, including the battalion commander, who was shot
through the head. "Every other officer and man was accounted for as having been buried or evacuated wounded. There were no stragglers," Wainwright reported.[31] At about the same time as the Battle of the Points came
the Battle of the Pockets.

When Homma discovered that MacArthur was pulling back he ordered his field commander to closely pursue the Americans and not give
them a chance to dig in. They hugged the Americans tightly through the
maze of bamboo thickets, creepers, vines, and jungle brush, all the way to
the Bagac Line, and, in so doing, created several "pockets," which were
actually a mile behind the U.S. main line of resistance. These pockets also
took twelve days to annihilate, at great cost to the Americans because the
Japanese had dug tunnels and so were almost impossible to ferret out. The
U.S. forces did so by dropping bags of hand grenades into the tunnels and
fighting with the Japanese hand to hand.

By now many American commanders, especially those who had
served in World War I, were beginning to realize that they were fighting an entirely new kind of enemy. Wainwright addressed himself to this

fact: "The old rules of war began to undergo a swift change in me. What had at first seemed a barbarous thought in the back of my mind now became less unsavory. It had at last dawned on me, as it would on so many commanders who followed me into the Pacific, that the Jap usually prefers death to surrender."

As the Battles of the Points and the Pockets drew to a close, Homma decided he had had enough for the present. These two actions had cost him thousands of men, practically all of them killed; his offensive on Bataan was getting nowhere. Accordingly, on February 8, he ordered his entire army to withdraw back up the peninsula for reorganization. At the same time, with his fifty-day deadline expired, he asked Tokyo to send him more troops. Alarmed and irritated by Homma's lack of progress, Imperial General Headquarters complied by transferring troops from China, but clearly they were unhappy with Homma's performance. To that end they also sent him the ubiquitous Colonel Tsuji who, during his stay in Singapore, had incited the murder of more than five thousand Chinese (whose severed heads were stuck up on pikes around the city) on grounds they had been supporting British colonialism.[32]

Meantime, a perplexing question arose in Washington: With the Philippines clearly on the verge of collapse, what should they do with MacArthur? The spectacle of him being paraded in irons through the streets of Tokyo was bad enough. And what if he should die with his men, as he had promised? The army would lose one of its most prestigious and brilliant commanders. It was a sticky problem because no one knew how to tell MacArthur he would have to leave Corregidor; the general himself would certainly see it as the blackest mark in his long career, virtually a desertion of his troops in the face of the enemy. It was decided that President Roosevelt himself would give the order, which he did on February 23, telling General MacArthur he was to go to Australia and assume command of all new U.S. forces bound for the Far East.

As expected, MacArthur protested but in the end was forced to see the logic of the order. On March 12, rather than wait for a submarine the navy was sending to take him away, he boarded the PT boat commanded by Lieutenant John D. Bulkeley and, with his wife and son and seventeen of his staff members, roared off into the night. The plan was to take MacArthur six hundred miles south to the large island of Mindanao where, from an airfield on the Del Monte pineapple plantation, he would meet four B-17s sent from Australia to complete his deliverance. But all this was easier said than done.

There were four PT boats in the little flotilla. Normally they could make about 50 knots, but because they were so long out of overhaul they could make only half that speed. Next they had to thread their way through the Japanese blockade, including a heavy cruiser that could have blown them out of the water anytime it wanted, and they had to hide from a Japanese destroyer in broad daylight. Worse were the extremely rough seas, which separated the flimsy wooden PT boats and tossed them about like corks. Almost everyone got seasick and MacArthur himself described the voyage as being like "spending two days inside a cement mixer."

Playing hide-and-seek with Japanese planes and ships, laying up under cover of coves in daytime, navigating without proper charts, Lieutenant Bulkeley's flotilla reached Mindanao at dawn of March 14 and were taken to the Del Monte plantation where, instead of meeting four B-17s, they found only one plane—two were missing and a third had crashed. Even the one that had arrived was in bad shape. MacArthur was furious and demanded in a missive to Washington that "the best three planes in the United States or Hawaii should be made available." He further stated that to fly on such planes as had been sent "would amount to consigning the whole party to death and I could not accept such responsibility."

Presently three brand-new B-17s arrived and by nine A.M., March 16, MacArthur and his party were safely in Darwin, Australia—or so they first thought. They had landed just in time for a major Japanese air raid on that city, which caused them all to flee inland, but not before MacArthur made his famous proclamation, "I came through, and I shall return."* MacArthur

---

*This was vintage MacArthur. The "I shall return" remark was printed and broadcast all over the world. It was stamped on matchbooks provided by the army for soldiers in the Pacific theaters. It was glazed into commemorative china and scrawled on the walls of outhouses and public toilets. The general certainly had a way with words and, like "Remember the Alamo" or "The British are coming!," it slipped easily into the American lexicon.

waxed stoic about the whole thing, telling his traveling companions, "It was close, but that's the way it is in war. You win, you lose, live or die—and the difference is just an eyelash."[33]

Back on Bataan, command of the army had been turned over by MacArthur to his old friend General Wainwright, who had been told, "We're alone, Jonathan, you know that as well as I. If I get through to Australia you know I'll come back as soon as I can with as much as I can. In the meantime, you've got to hold." As he left, MacArthur gave Wainwright a box of cigars and two large jars of shaving cream, and in thanking him Wainwright replied, "I'll be here on Bataan if I'm alive."[34]

Skinny Wainwright was one of the most beloved soldiers in the army, and for good reason, as best expressed here by a young navy lieutenant who, without another job, had recently been selected to serve on Wainwright's staff. One day during the height of a Japanese bombardment Wainwright decided to visit his front lines on Bataan. Japanese artillery shells were coming in at treetop level and exploding all around them and as soon as the jeep came to a halt the navy lieutenant and everybody else wisely dismounted and jumped into foxholes—all except for Wainwright, who had noticed a captain he had known back in Virginia.

"He went over and took this captain by the arm and said, 'How are you, Captain?' and he sat on the sandbags with his back to the Japanese. We were all in the foxholes." Wainwright sat there, patiently talking to the captain during the length of the Japanese bombardment, completely exposed to enemy shellfire. When it finally stopped, he got back into his jeep and set off for his headquarters.

On the way back the navy lieutenant told him: "'General, I am a lieutenant in the navy. I admit I do not understand your situation here. Do you realize sir, that you are loved by your men, you are in command here on Bataan, you are risking your life, and I don't understand why? The men love you. They want you alive. Why do you expose yourself in the way you did a few minutes ago?'

"He said, 'Young man, you don't understand what we have to give to our men. A general in the Army of the United States does his best to give his men arms and ammunition, food, medicine and recreation. We have none of those things. The men are starving. We are running out of ammunition.

As you saw, they are dying. What can I give them? What can I do for my men? The only thing I can give them now is morale. My life is not worth as much as you think it is. I can give them morale and my presence on that front line is not the waste you think it is. When I sat on the sandbags, I did it deliberately. They want their general and they want to know he is here. I do that, and I do it for a good reason.'

"I said, 'Thank you, God bless you, I understand.'" So said the navy lieutenant, tears in his eyes.[35]

Chapter Ten ★

On the evening of February 23, 1942, just as President Roosevelt was about to broadcast one of his famous fireside chats, a large Japanese submarine appeared off the coast of Santa Barbara, California, and for about twenty minutes bombarded an oil field and refinery there. It was naturally big news on the West Coast, whose citizens expected an impending invasion, but for the rest of America the news had been so bad everywhere that the Santa Barbara shelling paled by comparison. Pearl Harbor was still fresh in everyone's minds; since then the Japanese had taken Wake, Guam, Hong Kong, Malaya, Singapore, and Thailand and were successfully invading Burma, oil-and-rice-rich Sumatra, Java, Borneo, and New Guinea as well as hundreds of smaller islands in the southwest Pacific. The continent of Australia, which the Japanese had begun bombing the day of MacArthur's arrival, seemed next on the list, in addition to New Zealand. The American situation in the Philippines seemed hopeless.

On the other side of the world the German general Erwin Rommel was wreaking havoc on the British army in the North African deserts, and the Nazis, having occupied much of the Soviet Union, were poised on the doorsteps of Moscow and Leningrad and the tremendous battle for Stalingrad was about to begin.

*   *   *

Four days before the Japanese submarine shelled the California coast, President Roosevelt had signed an executive order, no. 9066, which subsequently came to be one of the most bitterly controversial orders ever issued by an American president, though it wasn't considered at all controversial at the time. At the outbreak of war there were some five million people of German descent living in the United States, as well as five million of Italian lineage. Most of these were hardworking, law-abiding people, but some thousands (including numerous noncitizen aliens) were not, and these were rounded up as potential spies, saboteurs, and troublemakers and placed in internment camps.

On the West Coast, however, there arose a thorny problem: what to do about the large colony of Japanese, citizens and noncitizens alike. As we have seen, the FBI and the military counterintelligence services had been intercepting secret Japanese communiqués regarding the use of Japanese civilians in espionage work. Since the West Coast ports were now the jump-off points for the whole Pacific war, it was disturbing to know that they could be (and probably were being) watched with impunity by any number of unfriendly Japanese.*

Just after Pearl Harbor the FBI—as they had with certain Germans and Italians—rounded up several thousand Japanese on the West Coast and in Hawaii who were suspected of enemy activity and put them in internment camps, where they remained until the end of the war. But that still left more than 100,000 Japanese or people of Japanese ancestry and it was here that the problem became sticky. Sixty years ago, America as a whole was far less tolerant than it is now. Blacks, Jews, Hispanics, Orientals, as well as Italians, Germans, and Eastern Europeans were often targets of racial or nationalistic slurs. The Japanese came in for particular malediction because they did not assimilate well into American culture; they tended to isolate themselves, forming Japanese clubs and other social organizations, and a few, in one degree or other, remained loyal to their emperor and homeland. They therefore immediately became a target of suspicion when America was attacked and a movement began to have them ejected from the West Coast states.

*For instance, on Terminal Island in Los Angeles there were thousands of Japanese, mostly fishermen, who could plainly see any warship or troop transport leaving the harbor.

Few Americans objected to this; even the American Civil Liberties Union demurred when asked to intervene after Roosevelt signed his now-infamous presidential order. From San Diego to Seattle, West Coasters had the war jitters. Not only were there news stories of enemy aircraft and ships operating in the area, there were rumors of every imaginable stripe. The possibility of a Japanese invasion was given widespread credence and it was even suggested by some in the military that the U.S. main line of defense should be the Rocky Mountains. Japanese civilians were treated with iciness and contempt and were repeatedly attacked in the streets—mostly by Filipinos, who resented the Japanese attack on their own country. Many Chinese were observed with handwritten signs attached to their persons, stating: "Chinese—not Jap." U.S. Secretary of War Henry Stimson recorded that "anti-Japanese feeling had reached a level which endangered the lives of all such individuals; incidents of extra-legal violence were increasingly frequent."*

The presidential order itself did not, as many still believe, mandate that the West Coast Japanese be rounded up and thrown into "concentration camps." What it did was allow military authorities to instruct the Japanese that they must evacuate certain excluded areas of the West Coast, including the western parts of Washington, Oregon, Arizona, and all of California and Alaska. They were free to do this on their own, and some ten thousand Japanese did, moving east toward they knew not what. But the remainder, about a hundred thousand, did not comply with this order. Some simply did not know where to go, did not speak English, did not have the money, or had other good reasons, such as businesses or farms to attend. Further complications arose when Japanese who were voluntarily relocating themselves received less than enthusiastic welcomes in other parts of the country.

Within the month it became apparent that the volunteer evacuation was not working, so further orders were given by the Justice De-

*Curiously, one person who did not agree with the relocation was J. Edgar Hoover, dictatorial director of the FBI. But his reasons were probably not as pure as might at first be supposed. According to biographer Curt Gentry, Hoover believed that all Japanese who might be involved in espionage had already been arrested by his agency, which had responsibility for domestic security, and thus the mass relocation somehow "implied criticism" of his agency; i.e., that the FBI hadn't done its job.

partment to physically relocate the West Coast Japanese. These orders stated: "No military guards will be used except when absolutely necessary for the protection of the evacuees. You will, to the maximum, provide assistance. For those who do not relocate themselves comfortable transportation will be provided to temporary assembly centers. Families will not be separated, medical care, nutrition for children and food for adults will be provided." Once assembled, the Japanese were parceled out to ten War Relocation Centers in various far-western states from where, if they wished, they could still relocate voluntarily anywhere in the United States except back to the West Coast exclusion areas (about a third—more than thirty thousand—chose this option). The man selected by Roosevelt to be in charge of all this was Milton Eisenhower, brother of General Dwight D. Eisenhower.*[1]

If the West Coast was infected with rumors of invasion and bombs (with the exception of the reality of the shelling by the Japanese submarine), citizens of the East Coast were experiencing a real-life nightmare. The Nazis had been taken with complete surprise by Japan's attack on Pearl Harbor and though Hitler responded promptly by declaring war on the United States, the German navy was not prepared. This, however, was remedied in short order by Admiral Karl Dönitz, the ruthless fifty-year-old commander of German submarines who, contrary to all treaties, rules, and customs of the sea, had ordered his U-boat commanders to machine-gun any survivors of merchant ships they sank on the theory that these men could not then be put back to sea.[†]

---

*Part of the controversy over the Japanese relocation stems from the fact that many were U.S. citizens, either by virtue of naturalization or by being born here. A few years after the war was over the Japanese were given compensation by the U.S government for problems associated with the relocation. Then, some forty years later, descendants of the relocated Japanese began a campaign for reparations for their removal, which resulted in further compensation.

†Fortunately, most German submarine commanders ignored these repellent orders. In 1945, after the death of Hitler, Dönitz became the temporary leader of Germany, which he quickly surrendered to the Allies. At the Nuremberg trials he was sentenced to ten years in prison for war crimes.

It took Dönitz until the first of January 1942 to reposition his submarines off the American coasts, but soon freighters, tankers, and other cargo ships began exploding at an alarming rate from New York to the Gulf of Mexico. More alarming was the fact that the U.S. military was almost totally unprepared to defend against this menace. In the scramble since war broke out, military services were clamoring for men and matériel of all kinds, but the sorts of planes, ships, and guns needed for antisubmarine warfare were in woefully short supply.

One merchant seaman described the ordeal this way: "We was carrying fifty thousand barrels of Oklahoma crude and fifty thousand of high-test gasoline. It sure gives you a funny feeling. I thought we'd get it any minute. Man, those nights are killers! You sleep with your clothes on. Well, I don't exactly mean sleep. You lie there in bed with your clothes on. All of a sudden the old engines slow down and your heart speeds up. Someone knocks on the door and you rise right up in your bed and seem to lie there in the air. So it turns out it's only the watch. You settle down and try to light a cigarette if your hand don't shake too much. Not that you're scared of course. Oh nooooh!"[2]

Soon beachgoers from Atlantic City to Miami were treated to the grisly souvenirs that washed ashore: oil slicks, clothing, bodies and parts of bodies. The press cried for solutions, but few were forthcoming. The military could muster only a handful of patrol planes, some of which were practically falling apart. The U-boats generally would lie by day on the ocean bottom outside such ports as Newark, New York, Norfolk, Jacksonville, Miami, or the mouth of the Mississippi River, then at night surface to conduct their grim work. Soon it became a massacre, of course, the merchant ships being unarmed. The Civil Air Patrol, a civilian group of airplane buffs, volunteered to run patrols but these generally were ineffective: their planes did not have the range to get out far and were not equipped to deal with a U-boat even if they spotted one. By the time word got back and military planes reached the area, the U-boat was long gone.

The navy tried various measures to stop the slaughter but with limited success. It decreed that shipping would be suspended during daylight hours and the ships must come into harbors from the Chesapeake Bay to Jacksonville, Florida, and sail only at nighttime, when they would be harder to spot. With the days getting longer sometimes this was not possible, and the U-boats would surface brazenly in broad daylight and sink ships with little fear of being attacked themselves. A merchant sailor told his story of the sinking of the *Empire,* a Cities Service oil tanker, off Fort Pierce, Florida. "I was asleep when the torpedoes hit us—three of them. I rushed up on deck and helped get one of the lifeboats over the side. I saw our captain on a life raft. He and some of the other men were on it. The current was sucking them into the burning oil around the tanker. I saw the captain going into a sheet of orange flame. Some of the fellows said he screamed . . . Monroe Reynolds was with me for a while. His eyes were burned. He was screaming that he was going blind. The last I saw of him he jumped into the fiery water. That was the finish of him, I guess."[3]

Hundreds of ships were being lost, many in plain view of shore where sunbathers from the Jersey Capes to Virginia Beach to Florida witnessed the horrifying spectacle of seeing large merchant ships explode before their very eyes. One of the most obvious defense measures was shamefully ignored until late spring of 1942. This was the dousing of shore lights, which would silhouette the merchant ships for the German submarines. Municipal and commercial interests from Atlantic City to Miami refused to turn off their glowing neon signs and waterfront lights on grounds that it would hurt their tourist business. The navy finally got around to ordering a total blackout in late April, but not before many ships were sunk and many sailors died. This was a puzzling attitude (many said flagrant selfishness) on the part of some Americans, who simply would not believe that the war could come directly to them.

They were soon to find out, however—and in more ways than one. Many of the ships being sunk had cargoes of oil from the Texas and Oklahoma fields bound for the great refineries of New Jersey, or had come from South America or the Caribbean carrying sugar, coffee, or bauxite ore (used to make aluminum). Within a few months gas would be limited to fewer than five gallons per week, per family—hardly enough for a Sunday drive. Sugar and coffee were severely rationed and the supply of aluminum electric toasters, garbage cans, and pots and pans quickly dried up. During the six months from January of 1942 until July, some 380 merchant ships were sent to the bottom and several thousand seamen were lost. Clearly something had to be done.*

Meantime, American life was changing so dramatically that people were stunned. Ten million men either enlisted or were inducted into the military. Businesses had to be sold or shut down because there was no one to run them. Dairy farms went out of business because there was no one to milk the cows. Circuses closed. HELP WANTED signs were posted everywhere but generally went unheeded. The most popular ditty of the day was:

> *You're in the army now;*
> *You're not behind a plow;*
> *You'll never get rich, you son-of-a-bitch*
> *You're in the army now!*

Almost overnight manufacturing firms that had been turning out electric fans, bicycles, ovens, automobiles, zippers, eyeglasses, and the like, were converted to make guns, planes, tanks, trucks, jeeps, field glasses, canteens, and so on. Some twenty thousand industries were so converted. Others were begun from scratch, one being the giant Willow Run aircraft production plant near Detroit, Michigan, which was run by the Ford Motor Company. The Willow Run building was more than a mile long and a quarter mile wide and was expected at its peak to turn out a thousand B-24 medium bombers a day.† Fifty thousand people worked there, including a small army of midgets, many rounded up from circuses or Hollywood, who were useful in putting the finishing touches on hard-to-get-at places within the fuselages.

---

*After the war, a stupendous public works project was set in motion to guard against these deadly attacks against American shipping. This was the completion of the Intracoastal Waterway System, first authorized by Congress just after World War I but which became a thirty-year-long, three-thousand-mile system of inshore canals that connect vital ports from Boston to the Texas border with Mexico, inaccessible to submarines.

†Ultimately it turned out only five hundred bombers a month at its peak.

Women flocked into the workplace in unprecedented numbers. By 1942 millions had left rural farming or mining communities to seek high-paying employment in munitions plants, shipyards, aircraft factories, or other war-related enterprises. "Rosie the Riveter" became a staple image for posters extolling the virtues of defense work. A concomitant problem quickly became how to house all these newcomers. Home owners took up some slack, living in one or two rooms and renting out the rest. The federal government tried to build dormitories and even some shabby types of houses,* but they lagged far behind and people shared what sleeping quarters they could find by working and sleeping in shifts or living in cars, tents, and trailers. Blacks were especially hard put, for white owners would generally not rent to them under any circumstances. By this time, though, the Rosie the Riveters were making more money than they had ever imagined possible; they met and married servicemen from every state in the Union and soon enough it was becoming clear that the face of America was changing forever.

At army and navy training posts the atmosphere was chaotic. On paper there was now a huge American army, but it was training with broomsticks for rifles and stovepipes for mortars and stumbling all over itself on the drill fields. Many officers were simply deadwood—the old "brown shoe army"—and others were green and barely trained themselves. A stark reminder of the Great Depression was that 40 percent of the men who went before their draft boards were rejected for physical reasons: hernias, tuberculosis, dropsy, venereal disease, lack of teeth, flat feet, sight problems. Two million were rejected by psychiatrists. The building of military camps and bases was often scandalous, marked by contractors' shoddy work, price gouging, and fraud. Residents of towns nearby were frequently disagreeable, putting signs in storefronts such as "No Dogs or

---

*Typical of these "housing projects" was a place named Birdville, near Brookley Air Base in Mobile, Alabama. All the streets were named for birds, e.g., Robin Drive, Red-bird Street. The houses were identical single-story, two-bedroom wood structures on tiny lots, but they were occupied quickly and gratefully by workers at the base. They remained after the war as a sort of low-income alternative but over the years fell prey to the usual urban blight of dilapidation, drugs, and crime. The Birdville housing remains today.

Soldiers Allowed." Beer halls and nightclub strips sprang up almost overnight, as if by wicked magic. Also, not all the women who joined the war
effort went to work in munitions factories. "Girlie Trailers" filled with
prostitutes quickly appeared on the scene. In Norfolk, Virginia, the police chief demanded that the federal government provide him with "a concentration camp large enough to handle two or three thousand women."[4]

Especially in the South, where Jim Crow laws were in effect, there
was tension between white and black soldiers. Because of the milder climate, many of the new military bases had been built there, but when
northern black soldiers arrived in southern states they found that they
were segregated into separate units and usually given menial tasks. Their
mess halls were separate and they even heard via the Negro press that
the Red Cross was segregating black and white blood. There were rumors
of lynchings and various incidents such as the black MP who was shot by
a white civilian policeman. And it wasn't just in the South, either; riots
broke out at Fort Dix, New Jersey, and people were killed. Japanese
propagandists were quick to seize on this strife; shortly after a Mississippi lynch mob burned to death a black man, the Japanese were broadcasting the news worldwide in an attempt to disaffect black Americans
from whites.[5]

Nevertheless, war or not, the old ways still gripped the southland.
Senator John Bankhead, Alabama Democrat, wrote to U.S. Army chief of
staff General Marshall: "Our people feel that the government is doing a
disservice to the war effort by locating Negro troops in the South in immediate contact with white troops at a time when race feeling among the
Negroes has been aroused and when all the energies of both the whites
and blacks should be devoted to the war effort." If, "as a result of political
and social pressure," black soldiers must be trained in the South, Bankhead
continued, "can't you place Southern Negro soldiers there, and place the
Northern Negro soldiers in the North, where their presence is not likely
to lead to race wars?"[6]

Meantime, all kinds of "win the war quick" schemes were being hatched
by inventors and innovative people far and wide. There was the inevitable

so-called death ray, which had been proposed as far back as World War I. One man even got so far as to hold a demonstration of his death ray before a group of army officers in rural Maryland, where he proposed to kill a herd of sheep grazing on a hillside. The death ray was turned on, the sheep were unaffected, and the inventor packed up his death ray and went back to the drawing boards.

A Pennsylvania dentist named Adams became convinced that bats could be used to carry small incendiary devices to ignite the paper-and-wood cities of Japan and persuaded President Roosevelt that this was feasible. Accordingly, Adams and a Harvard biologist named Griffin went to Carlsbad, New Mexico, wherein lived some ten million Mexican free-tailed bats and captured five hundred of them in nets. Unfortunately, it was found that these bats could not carry enough payload of incendiary bombs, and there the matter might have rested. But once government bureaucracy sets into motion it is, as proven time and again, hard to stop. Larger bats from Central America were tried, but they were temperamental and did not work well either. Not to be deterred, the Marine Corps leased four huge caves in California and four others in Texas to collect more bats, each site classified as top secret and manned by armed guards. In the end, the project was canceled, but not before the government spent some $2 million ($20 million in today's dollars) on research and bat collection.

One of the most curious schemes was the Dog Army, proposed by a Swiss citizen named William A. Prestre, a resident of Santa Fe, New Mexico. He managed to persuade the Pentagon to lease an entire island, named, of all things, Cat Island, lying in the Mississippi Sound, just south of Gulfport and not far from New Orleans.* There Prestre, aided by hundreds of U.S. Army troops, hoped to train—just for starters—an army of 40,000 large attack dogs. (The government had already put out a call for 125,000 dogs, but Prestre estimated that with some sixteen million dogs available in the United States a much vaster army of up to two million dogs could be organized once the kinks were worked out.)

---

*Later the project expanded to include nearby Ship Island as well, which had been used by the British to launch their expedition in 1814 that culminated in their ill-fated Battle of New Orleans and, forty-eight years later, was the launching point for Admiral David Farragut's successful capture of New Orleans during the American Civil War.

Prestre's underlying thesis was that, with the Japanese now holding so many Pacific islands, large forces of infantry would have to be employed to invade and eject them. But what about this: when the hundreds of landing craft began streaming into the beaches of one of these enemy islands, and their ramps flopped down, instead of disgorging thousands of marines or soldiers they would instead disgorge tens of thousands of vicious dogs, who would race across the beaches and attack the horrified Japanese at their machine guns and mortars.

Prestre worked it all out carefully, as one Private Harold House, a former dog trainer, testified before an army board: "Each dog was to be trained to kill Japanese only. The greyhounds were to lead the attack because of their speed, followed by the wolfhounds, who would aid in the confusion, after which the Great Dane packs were sent out as the main killers. Chesapeake Bay Retrievers were to be trained for beach landings." Bloodhounds and other tracking dogs would be used for mopping-up operations.

The first problem encountered was how exactly to train a dog to kill only Japanese. Accordingly, discussions began within army circles of how to acquire Japanese persons, with their particular looks and scent, to be trained on as "bait." Someone suggested using Japanese prisoners of war but, as we have seen, the Japanese did not surrender and thus there *were* no Japanese prisoners of war. Next, they considered using Japanese aliens, "preferably without families *in this country*." But that too was rejected on grounds that it "might cause adverse public sentiment." Finally it was decided that twenty-five Japanese-American enlisted men and three officers from a U.S. Army post in Wisconsin would be sent as "volunteers" to the Cat Island project.

The Japanese-Americans performed splendidly; the dogs did not. Wearing big padded suits and hockey gloves, the Japanese subjected themselves to being sicced on, over and again. An army report stated that "although their part in the entire project is distasteful," and while "several of them have been bitten severely . . . [they] continue the training without complaint."

The problem, though, was the dogs themselves—and Prestre himself, too, who, according to Private House's testimony, "did not know dogs or how to handle them." (Prestre had decided to use large French horns to incite the dogs to charge across the beaches, but these seemed only to confuse them.) It was also discovered that shellfire terrified most of the dogs, with the result that they became uncontrollable. Others were, well, just docile. In the event, after millions of dollars had been wasted, the Dog Army idea was abandoned as being incompatible with reality and Prestre returned to Santa Fe, but not before a "K-9 Corps Marching Song" was composed by the dog editor of the *New York Sun.*"*[7]

While MacArthur's army was beginning the fight for its life on Bataan, a daring and uplifting enterprise was gathering shape in Washington. It became the stuff that myths are made of.

Ever since Pearl Harbor, everyone and his brother had been wracking his brain trying to come up with some plan that would provide the Japanese a setback. But every idea had been nixed for one reason or another, and the Japanese octopus continued to crawl all over the Pacific. One bright and potentially successful idea had been to put big U.S. B-17s in Vladivostok, in the Soviet Union, only six hundred miles from Tokyo, and bomb Japan from there. When Roosevelt asked Stalin for permission, however, he was rebuffed—"Uncle Joe" was already deep in war with Germany and didn't want to provoke Japan, too. Then one cold January day a month after the war began, as brilliant ideas so often do, a lightbulb clicked on over the head of a certain navy captain named Francis "Frog" Low, who was in Norfolk to report on the navy's newest carrier, *Hornet,* which had just undergone her sea trials.

Low was waiting on the runway for his plane to take him back to Washington when he looked out the window and noticed that on an adjacent runway the outline of a huge aircraft carrier flight deck was painted on the surface. This was so that navy carrier pilots-in-training could practice-land there without the possibility of wrecking the deck of a real carrier. As Low's plane took off he suddenly saw two big army bombers coming in on the runway with the carrier deck painted on it. For Low it was like

*Dogs did prove very useful in all theaters, as sentries and scouts.

the tale of Isaac Newton conjuring up the law of gravity after being hit on the head by a falling apple.

A carrier operation against the Japanese mainland had been contemplated and dismissed because, unlike the Americans at Pearl Harbor, the Japanese were sure now to be on full alert and, with the types of smaller planes the carriers bore, they could never get close enough—not enough fuel range, not enough bomb power—to do any damage. But bombers, Captain Low suddenly wondered—army bombers, with their big payloads and fuel capacity . . . It had never been done, but it might just work.

When he got back to Washington Frog Low went to see his boss, Vice Admiral Ernest J. King, who had replaced Admiral Stark as chief of naval operations and commander of the U.S. fleet.* King, a hard-drinking, hard-boiled, no-nonsense sailor, "more feared than loved," was receptive to the notion. "That might be a good idea," he told Low, adding that he should study it further and get back to him.

The carrier people were skeptical. Bombers, they said, might take off from a carrier but they could not return because of too-fast landing speeds, among many other problems. Large bombers had wingspans too great to fit on a carrier or needed too much takeoff footage. Then, after studying the specs, somebody came up with a plane—the B-25. It was possible, just possible, and the beauty of it was that the B-25s could be launched beyond the range of Japanese fighter-bombers to retaliate. When Low informed Admiral King of this, King said, "Go see General Arnold about it, and if he agrees with you, ask him to get in touch with me. But don't mention this to another soul."[8]

General "Hap" Arnold—so known because of his smiling disposition—was the nation's chief air officer; only a month earlier he had recalled from civilian life one of America's most famous pilots—right up there with Lindbergh and Eddie Rickenbacker. His name was James H. "Jimmy" Doolittle, a man who, so far, had led a charmed life. Arnold had promoted him to colonel and made him his troubleshooter, and when Low and his team

---

*Unlike Admiral Kimmel and General Short, none of the blame for the Pearl Harbor disaster was placed on Stark's head. But he was quietly shipped out to a cushy job in London commanding the U.S. European fleet, of which there was none.

approached the commanding general with their proposal for a joint army-navy attack on Japan, Arnold immediately sent for Doolittle. It was a brilliant decision, for Doolittle was the epitome of a can-do man and the very idea of the ubiquitous interservice rivalries was anathema to him. They got down to planning right away, cloaked in a dense fog of secrecy.

The forty-five-year-old Doolittle was an old man relative to the young men who would serve as his flight crews. But few U.S. Army Air Corps officers had anything like Doolittle's experience. He grew up in a somewhat impoverished broken home in Alaska and—at only five feet, four inches—gained an almost impeccable record in his youth as a professional boxer. Always mechanically minded, Doolittle entered the University of California in hopes of becoming a mining engineer, but World War I interrupted and he found himself in the fledgling army air corps piloting fighter planes. Planes soon became his passion—not just flying them but everything about them. He earned master's and doctorate degrees in aeronautics from the Massachusetts Institute of Technology and applied his knowledge to achieve a number of firsts in aviation. He was the first, in 1927, to perform the dangerous—and then deemed impossible—"outside loop." Two years later he became the first pilot ever to "fly blind," using only instruments from takeoff to landing, wearing a bag over his head. This experiment basically defeated the problem of flying in fog, which had killed so many pilots. Not only that, Doolittle was celebrated worldwide as a famous racing pilot, holding several transcontinental records. Hap Arnold had described him as "absolutely fearless."[9]

In 1930 Doolittle resigned from the army and, during the Great Depression, made a small fortune as an official of the Shell Oil Company's aviation section. That was where Hap Arnold found him a few days after Pearl Harbor and asked him to return to duty. At an age when most people are looking forward to retirement, little did the former bantamweight boxer realize that before it was over he would find himself commanding three major U.S. air forces—in North Africa, Italy, England, and the Pacific—win the Congressional Medal of Honor, and be promoted to full general. But first came the famed Tokyo Raid, renowned in books and movies.

The strategy that evolved would utilize two aircraft carriers, the *Hornet* for the bombers and the *Enterprise* to provide fighter cover in case the Japanese discovered them. They would sneak across the Pacific using essentially the same northern route the Japanese had taken on their way to Pearl Harbor five months earlier. About five hundred miles off the coast of Japan, the bombers would launch and, barreling in right on the deck, bomb military installations, oil refineries, and factories in Tokyo, Yokohama, Osaka, and Kobe. Meantime, the carriers, after launching, would come about and steam full speed back toward Pearl Harbor, while the bombers would continue southwestward across the China Sea to airstrips in the Nationalist part of China, which would have been prepared for them in advance. It was, in effect, a variation on Yamamoto's original suicide mission against Pearl Harbor, without the suicide part of the plan.

April 18, 1942, was selected as launch date; data from U.S. submarines operating off Japan, specially equipped for weather observations, indicated this would be the ideal date as clear skies were expected over Tokyo. Only sixteen bombers could fit on the *Hornet,* and these had to be lashed to the flight deck because they were too big to fit on the hangar-deck elevators. The planes would have to be specially modified for the mission, most importantly to conserve fuel. The takeoff would be on Saturday evening; Doolittle would lead the raid, or so he thought, dropping incendiaries over Tokyo in order to guide the following bombers in.

There wasn't much time for gathering and training crews. Finding them was a problem in itself. After much consideration it was determined that the men and planes of the Seventeenth Bombardment Group in Pendleton, Oregon, were the most suitable for the mission because of their flying experience—especially over water. They were told only that "volunteers were needed for an extremely hazardous mission." Almost to a man, the Seventeenth Bombardment volunteered and were told to report to Eglin Field, a navy flying facility in the Florida panhandle that met Doolittle's specifications for isolation and secrecy. When they got there, the eighty men were assembled by Doolittle and told again that they would be volunteering for an exceptionally dangerous mission and that anyone could drop out "for whatever reason and nothing would ever be said about it."* No one did, "but one young man raised his hand and asked if I would give them more information. I told them they might guess why they were doing certain

*Doolittle himself gave as odds only fifty-fifty that anyone would make it back alive.

things, but the entire operation was top secret and they were not even to discuss their guesses among themselves."[10]

For these young pilots, the training they were put through was both startling and difficult. The normal takeoff speed of a B-25 was around a hundred miles per hour on a mile-long runway. Now they were being asked to jerk the thing off the ground in less than five hundred feet at fifty miles per hour—near stalling speed—which, Doolittle observed, "took some courage and was very much against their natural instincts." The crews had barely a month to train, practicing takeoffs, gunnery, and low-level bombing. With only two weeks to go, Doolittle himself got a scare when he discovered that Hap Arnold had not expected him to lead the mission, only to organize it. In Washington to give General Arnold a progress report, Doolittle "launched into a rapid-fire sales pitch" about why he should be in charge of the raid. Finally Arnold seemed to give in. "All right Jim. It's all right with me if it's all right with Miff [Brigadier General Millard F. Harmon, Arnold's chief of staff].

"I smelled a rat so I saluted, about faced, and ran down the corridor to Miff's office," Doolittle said.

"'Miff,' I said breathlessly, 'I've just been to see Hap about the project I've been working on and said I wanted to lead the mission. Hap said it was okay with him if it's okay with you.'"

"Miff was caught flat-footed, which is what I intended. He replied, 'Well, whatever is all right with Hap is certainly all right with me.'"

Doolittle closed the door just in time to hear Arnold's voice on Harmon's intercom. "But Hap," Harmon said plaintively, "I just told him he could go."[11]

On April Fools' Day, the planes and crews arrived in San Francisco after hedge-hopping across the country. Gigantic cranes swung out and loaded the big army bombers onto the flight deck of the *Hornet,* where the astonished and uninformed sailors began lashing them down. At noon, April 2, 1942, the *Hornet* task force, Doolittle included, cruisers and destroyers first, then the *Hornet* herself, steamed westward out of San Francisco Bay. By late afternoon, when they were out of sight of land, the skipper, Captain Marc Mitscher, sent a signal to all ships: "This force is bound for Tokyo." Within moments great cheers began to rise toward the darkening Pacific skies.[12]

Chapter Eleven ★

While Doolittle was still training his fliers back in Florida, one of the worst sea disasters thus far in history befell the Allies in the southwest Pacific.

When the American admiral Thomas Hart took his small Asiatic Fleet south to avoid destruction in the Philippines, he linked up with forces of the Dutch, British, and Australian navies. You could hardly call a fleet of nine cruisers and eleven destroyers ragtag but, considering that they had never trained together, the language problems involved, and that the Japanese had a fleet of six aircraft carriers and superior numbers of cruisers and destroyers operating in the region, it was not the ideal striking force, either. But strike it did.

In what would come to be known as the Battle of the Java Sea, and its sequel the Battle of Sunda Strait, practically all of this combined Allied force ended up at the bottom of the ocean with a terrific loss of life, including its commanding officer, Rear Admiral K.W.F.M. Doorman, Royal Netherlands Navy. This also signified a dismal end to the U.S. Asiatic Fleet and her flagship, U.S.S. *Houston,* which went down with 632 men. All these ships fought with inspiring bravery against bad odds. The *Houston* certainly went down fighting; it took four to six torpedo hits, three full salvo hits, eleven individual shell hits, and various other damage to sink her, but not before the *Houston*'s crew had fired up "every bit of ammunition they had, even starshell, until it was expended," her skipper was killed, and the entire engine-room crew scalded to death by steam.[1]

What had caused this awful misadventure? First, one would have to suggest, was the almost total Japanese control of the air over the Java Sea. Japanese scout planes not only located the Allied ships and forewarned their fleets, but those fleets could send aircraft to bomb and torpedo the Allies. Second was the Japanese supremacy in surface-ship torpedo warfare. In the period between the wars the Japanese had developed a destroyer-launched, oxygen-powered torpedo that was twenty nine and a half feet long and two feet around with a 1,250-pound explosive charge; it ran at fifty miles per hour and was accurate at more than a mile.* It was called the Long Lance. Moreover, the Japanese navy had for years generously expended live torpedoes in maneuvers and on practice targets and had worked out all the kinks.

On the other hand, the U.S. Navy, operating on its parsimonious between-the-wars budget, did no such thing. To save money (a torpedo then cost approximately $10,000 ($100,000 today), before the war there had not been a live-torpedo test-firing since 1926 and, where practicable, navy orders had been for torpedo-firing vessels to practice-fire at beaches or other places where the dummy "fish" could later be collected and reused. A heavy price was paid in lives and ships for this folly. A third reason for the resounding defeat of the combined southwest Pacific fleet was the lack of communication caused by language differences. For example, Admiral Doorman on his doomed Dutch cruiser *De Ruyter* could lead the Allied forces into the Java Sea battle only by flag signaling to his fellow vessels, "Follow Me," like something out of eighteenth-century warfare.

In retrospect, it could be argued that the wiser choice would have been for the British to have evacuated the Malay peninsula and saved its 85,000 troops to fight another day, for the 32,000 Dutch, British, and Australian troops on Java to have done the same, and for the 12,000 American troops in the Philippines, who could have left on Hart's warships before

---

*Some say twenty miles, but that seems a bit of a stretch.

the Japanese invasion, to have done so as well.* And it certainly might have been smarter to have sailed the nine cruisers and eleven destroyers of the Allied forces to Australia, where they could one day be assembled along-side a mightier armada.

One factor as to why they did not can probably be laid to pride or, if you prefer, arrogance. Malaya, Singapore, the Dutch East Indies, and the Philippines were colonial possessions and, as such, were "property." Few responsible persons or authorities are willing to see their property stolen before their very eyes. Finally, the Allied nations never quite understood the forces Japan was marshaling against them, and by the time they did it was too late. But all that was in retrospect.

In the Philippines, from early February until April 1, an ominous calm descended over Bataan. There was only sporadic artillery fire and patrolling by the Japanese, but everyone understood that with reinforcements they were regrouping for a big push. The American food shortage naturally grew worse. Reports circulated that practically all the monkeys, lizards, and snakes on the peninsula had been devoured. Fewer and fewer held out hope for the big relief fleet from the United States.

The big push began on April Fools' Day, just as Doolittle's fliers were steaming toward Japan. Suddenly the entire American line erupted with explosions from Japanese heavy guns. Enemy airplanes circled above Bataan hundreds at a time, from dawn to dusk, bombing and strafing anything and everything, and "a gray pall of smoke and dust hung over the peninsula."[2]

The Japanese began dropping incendiary and phosphorous bombs, which, it being the dry season, started great forest fires, causing the American forces to flee or be burned alive. Then large columns of Japanese infantry and tanks began crashing through the American lines, isolating units

---

*There was another reason, which MacArthur expressed directly to Roosevelt: the notion of abandonment. If the Western nations in the Pacific had simply turned tail and run, the Asian peoples from China to Borneo to India would lose all respect for them and probably side with the Japanese because there was no one else to turn to.

from one another. Not knowing what else to do, Wainwright on April 8 ordered an attack. He must have known it was futile, but nothing else was working and, from Australia, MacArthur had ordered him a week earlier: "If food fail[s], prepare and execute an attack upon the enemy."[3] The men on Bataan complied but only halfheartedly and, by day's end, their firing dropped away; they jammed the roads and trails in a mad rush to get away from the advancing Japanese. That night a gigantic series of explosions rocked southern Bataan and reverberated to Corregidor. Fire and flames shot thousands of feet into the air and the event startled all who witnessed it. An artillery major asked what was going on and was told, "It's all over." They had blown up the ammunition dumps.[4]

The same artillery major who was at headquarters in the Malinta Tunnel watched General Wainwright speaking on the phone with General Edward P. King, senior commander on Bataan. "'You can't surrender!' he shouted. 'You can't!' As he listened intently his gaunt frame seemed to sag in on itself. Tears rolled down his cheeks. 'Why don't you attack with I Corps?' he asked. We clearly heard a voice say: 'I Corps no longer exists.' General Wainwright slumped into his chair."*[5]

In fact it was all over—at least the fighting on Bataan. Every fiber of Wainwright's body and soul told him that American soldiers do not surrender, had never surrendered; at Valley Forge, Gettysburg, even during the slaughters at Fredericksburg, both Manassas battles, Chancellorsville, and on and on, there had been setbacks, defeats, retreats, but not surrender—never before in the history of the United States had an entire army surrendered. But Wainwright accepted the inevitable. "Let me say here that I have no criticism of General King for accepting the situation and surrendering. It was a decision which required great courage and mental fortitude. He had either to surrender or have his people captured or killed piecemeal [and] this would most certainly have happened to him within two or three days."[6]

---

*There are conflicting accounts as to whether or not King and Wainwright spoke about the surrender. King says they did not. Wainwright's account is somewhat confusing. The account above comes from Brigadier General (retired) Steven Mellnik, the artillery officer who was on the scene.

After more than a week of constant combat the starving and sick soldiers on Bataan could go on no longer. Ninety percent (mostly Filipinos) had no shoes and their clothes were in tatters; their ammunition was mostly used up; many had had no sleep whatsoever for the past two or three days. One unit reported taking 2 percent casualties per *hour* from Japanese artillery fire alone. The two U.S. Army corps on Bataan simply ceased to exist for purposes of organized resistance, and it became practically "every man for himself."

By dawn next day General King was in a jeep with two other officers in search of the Japanese commander. All he could find was a Japanese colonel who offered no negotiations or terms except unconditional surrender. Under the circumstances, King had to comply. The colonel also demanded King's sword and became furious when the general told him he did not have one. The matter was finally settled when King offered the Japanese officer his pistol instead.

Those on Corregidor—there were some 10,000 to 15,000 of them now, their ranks swelled by those lucky enough to find a craft to help them escape, as well as several dozen army nurses who had been evacuated— watched in grim fascination as the firing finally stopped. One officer remembered, "As the afternoon drew to a close, we saw long columns of men moving north from Marivales [the little port town on the tip of Bataan]. White flags dotted the columns. I was glad that the ordeal for those men was over. They could rest now, and receive medical attention."[7]

This last observation raised perhaps the grossest example of false hopes in the history of the world. The men got no such things. Instead they became victims of the most studied cruelty that Americans and Filipinos alike had ever had or would ever have to endure. Starving and ill, the 78,000 U.S. troops started northward on the infamous sixty-five-mile Bataan Death March, in which about 10,000 of them either perished from starvation, thirst, or other health problems or were murdered by sadistic Japanese guards. Because this monstrosity has no dearth of firsthand accounts, no doubt exists that the ordeals these soldiers experienced were beyond embellishment. If any of those men had thought that stories they had read of Japanese atrocities in China might have been exaggerated, he would soon find out, to his dismal regret, that they were not.

In the beginning, what most members of the Death March remembered was the noise and confusion. And the dust. As Homma's army poured south into lower Bataan by the tens of thousands there was scarcely room on the roads for both them and the 78,000-man chain of prisoners moving north. The Japanese came marching in units, interspersed with truck convoys or tanks or jeeplike vehicles carrying officers. The Japanese guards were constantly shouting and screaming in a language unintelligible to the Americans and Filipinos, so that when the guards wanted their prisoners to move off the road to let a Japanese column pass, they resorted to clubbing the men or prodding them with bayonets.

Then there was the eternal dust stirred up by so many thousands of feet and by the Japanese vehicles, a fine, powdery dust four to six inches deep, which nearly strangled the men and burned their eyes and clogged their pores in the 90-plus-degree heat as if they were wearing a rubber suit. Ralph Levenberg, an air corps sergeant who had been fighting as an infantryman since the destruction of the planes, remembered, "It reminded me of what it might have been like when the Jews exited Egypt into the desert—no one knowing where they were going or what they should take or how long it would take to get where they were going. The Japanese were just in a rush to get us out of their way."[8]

Private First Class Blair Robinett's first encounter with a Japanese soldier did not go well. "He stepped out, came across, and took my canteen out of its cover. He took a drink, filled his canteen from mine and poured the rest of my water on the ground and dropped the canteen at my feet. When I bent down to pick up my canteen he turned around and hit me on the head with his rifle butt."[9]

Presently the Japanese became a little more organized. They began to separate the prisoners into groups of a thousand or so, with about sixteen guards each, whose tempers did not improve but became demonstratively worse. "A short distance away, an American fell behind. He was bayoneted in the throat. He gasped for air, then was dead." The Americans could not comprehend the Japanese. As Homma's convoys passed the prisoners, some of the Japanese soldiers would wave and smile while from the next truck men would strike out with rifle butts or bayonets, which left many Americans lying in the dust after the truck drove on by. At one point the marchers passed a sugarcane field and several men, including an air force pilot, tried to get at the cane. "When they got to the edge of the field, the Jap guards shot them down and clubbed the wounded survivors to death." And yet: "Another group, seeing the sugarcane field, ran over and cut some of the juicy stalks. The Jap guards entered the field to help themselves."[10]

A young infantry lieutenant on the march chronicled what he saw and felt throughout his ordeal as a prisoner of the Japanese. His name was Henry G. Lee, from Los Angeles, and his poems were written in POW camps on scraps of paper and sometimes on shreds of cloth or canvas. Late in the war, before he was starved to death by the Japanese, Lee buried his collection of verse for what he hoped might be posterity, which he finally achieved after the war, when U.S. soldiers investigating the Japanese prison camps dug up his works and sent them to his father. They were published in 1948 under the title *Nothing But Praise* and represent some of the best poetry to come out of World War II. He wrote of the Bataan Death March.

> *Prisoner's March*
> *(Death of a Friend)*
> So you are dead. The easy words contain
> No sense of loss, no sorrow, no despair.
> Thus hunger, thirst, fatigue, combine to drain
> All feeling from our hearts. The endless glare,
> The brutal heat, anesthetize the mind.
> I cannot mourn you now. I lift my load,
> The suffering column moves. I leave behind
> Only another corpse, beside the road.[11]

Several accounts refer to a grisly incident in which an American soldier, obviously ill, was staggering and reeling along when a column of Japanese tanks appeared in the opposite direction. A Japanese guard "grabbed this sick guy by the arm and guided him to the middle of the road. Then he just flipped him out across the road. A tank pulled across him. Well, it killed him quick. There must have been ten tanks in that column and every one of them came up there right across the body. When the last tank left there was no way you could tell there'd ever been a man there. The man disappeared, but his uniform had been pressed until it had become part of the ground."[12]

The guards used the occasion to enrich themselves from their pitiful charges. Wristwatches and rings were taken. One man had his teeth knocked out because a Japanese admired his gold fillings. Rings were often a source of consternation because many of the men's fingers were swollen as a result of suffering from edema and the rings would not come off. In that event, the guard sometimes chopped off the finger to get at the ring. Sometimes he chopped off more than one. Another great fear was being found with anything of Japanese origin, as the first-in-line marchers soon found out. The Japanese immediately assumed the item had been taken from the body of a dead Japanese soldier and the prisoner was killed on the spot. The fact is, many of the prisoners had been in Manila for months or longer and had purchased watches, pens, wallets, combs, shaving mirrors, and such from the many Japanese-owned shops that lined the streets. Word spread back along the line of march and all things Japanese were quickly disposed of.

The prisoners quickly learned to help their weaker comrades along since those who dropped out were not allowed to rest but instead were routinely murdered, often in grotesque fashion. The Japanese were fond of using their swords, and the march slowly began to wind past dozens of decapitated American bodies. Rifle shots cracked out incessantly, for behind each group of marchers was a squad of Japanese guards, finishing off any stragglers. Two soldiers were carrying between them their captain, who was almost prostrate with dysentery, but they were falling farther and farther behind. "Finally, one of the men at the rear of the column, who kept watching for guards, yelled to us that a Jap was coming. By now we were dragging [him]. When the guard got to us he rammed his bayonet right through the captain. Naturally we dropped [him] and ran up and got into the middle of the column." For the men near the rear of the march it was even more traumatic, since they had to pass by all the thousands of bodies killed ahead of them. Practically all of the men had dysentery. If they stopped by the roadside to relieve themselves, they "were ordered to eat their own excrement. If they refused, they were either bayoneted or shot." On more than one occasion Americans were ordered at bayonet point to dig holes and bury their sick comrades alive.[13]

This went on, day after day, night after night, for nearly a week under the broiling sun for sixty-five agonizing miles. The Japanese rarely allowed the men to stop for water. If the marchers ahead had halted for some reason, and the prisoners behind found themselves beside a stream, or even a slimy ditch, it was risking almost certain death to try and get at the water. On more than one occasion, when the men were finally allowed to drink from a ditch or stream by the roadside, more often than not they found the water contaminated by bloated, maggot-infested bodies. There was no food from the Japanese, except an occasional small rice ball. The only bright spot in the whole affair was that when the marchers passed the dozens of little Filipino villages along the route they were often greeted by women and children offering them gifts of rice, water, sugarcane, or fruits.* Some of the women cried, and some of them died—the Japanese did not take kindly to Filipinos helping their enemies. One pregnant woman trying to help was shot and then bayoneted in the stomach for her kindness.

One officer recorded later, "Some people think there was one Death March. There were many Death Marches." This was all too true, even when the march was over. Finally they reached the town of San Fernando, where there was a railroad with a line of old-time steel boxcars baking in the tropical sun. "Into the oven we went. The heat from inside hit us in the face. They packed us in just as tight as you can be packed in. In fact, I know there were people who never stood on the floor. They were being held up by their friends. Everyone at first started yelling and screaming. It was worse than anything that had gone on before. Once in a while the train would stop and some Jap guards would open the doors so we could get some fresh air. Then is when we'd get the dead ones out. If we could we'd lift the corpses and pass them over to the door." The men were panicky, vomiting and excreting until everyone's shoes were filled with filth. Some hours later they reached their destination, a hellhole called Camp O'Donnell.[14]

---

*It must also be said that in some of the accounts the Filipinos *sold* these items to the American soldiers.

Actually, they did not reach O'Donnell proper but were still eight miles west of it. The "camp" was a partially completed American airfield and here the 78,000 (less some thousands dead) soldiers were incarcerated. The Japanese had decided that O'Donnell was to be the POW camp until the remaining 10,000 holding out on Corregidor were taken; then some other plan would be made. Meantime, they would stay in this place, featuring long and partially completed barracklike huts with thatched nipa-palm roofs enclosed by barbed wire and machine-gun-ready guard towers.

When they got to Camp O'Donnell the men learned for the first time what their status was vis-à-vis "prisoners of war." They had none. The Japanese had refused to ratify the Geneva Convention of 1929 in which prisoners of war were to be treated humanely, with honor, and maintained by the imprisoning country according to the standards of the International Red Cross. Instead, on that occasion the Japanese stated that "real improvement of prisoners depends, in the final analysis, on the humanitarian sentiments and goodwill of the belligerents." The reason was that in the Japanese mind surrender was a criminal act; the surrenderer was a traitor; his family would live in perpetual disgrace and his name would be erased from any mention in his village records; he should first have committed suicide (hara-kiri). This attitude did not lead to "goodwill," or to any sentiments most people recognize as humanitarian.

General King tried to address this notion in a speech to the prisoners at O'Donnell when he told them, "You may remember this. You did not surrender. You were surrendered. You had no alternative but to obey my order. I did the surrendering. I am the one that has the responsibility, let me carry the responsibility."[15] The Japanese were unmoved. The camp commander, Captain Yoshi Tsuneyoshi, soon delivered a ranting jumping-up-and-down harangue in which he compared the prisoners to dogs and told them, "You think you are the lucky ones? Your comrades who died on Bataan are the lucky ones!"[16]

For the prisoners, Camp O'Donnell was as close to hell on earth as they would ever remember. For the tens of thousands there was exactly one water spigot. Sergeant Charles Cook recalled, "If I wanted a drink of water, I got up in the morning and headed for the water faucet. There would already be hundreds waiting in line. I'd wait in line all day. The water would run a while, then they'd turn it off. So I just waited and took my chance."[17]

At O'Donnell the American and Filipino troops were segregated. By now there were fewer than ten thousand American soldiers, and at first they began dying at a rate of about thirty to fifty per day. There was no medicine except for what the surgeons had managed to bring with them and this quickly ran out. "The camp became one vast sewer, foul and stinking. Clouds of flies buzzed everywhere: in the latrines, where they dropped their eggs in teeming filth; on the faces of those in coma, rimming their lips and drinking from their half-open eyes; over open, dripping ulcers of arm and leg; in filth-soaked clothing. They settled in an almost solid mass on the rice buckets as they were loaded by shovel from the steaming *kawalis* [open kettles], refusing to rise as they were waved away by KPs. Eating became a tricky maneuver; one hand rapidly shoveling rice from the mess kit into mouth while the other moved back and forth over a rag with which the rice in the mess kit was kept covered."[18]

This last description was written by an army physician named Captain Alfred Weinstein, who goes on, "Men standing quietly in the chow or water line toppled over dead. Others straddling the slit trenches slithered into their fecal graves. Still others struggling back from a work detail would silently lie down on their filth-covered pallets and die. On scraps of paper the medics copied the serial numbers of the dead which had been painted on gaunt chests with the pitifully tiny supply off iodine husbanded on the long, long road from Bataan. If the Angel of Death ever had a caldron of victims ready for him, it was in Camp O'Donnell during these first twelve weeks after the surrender. Why all of them didn't die remains a mystery to those of us who watched and tried to help make their last death agonies less painful. The death toll rose—fifty, two hundred, three hundred, four hundred lifeless skeletons to be buried a day—until it reached a peak of five hundred and fifty."[19] The Japanese had by now captured and inventoried the vast stores of American medicines from the hospitals on Bataan but none of this was forthcoming to the diseased and dying men in O'Donnell; the Japanese used it for themselves.

There are enough recorded stories of this sort to fill dozens of books, but the picture so far is clear enough: the Japanese had little or no humane concerns regarding their disarmed and helpless charges. One reason as to why was, as mentioned, that the Japanese never ratified or agreed with the provisions of the Geneva Convention. Another was answered later, at the war crimes trial of General Masaharu Homma, which was that while the Japanese had expected to have prisoners after the fall of Bataan, they had expected only about 40,000—about half of what they got—and had made no provisions for so many men and didn't bother to do so afterward. As to the Death March itself, General King had offered to transport the American and Filipino prisoners to whatever point the Japanese designated in U.S. Army trucks, but the Japanese refused; they had little transportation of their own and wanted to utilize whatever they had captured to move their own troops. Finally, the arrival of the ever ubiquitous Colonel Tsuji, of the Singapore Chinese massacres, may have had something to do with it.

It was said that after Tsuji came to the Philippines he became even more of a rogue officer, using his position as director of war planning to dictate recommendations and even orders to his superiors as though, through him, they came directly from Imperial Headquarters in Tokyo. It was said that he considered Homma weak and tried to undermine his authority and get him fired. It was said, too, that Tsuji "convinced several admiring officers on [Homma's] staff that this was a racial war and that all prisoners in the Philippines should be executed: Americans because they were white colonialists and Filipinos because they had betrayed their fellow Asians." To that end, it was then said that from Tsuji many Japanese commanding officers had received some kind of indirect order to "kill all prisoners and those offering to surrender." One officer, it was said, Major General Torao Ikuta, refused to obey this order unless he received it in writing.*[20]

*The source material for the role of Colonel Tsuji seems to originate with the historian John Toland, who revealed it in his 1970 book *The Rising Sun.* Subsequent authors, including myself, have gone by Toland's accounts. But it also seems that Toland did not interview Tsuji himself, and used for his authority an unpublished article by one of the Japanese officers on Bataan. What historical weight should be given this article is debatable, since after the war the Japanese tried to distance themselves from atrocities in the Philippines and elsewhere. It should also be pointed out that Toland, of all the Pacific war historians, tended to be more sympathetic to the Japanese as a whole.

All this might be quite true; still, it does not explain the barbaric and heartless behavior of so many individual Japanese guards and soldiers, or their officers, who should have known better. It is one thing to execute people; it is another to torture and brutalize them beforehand. It has also been mentioned by way of excuse that the typical Japanese soldier was himself brutalized by his own officers and thus was hardened to brutality.

Listen again to our defiant poet-lieutenant Henry Lee.

An Execution

Red in the eastern sun, before he died
We saw his flinting hair; his arms were tied.
There by his lonely form, ugly and grim,
We saw an open grave, waiting for him.
We watched him from our fence, in silent throng,
Each with fervent prayer, "God make him strong."
They offered him a smoke, he'd not have that,
Then at his captor's feet he coldly spat,
He faced the leaden hail, his eyes were bare;
We saw the tropic rays glint in his hair.
What matter why he stood, facing the gun?
We saw a nation's pride, there in the sun.[21]

While all this dreadfulness was going on in the Philippines, eleven days out in the far North Pacific the carrier U.S.S. *Hornet* rendezvoused with Admiral Halsey's *Enterprise* task force, which had left Pearl Harbor several days earlier to conduct Colonel Doolittle's Tokyo raiding force. Five days later, on April 17, the two carriers were within Japanese home waters. The bombs and ammunition had been loaded, gas tanks topped off, last-minute checks made. Doolittle gave his final instructions, which included, "Under no circumstances [are we] to bomb the emperor's palace." Also, he gave them a last chance to drop out. "No one did." Then snags began to develop. At three A.M. on the eighteenth, the *Enterprise* flashed a message: TWO ENEMY SURFACE CRAFT SIGHTED. Radar on the carrier had picked up Japanese ships about four miles away. The task force immediately went to general quarters and swung north to keep from being

spotted. By dawn a forty-knot gale had blown up and the seas were mountainous. The *Enterprise* sent up patrol planes, which soon spotted other Japanese ships; what initial intelligence had not revealed was that the Japanese
had established an early-warning picket line of fishing ships approximately
seven hundred miles offshore. The task force was running into them now,
more than two hundred miles away from their designated launch point.[22]

Suddenly, at six-thirty A.M., the cruiser *Nashville* roared to life with
her big guns. People on the other ships ran to the sides to see what was
going on. Less than two miles away was a seventy-ton Japanese picket ship.
The jig was up now; if they could see it, certainly it had seen them. Radio
scanners were picking up messages in Japanese code; obviously the presence of the task force was being reported. The Japanese picket would have
to be sunk, but this was easier said than done. In thirty-foot swells, the
ship was bobbing so much that it took 934 six-inch shells before one finally hit. One of the Japanese survivors who was fished out of the water
told of how he had spotted the American task force and ran to his captain's
quarters to report "two beautiful Japanese carriers" passing by. The captain went topside and after taking a look said to the seaman, "Yes, they are
beautiful, but they are not ours." Then, according to the sailor, the captain "returned to his cabin and shot himself in the head."[23]

Here was an awful predicament. The carriers had been expected to
get the raiding force inside of five hundred miles from Japan, but they were
still eight or nine hours away from their launching point. The Japanese
picket ship had reported their presence and Japanese bombers were certainly being scrambled at this moment. Fuel for the B-25s had been calculated down to the last drop to carry the planes across Japan and on to China.
But if they launched now the planes might run out of gas; almost worse,
instead of arriving over the Japanese cities at night, when they would be
fairly safe from Japanese antiaircraft and fighter attack, they would arrive
in broad daylight. The decision was agonizing, but Doolittle made it instantly. Word blared over the *Hornet*'s loudspeaker system: "Army pilots,
man your planes!"

The *Hornet* immediately became a hive of activity. From below, sailors
lugged up hundreds of five-gallon jerricans of aviation gasoline to give each
plane a boost in fuel capacity. Doolittle warned his pilots to make sure

someone punctured holes in the the cans before tossing them out, so that they would not leave a trail in the ocean leading back to the carriers. The twin engines were started and revved up; the startled army pilots, some of whom had been shaving, others eating breakfast, dropped everything and got their gear together. By eight A.M. Halsey, on the *Enterprise,* flashed a message over to the *Hornet:* LAUNCH PLANES X TO COL DOOLITTLE AND GALLANT COMMAND GOOD LUCK AND GOD BLESS YOU. Watching the planes taking off, Halsey called it "one of the most courageous deeds in military history."[24]

Officers and crew on the *Hornet* gaped in breathless consternation as the first plane, Doolittle's, started down the runway. The carrier was dipping and bobbing so much in the thirty-foot seas that Doolittle described it as "like taking off on a moving see-saw." At the far end of the flight deck a launch chief was waving a checkered flag in a circle, faster and faster, telling Doolittle to keep revving his engines, higher and higher. Then, timed as daintily as a minuet, when the bow dipped into a huge wave he signaled for Doolittle to release the brakes and put full speed on the throttle. The fully loaded bomber lumbered down the deck, its left wing sticking out over the side, and, just as the bow rose again from the wave trough, went airborne. Lieutenant Ted Lawson, piloting *Ruptured Duck,* was seventh in line; he remembered, "We watched him like hawks, wondering what the wind would do to him, and whether he could get off in that little run toward the bow. If he couldn't, we couldn't. He had yards to spare. He hung his ship almost straight up on its props, until we could see the whole top of the B-25." Huge cheers reverberated throughout the *Hornet* and the other American ships.[25]

A takeoff by a 25,000-pound plane in such a short space would have been impossible except from an aircraft carrier. By plowing ahead at full speed—nearly thirty-five miles an hour at that small length of ship—into the teeth of the gale-force wind, the *Hornet* was giving the bombers' wings double extra lift, the aerodynamic factor that allows planes to leave the ground or, in this case, the deck. The rest of Doolittle's squadron took off without serious incident until the turn of the last plane, *Bat Out of Hell.* She was revving high and her props were spinning in a blur when one of the sailors assigned to remove the restraining ropes slipped on the soaking deck and was sucked into the *Bat*'s propeller. It chopped off his arm, but the horrified airmen on the *Bat* took off anyway, following their fellows toward the empire of Japan.

Five and a half hours later Doolittle's bombers, flying at treetop level, began to cross the coast of Japan. People in fishing boats and crop fields smiled and waved up at them. As the Americans neared Tokyo it was a strange, almost surreal feeling to spot the snowcapped peak of Mount Fuji, just as Commodore Perry had first done ninety years earlier. Now bicyclers and children looked up and waved at them; many assumed the B-25s were some kind of new Japanese airplane. The citizens of Tokyo had just experienced an air-raid drill that morning, and most people thought this had something to do with it. Soon the American fliers began to see flights of Japanese warplanes, but the warplanes took no notice of them. Just as the Japanese had at Pearl Harbor, Doolittle's fliers were using Tokyo radio to home in on the city. And just as at Pearl Harbor, the Japanese were expecting nothing more than another lovely spring day. They were taken completely by surprise. Then the bombs began to fall.

There wasn't a whole lot of damage with only 32,000 pounds of bombs dropped on a city like Tokyo, whose eight million inhabitants were spread out in an area the size of Los Angeles. But damage was done. Oil refineries, electrical plants, steel mills, railroad centers, port facilities, airplane factories—all would take hits. Slowly but steadily the Japanese antiaircraft cannon began to come to life; flak exploded near the planes but they were flying so low and fast that it was generally ineffective. The last planes to go in saw flames and smoke belching up all over the city, but by now the Japanese antiaircraft fire was thick and the skies were filling with dozens of enemy fighter planes. But once the B-25s had dropped their payloads, their speed picked up dramatically and the Japanese pursuit planes were no match for them.

Right in the middle of all this the Japanese dictator, Prime Minister General Tojo, was riding in a small official plane that was trying to land at the Mito Aviation School on the far side of Tokyo, where he had intended to conduct an inspection. When his plane descended toward the runway, one of Doolittle's B-25s "roared up on its right side and flashed by without firing a shot." Tojo's secretary, an army colonel, reported that the plane was "queer looking."[26]

At the U.S. embassy, where diplomats and their staffs were being kept prisoner until they could be exchanged for Japanese diplomats in the United States, there was divided opinion as to whether the attack was a real one. When, going out on the roof, they discovered that it was true, Ambassador Joseph Grew reported, "We were all very happy and proud in the embassy and the British told us that they drank toasts all day to the American fliers."[27] The wife of the American naval attaché recognized the planes and said to a friend, "Those planes are American bombers and I bet you that Lieutenant Jurika is in one of them." She was wrong, but not by much. Jurika, who had spent years in Tokyo as naval attaché, was now Lieutenant Commander Jurika, the intelligence officer aboard the Hornet, who had briefed Doolittle's pilots on what they might expect if they were shot down and captured by the Japanese.[28]

Jurika's remarks had not been comforting. He informed the pilots that in the skies over Tokyo alone, "military intelligence had determined that they would be greeted by three hundred 75mm anti-aircraft guns and five hundred Japanese planes" and that "if they were captured dropping bombs on Japan the chances of their survival would be awfully slim; very, very slim. I figured they would be, first of all, paraded through the streets as Exhibit A, and then tried by some kind of kangaroo court and probably publicly beheaded."[29]

In any case, now that the raid had been successfully carried out without loss, the most serious part of the mission began—escape. Authorities in Washington had prearranged, or so they thought, for a landing field about seventy miles inland from the coast, still in Chinese Nationalist hands, to be prepared to receive the bombers. It would broadcast a homing beacon, be lit up for a possible night landing, and have on hand enough aviation gasoline to refuel the planes so that they could continue on to the Nationalist capital of Chungking, far into the interior of China. There the bombers would be turned over to the American air forces in China and the pilots picked up by planes flying from India and returned, via the western route, to the United States.

It did not work out that way; their luck had been too good to last. The weather began to turn and rain squalls set in. There was no beacon broadcast from the Chinese airfield, and neither was it lighted. Since the thing was in a valley flanked by steep mountains, locating it would be impossible. More ominous, the pilots would soon be approaching large mountain ranges and the maps they had were faulty. On one map, for instance, the altitude of a peak would be given as 5,000 feet; on another the same peak would be measured at 10,000 feet. At about eight-thirty P.M. they began to spot the first islands off the China coast. They had been in the air a full twelve hours and now the only chance for survival was either to fly down on the deck and try to find a spot to land in the fast-approaching darkness or to fly up high on instruments, hoping to get above the jagged peaks, and when the gas was almost gone to bail out and take their chances. Some took the first option, most took the second, and one plane whose gas situation was so critical that an escape to China became impossible veered far north and managed to land in Vladivostok, Russia, despite what Uncle Joe Stalin had said.

Lieutenant Ted Lawson piloting *Ruptured Duck,* who had so anxiously watched Doolitte's takeoff from the *Hornet,* decided to try a landing on an empty beach. But just as he was coming in both engines quit and the plane smashed into the water some hundred yards offshore, "with the most terrifying noise I have ever heard." Lawson, his copilot, and his navigator were hurled through the sturdy Plexiglas windshield. The bombardier was also thrown, headfirst, from his position in the nose cone. Lawson awoke from the impact still strapped into his seat under ten or fifteen feet of water. At first he thought he was dead; then he managed to unbuckle his straps and "drifted up off the seat and started to the surface."

Lawson was more or less paralyzed but his life belt and the big waves carried him to the beach. It was pouring rain. He managed to stand but his legs were numb. He put his hand to his mouth and realized that his lip had been cut clear through to the chin, "so that the skin flapped over and down." His upper teeth were bent in and, when he put his thumbs into his mouth to push them out, "they broke off in my hands." So did his bottom teeth. His navigator, Dean Davenport, came walking down the beach, took a look, and said, "God damn! You're really bashed open. Your whole face is pushed in." And that wasn't the worst of it.[30]

Doolittle, meantime, had chosen the second option—going high and bailing out when the engines started to sputter. Visibility was zero and it was dark when they started bailing out of the plane. Doolittle was the last one out; he pulled his rip cord and began floating down into he knew not what: mountain peak, river, forest, or the waiting arms of Japanese soldiers. In fact he landed in the soggy mess of a rice paddy, "in a not-too-fragrant mixture of water and 'night soil.'" He looked around, saw a light, got up, and knocked on the door of some kind of farmhouse, shouting, "*Lushu hoo megwa fugi*," which they had been taught aboard the *Hornet* by Lieutenant Commander Jurika meant, "I am an American." There was some rustling inside the house and then he heard "the sound of a bolt sliding into place. The light went out and there was dead silence," leaving Doolittle standing there in the rainy Chinese night in his stinking uniform. For this he had come more than two thousand miles.[31]

Men from the fifteen other planes were having similar experiences. One man landed in a tree and was caught, but before he tried to free himself and climb down he smoked a cigarette. When he threw away the butt he watched its orange glow descend into some unfathomable depth; turns out he dropped onto the edge of an enormous rock cliff. He decided to spend the night in the tree. Here may be the world's only example of a cigarette saving someone's life.

Peasants and farmers all over that part of China were startled to see and hear the violent crashes of the planes against their mountains and into their rice fields, and they had no idea what to make of it. Practically all of the bailed-out crews found one another next day, but *Lushu hoo megwa fugi* seemed to make no impression whatsoever on any of the Chinese. Many of the crews were rounded up by Chinese militia, who did not comprehend who they were or what they had just done. A few were robbed by Chinese bandits or guerrillas. Many were injured in the landings and, miraculously, only three were killed. Gangrene set in on

Lieutenant Lawson's leg and it had to be amputated under the most trying conditions.*

Eight of the crew members were captured by Japanese troops in China
and three of these were executed on the basis of a trumped-up document
concocted by the Japanese army after the raid and entitled "Japanese Regulations for Punishment of Enemy Air Crews." Five of the prisoners were sentenced to death but for no particular reason the sentence was commuted to
life in prison. Lieutenant William G. Farrow and Sergeant Harold A. Spatz
of *Bat Out of Hell,* the unlucky plane that had cut off the *Hornet* sailor's arm,
and Lieutenant Dean E. Hallmark of plane number 6, *Green Hornet,* were cere-
moniously marched to a cemetery where three white wooden crosses had
been set up. They were made to kneel while their arms were tied to the
crosses. Then they were blindfolded and a firing squad of six Japanese soldiers shot each in the head. When Roosevelt heard the news he announced
it in one of his fireside chats, which began with, "It is with the deepest horror . . ." The unrepentant Japanese responded with a radio broadcast of their
own: "Don't forget America you can be sure that every flier that comes here
has a special pass to hell. Rest assured that it's strictly a one-way ticket."[32]

The crew of the B-25 that had landed in Russia were greeted initially
with welcome by the Soviet army, but this treatment quickly changed as they
were shifted through higher and higher levels of that strange and brutal government. At first they were given borscht and vodka and shown American
movies, but soon they were transported to the bleak and freezing interior of
the Soviet Union, where they were put under guard in a dismal house. The
food was so poor that their gums bled and they began to lose weight and
become ill. Out of desperation—and to the horror of their warden—the
chief pilot, Edward J. "Ski" York, decided to write a letter to Stalin himself,
asking that they at least be moved to a warmer climate. To everyone's surprise they were, and the tale of their escape is right out of a movie.[33]

By some miracle the rest of Doolittle's bunch—sixty-seven pilots and
crewmen—managed to find their way into the hands of friendly Chinese
forces and were escorted in everything from junks to sedan chairs across the

*When he returned to the United States Lawson wrote the best-selling book *Thirty
Seconds Over Tokyo,* which was published in 1943 and soon made into a major motion picture.

mountains, often through Japanese-occupied territory, to Chungking, a thousand miles distant. There they got to meet Chiang Kai-shek and his famous wife, Madam Chiang,* and were given medals and then flown back to the United States.

For their part, the Japanese were furious. Emperor Hirohito himself approved orders for a punitive bloodbath against all Chinese in the areas near where the Americans had come down and were helped to safety. Accordingly, an army of 100,000 Japanese marched into the region and in a carnival of boiling vengeance turned the entire province—large as Tennessee—into an abattoir. When they were finished four months later some 250,000 Chinese civilians had been murdered, many by the most barbaric methods. One old man, a schoolteacher who had fed some of the Americans, told two Catholic priests the monstrous story of how Japanese soldiers had "killed my three sons; they killed my wife, Ansing; they set fire to my school; they burned my books; they killed my grandchildren and threw them in the well." (The schoolteacher himself escaped death only by hiding in the well with his slain grandchildren.) Another man was immolated by being wrapped in a kerosene-drenched blanket that the soldiers then ordered his wife at gunpoint to set afire.[34]

Barbaric as the Japanese reprisals were, the Doolittle raid achieved the desired effect on American morale. The first newspaper reports were sketchy and overstated the damage done, but all Americans felt that somehow Pearl Harbor and all the rest of it had been at least partially avenged. It gave Roosevelt a chance to engage in his favorite sport—tweaking newsmen. When everyone clamored to know where Doolittle's planes had come from in order to get to mainland Japan, the president, flipping his famous cigarette holder Groucho Marx–style, told them, "From Shangri-la."†

Doolittle had no sooner gotten back to Washington when he received a call from Hap Arnold to await his staff car outside his apartment. Doolittle

*Said by some to be the model for the "Dragon Lady" in Milton Caniff's comic strip *Terry and the Pirates.*

†Name of the legendary kingdom in James Hilton's novel *Lost Horizon.* Also the name of the U.S. presidential retreat in Maryland, which is now known as Camp David.

did as he was told and was astonished to find not only Arnold but General Marshall sitting in the backseat. When they drove off, Doolittle inquired where they were headed.

"We are going to the White House," Arnold said.

"What are we going to do there?" Doolittle asked.

"The president is going to give you the Medal of Honor," said Marshall.

Doolittle was shocked and began to protest that the medal "should be reserved for those who risk their lives trying to save somebody else." He continued by praising all the men who had flown the mission, then began to notice that not only was Arnold beginning to look flushed and angry but so was Marshall, who was scowling.

"I don't think I'm entitled to the Medal of Honor," Doolittle concluded, by now a little hesitant.

"I happen to think you are," Marshall said icily.

The trio rode on in stony silence while Lieutenant Colonel Doolittle blanched at the gaffe he had just made.

"The highest ranking man in Army uniform had made his decision. It was neither the time nor the place for me to argue."[35]

Chapter Twelve ★

By the spring of 1942 the Germans seemed poised on the edge of victory in their war against the vast Soviet Union. Their attack the previous summer, before America entered the war, had left them a thousand miles inside Soviet borders, poised at the gates of its most important cities, Moscow, Leningrad, and Stalingrad. Then the Russian resistance stiffened and, more ominiously, the Russian winter closed in, just as it had for Napoleon a century and a half earlier. But with springtime the thaw arrived, and the Germans again began their relentless attacks. The Roosevelt administration had quickly recognized the danger and pledged to Stalin a billion dollars in Lend-Lease aid, a stupendous sum for the times. American tanks, warplanes, clothing, guns, and ammunition were pouring into ports in northwest Russia, but would it be enough and in time?

The Nazi armies steadily made progress against the more poorly equipped, trained, and led Soviets. They swept into the town of Tula, birthplace of the revered Russian novelist Leo Tolstoy, entered his shrine, flung the original manuscripts of such celebrated novels as *War and Peace* to the winds and snow, and burned his furniture for heating fuel; they treated likewise the home of the immortal composer Tchaikovsky, near Moscow. Few observers at the time gave the Russians much chance against Hitler's powerful armies, and the great fear of the time was that if the Soviets were defeated, those same German armies would be free to turn on the Allied forces, prin-cipally Great Britain, then fighting for its life in the North African deserts.[1]

By late spring of '42 General Rommel had captured the British strong-hold of Tobruk, in Libya, took 25,000 Allied prisoners and an immense amount of supplies, and pushed the British army back into Egypt. It began to appear that the British might not be able to hold the Middle East, with all its crucial oil reserves, nor for that matter India itself, which the Japa-nese army was also pushing toward from the east. All in all, it had been an abominable year and prospects looked bleak.

By March of 1942, the Americans and British had concluded an agreement: the United States would assume responsibility for driving the Japanese out of the Pacific while the British would take on the Germans and Italians in the Middle East and defend the Mediterranean and the Indian Ocean. Both would continue fighting the Germans on the Atlantic and cooperate in tak-ing the French North African colonies from the Vichy French to (possi-bly) use as a launching pad for operations against Italy. The Americans were also champing at the bit to cross the English Channel, drive the Germans from France, and begin a thrust against Germany itself. (They were wisely talked out of this by Churchill, who warned that such a premature inva-sion would cause the Channel "to run red with blood.")

These were bold commitments since, with exception of the pitiful American soldiers and marines hanging on in Corregidor, the Japanese had everywhere conquered the Pacific beyond their wildest dreams and were knocking at the door of Australia itself. As well, Rommel was still driving for the Suez Canal and the Japanese had by now sunk every decent war-ship the British had in the Indian Ocean. Moreover, every month German U-boats were sending hundred of thousands of tons of Allied shipping to the bottom of both the Atlantic and the Gulf of Mexico and there seemed to be no way to stop them. For their part, the Japanese had persuaded themselves that they were invincible and quickly succumbed to what was afterward called, by the Japanese themselves, "Victory Disease," the manifestation of which was to expand and speed up their conquests be-yond what they could prudently handle.

The Americans had so far to content themselves with small raids against the Japanese, such as the one Doolittle had conducted, as well as a series of hit-and-run carrier strikes against Japanese-held islands in the Marshalls chain as well as the areas around Australia. With the exception of Doolittle's raid, these were successful only inasmuch as they gave the navy pilots valuable on-the-job training and because no American carriers were lost. The Japanese considered these raids of no more importance than being attacked by gnats, but gnats could be obnoxious and they resolved to eliminate them.

To that end, in May 1942, the Japanese decided to expand their empire even further to the small island of Tulagi in the Solomon chain, and to Port Moresby, on the southern tip of New Guinea, in order to extend their mastery of the air over the vast Coral Sea and presumably give them protection from any aerial bombing or surface-ship attacks from the new and growing American presence in Australia. It would also give them a launching point for the further conquest of eastern Pacific island chains including Fiji, Samoa, New Caledonia, and the New Hebrides. Once accomplished, this would completely isolate Australia and New Zealand from further American support or interference. It would also be the beginning of the Japanese military's unraveling.

The Doolittle raid, meanwhile, was having consequences in Japan far beyond its modest intentions. Aside from achieving the desired boost to American morale and damaging some Japanese facilities, the raid created near panic among top Japanese military officers, particularly in the navy, since it was quickly learned that the planes had been launched from aircraft carriers and thus had been their responsibility. Immediately after the raid the Japanese, like a disturbed colony of ants, sent practically every plane and warship in their fleet out looking for the American task force, but of course Halsey was far away by then. Importantly, all these Japanese ships generated a huge amount of radio chatter and American radio-intercept stations from Australia to the Aleutians, from Midway Island to Hawaii, plucked thousands of signals out of the air and quickly began to piece together the missing parts of the top-secret Japanese naval code puzzle.

It will be remembered that at the time of Pearl Harbor Lieutenant Commander Rochefort and his team of cryptologists back in Honolulu could read less than 10 percent of the Japanese code; a week after Doolittle's raid they were reading nearly half of it, and by June they were reading almost all of it. This was an incredible stroke of good luck as well as masterful work by the code breakers, for they soon divined that the Japanese were planning a big naval operation somewhere in the mid-Pacific. Reading the code, however, did not mean reading Japanese intentions; they had a code within their code, as all codes do, which told what it actually meant, and this would prove far more perplexing.

Here manifested the second unintended consequence of Doolittle's raid. Admiral Yamamoto had been the instigator of this big mid-Pacific operation in order to lure the remains of the U.S. fleet into a trap where he could annihilate it thoroughly. Yamamoto's naval colleagues and superiors on the Naval General Staff, however, were not warm to the notion. They felt the Japanese navy would be better employed supporting the continuing Southward Movement, gobbling up more territory, probably even Australia. After the Doolittle business, however, these naysayers either changed their minds or kept their counsel. The Japanese homeland had been attacked and Yamamoto's scheme suddenly made sense: to extend the defensive ring around Japan thousands of miles farther northeast toward Hawaii—from whence the U.S. carriers had come and from where they could better monitor and deflect U.S. naval movements. To accomplish this, they would need to capture the important American fighter-bomber, air reconnaissance, and naval outpost of Midway Island, stuck way out in the central Pacific, too close for comfort and a thorn in the side for Japan.

Equally important, the Japanese at the same time were determined to continue their expansion in the South Pacific and, to that end, dispatched three of their aircraft carriers to support an invasion of southern New Guinea—almost within shouting distance of the north Australian coast as well as a series of Australian-controlled islands in the Solomon chain just to the eastward, including one whose name would soon become infamous, Guadalcanal.

Now that they were able to read much of the Japanese code, the U.S. Pacific Fleet headquarters in Pearl Harbor quickly formed a picture of the expanded Southward Movement: a Japanese fleet built around the three carriers, two large and one small, guarding a flotilla of troop transports for the invasions. In other circumstances this precious information would have been a godsend, but at the moment the U.S. Navy did not have enough available carriers in the Pacific to ensure superiority against the Japanese force now headed south. Of the five now on hand, *Saratoga* was laid up in a West Coast shipyard after being torpedoed and almost sunk a month earlier. Halsey's task force, including the *Enterprise* and the *Hornet,* was still making its way back across the Pacific following the Doolittle raid, and it would have to be replenished before putting to sea again. That left only the *Yorktown,* already operating in the Coral Sea, and the *Lexington,* which was ready and waiting at Pearl. Admiral Nimitz decided to send these two anyway, against a superior Japanese fleet, with hopes that surprise would be a deciding factor. On May 1,1942, the two U.S. task forces rendezvoused in the Coral Sea.

The Coral Sea, described here by the official naval historian Dr. Samuel Eliot Morison, who sailed it, "is one of the most beautiful bodies of water in the world. Typhoons pass it by; the southeast trades blow fresh across the surface almost the entire year—raising whitecaps from the lee shores of the islands, that build up into a regular, gentle swell that crashes on the Great Barrier Reef in a 1,500-mile line of white foam. There is no winter, only a summer that is never too hot." He goes on to describe the various island and island groups: "Here the interplay of sunlight, pure air and transparent water may be seen at its loveliest, peacock-hued shoals over the coral gardens break off abruptly from an emerald fringe into deeps of brilliant amethyst."[2] And here, he could have added, among all that beauty, two large naval fleets were on a collision course, and many men would die violent deaths and large ships would go down to the deeps.

On May 3, 1942, a Japanese invasion force of fourteen troop transports left the big naval base at Rabaul at the northern end of the Solomon Island chain and headed south to invade Port Moresby and capture its airstrip on the southeastern tip of New Guinea, only a few hundred miles from the Australian coast. Protecting the troop transports were the three carriers, eight cruisers, and twelve destroyers under Vice Admiral Takeo Takagi. To meet this force and stop the invasion of eastern New Guinea, Rear Admiral

Frank Jack Fletcher had sailed his task force, built around *Lexington* and *Yorktown,* into the sparkling emerald waters of the Coral Sea.

Neither commander was aware of the presence of the other. Fletcher had been receiving intelligence reports from William Friedman's code-breaking operation at Pearl Harbor, giving the size and intentions of the Japanese force but no precise location for it. For his part Takagi had no idea that there were any American warships in the Coral Sea at all, until on May 3 the newly captured island of Tulagi was bombed by U.S. planes that could only have come from a carrier. Accordingly, he barreled south-ward at full steam to do battle. What ensued could be described as a comedy of errors if the stakes had not been so high and the consequences so deadly.

First, Takagi's fleet was sailing under protection of a weather front, which prevented him from being spotted either from Fletcher's planes or by land-based aircraft from Australia. By the time Takagi pulled out of the front, Fletcher's search planes had been recalled just a few miles from the Japanese force and any chance for a surprise strike was lost. Likewise, Takagi had launched no search planes at all; if he had he likely would have caught Fletcher's carriers refueling, a prime opportunity for attack. As night closed in over the Coral Sea the two opposing fleets lay a mere sev-enty miles from each other, though neither knew it at the time.

Next day, May 7, Takagi finally sent out search planes, which spot-ted the big U.S. Navy fleet oiler *Neosho* and her escort, the destroyer *Sims,* which had been detached from Fletcher's group and ordered to rendez-vous later at a prearranged position much farther south. However, the Japanese search planes radioed back that they had located an "American aircraft carrier and a cruiser" and within the hour Takagi had launched nearly seventy planes to deal with this grand prize.

First to be struck was the destroyer (reported as a cruiser) *Sims,* which exploded with a terrific roar and was "lifted ten to fifteen feet out of the water" after being hit by three 500-pound bombs. Only fifteen out of her crew of two hundred and fifty were rescued. After the *Neosho* (reported as a carrier) was similarly hit, burning and listing, the captain ordered, "Prepare to abandon ship," at which point scores of sailors, horrified by what had just happened to the *Sims,* leaped into the sea without further orders; many of them were hauled back aboard but others drifted away in life rafts.* Not only that but in the confusion the *Neosho*'s nervous navigator, trying to plot the ship's position, reported the coordinates incorrectly by some hundreds of miles, which made eventual rescue problematic.

Meantime, all kinds of strange things were happening to Fletcher's task force. For one, a U.S. cruiser was attacked by several high-flying bombers, which, maddeningly, turned out to be American B-17s from a U.S. air base in Australia under MacArthur's command. For another, a search-plane pilot radioed back that he had just spotted a Japanese fleet of "two carriers and two heavy cruisers," proving yet again that misidentification of ships was not confined to the Japanese navy. Fletcher promptly launched nearly a hundred planes at this fat and seductive target, only to discover when the search plane returned that the pilot had meant to communicate that he had seen only "two heavy cruisers and two destroyers."[†3]

Fletcher's search planes, however, did come upon a genuine prize a while later, the Japanese light carrier *Shoto,* which was escorting the invasion transport ships. Ninety-three American planes jumped on her and in less than twenty minutes she sunk to the bottom of the Coral Sea. Both the *Yorktown* and *Lexington* broadcast the action over their public address systems so that thousands of anxious sailors could hear the battle. Because of radio static and the somewhat frenetic squawking among ninety-three pilots, most of the conversations were garbled; then, suddenly, the voice of Lieutenant Commander Robert E. Dixon came through loud and clear with these famous words: "Scratch one flattop! Dixon to carrier! Scratch one flattop!" One can imagine the cheering.

Five months to the day since the Japanese had bombed Pearl Harbor, the *Shoto* became the first and only major Japanese warship sunk so far. For Admiral Takagi it was a mortifying development. He immediately

---

*Sixty-four of the sixty-eight sailors who had jumped into the life rafts perished after a nightmare of ten days adrift in the Coral Sea. It caused the navy to rethink its entire practice of survival-at-sea tactics.

†Even this proved to be in error, for when the American planes got there all they found were two antiquated Japanese cruisers of World War I vintage and a couple of rickety gunboats.

ordered the troop transports to turn back from harm's way until the Americans could be cleared from the Coral Sea—thus the invasion of Port Moresby, New Guinea, was postponed; though Takagi could not know it at the time, the postponement would be permanent.

That afternoon rain squalls and heavy weather closed in around both fleets but Takagi was determined to cripple or sink the American carriers if possible. Late that afternoon he sent off twenty-eight planes, which, owing to U.S. radar, were picked up and thwarted by a squadron of U.S. Navy Wildcats from the *Lexington* and *Yorktown.* The Wildcats shot down nine of them, at a cost of two of their own. The dogfights were so confused that at one point a squadron of six Japanese planes actually tried to land on the *Yorktown,* thinking it was one of their own carriers; they were ignominiously chased off with the loss of one plane. Of the remaining Japanese planes, eleven crashed into the ocean trying to land on their carriers, that is, after they finally found them in the dark. Thus, out of the original flight of twenty-eight, only seven returned safely.

At dawn next morning both Takagi and Fletcher, each still itching for a fight, sent out search planes. Fletcher had evened the odds with the sinking of the *Shoto,* but he knew there were still two Japanese carriers to be reckoned with. These were the *Zuikaku* and the *Shokaku,* both large, modern ships, which had taken part in the Pearl Harbor attack. What ensued was the first major battle in naval history where the opposing ships were never in sight of one another.

Half an hour before sunrise, May 8, Fletcher's task force began to launch planes (eighty-four). So did the Japanese (seventy). They found each other's ships at almost precisely the same time, actually passing by each other in the air from opposite directions. The Americans reached the position of the *Zuikaku* and *Shokaku* about a hundred and seventy miles distant, just before ten-thirty. Their attack was not a spectacular success, as of the day before. The U.S. torpedo bombers failed to damage a single target; either the torpedoes failed, as usual, to explode or, as one Japanese aboard stated later, they were so slow that "we could turn and run away from them."[4] The dive-bombers faired a little better, scoring two hits on the *Shokaku,* which did not cripple her but, luckily, set some fires and put her plane-recovery operations out of business. However, she was still able to launch, and after putting her remaining planes into the air to land on the *Zuikaku,* the *Shokaku* was ordered to retire northward out of the battle area. *Zuikaku* escaped damage altogether by sailing into a fierce thunderstorm. For this the American forces sacrificed forty-seven planes and their pilots.

The Japanese were more successful. In the brilliant morning sun they spotted the *Lexington* cruising along in a light breeze, small whitecaps dancing around her. Lady *Lex'*s fighter control had picked up the approaching Japanese planes on its radar twenty minutes earlier but that was not time enough for them to launch enough Wildcat fighters—the time necessary for them to gain altitude—to blunt the Japanese assault, which came in quickly and straight out of the sun. Lady *Lex,* at 40,000 tons, was slow to the helm and unable to dodge two of the eleven torpedoes launched by the Japanese planes, which hit her portside. Men below were so grotesquely scorched by the conflagration that followed that their "skin [was] literally dripping from their bodies." Then the dive-bombers began to come in.

Meantime, the *Yorktown,* a dozen miles astern, was enduring the same treatment. Being a lighter and more agile ship she was able to dodge the torpedoes but took an 800-pound bomb near the conning island, which tore through the flight deck, the hangar deck, and the galley before finally exploding in the ship's soda fountain. Sixty-six sailors were killed or wounded by this blast. It was all over in less than fifteen minutes and the exultant Japanese pilots headed home, reporting that they had sunk *two* U.S. aircraft carriers. This erroneous information would lead to much trouble later on for Admiral Yamamoto.

Lexington, meantime, though severely crippled, had managed to shore up her damages, was making good speed, and seemed destined to fight another day when, at 12:45 P.M., a huge explosion ripped through her innards. The ship shuddered so violently that the captain thought they had been attacked by a submarine; instead it was aviation gasoline vapors, which had been ignited by a generator belowdecks that someone had thoughtlessly left running. Smoke billowed from all vents and many men below were killed. Even this did not sink her, and the Lady continued on at twenty-five knots, billowing enormous columns of white, black, gray, and yellow smoke from every pore while her crew frantically fought the raging fires below.

In the middle of all this came a remarkable and heart-wrenching conversation between the *Yorktown*'s radio room and one of the pilots, Commander William B. Ault, who had led the dive-bombing strike on the *Shokaku*. Both he and his radioman had been wounded by antiaircraft fire; his plane was shot up, losing altitude, and almost empty of fuel, and he was trying to find somewhere, anywhere, to put it down.

Radioman: "Nearest land is over 200 miles away."

Ault: "We would never make it."

Radioman: "You are on your own, good luck."

Ault: "Please relay to *Lexington*. We got one 1,000 pound bomb hit on a flattop. We have both reported 2 or 3 times. (a pause) Enemy fighters. Am changing course North. Let me know if you pick me up."

Radioman: "Roger. You are on your own. I will relay your message. Good luck."

Ault: "OK, so long people. We've got a 1,000 pound hit on the flattop!"[5]

Commander Ault was never heard from again. But if anyone, Japanese, Nazi, or otherwise, including a small cranky few in the United States itself, ever thought the American fighting man was soft, that exchange should have set them straight,

Lady *Lex* was fighting a losing battle against the great fires that raged within her. Later in the afternoon two more stupendous internal explosions rocked her and the commanding admiral Aubrey Fitch phoned Captain Frederick Sherman on the bridge. "Well, Ted, let's get the men off." It was a sad day indeed for *Lexington*'s crew, many of whom had been with her since she had been commissioned in 1927. As Dr. Morison points out, "This happy ship was loved as few ships have been before or since." The abandonment was orderly and businesslike, as opposed to the panic aboard the oiler *Neosho* the day before. The thousands of sailors took off their shoes and lined them neatly on the deck; neatest of all were the shoes of the company of marines aboard.* They either jumped or climbed down ropes suspended from the

*Many of those several thousand men last in line regretted removing their shoes; the decks were becoming intolerably hot from the belowdecks fires and many feet were scorched.

five-story-high flight deck. The ship's pay officer even tried to take his records with him, as well as hundreds of thousands of dollars in the purser's safe. The captain's dog Wags was rescued along with everyone else not killed in the attack. Men waiting their turn to go overboard dug generously into portions of ice cream from the ship's store. Last to go was Captain Sherman, who went hand over hand down a lifeline to a waiting destroyer.[6]

Whaleboats from the destroyer squadrons fished the men out of the ocean; by sunset the great aircraft carrier was dead in the water, deserted and abandoned, still belching smoke and flames. As everyone watched choked with emotion, many with tears in their eyes, a destroyer ordered by Captain Sherman to finish off the *Lady* did so by firing four torpedoes at close range. Unlike most, these hit home and the *Lexington* quickly began to settle by the stern. Within minutes, as darkness closed over the Coral Sea, she slipped beneath the waves into fifteen thousand feet of water.

Fletcher now sailed his one remaining carrier, *Yorktown,* east and then north, away from the Japanese, as he had received a message from Nimitz back in Pearl to come home quick; something very nasty was brewing in the mid-Pacific. Nimitz sent the same message to Halsey, commanding the *Enterprise* and the *Hornet,* whose task force was finally racing south to help Fletcher after reprovisioning in Hawaii.

The Coral Sea Battle had cost the Americans one large aircraft carrier, an oiler, and a destroyer; sixty-six airplanes and 547 men killed; as well as serious damage to the *Yorktown.* The Japanese lost a light carrier, 1,047 sailors and airmen killed, and seventy-seven airplanes, but they had caused the *Lexington* to be scuttled and believed they had sunk *Yorktown* too, which then led them to conclude that there were probably only two U.S. carriers left in the Pacific (since they also believed that they had sunk the *Saratoga* by submarine attack a month earlier). This misinformation would figure critically in their calculations for the impending Midway battle.

Not only that but the American bombing of the *Shokaku* was so severe that it would take months to repair it, and the *Zuikaku* had lost so many pilots and planes that, like *Shokaku,* it would have to sit out the Battle of Midway. With the destruction of the *Lexington* the Japanese had won a tactical victory; strategically, however, they had lost the battle, as they would soon find out.

As in so much of war from time immemorial, ramifications of the Coral Sea Battle were not apparent to either side at the time; both publicly announced a great victory, but privately the U.S. Navy was not well pleased at having one of its few Pacific aircraft carriers resting at the bottom of the ocean. And there was worse news to come. General Wainwright and his 15,000 on Corregidor were on their last legs, facing an army that now numbered 250,000 Japanese, and everybody understood that aside from prayers there was nothing anyone could do to help them.

Immediately after the fall of Bataan, General Homma turned his attentions to reducing Corregidor with relentless air and artillery bombardments. He could not claim victory in the Philippines to Imperial Headquarters in Tokyo until he had captured the big rock island at the entrance to Manila Bay and also caused the surrender of the remaining U.S.-Filipino forces operating in the vast islands south of Luzon. This of course was easier said than done, and was made all the more annoying by the pressure exerted by Tokyo for Homma to wrap it up.

With Bataan now in his hands, Homma lined up more than one hundred huge artillery pieces at the peninsula's tip and other strategic points and began an around-the-clock bombardment of Corregidor's three-mile length.* Not only that but with beefed-up airpower newly provided by Tokyo, Homma ordered round-the-clock aerial bombing too. This caused many American soldiers, sailors, and marines to adopt a molelike existence underground; for those manning the many artillery and antiaircraft batteries, this was not possible, so they just stood outside and took it and fired back whenever they could. One antiaircraft battery captain described it this way: "The bombers come over; we see them drop their bombs—all the while we are tracking them with our instruments . . . the bombs con-

---

*What this meant was that, more or less, every 150 feet of Corregidor land had at least one large-caliber Japanese artillery piece firing on it nonstop, day and night.

tinue downward on their way towards us. We open fire. In about 15 seconds our guns are pointing as nearly straight up as they can. We cease firing. The bombs whistle; we duck for a few seconds while the bombs burst, and pop up again to engage the next flight. When fighters come in one after the other we stay up while the bombs hit all around us."[7]

The Japanese artillery bombardment was horrific and certainly frightened the men more than the aerial bombing because of its accuracy. It had begun shortly after the fall of Bataan and for the next month increased in fury until, by May 1, the three-mile-long island received more than 3,600 shells during a five-hour period from the behemoth 240mm guns alone.* Their shells were so large that men could actually follow them with their eyes and watch the flickering shadows they cast on the ground. Slowly but inexorably the Rock began to crumble. All aboveground buildings were destroyed. Phone lines were cut and transportation was practically nonexistent. Trees were flattened and shrubbery blown to smithereens. It was hauntingly reminiscent of the sort of destruction seen during the First World War in Flanders and northern France, a kind of moonscape of craters and wreckage for miles around. Beach defenses were shattered. At one point a direct hit by a large Japanese gun tossed a ten-ton American rifled artillery piece hundreds of yards into the air, until it finally landed in the middle of the golf course; another was blown into the ocean. All wildlife disappeared or went below ground; the island's power plant came in for particular attention and was out of order most of the time, causing surgeons in the tunnel to operate by flashlight and fire-control directors to operate not at all.

The most maddening thing was that there was not much the Americans could do about it. All of their larger guns were fixed—the "concrete artillery," was what old-timers called it. As in Singapore, the biggest guns, the ones with the range and power to inflict serious damage, all pointed out to sea, while the Japanese could move their guns around and hide them in

*These enormous weapons fired a shell weighing in excess of 800 pounds and could destroy a city block when exploded. Wainwright himself estimated that on May 1 the Japanese had hit Corregidor with 1,800,000 pounds of explosive shells.

foliage. Their smokeless powder made them all the more elusive while the U.S. guns were easy to spot. At one point a huge balloon began appearing every day over Bataan, carrying a basket of Japanese artillery observers to pinpoint their prey and adjust fire. One by one, the American batteries and searchlight sections were silenced.

By most accounts the Malinta Tunnel was a hellish place, almost always choked with dust and fumes and otherwise humid and vermin infested; it was noisy from motor traffic and diesel generators, smelly from thousands of unwashed bodies, and maddeningly illuminated day and night from long bluish-hued lights that laced its ceilings. Flies and mosquitoes were rampant; the latrines were horrid, even when they worked. At least it was bombproof, which was good fortune since it was now difficult even for a rat to survive on the surface for any length of time. With Bataan now lost, every man on the island knew he was doomed; the "great naval relief convoy" had proved to be a cruel hoax. There was food enough for only about two months, even on half-rations, and the artillery and antiaircraft batteries were being destroyed at an alarming rate.

Though they knew all this, the men trudged on, joking and cursing darkly among themselves and trying to make the best, as soldiers will do, until this became one of the proud moments in American history: one afternoon, as General Wainwright looked on, a huge Japanese artillery shell exploded on the parade grounds near the ten-story-tall flagpole that flew an enormous American flag. "A fragment from the bomb cut the halyard and 'Old Glory' slowly, terribly, began to descend down the pole as if drawn by some ghostly and prophetic hand." But before it touched the ground three men, a captain, a sergeant, and a Filipino civilian, raced out in the middle of the bombardment and gathered it up, fixed the halyard, and raised the flag again smartly to the top. For this Wainwright awarded each of them the Silver Star.[8]

A more prudent Japanese military would simply have conserved lives and property and starved the Americans out, since they had a pretty fair notion of how long the Corregidor foodstuffs would last. (After all, where would they be going?) But Tokyo wasn't interested in anymore waiting; it wanted victory and wanted it now, one reason being that until the big guns of

Corregidor could be silenced, the Japanese would be denied the use of Manila Bay and its harbor,* said to be the finest and most protected in the Far East. So nothing was left to Homma but to attack Corregidor by seaward invasion, a plan he knew would be costly. Nevertheless, he ordered it done.

A problem most critical to survival on Corregidor was drinking water, and the prospects were looking bleak. Before the war, water was shipped in from the mainland, but of course that was no more. The island had a number of deep wells but these were all driven by diesel pumps and diesel fuel was running perilously low due to heavy use of generators needed to provide power to all the guns and artillery. By early May '42, engineers estimated that there was scarcely a week's supply of diesel fuel; after that, no water. Each man was already reduced to a single canteen per day, scarcely enough "for men who had to do heavy physical work in the open on a sun-baked tropical island where the temperature soared up to 100 degrees during midday. The lack of water was not only a major inconvenience but a serious threat to health."[9]

Yet before water could become the surrender-forcing issue, Homma's people launched their attack. On May 4, the Japanese ratcheted up their bombardment yet again, which even those on the Rock believed was impossible. Before that day was out some sixteen thousand shells had landed on Corregidor with such intensity that the explosions seemed almost a continuous roar. Many were concerned that the tunnel itself, shaking as in an earthquake, would collapse and kill them all.[†] During the afternoon observers reported seeing a number of Japanese landing barges along the Bataan coast. As a result of the stupendous bombardment during the past several days, morale had plummeted and "men were living on nerve alone."

*Almost all of these guns were of World War I vintage, or even earlier, but they were large and powerful and certainly intimidated Japanese ships that might want to try and enter the bay.
†This was no idle fear. One smaller tunnel not far away from Malinta had done just that a few days earlier, burying alive forty-six men, who were suffocated to death.

The atmosphere in the tunnel was described as "morgue-like gloom," and a captain wrote of "a feeling of doom, mingled with wonder." Even Wainwright's resolve was wavering; he reported by cable to Marshall in Washington that the "situation here is fast becoming desperate. I estimate that we have something less than an even chance to beat off an assault." On second thought, "wavering resolve" might be too strong an expression; more likely he was just being realistic.[10] In a later message to the president, Wainwright told him, "There is a limit to human endurance, and that limit has long since been past [sic]."

The night of May 4, following yet another exceptional barrage, the Japanese launched two thousand men in assault boats and barges to finish off Corregidor. This was to be only the first wave of a continuous ferrying operation until they had superiority over the Americans. But the Japanese had not taken into account the strong currents that rushed between the Rock and the tip of Bataan and they landed more than a mile away from their intended destination at the thin tip of Corregidor's tail and, as luck had it, right into the positions of the First Marine Battalion, which mowed them down with ferocious machine-gun fire and sank or damaged most of the barges and boats. Of the original two thousand, only six hundred Japanese survived to crawl across the beaches.

As it turned out that was enough. With communications yet again cut by artillery fire, conflicting and erroneous reports came in about other Japanese landings. Fierce firefights ensued; foxholes and trenches were overrun and artillery batteries and machine-gun positions were taken. Before the sun rose Japanese tanks could be heard moving off the beaches toward the American lines. There was no shortage of heroism that night, or the next morning, either. Of the 15,000 U.S. forces on Corregidor, only 3,600 were trained combat troops; the rest were a grab bag of command and support personnel, doctors and nurses, cooks and bottle washers, communications and finance people, engineer troops and civilians left over from the Philippine government. To make it all the more difficult, those 3,600 had to protect nearly six miles of beaches, not knowing where the Japanese would actually land.

All through the night beneath a brilliant tropic moon there was confused and desperate fighting as the Japanese slowly clawed their way up the heights toward the Malinta Tunnel. It was a battle of small arms: rifles, bayonets, knives, rocks, even fists and choking hands. Against the tanks, the Americans had only improvised Molotov cocktails—bottles filled with gasoline or oil and lit with a paper or cloth fuse.

As dawn broke on May 5, 1942, more Japanese were seen to be arriving on the landing barges, but their forward progress toward the tunnel had been stopped at a lesser eminence called Water Tank Hill. There, as the heat rose, men on both sides fought and died in a bloodthirsty battle that lasted all morning, but the Japanese still had not broken through. While General Homma paced nervously at his command post at the tip of Bataan and worried that his assault would end in failure, up in the tunnel Wainwright made a fateful decision.

Concerned that a breakthrough would expose the thousands of badly wounded soldiers in the tunnel to a Japanese massacre and aware that, even if the water situation had not been critical, there was no way they could hold out against the now quarter-million-man Japanese army in the Philippines, which could land its troops at will, he decided on a course of action that was as repugnant to him as it was sensible. He would surrender.

"Tell the Nips we'll cease firing at noon," Wainwright informed his commanders. As the news spread through the tunnel many men burst into tears and the radio operator who had faithfully kept up communications with Washington through the Pacific network tapped out his home address in Brooklyn, then signed off with his final message: "Tell Mother how you heard from me."

The men fought right up until the end. Major William "Wild Bill" Massello's last remaining twelve-inch mortar was now manned by an assortment of motorpool personnel, cooks, and clerks after one regular gun crew after another had been killed or wounded. The gun pit had become a shambles of blown-up or collapsed concrete, torn bodies, and burning ammunition cases. Still they kept on firing the twenty-five-year-old piece, raining destruction on the Japanese invasion forces. Major Massello himself remained in the gun pit, directing fire; at one point, after hearing a rumor of the impending surrender, he ordered the telephone to be ripped from the wall so as not to receive such a detestable order.

Determined to fight it out, Massello kept up a steady fire until he, too, was put out of commission with an arm almost severed and a leg split completely open by a Japanese shell. Nevertheless, he remained to direct the action from a stretcher until the weapon's breechblock froze and it fell silent. "The old mortar had finally quit on us," Massello remembered, "but it had lasted long enough to be the last big gun on Corregidor to fire on the enemy."[11]

At noon, an American colonel and his aide, accompanied by a bugler, went out from the tunnel through the fierce Japanese shellfire to the big flagpole on the parade ground and, while the bugler played taps, hauled down Old Glory and ran up a white bedsheet. Soon white flags began appearing all over the island, but the Japanese ignored this universal signal of surrender and continued their shelling with unabated fury. After more than an hour of this, Wainwright sent out two officers to find the Japanese commander and ask for a truce. When they found him, the Japanese stated that only Wainwright himself was acceptable to conduct the surrender. It was past two in the afternoon when Wainwright finally reached the Japanese command post; he was treated rudely by the Japanese colonel who received him but was soon ferried off Corregidor to Bataan for a meeting with General Homma.

Once on Bataan Wainwright and his party were driven a few miles north to a "dingy white house not far from the beach," where they were given some water to drink, then made to line up in the yard for the benefit of Japanese cameramen and newsreel photographers. Presently General Homma arrived, "dramatically, in a beautiful shiny Cadillac, accompanied by three overdressed aides." The most striking impression Wainwright and the Americans recalled was Homma's size. "He stood nearly six feet tall and must have weighed close to two hundred pounds," Wainwright remembered. "He stood there for a moment, giving us a look of bored contempt," then motioned for the Americans to follow him to the porch of the house.[12]

Wainwright had prepared a formal document surrendering Corregidor and its small outlying forts, but Homma angrily rejected it, telling Wainwright he must surrender all U.S. forces in the Philippine Islands. (There were some 50,000 of these, posted in islands farther south.) Wainwright replied that he no longer commanded those men, that they were under the command of General William F. Sharp on Mindanao. At this, Homma became livid and, calling Wainwright a liar, informed him that unless and until all troops were surrendered, he considered the battle still on. Wainwright knew what this meant; all those defenseless thousands on Corregidor, who by now had destroyed their own weapons, would face the same fate as had the helpless civilians of Nanking.

Homma rose up brusquely and returned to his shiny Cadillac while Wainwright asked a Japanese colonel what they should do now. "We will take you and your party back to Corregidor and then you can do what you damn please," the Japanese spat, and told Wainwright that if he still wanted to surrender, he must now do so to the Japanese officer commanding the troops on Corregidor. Returning to the Rock, Wainwright was shocked to find lines of Japanese infantry blocking both entrances to the Malinta Tunnel. There was no question of escape or further fighting, and no question in Wainwright's mind of what he must do next. He found a Japanese colonel and surrendered the entire Philippines.

MacArthur's reaction to Wainwright's capitulation was both curious and strange. Even though he knew of the critical water situation and the heavy odds against Wainwright's force, he suggested to General Marshall in a cablegram that Wainwright must have become "unbalanced" by all the strain. Coming on the same day that the *Lexington* was sent to the bottom of the Coral Sea, the news for the first half of 1942 was uniformly bad for the Allies, but most Americans still did not lose cheer. The newspaper and radio media in those days were quite different than they are today. What naysaying there was, was generally confined to squabbles between political parties or general grousing over conflicting rules and regulations among the many war-related federal agencies. Victories were often touted when the results were murky and defeats were turned into victories in the press or kept out of it entirely by censorship. Still it was impossible for the media to deny the losses of the Pacific islands and the Philippines, nor the strained situation in the Middle East and Mediterranean and the awful plight of the Russians, besieged at the gates of their largest cities. As well, on the

American East Coast the tragedy of merchant shipping continued daily, visible from the beaches from Texas to New England. Nevertheless, Americans are an optimistic people and seemed to view the war in the way a football fan might assess the situation when his team is thirty points behind in the first quarter: there are still three more quarters left to play.

In schools public and private across the land students recited the Pledge of Allegiance each morning and prayed for American victory, sang patriotic songs and plotted with pins on maps the battles for the Pacific islands with unpronounceable names. Many looked forward to becoming old enough to join the armed forces while some of the girls planned to become nurses, or at least to wrap Red Cross bandages or perform other useful services. Within a few years there were more than 200,000 in the various women's service auxiliaries and many more in the Red Cross. College sports suffered dramatically as the draft and enlistments dwindled the numbers of available players. As in all bureaucracy, some colleges soon found a way to capitalize on this situation: the military services, in particular the navy, had set up officer training programs at a few universities, and standout football players from various colleges were actively recruited to participate—provided they would play sports. Thus colleges like Duke became football powerhouses during the war.

The tempo of total war on a nationwide footing seemed to increase by the hour. Millions began planting Victory Gardens and donated to the incessant rubber and scrap-metal drives. Entire cities were transformed forever by an influx of workers in war-related industries. More than a hundred military training bases and camps were established, most of them in the South. Shipyards sprang up in every city or town with a harbor, especially along the Gulf Coast, which had never before turned out a serious oceangoing vessel.

The shipbuilding industry nearly doubled the population of Mobile, Alabama, within a few months, to more than 100,000. This of course put impossible strains on the infrastructure: the city's main public high school, for example, completed a decade and a half earlier to educate several thousand students, suddenly found itself with twice the planned number. There was such scant housing available that workers lived in tar-paper shacks on vacant lots or, if they were lucky enough to find a boardinghouse, shared so-called shift rooms, named for the round-the-clock work schedule.

For want of alternatives, mothers working Rosie-the-Riveter shifts after school hours often dumped their children in what had become twenty-four-hour-a-day movie theaters. The children, often bored by watching eight hours of the same movies, frequently became rowdy and vandalized the premises, causing police to become overworked as well. A Mobile County truant officer with the wonderful name of Miss Bessie Rencher* reported that on any given day at least a third of the students were absent from classes.

With all the excitement, many young women in the forty-eight states, some barely in their teens, strayed into a life of prostitution, or at least semi-prostitution, hanging around bus stations, ports, and rail terminals; what with the millions of young servicemen with money in their pockets passing through all over the country, they earned themselves the name Victory Girls. And with the large numbers of blacks flocking into the war workforce, racial tensions heightened and often spilled over into sometimes deadly race riots. These and similar episodes were not only common but prevalent in many towns and cities across America as the nation adjusted, or at least tried to adjust, to life during wartime.

There were, of course, some grousers—mostly die-hard anti-Semites and British-hating American Irish radicals, as well as antiwar religious sects such as Quakers and Seventh Day Adventists, who continued to question and even disparage the war aims, but they were roundly told to shut up in publications ranging from *The Nation* to the *New York Times*. Roosevelt himself pooh-poohed them as "defeatists" and suggested that they constituted a pro-Axis fifth column.

By mid-1942 America and her allies were badly in need of a lift, and they were soon to get one. In fact, a bright new sun was rising to shine on the free world, or what was then left of it. It would certainly not shine without further peril, misery, and sorrow, but shine it would, very suddenly, near a remote speck of land in the mid–Pacific Ocean called Midway Island.

---

*The author grew up in Mobile and though the war was finished by then, Miss Bessie Rencher was not; she stayed on as truant officer for many more years, patrolling known hangouts of delinquents and striking a note of fear, even terror, in the hearts of layabouts.

★ Chapter Thirteen

By early May 1942, Admiral Chester Nimitz knew he had the tiger by the tail. The Japanese were planning something very nasty and sinister in the mid-Pacific and, though he did not know exactly when or where it was to be, Nimitz understood that the whole course of the war could hinge on the outcome. This was not good news, coming on the heels of the Pearl Harbor disaster, the annihilation of the Allied fleet in the Java Sea, the loss of the entire Philippine army, and the sinking of the *Lexington* and serious damaging of the *Yorktown*. What U.S. intelligence was able to develop was that the Japanese were mustering about two hundred warships for this operation, more than they had ever mustered thus far, and certainly far more than the United States could hope to bring against them.

As we have seen, Commander Rochefort's combat intelligence section at Pearl had been working round-the-clock since war broke out and had made good headway on breaking the main Japanese naval code, which could of course be changed in Tokyo at any moment and set the Americans back to square one. In fact, that was just what the Japanese had in mind, but owing to bureaucratic delays the projected change on May 1 was postponed to June 1, which would prove an incredibly fortuitous stroke of luck for the Americans.

Wearing his trademark red smoking jacket and carpet slippers, Rochefort spent most of his days in the dank underground intelligence room amid the clatter of IBM punch-card machines and teletypes and the growl of primitive air conditioners. His army of clerks now included members of the band of the wrecked battleship *California,* whose musical training turned out to be extraordinarily compatible with deciphering Japanese communications. Slowly Rochefort's team pieced things together from the seemingly unfathomable jigsaw puzzle that made up the Japanese naval code and what they began to discover was startling. Sometime in June 1942, they learned, less than a month away, Admiral Yamamoto intended to attack the American base at Dutch Harbor, in the Aleutian Islands chain off Alaska, and occupy several of the U.S.-owned islands there. At the same time, and far more importantly, the Japanese would attack and occupy Midway Island, the last remaining U.S. outpost in the western Pacific. From there they could bottle up the U.S. Pacific Fleet at Pearl Harbor, if not occupy Hawaii itself, and that, too, was part of Yamamoto's plan.

At least that's the way Rochefort's people saw it; others, including the new chief of naval operations, Admiral Ernest King, weren't so sure and were reluctant to risk what remained of the Pacific fleet on pure signal intelligence interpretation alone.* King, back at his desk in Washington, was actually of the opinion that the main Japanese attack would fall on Hawaii itself. But Rochefort had a plan to ferret out the truth, a trick, as it were, that would cause the Japanese to reveal once and for all their darkest secret.

The problem with the U.S. decoding of the "when and where" was that this most precious information lay deeply embedded in a special Japanese

---

*King was a gruff sailor of the old school, of whom it was said, "Not only did he not suffer fools gladly, he did not suffer *anybody* gladly." In the navy of King's day "intelligence" was not considered a proper job for career officers, i.e., professional Naval Academy graduates. Service aboard ships, preferably battleships, was. Thus, only the more mediocre officers were assigned to the intelligence branch, although as it turned out many of these were anything but mediocre. It is therefore all the more remarkable that intelligence had as much to do with winning many World War II battles as the actual fighting ships did.

encoding system, layers and layers of intricate cryptology wrapped so thickly that American code breakers had previously not even wanted to waste time trying to figure it out. But the beauty of Rochefort's method lay in its stunning simplicity. He sent a top-secret cable to the commander at Midway, telling him to report back, falsely, to Pearl headquarters over the open airwaves a matter of minor housekeeping: that the fresh water distillation plant on Midway was broken. Rochefort knew from his deciphering that if his conclusions were correct, the Japanese code word for Midway would be "AF," and if the Japanese took the bait "AF" would be confirmed. A day or so after Midway broadcast Rochefort's trick message, U.S. radio intercepts picked up a Japanese report to Tokyo noting that "AF" was running low on fresh water.

The excitement at Rochefort's shop was electric, and soon it was as well in Nimitz's Pacific fleet headquarters. When Nimitz got the news his eyes lit up with the old "blue light of battle," and his intelligence officer remembered that at that moment his smile was "nothing less than radiant." Now the battle would be joined; now the location and intention of the enemy fleet was known. Chester Nimitz always liked a good fight, and this was one he'd been waiting for.

There was still the critical information of the date and time of the attack yet to be divined. Up until May 27, almost the last day the U.S. Pacific Fleet could act, the code breakers had not succeeded in breaking the ultrasecret cipher that contained this information. Then one of Rochefort's senior cryptologists took a crack at it, after already putting in his regular twelve-hour shift. He was Lieutenant Commander Wesley A. Wright, and to give an indication of the complexities of his Herculean task, let us turn to David Kahn's description of it in *The Code Breakers*: "As the night wore on Wright worked it out. He discovered that the date-and-time cipher comprised a polyalphabetic with independent mixed-cipher alphabets and with the exterior plain and key alphabets in two different systems of Japanese syllabic writing—one the older formal *kata kana*, the other the cursive *hira gana*. Each has 47 syllables, making the polyalphabetic tableau a gigantic one of 2,209 cells, more than three times as extensive as the ordinary Vigenere tableau of 676 cells. Nevertheless, by 5:30 A.M. he had a solution."[1]

What Commander Wright had deciphered told Nimitz that the Japanese attack against the Aleutians would commence at daybreak June 2 and the attack on Midway at daybreak June 3. This priceless information was clouded only by the staggering inferiority of the American fleet compared with the Japanese juggernaut. Against Yamamoto's eight aircraft carriers, eleven battleships, sixteen cruisers, and forty-nine destroyers, the most Nimitz could muster were three aircraft carriers, eight cruisers, fourteen destroyers, and zero battleships—twenty-five ships against eighty-four. If surprise ever counted for anything, it had better be now.

As a matter of fact, after the Coral Sea battle just three weeks earlier, Nimitz was left with only *two* carriers instead of three. Damage caused by the 800-pound bomb that exploded deep in *Yorktown*'s bowels had been so severe it was estimated by the experts that it would take three months to repair. But after personally inspecting the ship when it returned to Pearl, Nimitz ordered the navy yard to do whatever it took to make the thing seaworthy again. This they did immediately, working more than three thousand men around the clock, shoring up structural damage with timbers and bailing wire, rewelding twisted bulkheads, splicing miles of broken cables, and producing a ready fighting ship in a little under three days!

As the planes, bombs, ammunition, and fuel were frantically being taken aboard the carriers and the thousand and one minute details worked out for such a huge undertaking, Nimitz still had two crucial decisions to make. First was where, assuming the cryptoanalysts' information was correct, to place the fleet to best intercept Yamamoto's force with the maximum of surprise and, second, who possibly could replace Bill Halsey?

Admiral Halsey had been the natural choice to lead this most important of missions, but at the last moment he had come down with a wretched skin ailment that rendered him temporarily unfit for command and landed him in the base hospital, fuming and fulminating. He was, however, able to give Nimitz a recommendation for his replacement, and it turned out to be a good one: Rear Admiral Raymond A. Spruance, a fifty-six-year-old 1907 graduate of Annapolis, who was not an aviator and had never commanded a carrier, let alone a carrier fleet. But Spruance was "intense and single-minded of purpose," and his habit of pacing as exercise and letting off steam was frequently remarked on by those around him: pacing, always pacing, whether in his cabin or on the decks of his ships, seemingly lost in thought. However, he was not to lead the Midway operation. Instead, owing to the navy's rigid rank-and-command system, Rear Admiral Frank Fletcher, who had just fought the carrier battle of the Coral Sea, was picked because he was senior to Spruance. Nevertheless, Spruance's selection to replace Halsey was certainly testimony that "his virtues as a tactician were not lost on his seniors."[2]

The other decision—where to position the fleet to best ambush the Japanese—was equally vexing. Nimitz made a calculated guess that Yamamoto would approach Midway from the northwest, just as he had done at Pearl Harbor, and therefore the best place to attack him was on his northeastern flank, meaning that the Japanese fleet would be caught between the attack planes from Midway—which, owing to recent reinforcements, had become virtually an unsinkable aircraft carrier—and the planes from his own fleet. The plan was for Fletcher and Spruance to rendezvous their carriers at sea (Spruance commanding Halsey's old force, the *Enterprise* and the *Hornet,* and Fletcher in the *Yorktown* with overall operational command), then steam to an imaginary spot labeled Point Luck, about 350 miles northeast of Midway, and wait there until the long-range reconnaissance planes from Midway had located the Japanese fleet. In this way they could box them in and hammer them from both ends. It was a good plan, perhaps even a brilliant plan, providing the Japanese cooperated and showed up when and where Nimitz thought they would.

The Japanese, meanwhile, were not just sitting around like cardboard dummies; they had their own plans to foil any attempt by the American navy to surprise them, although in retrospect these were faulty. First, Yamamoto believed that his diversionary attack on the Aleutian Islands would draw at least some if not all of the U.S. fleet far northward, out of the Midway battle area. In addition, he did not believe that Nimitz would react to the attack on Midway until the attack had already begun—that was his passionate dream, his vision, not only to capture Midway but in the process to lure the Americans into the decades-old Japanese notion of the Great Sea Battle, in which the remainder of the U.S. Navy would be sunk and the entire Pacific turned into a Japanese-held lake.

Just in case, though, the Japanese had taken careful precautions lest the Americans not behave as expected. They sent a fleet of twenty submarines to sneak in and scout out Hawaiian waters, reporting back on any U.S. movements. Too, their master plan called for their cruisers to catapult-launch reconnaissance planes to scout westward from north to south in any direction from which the Americans might appear. On paper the plan worked, but its operational faults were glaring. For one thing the submarines arrived off Hawaii later than expected, and as a result they completely missed the American fleet, which, in any case, based on Rochefort's information about the Japanese submarines' pending arrival, was already put out to sea, steaming for Midway. For another, not all their cruiser-launched reconnaissance planes were able to get into the air on time; thus there were critical holes in the coverage. Most important, they hadn't the foggiest notion that U.S. intelligence had been reading their mail.*

What was going through the two U.S. admirals' minds as their carriers bucked and wallowed through the great swells of the North Pacific has not been recorded. Fletcher only a few weeks earlier had seen the burning hulk of the *Lexington,* for which he was responsible, go down in the Coral Sea, a commander's worst nightmare. This must have been in his thoughts as they steamed west toward Midway. Spruance, for his part, detested publicity and, in turn, distrusted "the press," as it was called in those days. He gave no interviews and thus was often characterized as being aloof or stand-offish. Yet one can imagine him thinking that he and Fletcher commanded the only ships in the entire Pacific Ocean—the aircraft carriers—capable

*Another Japanese failure was wrapped up in a scheme to send one of their own flying boats to Hawaii to report on whether the U.S. carriers were there or not. But the flying boat would obviously need refueling and the Japanese had planned to do this at a remote pile of rocks in the ocean well northwest of Pearl Harbor called French Frigate Shoals. When the Japanese submarine carrying the fuel surfaced at French Frigate Shoals, however, the captain was unpleasantly surprised to find that the U.S. Navy was already there, occupying it, and so this scheme unraveled; consequently, neither Yamamoto nor the Japanese Naval Staff in Tokyo had any precise information as to where the U.S. carrier fleet actually lay.

of inflicting serious damage on the Japanese; if they were lost it would be catastrophic to the U.S. war effort. Nimitz's orders to Fletcher and Spruance had been no more than the ages-old simplified dictum of warfare: to attack the enemy, but only if there was a reasonable chance to inflict more damage upon him than he could inflict upon you. Both admirals knew perfectly well that great dangers lurked; that a battle at sea was unforgiving; that planes would go down in flames and ships would sink into fathomless depths; that there would be suffering and anguish and grief; that many men probably would die—all these things were certainly in their minds and upon their shoulders.

On Midway Island tensions were equally charged; everyone knew an attack was forthcoming and, unlike at Wake Island six months earlier, they knew this was going to be a big one. The reason they knew it was that Nimitz had personally paid a visit to Midway a couple of weeks earlier and informed its commanders of the impending invasion. He asked what they needed, within reason, and they told him; Nimitz said, "And if I deliver all these things to you, can you hold the island?" They replied that they could and would. So seventeen of the precious long-range B-17 Flying Fortresses were delivered to Midway, as were twenty-five big Catalina flying boats, the most effective reconnaissance plane in the U.S. arsenal. More fighting troops were sent, bringing the total up to about three thousand, as well as five tanks, more antiaircraft guns, more fighters and dive-bombers, more coastal guns and sea mines, more cement and steel reinforcing for bunkers and barbed wire for the beaches, and more machine guns and ammunition. Nimitz delivered all he had, nearly stripping himself bare at Pearl Harbor.

Yet with all that, if the Japanese launched a full-scale invasion—which they intended to do—Midway was still not fully equipped to defend against it. Many—but not all—of the island's 121 planes were either obsolete or, in many cases, practically antiques from the early 1930s; most guns were of First World War vintage and the men were equipped with First World War rifles and tin-plate helmets and wrapped leggings, just like the doughboys of 1917. Such was the continuing state of American unpreparedness,

despite the fact that U.S. factories were just now pouring forth a remarkable and unprecedented array of modern weaponry, which had yet to find
its way into the remote Pacific supply chain. Still, for all the shortcomings
the marines and other military personnel on Midway felt they were up to
the task, and certainly would have given a hot reception to the 5,000 Japanese special assault troops that were at that very moment headed their way.

For most of modern history Midway Island, like Wake, had been little
more than a speck upon the ocean, uninhabited except by birds and once
frequented by Japanese feather hunters. It was so remote that it wasn't
even "discovered" until 1859, when an American sailing captain blundered
into it, marked it on a chart, and claimed it for the United States; even
then, it was another eight years before we got around to formally annexing it by sending a U.S. warship to steam out, run up an American flag,
and conduct the usual ceremony.

Like Wake Island, Midway is an atoll, kidney-shaped, about fifteen
miles north to south and a bit longer east to west, with a big lagoon in the
middle; however, the only habitable parts are two islands about three or
four miles long, for the rest is low-covered shoals. With the arrival of steam
propulsion it took on new importance as a mid-Pacific coaling station and,
later, as a trans-Pacific undersea cable station; later still, it was used as a
stopover and refueling point for the giant trans-Pacific Pan-American clippers, which could set down in Midway's big, protected lagoon. As at Wake,
the airline built a seaplane ramp, a hotel for passengers, storage facilities,
and other amenities.

By this time the various workers and employees had turned bleak
Midway into a veritable garden spot by planting eucalyptus and ironwood
trees and all sorts of flowering shrubbery and lawns; they even built tennis courts. In the 1930s, as tensions with Japan rose, the U.S. military began
to take an interest in Midway as a forward reconnaissance base and the navy
revamped the seaplane ramps and began building runways and other facilities so they could station a small number of their big PBY flying boats
there to keep an eye on what the Japanese were up to in the Marshall Islands
to the south. In 1942, after the fall of Wake, a thousand or so miles to the
southwest, Midway took on enormous significance because it was now the
farthest U.S. Pacific warning station, guarding Hawaii against another

surprise attack or even invasion. From its modern runways the lagoon scout planes and the long-range PBYs could patrol the ocean for more than seven hundred miles in any direction and hope to pick up a Japanese fleet sailing across the international date line.

This development was not lost on the Japanese, which was why, at this very moment, they were steaming eastward to put Midway out of business. They expected rough going and so, in addition to the 5,000-man invasion force with all of its supporting ships, they sent the greater portion of their fleet, with all its aircraft carriers and battleships, to pound Midway into submission. What they did not expect was that the U.S. Navy, such as was left of it, would also be there in a timely way to greet them.*

As they approached Midway the Japanese were sailing into the "fog of war"—this time literally. The north-central Pacific mists closed in upon them so thickly that neighboring ships could not be seen at all, despite the use of powerful searchlights, and their officers craned out of conning towers and bridges straining to get a glimpse of anything ahead, abeam or astern. Because of the strict radio silence imposed by Yamamoto, the situation became extremely dangerous since the prospect of midsea collision was quite real.

The Japanese assault force was four-pronged. First to sortie was the group of ships attacking the Aleutian Islands in Alaska—carriers, cruisers, destroyers—in hopes of confusing and diverting the Americans into thinking that the big movement was headed there. Next was the main Midway striking force, consisting of the carriers *Akagi, Kaga, Hiryu,* and *Soryu,* which had all taken part in the attack on Pearl Harbor. As well, there were two battleships, three cruisers, and eleven destroyers. Missing from this formidable armada were two more carriers, which well might have made the difference in the outcome of the battle: the *Zuikaku* and *Shokaku,* which had been so shot up and depleted at the Battle of the Coral Sea a month

*Midway Island is scarcely mentioned in most Pacific Ocean history books. The physical description I have used here comes from Dr. Morison's volume on the battles of Coral Sea and Midway, in which he notes that he culled his historical data from the *American Neptune* of July 1948.

earlier that they were still in dry dock.* If Yamamoto had suspected the Americans would arrive on the scene with *three* carriers, he might well have canceled the Aleutian invasion and brought his whole force to bear at Midway. But he did not suspect this, because of the recent sightings of the *Enterprise* and *Hornet* so far away in the South Pacific.

Third to sortie was the Midway invasion force itself, assembled well to the southeastward in the Marshall Islands and consisting of a carrier, a battleship, ten cruisers, twenty destroyers, and various seaplane carriers and other support ships to escort the 5,000-man invasion force in fifteen transport ships.

Finally was the heavy artillery, that which Yamamoto envisioned as finally winning the Great Sea Battle, the sinking of the remnants of the American fleet and destroying entirely American sea power in the Pacific. This consisted of Yamamoto's flagship, the *Yamato*, the most powerful battleship ever built, before or since, a gargantuan metallic behemoth bristling with eighteen-and-a-half-inch guns—which outranged and outpowered anything else afloat—and armored so heavily that it weighed nearly twice as much as any other battleship of any navy. Added to this were six other battleships, three cruisers, twenty-one destroyers, a carrier, and all the attendant support ships.

Yamamoto's plan was roughly this:

1. The Aleutian force would attack the Americans at Dutch Harbor, Alaska, then occupy several islands at the western end of the chain to give the Japanese a firm base in the North Pacific. It was also hoped that this action would confuse the Americans and cause them to speed north with their fleet, only to find that the main attack was at Midway; then, when they sped back to Midway, they would head into annihilation.

2. The Midway Striking Force with the big carriers would first lend support to the invasion fleet by bombing Midway, knocking out its planes and installations, and eliminating Midway as a danger from land-based aircraft and then—most important—turn, face, and destroy the U.S. fleet,

---

*That Nimitz was able to get the *Yorktown*, which was more severely damaged than either of the above-mentioned Japanese carriers, seaworthy in just two and a half days, is testimony enough to American ingenuity, perseverance, and resolve.

which was sure to come rushing toward them either from Pearl Harbor or from its fool's errand in the Aleutians.

3. Finally, Yamamoto's big battleship fleet, steaming a day or so behind the Midway Striking Force, would suddenly appear on the scene to blow out of the water any remaining U.S. ship still afloat. That was the way it was supposed to work, and might have, too, except for the sort of prophetic dictum tersely expressed by MacArthur to his aides when they finally reached Australia after the harrowing voyage from the Philippines: "You win, you lose, live or die, and the difference is just an eyelash."

Or, in the case of Midway, a lot of eyelashes, batting not all at once but fluttering over a period of weeks, months, even years: the agonizing deliberations of code breaking, ship repairing, pilot training, reinforcing remote outposts such as Midway. For the Japanese, "Victory Disease" had set in to the point that most believed themselves invincible. One who did not share this conviction was the commanding officer of the Midway Striking Force, Vice Admiral Chuichi Nagumo, who had commanded the wildly successful sneak attack on Pearl Harbor and now found himself in the position of mother hen, protecting his priceless brood of capital ships and worrying himself over what would happen out on the ocean blue, so far from home, if the United States Navy showed up with any kind of powerful forces.

Commander Mitsuo Fuchida, who had led the Pearl Harbor attack and was expected to play a major role in the Midway operation, was aboard Nagumo's flagship, *Akagi,* when first night out to sea he had to have an emergency appendectomy. This left him out of the action but in a perfect position to observe and reflect on the operation as a whole, which he did in his fascinating narrative *Midway: The Battle that Doomed Japan.*

Nagumo was, Fuchida reported, during the ten years he had known him, a tough, intelligent, and highly capable naval officer but "it was not long, however, before I noted that Nagumo had changed, and I began to feel dissatisfied with his apparent conservatism and passiveness. It might have been because he was now commanding an air arm, which was not his specialty. Personally he was as warmhearted and sympathetic as ever, but his once-vigorous fighting spirit seemed to be gone, and with it his stature as an outstanding naval leader. Instead he seemed rather average, and I was suddenly aware of his increased age."[3]

Those are harsh words for a subordinate to use to describe his superior, especially one of the leading admirals in the Japanese navy, but Fuchida's observations have a ring of truth about them that is hard to dispute, especially because they were echoed by Nagumo's air officer and the chief architect of the Pearl Harbor operation, Commander Minoru Genda.

Because of the foul weather the Japanese attack was delayed for a day, but on June 3 the assault on the Aleutians commenced, in heavy fog, with a Japanese bombing of the U.S. base at Dutch Harbor. This killed a score or more of American soldiers and sailors and did a considerable amount of damage but fooled no one, especially not Admiral Nimitz, who knew the major blow was to fall on Midway, particularly since one of the patrolling PBY flying boats out of Midway had already spotted the Japanese invasion force some seven hundred miles out that same morning. The fog, however, had concealed the main Japanese striking force, though the Americans knew they were out there, somewhere.

Thus the U.S. carrier fleet was now on station at what was designated Point Luck, waiting for dawn, and for the other shoe to drop. Tension aboard the big ships was pervasive since everyone knew that a big sea battle was brewing. Aboard the *Hornet* a torpedo bomber squadron leader, Lieutenant Commander John Waldron, wrote a letter to his wife back in South Dakota: "I believe that we will be in battle very soon. If I do not come back—well, you and the little girls can know that this squadron struck for the highest objective in naval warfare—to sink the enemy. . . . I love you and the children very dearly and I long to be with you. But I could not be happy ashore at this time. My place is here with the fight."[4]

The Japanese, too, were beginning to sense that something was afoot. They knew that the invasion troop transports had been spotted because they saw the American plane that spotted them,* and their own radio

---

*Unfortunately for the Japanese, the strict radio silence imposed upon the fleet by Yamamoto did not allow this important news to be conveyed to the Midway Striking Force under Admiral Nagumo; thus, the commander with the most to lose was lacking this crucial information.

rooms were picking up all sorts of "urgent" signals from U.S. ships directed to Midway. Though they could not decipher these communications they realized that the Americans might be closer than they expected.* Admiral Nagumo, for his part, was getting cold feet about what he should do the following morning. His main objective, as he understood it, was to attack and sink the American fleet when it presumably would rush out from Hawaii to try to defend Midway, but he was also charged with using his carrier's planes to bomb and neutralize Midway Island itself.

Yet what if the Americans showed up in the middle of all this? The question Nagumo demanded of his subordinates was reasonable: "But where is the enemy fleet!" Nobody knew the answer—except of course the Americans, and they weren't saying—but Nagumo's chief of staff had reassuring words. The Americans, even if they had already figured things out and had sailed from Hawaii, must still be several days away; thus there was plenty of time to bomb Midway and still prepare to annihilate the U.S. fleet.[5]

Dawn broke on June 4, 1942, at five A.M. but the first wave of Japanese planes that were to attack Midway had begun taking off in the darkness half an hour earlier, 240 miles northwest of the island, just about where Nimitz had predicted: dive-bombers, level bombers, and their fighter escorts, 108 planes in all from four carriers. Commander Fuchida described the scene aboard *Akagi:* "Plane engines were started, and livid white flames spurted from exhaust pipes. The flight deck was soon a hell of ear-shattering noise. Flood lights suddenly illuminated the flight deck, making day of the night. *Akagi* was steaming full into the wind. 'Commence launching!'

---

*The Japanese had been lulled into a further false sense of security when it was reported, correctly, by one of their scout planes that an American carrier task force was operating in the seas near Samoa. This had been Halsey's *Enterprise* and *Hornet,* rushed fresh from the Doolittle raid to help out Fletcher at Coral Sea, but rushed just as quickly back north when Nimitz discovered the Japanese intentions toward Midway. It has been suggested that Nimitz actually ordered the *Enterprise* and *Hornet* to sail within reconnaissance distance of the Japanese in the South Pacific and *let* themselves be seen (and heard), in order to deceive the Japanese into thinking they were still there.

came the order from the bridge. Swinging a green signal lamp, the Air Officer described a big circle in the air. A Zero fighter revved up its engine, gathered speed along the flight deck and rose into the air to the accompaniment of a thunderous cheer from *Akagi*'s crew. Caps and hands waved wildly in the bright glare of the deck lights."[6]

Things weren't exactly idle on Midway, either. At 5:35 the radar shack picked up the first flight of Japanese planes ninety-three miles away, headed toward them. When the air-raid siren blew, the frenzied scramble was such that within twenty-five minutes every plane on the island that could fly—from the slow and stubby old Brewster Buffalo fighters to the lumbering B-17s—was in the air. The thirty-three big PBY flying boats and nineteen heavy bombers were ordered to fly out of harm's way, since they were no good for intercepting the incoming hardware and nobody wanted them sitting on the ground when the Japanese attack came in. But fifty-four Marine Corps fighters and dive-bombers and six navy torpedo bombers rose up into the morning sun to do battle with the enemy.

It was an unequal contest. The marine fighters tried to attack the incoming Japanese bombers, which they encountered thirty miles out, but they were hopelessly outnumbered, outgunned, and outmaneuvered by the Japanese Zeros pouncing on them from above. Soon the sky was filled with huge orange fireballs, planes trailing smoke splashed into the cold sea, and a flurry of debris rained down: torn-off wings, tails, canopies, engine parts, and, alarmingly enough, the bodies of American airmen themselves. Of the twenty obsolete Buffaloes and seven modern Wildcat fighters, only ten returned and, of those, most were so badly shot up they were useless for the remainder of the Midway operation. One of the surviving Buffalo pilots later declared bitterly, "It is my belief that any commander who orders pilots out for combat in an F2A [Buffalo] should consider the pilot as lost before leaving the ground."[7]

Meantime, the torpedo bombers and dive-bombers from Midway proceeded in the direction of the Japanese fleet, passing along the way their opposite numbers bearing the Rising Sun, which must have created a strange sensation. But the efforts of these bombers also proved a futile enterprise since there was no fighter escort for them, all the fighters having been wrecked in the first encounter with the first Japanese incoming flights.

The American marine and navy torpedo bombers were shot out of the sky—most before even reaching their launch points—by a murderous combination of Zero interception and the hail of fire from the carriers they were trying to attack as well as their escorting battleships, cruisers, and destroyers. Those torpedo bombers that did get close enough to launch were ineffective because the slowness of the U.S. torpedoes allowed the Japanese to dodge them easily. One dive-bomber squadron leader, Marine Major Lofton Henderson, who had decided that his young pilots had so little training in dive-bombing techniques, told them to just go straight in and "skip" or "glide" bomb the Japanese ships. This was a novel and very unorthodox method in which the dive-bomber, hurtling in low, just a little above the deck, releases his bomb in the same way as a torpedo bomber (but from a much closer range) and hopes that it will skip and bounce over the water and hit the enemy ship. It didn't work, and half the dive-bombers were shot down, including Henderson's; one pilot who managed to return counted 259 bullet holes in his plane.[8] In fact, of all the different types of U.S. attacks on Nagumo's fleet from Midway, none scored even so much as a near miss.

Nevertheless, this was a wake-up call for Admiral Nagumo—after all, it didn't take but one bomb or torpedo to sink a carrier, the more so since his air commander who had led the attack on Midway had just radioed back: "There is need for a second attack wave." What that meant to Nagumo was that if he didn't order a second attack wave on the island and put the American force out of commission, his fleet might expect more U.S. aircraft to fly out and keep trying to sink him.

The problem for Nagumo, however, was that most of his second wave, now sitting on the decks of his four carriers, had been armed with torpedoes against the (to him remote) possibility that the U.S. Navy might turn up at any moment. So far, his search planes had found nothing, but that didn't mean it was an absolute certainty that the Americans were not out there. For Nagumo it was a wrenching decision because if he sent his planes below now to have their torpedoes removed and rearm them with bombs for a second Midway attack, during that brief period he would be almost naked against a surprise appearance by American carrier aircraft.

Worse, the determination had to be made quickly since the planes from Nagumo's first Midway sortie would soon be returning and all decks would have to be cleared to recover them. It was the sudden U.S. aerial attack from the Midway-based planes that made Nagumo's mind up for him: Midway was the immediate problem and Midway must be shut down. It was 7:15 A.M. when he flashed the fateful message: "Planes in second attack wave stand by to carry out attack today. Re-equip yourselves with bombs."[9] All those American pilots who had bashed themselves to death against the full fury of the Japanese fleet had served a good purpose after all; as at the Coral Sea battle, which had led the Japanese to think that both U.S. carriers had been sunk, their sacrifice was not in vain, as we shall soon see.

Thirteen minutes after reaching his decision to rearm his second wave of planes, Nagumo received shocking news. One of his search planes, which had gotten off half an hour late because of a faulty catapult on the cruiser *Tone*, tapped out a message: "Ten enemy ships 240 miles from Midway," and gave bearings, speed, etc. Nagumo stewed for fifteen minutes, demanding to know what kinds of ships. Presently the search plane reported, "Enemy composed of five cruisers and five destroyers." No mention of carriers. Nagumo was now in a quandary. He knew the Americans had found him from the earlier attack from Midway. He also knew that the U.S. Navy was in the vicinity, but in what strength? That many cruisers and destroyers often meant a carrier task force, but the search plane had made no mention of one, so Nagumo allowed the rearming to go on.

Suddenly there were huge explosions and gray geysers of water around the carriers *Hiryu* and *Soryu*. These were caused by a flight of fourteen B-17s, which had been milling around in the air during the Midway attack and were now ordered to bomb the Japanese fleet from an altitude of 20,000 feet. From his vantage point aboard *Akagi* Commander Fuchida noted that of the more than 100,000 pounds of bombs dropped by these planes none scored a hit, and the two big carriers emerged from the towering water geysers into the sunshine. Fuchida noted afterward, "We had by this time undergone every kind of air attack by shore-based planes— torpedo, level bombing and dive bombing—but were still unscathed. Frankly it was my judgment that the enemy fliers were not displaying a very high level of ability, and this evaluation was shared by Admiral Nagumo and his staff. It was our general conclusion that we had little to fear from the enemy's offensive tactics."[10]

Ironically, for all the death and sacrifice so far that morning, the Americans had actually lured the Japanese into a false sense of security, for already flights of U.S. Navy dive-bombers and torpedo planes were winging their way from the three American carriers, after having picked up the radio traffic from Midway regarding the location of the Japanese fleet.

This might not have been so were it not for the intervention of Admiral Halsey's chief of staff on the *Enterprise,* Captain Miles Browning, described almost universally as a "temperamental but brilliant" air officer. This was because Admiral Spruance had concluded that he wanted to get much closer to the Japanese before launching his attack, so as to make sure his planes had enough fuel to get back to the carrier. But Browning argued that to get within one hundred miles would take until at least nine A.M. and he had calculated from the Midway radio intercepts that if they launched earlier, nearer to seven A.M., they would likely arrive on the scene just in time to catch the Japanese with their pants down: either recovering or refueling their planes on deck from the first-wave Midway attack.

Now it was Spruance's turn to be in quandary. If he launched two hours early, as Browning suggested, it was almost certain that some of the planes would run out of fuel and have to ditch in the sea (his torpedo bombers had a combat range of only 175 miles out, allowing time to find the target). It was small consolation that the planes carried an inflatable life raft; ditching at sea is a terrifically dangerous business even under the best of circumstances. But Spruance made the decision anyway because, if he waited and was sighted by the Japanese, then *he* would become the hunted, instead of the other way around. It was a tough and difficult choice, but a smart one, and at 7:02 A.M. the full complement of torpedo and dive-bombing squadrons began taking off from the *Enterprise* and the *Hornet.* Admiral Fletcher, aboard the *Yorktown,* decided to hold off for a while, in case there were more Japanese carriers lurking out there than so far reported. But at about nine o'clock he began launching a partial strike of his own.

*   *   *

At 8:20, nearly an hour after he had first reported sighting U.S. ships, the pilot of the *Tone* search plane signaled back to Nagumo: "The enemy is accompanied by what appears to be a carrier."* Nagumo hardly had time to digest this unpleasant news when the planes† from his first Midway strike appeared on the horizon, eager to land. There was nothing for it but to turn all the carriers into the wind and begin the recovery operation, while the sailors belowdecks feverishly tried to remove all the bombs they had just loaded the torpedo planes with and replace them, yet again, with torpedoes. During the delicate recovery operation Nagumo did not want any more attacks from the Midway planes, so he ordered his fleet to turn away from the island, speeding on a northward course, which would soon have consequences for the American attackers.

Before leaving the *Hornet* Lieutenant Commander Waldron, one-quarter Sioux Indian, had not only written to his wife the night before, but also sent a Nelsonian message‡ to his fifteen pilots in Torpedo Squadron 8: "We have had a very short time to train and we have worked under the most severe difficulties. But we have truly done the best humanly possible. My greatest hope is that we encounter a favorable tactical situation, but if we don't and the worst comes to the worst, I want each of us to do his utmost to destroy our enemies. If there is only one plane left to make a final run in, I want that man to go in and get a hit. May God be with us all. Good luck, happy landings and give 'em hell."[11] With that they had taken off, without any fighter escort (there were only twenty fighters available aboard both *Hornet* and *Enterprise* to protect the ninety-odd dive- and torpedo bombers; the rest were needed to fly air cover for the carriers).

---

*Perhaps the pilot's qualification stemmed from the embarrassing episode in the Coral Sea, where the Japanese attacked the U.S. oiler *Neosho* and had reported sinking a carrier.

†All 108 did not return. The exact number shot down has never been determined but it is believed to be about thirty. The antiaircraft fire from Midway was formidable.

‡Before the Battle of Trafalgar, Admiral Horatio Nelson signaled to all ships in his fleet: "England expects every man to do his duty."

Before takeoff all pilots had been given a last-minute briefing concerning the location of the Japanese fleet, based on the latest information from Midway-based planes. At about nine-thirty a heavy force of thirty-five dive-bombers from the *Hornet* arrived at the spot where Nagumo's carriers should have been, but they weren't there. Their leader, Commander Stanhope Ring, saw only low clouds to the north and made a judgment that Nagumo had kept heading southeast to get closer to Midway, when in fact Nagumo had done just the opposite. Accordingly, Ring turned his powerful force in that direction, away from the low bank of clouds in which Nagumo was hiding, effectively taking himself and his dive-bombers out of the action. Ultimately, running out of gas, Ring had to land his planes on Midway itself to refuel before finally returning to the *Hornet* later in the afternoon, empty-handed.

However, three of the slower torpedo-bomber squadrons—including that of Lieutenant Commander Waldron—soon arrived at the same position where Commander Ring had made his decision to turn the wrong way. Instead of following him southeastward (they had evidently picked up Ring's radio traffic about making the turn), Waldron continued north, maybe on a hunch, or perhaps on the theory that if Ring were correct, they would have heard his radio traffic if he'd spotted the Japanese ships, and vice versa. In either case, Waldron guessed right, for presently below him he caught a breathtaking sight: four Japanese carriers in box formation with their escort of big-gun ships.

The Japanese had already begun to zigzag, or circle violently, as if expecting the American planes. In fact, they *were* expecting them, according to the account of Commander Fuchida aboard *Akagi,* who had been listening to the frenetic radio chatter of the Japanese destroyer screen to the southwest. "Reports of approaching enemy planes increased until it was quite evident that they were not from a single carrier. When the Admiral [Nagumo] and his staff realized this, their optimism abruptly vanished. The only way to stave off disaster was to launch planes at once."[12]

Waldron and the men of Torpedo Squadron 8 started their run far out to sea off *Akagi*'s starboard bow. Fuchida remembered that they appeared "as tiny dark specks in the blue sky. The distant wings flashed in the sun. Occasionally one of the specks burst into a spark of flame and trailed black smoke as it fell into the water. Nearly 50 Zeros had gone to intercept the unprotected enemy formation."[13]

One by one Waldron's squadron was shot down; still the bombers came on, now facing not only the ubiquitous Zeros but unwithstandable antiaircraft fire from every Japanese ship within range. Waldron's plane suddenly burst into flames and spun into the sea. Weeks after her notification of his death, his wife would finally receive the letter he had written to her and their two little girls.

Finally only one plane out of Torpedo 8's original fifteen was still aloft, piloted by Ensign George Gay who, last in line and with Waldron's admonition "If there is only one plane left I want that man to go in and get a hit" still ringing in his ears, resolutely bore in toward *Akagi,* skimming only a few feet above the waves with a swarm of Zeros on his tail. His gunner-radioman had been shot dead and Gay himself was hit in the arm by a bullet from one of the Zeros. As Gay, one of the many rookie fliers that day, recounted later, "It was the first time I had ever carried a torpedo on an aircraft, and the first time I had ever taken a torpedo off a ship. I had never even seen it done. We had no previous combat flying."[14]

About half a mile from the big carrier, Gay hit the electric launch button to release his torpedo and waited for his plane to lurch upward from the lost weight of the twelve-foot-long, 1,200-pound "tin fish." He was now staring ahead into an orange sheet of flame from every gun on the carrier's starboard side and flack puffs burst all around him. But no lurch was forthcoming. Gay then frantically grabbed for the emergency release lever. This time he felt the rise of the torpedo launch, but now he was coming right up on the carrier. Somehow he managed to pull up and just skip over the *Akagi*'s five-story-high flight deck by a mere ten feet. But the Zeros were still on him, soon shooting out his left rudder pedal. Out of control, Gay's plane pancaked into the water no more than a thousand feet from the huge carrier. The plane rapidly sank but Gay was able to struggle out and pop to the surface holding on to a black rubber seat cushion, which he promptly put over his head and hid under while Japanese cruisers and destroyers roared past him, their crews pointing and laughing. The sole survivor of Torpedo Squadron 8, like his dead comrades, had failed to get a single hit.

The two other torpedo squadrons just behind Waldron fared little better. Of fourteen from the *Enterprise* only four made it to their launch points before being shot down, but the Japanese carriers dodged the agonizingly slow American torpedoes. Next, a flight of twelve from the late-starting *Yorktown* appeared and made a run at the Japanese carrier *Hiryu.* They faired worse than their *Enterprise* companions, losing ten of twelve planes, and even though they had managed to launch five torpedoes, all missed. Clearly there was something wrong with the American torpedoes.

Of the forty-one torpedo-bomber aviators, all but seven were killed (along with their gunner-radioman crewmen), and thirty-five planes were lost, with Ensign Gay still bobbing in the cold Pacific, hiding under his cushion. No Japanese ship was as yet even touched; the Zeros had a field day.* So far, the American attacks had been a miserable disaster, from the slaughter of the Midway-based planes earlier that morning to the annihilation of three full carrier-based torpedo squadrons in the span of a few minutes. The Japanese naturally breathed a collective sigh of relief, but now the curtain was about to rise on the second act of the drama, with great surprises in store.

The extremely violent high-speed maneuvering by Nagumo's carriers trying to evade the torpedo planes had made it impossible for them to launch bombers of their own to go after the American carriers; if nothing else, this vindicated the awful sacrifice of the torpedo planes.† But there was another consequence, too, even more important. Because the torpedo planes had come in at wave-top level, all fifty covering Zeros had to get

---

*This attack proved the futility of sending in slow torpedo bombers to attack big ships against a superior cover of fast enemy fighter aircraft. The U.S. Navy learned the lesson the hard way, but from then on their tactics would improve.

†Few other than naval officers and seamen can appreciate the strains and stresses of a large ship jerking and lurching at speeds of up to nearly forty mph trying to avoid an aircraft attack. These ships, up to 45,000 tons and more, can list as much as fifteen degrees, throwing men down on the decks, while planes, gear, supplies, and armaments are often heaved about with the enormous force, making it sometimes impossible for men to do anything but hang on and hope not to break an arm or leg, which frequently happened.

down on the deck to fire at them; thus they were still down low, trying to regain altitude, when American dive-bombers suddenly arrived on the scene.

Earlier, Lieutenant Commander Clarence McClusky, with thirty-seven dive-bombers from the *Enterprise,* had arrived, like Commander Ring from the *Hornet* before him, at the spot where the Japanese fleet was supposed to be and, finding nothing, had decided to keep his force flying westward to see what that would yield. It yielded nothing, so McClusky decided to turn back north. He was pushing the limits of his return fuel capacity when suddenly through the clouds he saw below him the last tragic moments of the American torpedo-bomber attacks. He immediately ordered half of his planes to attack the *Akagi* and the other half to concentrate on the carrier *Soryu.* At almost the same instant, perhaps even a few moments earlier, Commander Maxwell Leslie with seventeen dive-bombers from the *Yorktown* arrived and saw the big carrier *Kaga* readying to launch planes.*

For the Japanese carrier fleet it was the worst possible situation to be in—no high-altitude fighter cover, and planes all over the decks in the process of being refueled, rearmed with torpedoes, or waiting for takeoff to go after the American carriers. McClusky's dive-bombers, in a long line one after the other, leveled off at an altitude of 14,500 feet, then pushed their sticks over and at full throttle began to plummet down hawklike at a seventy-degree angle, making for the big ships at three hundred miles per hour. One of the few American fighter pilots to witness the attack described it as "a beautiful silver waterfall." Commander Leslie's group was doing the same. The carrier *Hiryu,* far ahead of the other three and temporarily out of sight, was spared the ordeal—temporarily. The time was now ten-thirty A.M.

*There remains today some controversy over which carriers were attacked by whom. Dr. Morison asserts that McClusky attacked both *Akagi* and *Kaga* but other experts, including John Toland and Thaddeus Tuleja, write that McClusky attacked *Akagi* and *Soryu* and not *Kaga.* The truth will probably never be known. The Japanese carriers didn't have their names on their sterns, and even if they had it would have been nearly impossible for the dive-bomber pilots to see them. But *Kaga* was a large carrier and *Soryu* a smaller one, and one of Commander Leslie's pilots was later quoted as saying the carrier they attacked "was one of the biggest damned things I have ever seen." On the other hand, Morison, the official naval historian, shows charts placing *Kaga* nearest to *Akagi,* which McClusky's group attacked.

Commander Fuchida, on the bridge of *Akagi* along with Admiral Nagumo and Commander Genda, the fleet air officer, remembered that the signal had just been given to have the planes take off when "a lookout screamed 'Hell-Divers.' I looked up to see three black enemy planes plummeting toward our ship. The terrifying scream of the dive-bombers reached me first, followed by a crashing explosion of a direct hit. There was a blinding flash and then a second explosion, much louder than the first. Then followed a startling quiet as the barking of guns suddenly ceased. I got up and looked at the sky. The enemy planes were already gone from sight."[15]

The damage wrought by McClusky's attack "horrified" Fuchida. The bombs had blasted the midships flight elevator into a mass of molten metal, drooping into the hangar. Planes waiting to take off or being refueled had been set afire and turned the flight deck into an inferno. Then explosions from below rumbled through the ship as bombs, torpedoes, and fuel-storage tanks began to explode and hundreds of men were incinerated alive. Flames and black smoke poured out of every orifice, eventually enveloping the bridge. It was obvious that the ship was doomed.

Nagumo's chief of staff urged the admiral to transfer his flag to one of the nearby cruisers, but the commanding admiral seemed in a state of shock and waved off his second-in-command. The captain and others pleaded with him, but to no avail. By this time the ritual removal of the emperor's picture from its sacred place on the bridge was already under discussion. The chief of staff then informed the admiral that all communications were out: "Sir, most of our ships are still intact. You must command them." Nagumo finally agreed but, because all the passageways below were afire, the only way he and his staff could make their escape was by climbing down a rope from a window on the bridge and then making their way down through masses of strewn bodies to where a boat was waiting to take them to the cruiser *Nagara,* which Dr. Morison rightly points out "must have been a severe strain on Japanese dignity."[16] During this ignominious boat ride, Admiral Nagumo and the others could see their companion ships the *Kaga* and *Soryu,* as well as their own, burning furiously from stem to stern. It had been scarcely fifteen minutes since American bombers had visited the fleet; such were the fortunes of war.

Kaga had been hit with four 500- and 1,000-pound bombs and *Soryu* with three, which started uncontrollable fires on both ships, and survivors described seeing many screaming men running around in flames, cremated alive in the burning aircraft. The *Kaga* sank about three hours later. *Soryu,* ablaze from the dive-bombing attacks, was also hit by three torpedoes from the submarine U.S.S. *Nautilus,* which had been lurking in the area for just such an opportunity; she blew in half and sank shortly after sunset. *Akagi* lingered on till past midnight, burning and out of control, until Admiral Yamamoto, still four hundred miles to the west, reluctantly gave orders for torpedo-destroyers to scuttle the ship, which had been his old command. Upon learning this news the *Akagi*'s captain returned to his carrier from the cruiser and "lashed himself to an anchor to await the end." Likewise, the captain of the *Soryu,* after the abandon ship order had been carried out, returned to his bridge and, sword in hand, began screaming, "Banzai! and singing *Kimigayo,* the Japanese national anthem," as the ship went down.[17]

For his part Commander Fuchida, still weakened from his appendix operation a week earlier, tried to follow the exodus of the admiral's staff, but when he began to climb down hand over hand he found that the rope itself was already smoldering. He got as far as the gun deck but then, when he began climbing down a metal monkey ladder to the flight deck, he found to his horror that the rungs too were red-hot from the fierce fires raging inside the ship. He let go and fell ten feet, breaking both of his ankles. Some sailors nearby helped Fuchida down to the anchor deck, where he was strapped onto a bamboo stretcher and joined with the others on the long boat ride to the *Nagara.*[18]

Surprisingly, the Japanese were still full of fight. They had one remaining carrier task force, *Hiryu,* which had pulled far ahead of the other three and thus was not seen by the American dive-bombers. Even while Nagumo was making the unenjoyable boat ride to his new flag headquarters, orders were issued by his chief of staff for *Hiryu* to attack the enemy carriers. By eleven A.M. eighteen Japanese dive-bombers had lifted off deck and by a stroke of good luck managed to find flying ahead of them several of the planes from Commander Leslie's *Yorktown* squadron and followed them home, the distance between the two fleets having now closed to 110 miles.

Admiral Fletcher was on his bridge studying a chart when an aide told him, "The attack is coming in, Sir!" Fletcher, who like everyone else had been alerted fifteen or twenty minutes earlier by a radar sighting, continued at his chart work. "Well," he said, "I've got on my tin hat. I can't do anything else now." The returning flight of Commander Leslie had already been waved off to either join the overhead combat patrol or land on the other carriers and the *Yorktown* began to take violent evasive measures.

The fighter patrol flying over *Yorktown* did yeoman's work that early afternoon, destroying or crippling ten of the eighteen enemy dive-bombing planes; antiaircraft fire from cruisers and destroyers shot down another two. Six, however, came through and that was enough to cause serious and gruesome damage. A doctor aboard the *Yorktown* reported going onto the flight deck not long after the attack and passing a gun emplacement: "A pair of legs attached to the hips sat in the trainer's seat. A stub of spinal column was hanging over backwards. There was nothing else remaining. The steel splinter shield was full of men, or rather portions of men, many of whom were not identifiable. Blood was everywhere. I turned forward and saw great billows of smoke rising from our stack region. We were dead in the water."[19] Three Japanese bombs had struck the big ship in less than a minute, one of them actually falling right down the smokestack, setting fires from soot and paint. So many boilers were knocked out by deep exploding bombs that the *Yorktown*'s speed slowed to six knots, then she went dead. Fletcher promptly transferred his flag to the cruiser *Astoria* because, like Nagumo on the *Akagi,* the *Yorktown*'s communications and radar had been put out of business.

Within an hour and a half after the initial attack, however, a Herculean effort by engineers and damage-control parties got the big ship up and running again at twenty knots, all big fires out, her radar repaired, and already refueling and launching planes. No sooner had these happy events transpired than radar picked up another flight of Japanese planes about twenty minutes away. These were a flight of ten torpedo bombers from *Hiryu,* and even though the fighter cover from *Yorktown* knocked down six of them, four got through. Two of their torpedoes missed, but two did not, and thus the ship was soon to be doomed. People aboard later recorded that it seemed as if the *Yorktown* was lifted a foot or more out of the water. All power was lost, the rudder was jammed, and the ship took on an immediate seventeen-degree list. Twenty minutes later the list had increased to twenty-six degrees and the captain, Elliott Buckmaster, fearing that the *Yorktown* would capsize with all aboard, ordered abandon ship. Some of the thousands of men who took to the water seemed amazingly cheerful, considering what they had just been through, calling out "Taxi! Taxi!" to the rescue boats from the destroyers and singing "Beer Barrel Polka."[20]

Others, however, suffered immensely, especially those many who had been wounded and were now weak and floundering in the water, and most everyone was covered by a thick and nauseating black slime of fuel oil, which could not be scrubbed away with soap and water. Captain Buckmaster remained aboard the *Yorktown* alone, wandering among the bodies, trying to find anyone alive, which he did not. He went down into the hangar deck to see how bad the damage was and found it likely fatal. But unlike the suicide-prone Japanese captains, Buckmaster had no intention of going down with the ship if he could help it and, after finding out everything he could, he summoned a whaleboat from a destroyer to take him off.*

While this was going on, Spruance on the *Enterprise* began launching a strike of his own. He had always suspected there was a fourth Japanese carrier and the attack on *Yorktown* had just proved it. Now one of the *Yorktown*'s search planes, sent out earlier, reported back the position of the *Hiryu* and her complement of battleships, cruisers, and destroyers. Meantime, Spruance contacted Fletcher asking if there were any further instructions for him. Fletcher, aboard the cruiser and now having lost his second carrier (the first was the *Lexington* in the Battle of the Coral Sea), messaged back, "None. Will conform to your movements," thereby effectively turning over command of the battle to Spruance. Using the same successful dive-bombing attacks they'd employed that morning, pilots from Spruance's *Enterprise*

---

*There were in fact three men left alive aboard *Yorktown,* somewhere down in the bowels of the ship. One of these was not badly injured and summoned rescue by firing a machine gun from the deck, which alerted one of the circling destroyers.

and *Hornet* soon had the *Hiryu* in uncontrollable flames from four direct hits as the sun sank in the west over the hard, gray Pacific Ocean.

Thus went the Battle of Midway on June 4, 1942. By shortly after dawn next day, all four Japanese carriers, which had formed the backbone of the Pearl Harbor attack, lay on the ocean floor, three miles beneath the surface. Like the commanders of the *Akagi* and the *Soryu,* the captain of the *Hiryu* went down with his ship, along with the division commander, Admiral Tamon Yamaguchi, who was said to be favored as Yamamoto's successor. These two lashed themselves to the *Hiryu*'s bridge in order not to be floated away when she sank. As the last of the eight hundred or so survivors of the *Hiryu* began departing the burning and sinking carrier, Yamaguchi declared to them that he was "solely responsible" for the loss of the ship, and that they must live to fight again another day, "for His Majesty, the emperor." To his staff, who pleaded to remain with him, Yamaguchi said the same thing. Then they all drank a silent toast from a water pitcher.[21] The captain of the *Hiryu* tried to persuade the admiral to leave the ship, but Yamaguchi's only reply was, "The moon is so bright in the sky!" The captain thought about it for a moment, then said, "We shall watch the moon together," and strapped himself onto the bridge beside his commander.[22] There is little doubt that the captain of the *Kaga* would likewise have committed himself to a watery hara-kiri, but he had been killed on his bridge in the first American dive-bomb attack that morning.*

Four hundred miles to the east, Yamamoto with his vast and powerful fleet of surface ships received the news of Nagumo's annihilation with surprising composure. In fact, he remarked only "Ah so," and resumed the game of chess he was playing with one of his staff officers. Concluding the game an hour and a half later, he calmly ordered the two small carriers then attacking Dutch Harbor in the Aleutians to sail southwest and join with the Nagumo force. Almost as an afterthought he instructed the Midway invasion force to turn around, and also to send up its two small carri-

---

*No one can know how these seemingly pointless suicides affected the ultimate outcome of the war, but it is reasonable to speculate that with so many senior commanders—not only in the navy but in the army as well—killing themselves after a loss (or, to them, a humiliation), or allowing themselves to be killed, the Japanese military lost an appalling number of first-class superior officers.

ers to the Midway scene.[23] Yamamoto must have been thinking that when those four carriers arrived, along with his own gargantuan battlefleet, he would have enough forces to deal with the Americans.

Meantime, Nagumo had also composed himself and was itching for revenge. Always a "big gun ship" sailor he still had a number of undamaged battleships and cruisers of his own to give Fletcher and Spruance a taste of their own medicine—if he could get in range of them, especially at night when their planes could do him no harm. So he ordered the remains of his striking force to head east at full speed to challenge the U.S. fleet.

Problem for the Japanese was that Spruance wasn't having any of it. He knew they had highly perfected night-fighting capabilities and that his cruisers were no match for their battleships. Accordingly, he retired eastward, out of harm's way, but just far enough so that the following day he could return to the Midway battle area in case the Japanese somehow went on with their intended invasion of the island. Also there had been reports of a *fifth* Japanese carrier, after some Midway-based planes went out late to see what they could catch and found a number of Japanese fighters and bombers still circling around the area where the *Hiryu* was experiencing her final death rattle. It turned out that these were only the remnants of the *Hiryu*'s own fighter cover and the few returning planes from the *Yorktown* strike, hovering pathetically over their stricken mother ship with nowhere else to go until their fuel ran out.

Yamamoto, meanwhile, was having second thoughts about his plan to get at the U.S. fleet. It would take several days for the carriers from the Aleutians operation to arrive and, during that time, they would have been subjected to all sorts of bombing from Midway, submarines, and probably from Spruance too. So Yamamoto reluctantly ordered a general withdrawal westward, back toward Japan. As with Nagumo's staff, there were angry and hysterical protests and one officer demanded to know, "How can we apologize to the emperor for this defeat!" Yamamoto quieted them down, saying evenly, "I am the only one who must apologize to His Majesty."

That night Nagumo's ships plowed all over hell and back where they thought the Americans would be and, finding nothing but dark ocean, finally retired northwestward. There was much hand-wringing among Nagumo's staff over this. One officer went around saying they should all commit hara-kiri and another foolishly suggested that they should take the big battleships and shell Midway, leaving themselves naked against air strikes from both the island and Spruance's fleet, as well as from submarine attacks. He was quickly disabused of the notion by more senior officers. In any case he conformed to Yamamoto's orders and began the general retreat westward.

Next day brought the first major American tragedy of the battle. Even after all the damage that had been done to the *Yorktown,* her captain, Buckmaster, still thought there was a slim chance to save her. Late in the afternoon of June 4, the destroyer *Hammann* tied up alongside and work began with an all-volunteer damage-control party of 29 officers and 141 enlisted men to try to correct the terrible list by counterflooding and pumping from the *Hammann*'s electric power. Just maybe, if they could get her upright and stabilized, she could be towed back to Pearl and repaired. Meantime, Captain Buckmaster boarded, intending to identify all the dead and conduct a funeral service at sea.

But this was not to be, for while the damage-control party made good headway all day on June 5, and had begun to correct the list, the next day a Japanese submarine sighted the *Yorktown* drifting helplessly and ducked under the destroyer screen to fire four torpedoes at the big carrier. One missed, one hit *Hammann* amidships, breaking her almost immediately in half with a terrible loss of life, and the other two torpedoes went underneath the destroyer to slam into the *Yorktown*'s hull.

That should have finished *Yorktown* then and there but it didn't. The venerable carrier seemingly refused to sink and Captain Buckmaster, marveling at her resilience, prepared to send another damage-control party aboard next morning. But by first light of dawn it was obvious that the list had increased to the point of hopelessness. By six A.M., June 7, the destroyer escorts had backed away and lowered their colors to half-mast while everyone stood at attention, many old-timers with tears in their eyes, as the big ship finally rolled over with all her battle flags still flying and slipped beneath the ocean waves with a cacophonous and bone-chilling roar.

It had been eventful elsewhere, too. The day after the Japanese carriers had been sunk big Catalina flying boats from Midway began combing the waters in the battle area looking for downed pilots. They rescued several, including the rookie Ensign George Gay, who had been floating around for forty-five hours after witnessing firsthand from his wave-top vantage point the destruction of three of the carriers. When asked by doctors what he did to care for the bullet wound in his arm, Gay told them he had used "the salt water treatment."

Not only that, but another Catalina flying boat spotted two big Japanese cruisers about ninety miles from the island, and Spruance, who had by now steamed back in the area to cover Midway, launched an attack against them. These ships were traveling slow because they were both seriously damaged, having accidentally collided the night before after spotting a U.S submarine. The *Enterprise*'s dive-bombers finished the job—or nearly did, anyway: one of the cruisers was sent to the bottom and the other so badly wrecked it would take more than a year in dry dock for repairs.

After the death of the *Yorktown* the U.S. Pacific Fleet headed back to Hawaii to savor their victory and ponder the lessons learned in the battle. One of these was the futility of sending torpedo bombers without a proper fighter escort against an enemy force that has full air cover. Another was the crucial role played by the code breakers, without which there would have been no Battle of Midway, or not much of one, in any event. Yet they had won a resounding victory. In exchange for 307 American lives and the loss of the *Yorktown* and 147 airplanes and most of their crews, the U.S. fleet had destroyed four Japanese carriers, along with 332 planes, a cruiser, and three destroyers, and killed 4,899 Japanese sailors.*

On June 6 (EST) Americans were treated to newspaper headlines describing the battle and got the uplift they so badly needed. Admiral Ernest King, chief of naval operations, gleefully pointed out that this was the first decisive Japanese naval defeat since 1592. (The only downside for the navy men was the galling fact that newspapers throughout the land, including the distinguished *New York Times,* led with headlines that screamed "Army

---

*The eminent historian John Keegan in his latest book, *Intelligence in War: Knowledge of the Enemy from Napoleon to Al-Qaeda* (2003), suggests that the American victory at Midway was as much due to luck as to the U.S. intelligence cracking of the Japanese naval code. This may be true, but if the code had not been cracked, then the American carrier fleet would not have been there, would it? And if not, of course, there would have been no luck to depend on in the first place.

Fliers Blasted Two Fleets Off Midway.") The mood was equally high at the White House, where Roosevelt's aide Harry Hopkins, in a letter to the U.S. ambassador to Russia, proclaimed that the victory "may change the whole strategy of the Pacific. After all," he added, "it is quite fun to win a victory once in a while. Nothing that I know of quite takes its place."[24]

The Japanese, for their part, quickly draped a cloak of secrecy around the affair. Having first announced publicly that the Japanese navy had anni-hilated the entire American fleet (prompting the usual victory parades in Tokyo and gloating commentary from Tokyo Rose) their navy proceeded to isolate all survivors of the Midway battle, including Commander Fuchida, who, with his broken ankles, was confined to a base hospital and not allowed contact with his family. Even the emperor was kept in the dark for several weeks, despite Yamamoto's stern declaration: "I am the only one who must apologize to His Majesty."

Admiral Nagumo, precisely two years to the day from the Battle of Midway, committed hara-kiri on the island of Saipan to keep from being captured by American troops after the remainder of his fleet was sunk by the U.S. Navy.[25] The Japanese never did figure out that they had come to grief largely because the Americans had been deciphering their naval code, which, ill advisedly, they still considered unbreakable.

Chapter Fourteen ★

It is timely now to revisit our redoubtable spy "Cynthia" (Amy Elizabeth Thorpe), she with the "explosive sexual charms." It will be remembered from chapter three that during the year before Pearl Harbor Cynthia, an American, joined the British counterintelligence agency in Washington D.C., being run by the British master spy William Stephenson. There, she had managed to obtain the Italian naval code by seducing the Italian naval attaché at the embassy in Washington. Now, in mid-1942, when America was fully into the war, Cynthia was given an even trickier assignment: obtain the Vichy French naval code in preparation for the planned U.S.-British landings in French North Africa later in the year.

The Vichy French were on high alert since the Roosevelt government was openly hostile to them and the embassy itself was within a hairbreadth of being booted out of the United States. Cynthia, posing as a newspaper reporter, managed to attract the attentions of the French press attaché, Captain Charles Brousse, while waiting to interview the Vichy French ambassador. An affair followed, as Cynthia worked on Brousse's patriotism and hatred of the Vichy French president, the wicked Pierre Laval. Slowly Brousse began to give Cynthia secret information—by now she had confided to him that she was an intelligence agent—but when she finally got around to asking for the naval code he was startled, and replied that it could not be done since only two people were allowed access to the code room; Brousse was not one of them.

Undaunted, the two concocted a plan that must go down in the annals of espionage as one of its most innovative and irregular schemes. They appeared late one night at the French embassy when only the night watchman was on duty. Brousse explained to him that it was impossible to find a hotel room in Washington during wartime and, besides, it would not do for the French press attaché to be seen going into a hotel in the first place. And so would it be possible for the two of them to spend some time on the couch in one of the embassy's first-floor drawing rooms? Frenchmen being Frenchmen, the guard was sympathetic; a generous greasing of his palm with a tip didn't hurt, either.

They used this ruse time and again until the watchman became accustomed to it (and to his tip). Then one night, just as the Battle of Midway began, Cynthia and Brousse arrived at the embassy in gay spirits and with a bottle of champagne, from which they naturally offered the watchman a glass. Just as naturally the champagne they gave him was drugged and in due time the guard was hors de combat. No sooner was this done than their "taxi driver" appeared. He was actually a skilled locksmith and second-story man working for Stephenson, and within a few hours he had managed to pick his way into the code room and crack the safe with the priceless Vichy naval code in it. Problem was, there was no time to take the codes out, get them copied, and return them before the possibility of their all being caught. They would have to do the whole thing all over again.

This time Cynthia was worried; she sensed that the watchman was becoming suspicious and didn't think the drugged-champagne trick would work a second time. So she conjured up a new plan for a few nights later. This time, when the watchman looked in on them, Cynthia was fully nude on the divan; the watchman quickly shut the door in embarrassment, leaving them to whatever it was they were doing. It was not, of course, what he expected, for Cynthia and Brousse immediately threw open a window and let in their taxi driver, who, having cracked the safe once before, now did it again quickly. They removed the naval codes and gave them to another of Stephenson's agents waiting beneath the open window. He took the codes to a nearby safe house, where they were photostated and, within an hour, returned to the safe in the embassy code room with nobody the wiser. Next day the Vichy naval codes were being pored over by intelligence officers in London, with very useful results when the British-American invasion of French North Africa began four months later.[1]

Meantime, let us also revisit the travails of Commander Columbus Darwin Smith, captain of the U.S.S. *Wake* at Shanghai, China, the first American to be taken prisoner of war by the Japanese. For the first month or so Smith was treated well—while he was a prisoner of the navy. When he was turned over to the Japanese army, however, which was responsible for all prisoners, things quickly changed. Along with the two thousand or so prisoners who had just arrived from the Wake Island battle, Smith was shipped upriver from Shanghai to a dingy prisoner-of-war camp at Woosung. "I had been treated as an officer by the Japanese naval authorities," Smith remembered, "but the Japanese army treated us all as pigs, except they didn't bother to fatten us up. We were living in the midst of the finest farming land in the world, but we never were given vegetables."

The behavior of the Japanese soldiers paralleled that in the Philippines: clubbing, bayoneting, beatings, starvation; the weather was freezing and they had scant clothes, especially the men from Wake, who arrived in tropical dress. It wasn't long before Smith began planning an escape. His coconspirators were Commander John B. Woolley of the British navy, Commander Winfield Scott Cunningham, who it will be remembered had been in charge of the Wake Island base, and big Dan Teters, the former University of Washington football star who had been supervisor of construction on Wake.

The escape problem was daunting: they would have to crawl through three hundred yards of sharp gravel to get through a barbed-wire fence electrified with 22,000 volts. They set about scrounging to make knee pads and stole a shovel with which to dig under the electric fence. They told no one else of their plan. On the night of March 10, 1942, they were ready. The men sneaked out of their barracks and past the Japanese guards, crossed the gravel, and reached the fence. Woolley with the shovel began scooping out a shallow hole under the wire and soon announced, "Here I go, boys."

"He lay flat and inched himself under the wire," Smith remembered. "If even a button of his shirt touched that wire there would be a blinding flash and Woolley would be burned to a crisp." The others followed, with only a two-inch clearance between them and instant incineration. The plan, as devised by Smith, who had lived in Shanghai for fourteen years and spoke Japanese, and Woolley, was to make their way to the Yangtze River, steal a sampan, and oar ten miles downriver to free Chinese territory. But when they neared the river, they met with what Smith declared was "the greatest enemy a seafaring man can ever meet. Fog!" It was so thick, Smith said, "that we could reach out a grab a handful of it."

After an hour of aimless floundering in the fog they finally reached the river, only to hear the voices of Japanese soldiers; they backed away about a hundred yards until they stumbled into a small abandoned outhouse, in which they decided to hide until the fog lifted. All night they stayed there, fog as heavy as ever, until about nine next morning when it finally lifted. They had decided to remain in the outhouse until nightfall, then continue with their plan, but this was not to be. A party of Chinese puppet soldiers, in Japanese employ, found them and at gunpoint marched them away. They had been told many times that the penalty for escape was beheading.

Next day, after questioning, they were taken back to the POW camp and forced to reenact their escape, including crawling again under the deadly electric wire. Following this, they were trucked down to Shanghai to a torture chamber, where they would await their fate. Smith, fifty-one years old, was jammed into a ten-by-ten-foot cell that contained thirteen other prisoners, some of whom he knew, including the director of Standard Oil of China and the American president of the Shanghai National City Bank.

"These men were as filthy as human beings could be," Smith later recalled. "We were only given enough food to sustain life" and were forced to sit cross-legged on the floor all day without support for the back; "any man caught standing was beaten." A man who became one of Smith's best friends during this enforced-yoga ordeal was a Chinese murderer named Wang Lee, who took tender care of another cell mate, a man who stank horribly and lived under a blanket all day, moaning and picking chunks of flesh from his feet and sticking them onto the stone wall. He was a leper.

Many of Smith's cell mates were given the "water treatment," a time-honored Japanese torture that often resulted in death. Smith described it this way: "They would roll up a bath towel into the form of a cone and place it firmly around his mouth and nose. Meanwhile they'd be filling a five-gallon can with water. They would add kerosene and urine to the water. They would pour this through the opening at the top of the cone and the victim had either to swallow or strangle. His belly would swell and then the guards would strike him sharply across the stomach with a light steel rod. Usually the man would lose consciousness. They had a sort of hoist and tackle in the rooms they used for giving the water treatment. They would hoist the man up by his heels and allow the water to drain out of him. As soon as he recovered consciousness they would repeat the dose. Sometimes they would hit him too hard with the steel rods and the stomach would burst. Two men who had been given the water treatment were thrown back into our cells. In each case the man was dead."

Every day Smith was stripped naked and taken to his Japanese inquisitors. They kept asking him over and over who had helped him escape; when he truthfully told them it was no one, his ordeal was prolonged. Smith was not given the water treatment himself but instead was given the "balance treatment," that is, being forced to kneel for hours at a time on a steel plate in front of the interrogator with arms folded tight. If he lost his balance and put his hands out to catch himself, he was beaten, or used as a human ashtray. "The guards stood on either side of me, smoking," Smith remembered. "While a man was being questioned the guards would put out their cigarettes on the man's naked body when they had finished them. I have met and talked to forty-five prisoners who had to endure that. They averaged 200 to 400 burns each. The Japs never considered it torture, and were amazed when I told them I thought it a pretty awful thing to do."

There was also the "electric treatment," consisting of applying electrically charged rods to a prisoner's body and private parts, and the "hoist treatment" in which the prisoners were hoisted up until "their own weight wrenched their arms out of their sockets." One of the Japanese interrogators Smith remembered as "the most vicious, cruelest man I have ever met. He had lived in America—had, in fact, graduated from Notre Dame. He had married a Japanese woman who was an American citizen. Their two daughters had attended the University of Southern California."

One day Smith and his companions were rounded up, stripped naked, handcuffed, and taken into a courtroom where their trial was to be conducted—on the ridiculous charge of "deserting from the Japanese army," generally a capital offense.

The military judge was a Japanese brigadier general. They were given a defense counsel who could not speak English, and when they complained they were provided with an interpreter, "but he knew no English either." The verdict was a foregone conclusion; so, apparently, was the sentence, which with some relief surprised the three men: "Ten years of penal servitude."

Next morning they were taken to Shanghai's Ward Road Jail, which with its 9,300 inmates was the largest prison in the world at the time and was reserved for the most dangerous and degenerate felons. No one had been known to escape from the Ward Road Jail, but Smith and his companions were about to give it a try. They arrived on June 8, 1942, the day after the Battle of Midway ended, and almost precisely the same time as the seductive Cynthia was writhing naked on her couch at the French embassy in Washington, half a world away.*[2]

Cynthia wasn't the only espionage agent at work in America. The week after the Midway battle a German submarine surfaced off the Long Island village of Amagansett, which is now part of the fashionable Hamptons, and disgorged four English-speaking German spies and saboteurs in a rubber boat. These men rowed to the beach, stripped off their uniforms,† and buried them in the sand along with half a dozen boxes of high explosives. Their mission was to blow up hydroelectric dams at Niagara Falls, several ALCOA aluminum plants, and the locks on the Ohio River near Cincinnati. A few days later a second German U-boat landed four more saboteurs at the now exclusive golfing community of Ponte Vedra, Florida, near Jacksonville. They

*Commander Smith's story is taken entirely from his fascinating account, *Officially Dead,* written with Quentin Reynolds and published by Random House before the war ended.

†Worn so that if they were captured upon landing they would be treated as prisoners of war, not spies.

were to bomb the Pennsylvania Railroad station at Newark and other important railroad connections and poison the water supply system for New York City. Then both teams were to meet up and continue bombing Jewish stores and public transportation terminals. It was the Nazis' notion that this would spread fear and panic among the American population.

From the beginning, the German sabotage plan began to unravel. First, the sub off Long Island was grounded on a sandbar. Next, as the saboteurs were burying their clothes and explosives, a young U.S. Coast Guardsman walking the beach noticed them and inquired what they were doing. The German headman informed him they were sailors whose ship had been sunk, but the Coast Guardsman was suspicious. The German, who was carrying more than $80,000 in U.S. cash, offered him a bribe and the young man took it. But instead of keeping quiet he reported the entire encounter to his superiors, who quickly returned to the spot and discovered the Germans' cache. They in turn reported this to the FBI, which began a frantic manhunt for the fugitives, who by then had caught a train to New York.

There, the team leader, one John Dasch, thirty-nine, who had grown up in America, got cold feet. He assumed that the Coast Guardsman had not fallen for his story and that if and when the FBI caught up with them they would be executed as spies. He was not far wrong. Dasch fretted over the situation for a few days, confiding to one fellow saboteur that he thought he should turn them all in and ask for mercy. The teammate agreed and Dasch caught a train to Washington and marched into FBI headquarters. At first nobody would believe his story until he produced the $80,000 in U.S. bills. After interrogation Dasch spilled the beans on the other members of his team and they were quickly rounded up by the authorities. He was also able to lead the FBI to the four members of the Florida team of saboteurs by offering up a contact list that was written in invisible ink on his handkerchief. They, too, soon found themselves in custody and it was only then that the would-be saboteurs' presence in the United States was revealed to the media.

The Roosevelt administration immediately ordered a military tribunal to try them, the first such body convened since the assassination of Abraham Lincoln. The evidence was overwhelming; six of the eight Germans were given the death penalty, and Dasch (who for some reason had been expecting a hero's reward) and his accomplice received thirty years to life at hard labor and were lucky to get that. On August 8, 1942, the six German spies were shown into the death chamber at the Washington, D.C., jail, where they were escorted, one after the other, to the electric chair.*

By now, halfway into the first year of war, Americans were learning to accommodate themselves to new realities. For the first part of the century nearly all middle-class families had at least a servant or two. Now virtually all the servants had gone off into war work or the military and the ladies of the house had to learn to cook their own suppers and make their own beds and wash their own dishes and clothes and answer their own doors. Owing to the fuel oil crisis brought on by the German submarine war along the East Coast, many families found themselves living in only two or three rooms and closing off the rest for lack of heating. The Roosevelt administration instituted daylight saving time "for the duration," in order to conserve electricity and fuel. With rationing of heating fuels, many restaurants, bars, schools, department stores, and other businesses had to reduce their hours of operation, a further inconvenience.

Colleges, high schools, even grade schools were undergoing dramatic changes in curriculum. Before the war elemental math problems were couched in terms such as, "If a man is running at such and such a speed, and stops to rest for fifteen minutes each five miles, how long does it take . . . ?" or, "If a car is heading cross-country from Detroit to Denver at 50 mph . . . . ?" Now questions were posed differently, such as, "If an airplane is flying at 200 mph with headwinds of 50 mph, and uses 20 gallons of fuel a minute, how long would it take . . . ?" Subjects such as trigonometry (used in calculating artillery firing tables), mechanical drawing, geometry, physics, chemistry, and other sciences useful to the war effort were emphasized. Boys were encouraged to enter technical training schools and take up such subjects as metallurgy and engine mechanics; girls were en-

*Three years after the war Dasch and the other turncoat Nazi were deported to Germany, where they were reviled as traitors.

couraged to go into nursing. Medical schools cut their graduation requirement for doctors from four years to three.

Whereas in 1940 only 7 percent of American production had gone into making war materials, by mid-1942 nearly 50 percent did so.[3] Immediately after Pearl Harbor the isolationists had shut up, at least most of them; and now instead of America First rallies in public arenas there were victory rallies, complete with orchestras and other entertainments, and of course the inevitable war-bond sales. Few people spoke of "defense"; they spoke instead of "victory." So-called canteens began opening up all over the country, the most famous being the Stage Door Canteen in New York City, where servicemen could go and mingle with Broadway stars. The one in Los Angeles was even more sought after, since a soldier or sailor could visit in hopes of bumping into Hollywood stars such as Betty Grable, Rita Hayworth, or Bette Davis serving sandwiches and hot coffee.

There were "drives" for just about everything. Throughout the country women lugged their aluminum pots and pans down to fire stations and other designated collection points, since well-meaning authorities had announced that these things were needed in the construction of warplanes. And there it piled up because the type of aluminum used in cooking utensils is no good for making airplanes, and soon it was simply sold to scrap dealers, who sold it back to the pots-and-pans people, who sold it back to the women who had donated it in the first place. Rubber was another much sought after item in the drives, but its value to the war effort was real, since the Japanese, by taking Malaya, had cornered most of the world's rubber supply. Women donated their rubber girdles and garters, Congress coughed up the rubber mats around its spittoons, and automobile owners forked over their rubber floor mats. A Hollywood studio even donated the giant rubber squid used in the hit underwater movie *Reap the Wild Wind*. All in all, a spirit of unity and determination predominated across the land.[4]

Hollywood, however, was not quite sure what to make of the situation. Before the war, and during its first few months, the studios had released a number of passionate anti-Axis films that were generally well received. Many of these became known as "flag-wavers," because at the end of such films there would be a cut to a big American flag with patriotic music playing in the background and, after Pearl Harbor, the ever-present pitch to buy war bonds. But when the reality of war began to sink in, Hollywood producers started to realize that what Americans really wanted were so-called escapist movies: musicals, comedies, and the like, and so began to make these, many of them with South American themes, featuring samba and rumba singers with a lot of fruit on their hats, such as Carmen Miranda. This was to encourage a sort of "hands across the sea" relationship with nations of the Southern Hemisphere, most of which had not yet declared their allegiances to one side or the other. One movie that filled both bills was the Academy Award–winning classic *Yankee Doodle Dandy,* featuring a stellar performance by James Cagney as the patriotic song composer George M. Cohan from the World War I era, with the hit songs "You're a Grand Old Flag" and "Over There." Another was the hit *This Is the Army,* featuring popular wartime numbers by Irving Berlin.

Reviving an old World War I custom, mothers were encouraged to stick colored tinsel stars on the windowpanes near their front doors: blue for sons who had joined the military services and, sadly, gold if they had been killed in action.

By mid-1942 many well-known movie stars had joined the fighting forces, such as James Stewart, Henry Fonda, Clark Gable, Robert Cummings, Douglas Fairbanks Jr., Robert Montgomery, and even Sabu, the Jungle Boy. Cowboy actor Wayne Morris became a pilot and was credited with downing six Japanese planes; Stewart left the air force as a colonel and Montgomery commanded a destroyer during the Normandy invasion. Even Gable flew at least one bombing mission before being put on troop entertainment duty. Hollywood women played their parts, too; in addition to USO and canteen duties they traveled the country appearing at war bond rallies, raising tens of millions of dollars. Carole Lombard, Gable's wife, died in a plane crash returning from one of these rallies in 1942. Bob Hope got up an entertainment troupe to tour overseas. Many sports figures joined up as well, including baseball's Ted Williams and Joe DiMaggio and boxing's champ Joe Louis. Professional football and baseball continued throughout the war but at a much-reduced quality of play.

By this time the radio and recording industries had chipped in their two cents also, with such wartime favorites as "Yokohama Mama," "Praise the Lord and Pass the Ammunition," "Pistol Packin' Mama," "Don't Sit

Under the Apple Tree (With Anyone Else But Me)," "The Boogie Woogie Bugle Boy of Company B," as well as novelty songs such as "You're a Sap Mr. Jap" and Spike Jones's immortal "Der Fuehrer's Face," which sold a lot of records but was not airable at the time, owing to the song's recommendation of what should be done in the Führer's face. Bandleader and composer Glenn Miller's "American Patrol" became a great hit, especially after Miller, who had joined the U.S. Army Air Corps, was killed over the English Channel. But the greatest hit of all in 1942 was a tune from the musical comedy *Holiday Inn,* called "White Christmas," sung by Bing Crosby.

In the meantime, unpleasant things had begun to brew in the South Pacific. The Japanese army, despite their navy's horrendous defeat at Midway in the central Pacific, still had designs on Australia and New Zealand, desiring to keep the Americans out of their newly won gains in the South Pacific area. To that end they decided to construct and fortify a series of air bases in the southern Solomon Islands from which they could bomb with land-based planes all U.S.-occupied territory and sea-lanes from Samoa to New Caledonia. This, coupled with the planned occupation of Port Moresby, New Guinea,* would give the Japanese control over the Coral Sea as well, and preface an invasion of Australia itself, as well as New Zealand. Clearly, this would deprive the Americans and their allies of any staging base in the South Pacific from which they could plan to eject the Japanese from their recent conquests.

The dire news about Japanese intentions in the Solomons was first conveyed to the Allied authorities in early May 1942 by Australian "coast watchers," operating from the dark and dank interiors of the six-hundred-mile-long eerie and remote island chain.

*As we have already seen, the Battle of the Coral Sea thwarted Japanese designs on a quick taking of Port Moresby by seaborne invasion, but this did not stop them from their plan to occupy all of the Solomon Islands. They soon developed an alternative and costly strategy to take Port Moresby anyway, from the north side of New Guinea.

Guadalcanal was discovered in 1568 by the young Spanish explorer Mendana, who had set out from Peru on a quest for the fabled gold mines of King Solomon. When his fleet reached the islands he found no gold but instead throngs of ferocious cannibals and headhunters, who welcomed him with a shower of stones and spears to celebrate their being "discovered." After chasing away most of these natives with his rudimentary European firearms, Mendana's men replenished their stores by carrying off the natives' pigs and other foodstuffs and burning their grass-hut villages before sailing away in disgust—but not before Mendana named the island chain the Solomon Islands, as a tribute, gold or no, to King Solomon, and one of his lieutenants christened the big island they had just left Guadalcanal, after his hometown in Valencia.

The Solomons were then forgotten for the next two hundred years; the British even erased them from their charts on the dubious theory that they never existed in the first place. A French expedition finally visited the islands in 1767 and the British twenty years later, but nobody could find any use for them and the various explorers sailed off in search of happier landings. But by the mid-nineteenth century a use had developed: coconut farming. The coconut was to the economy of the Pacific what the Shmoo was as illustrated in cartoonist Al Capp's fabulous comic strips of the 1940s: it became almost all things to all men. Nothing was wasted; no less than fifty different products are derived from the coconut palm, from soap to oil to furniture wood, sandals, hats, butter, yarn, insulation, doormats, preservatives, vinegar, glycerin, rope, tea, fiberboard, charcoal, lamp shades, milk, medicines, dyes, fans, and brooms.

The beauty of it was that the coconut grows naturally and quickly in the equatorial Pacific, requiring little or no tending, except to keep the jungle vines off it. The main drawback with establishing coconut plantations on Guadalcanal and the rest of the Solomons was the native people, who remained fiercely opposed to intrusions by white men (or anybody else, for that matter) and were ready to back it up. Many well-meaning missionaries and geological expeditioners were killed (and presumed eaten); in the 1850s a wealthy Australian entrepreneur who sailed to Guadalcanal in his private yacht with the idea of establishing his own nation for the purpose of coconut growing was attacked by the natives and roasted alive.

At the turn of the nineteenth century Great Britain declared a pro-
tectorate over the Solomons and slowly established small outposts on
coastal harbors, aided by England's giant Lever Bros. Corporation, which
went into the coconut plantation business for the coconut copra, used to
make soap. The remaining cannibals and headhunters retired sullenly into
the interior jungles to do their thing, and thus the Solomons remained,
until the outbreak of World War II, when the Japanese arrived. The Japanese were not as benevolent as their white counterparts, who had been
evacuated hastily back to Australia. They began by promising the islanders a share in their Greater East Asian Co-Prosperity Sphere but what the
natives got instead was rude and brutal treatment from the Japanese soldiers, forced labor, and confiscation of their food and meager belongings
whenever a Japanese wanted them.[5]

Naturally this did not endear the Japanese to the Solomon Islanders,
of which there were ten thousand to fourteen thousand on Guadalcanal
alone, and they responded, at least some of them, by actively warring
against their new oppressors. Of these, the natives who did the most good
were those recruited by the aforementioned Australian coast watchers, as
bold and persevering a band of fighters as have ever lived. The coast watcher
system had been set up during World War I, using coconut planters, post-
masters, district officers, and others to report any enemy activity in their
areas. Problem was, communications were so primitive then that by the
time the information reached Australian headquarters it was usually too
late to be useful.

By the time war broke out in the South Pacific in 1942, however,
the coast watchers were equipped with powerful radio transmitters* so
that intelligence could be reported almost instantaneously. Thus, the coast
watchers and their native scouts operated all along the hundreds of miles
of islands stretching from Bougainville in the north, through New Georgia

---

*These big vacuum-tube radios were so large and complicated—and included gaso-
line generators used to recharge their batteries and tall antennas enabling them to transmit
several thousand miles—that they sometimes required up to sixteen natives to bear them
through the rough and slippery terrain. But for the sailors and marines fighting at Guadalcanal, they were worth their weight in gold.

and Santa Isabel southward, to Florida Island, Malaita, and Guadalcanal. From their jungle hiding places along the mountainous coasts, the coast watchers could report the number, type, and direction of Japanese war-planes or warships departing the big Japanese bases at Rabaul and the Shortlands, providing the Allies with vital, timely warning as to what the Japanese had in store for them, and when. The importance of this infor-mation with respect to the Battle of Guadalcanal cannot be overstated. Coast watchers, or their native scouts and bearers, if caught, were sum-marily executed by the Japanese.

The first move the Japanese made, in May 1942, was to establish a seaplane scouting base at Tulagi, a tiny island about twenty miles north-east of Guadalcanal, separated by what became known as the Slot, a six-hundred-mile-long north-south patch of ocean dividing the two parallel chains of islands. Tulagi had been the British-Australian Solomon Islands commercial and administrative capital, consisting of a row of Chinese shops, a hotel, wharves and packaging plants, the district office, a cricket pitch, a golf course, soccer and rugby fields, and other things Anglophilic. On his way to the Battle of the Coral Sea Admiral Fletcher had sent planes to bomb the new Japanese installations at Tulagi but they did minimal damage. MacArthur from his headquarters in Australia sent B-17s but they fared little better.

Then in July 1942, coast watchers reported the Japanese landing troops on Guadalcanal itself, followed shortly by more troops, heavy con-struction equipment, and laborers, who began hacking an airfield out of the coconut plantations on the island's north shore.*[6] They came with bulldozers and trucks and even built a small narrow-gauge rail line for hauling fill and coral to be crushed for the runway's surface. This news alarmed the U.S. Pacific Fleet back at Pearl Harbor, because it was evi-dent that if the Japanese got the air base up and running, all shipping in the area would be in constant peril. So at the beginning of July of '42, Nimitz ordered Vice Admiral Robert L. Ghormley, commander of the South

---

*Because the Japanese language does not include the sound of the letter "L," Guadalcanal was to them "Guadacanar."

Pacific Area, to draw up plans for an invasion and occupation of Guadalcanal, Tulagi, and the Santa Cruz Islands. This was named Operation
Watchtower, a prelude to taking back all of the Solomons and the Bismarck
Archipelago, including the vast Japanese staging area at Rabaul. It would
be America's first offensive of the war, and the first of the Pacific island-
hopping stepping-stones to Japan itself.

Ghormley selected as his task force commander Admiral Frank Jack
Fletcher, fresh from his victory at Midway, and to command the amphibious landings on Guadalcanal he chose Admiral Richmond Kelly Turner, a
hard-nosed and profane sailor of the old school. The task force would consist of three carriers: the *Enterprise,* the *Saratoga,* and the recently arrived
Wasp, as well as the new battleship *North Carolina* and a number of cruisers,
destroyers, transports, cargo carriers, and miscellaneous other ships. The
ground forces selected for the invasion itself were the 17,000 men of the
First Marine Division, most still on their way to the South Pacific from
the West Coast, and their commanding officer, Major General Alexander
Archer Vandegrift.

Vandegrift was born to an old Virginia family in 1887 at Charlottesville,
in the foothills of the Blue Ridge Mountains. After two years at the University of Virginia, he took the exams to secure a commission in the Marine
Corps and became a second lieutenant in 1909. He served, as did most of
the marines of his day, in the boiling Central American and Caribbean military conflicts: Panama, Nicaragua, Haiti, and Veracruz, Mexico, as well as
in China, "quickly working his way up through the ranks"—it took him thirty-
two years in the Marine Corps before making general. Vandegrift received
his second star on March 23, 1942, and took over the First Marine Division,
then based at Quantico, Virginia.

Almost from the start, things began to go wrong. For one thing, Admiral
Ghormley didn't much like the plan, which was not a good thing when so
many lives were at stake. Neither, for that matter, did MacArthur, who
had conceived his own strategy not only for taking the Solomons but for
invading the great Japanese base at Rabaul itself. By now he had with him

in Australia three full infantry divisions but would need the amphibious expertise of the navy's marine division plus its warships. But the navy was very reluctant to put its marines, carriers, and other precious warships under command of an army man. Finally it was settled that the navy would be in charge of the Solomons campaign, but it still didn't sit well with MacArthur, who fumed that this was all part of a vast conspiracy "for the complete absorption of the national defense function by the Navy."[7] And poor General Vandegrift; imagine his surprise when—after having been promised by the highest authorities in Washington that his marines would not be expected to see combat until the following January—he was summarily informed upon arrival in New Zealand that he had exactly one month to get his men ready to launch a major invasion.

The marines themselves appeared to be a questionable force. To get the division hurriedly up to strength, raw recruits right out of boot camp were thrown into the mix. And old leatherneck marines were yanked from their duties on posts and bases far and wide and sent to the First Marine Division. Listen to the wonderful description according to then Lieutenant Colonel Samuel B. Griffith II, who was there: "They were a motley bunch. Inveterate gamblers and accomplished scroungers, who drank hair tonic in preference to post exchange beer ('horse piss'), cursed with wonderful fluency, and never went to chapel ('the God-box') unless forced to. Many dipped snuff, smoked rank cigars or chewed tobacco (cigarettes were for women and children). They had little use for libraries or organized athletics and would not have known what to do with a career counselor if they met one. They could live on jerked goat, the strong black coffee they called 'boiler compound,' and hash cooked in a tin hat."[8] On second thought, maybe they wouldn't be so bad after all.

Then there was the acute shortage of such necessary items as earth-moving equipment, fuel-storage tanks, runway material, and skilled personnel; the small and undeveloped harbors of the South Pacific simply didn't have the capacity to load and unload all the things necessary for a big invasion operation. To make matters worse, before the marines departed the States their cargo was "commercially loaded" onto the ships, in order to make use of every available bit of space, instead of "combat loaded," in which every item is placed aboard with a mind toward its immediate need when landing on a hostile beach.* Worse yet was the fact that now that the enormous cargo for the 17,000 marines had to be unloaded and reloaded, the idiot Stevedores Union in New Zealand—with the Japanese knocking at their very doorstep—refused to let their longshoremen work in the rain, when the weather there was terrible at that time of year. So the longshoremen were chased from the docks and the marines themselves began the tedious process of loading and reloading their own ships in the ceaseless downpour; cheap cartons fell to pieces, labels on cans soaked off, leaving a hundred-yard-long soggy mess of drenched cornflakes, powdered milk, flour, and other rations, as well as clothing, shoes and socks, blankets—so many of the things the marines would need to fight the battle.

Another problem was the lack of detailed knowledge of the islands themselves. Because they were so remote, no one had ever made proper maps and charts of them, marking the precise locations and dimensions of beaches, bays, coves, inlets, tides, depths, mountains, jungles, rivers, and other topographical and oceanographic information. An army aerial photography mission launched from Australia was turned back by marauding Japanese Zeros and a package of vital information on the islands' topography compiled in Australia somehow got lost in the mail.[9]

A further disaster occurred when the navy task force and marines attempted a dress rehearsal for their landing on Guadalcanal at the end of July. The site selected was a remote island in the Fiji group and according to Vandegrift the exercise was a complete fiasco. The various units involved had never worked together before; indeed, it was the first attempted U.S. amphibious landing since 1898. Landing craft broke down, or were impaled on coral heads, and most marines never reached the beaches; gunnery was wildly inaccurate; and there were worse things, too.

Four days before the fleet was to sail, and just as the rehearsal landings were taking place, a conference was held aboard the *Saratoga,* Admiral

*This gross error does not seem to attach itself to Vandegrift; he assumed, as he had been told by officials in Washington, that his marines would not be called on to fight for at least six months. On the other hand, as a senior commanding officer, he might have considered the possibility that in war things can change quickly.

Fletcher's flagship.* Fletcher, like Ghormley, was against the Guadalcanal operation—even more so; he simply did not think it would succeed. Perhaps the fact that he had so recently seen two aircraft carriers
sunk under his command had something to do with it.† But by all accounts, Fletcher appeared unduly pessimistic and dismissive. When told
by Admiral Turner that it would take a minimum of four or five days of
air cover from Fletcher's carrier task force to unload all the men and
their mountains of supplies, armaments, and equipment, Fletcher balked:
"Vice Admiral Fletcher then stated that he would leave the vicinity of the
Solomons after two days because of the danger of air attacks against the
carriers." Both Turner, who was overseeing the amphibious landings, and
Vandegrift, concerned for his marines, were shocked, if not horrified.
It could not possibly be done in two days; the 17,000 marines would be
left on the beaches of a hostile island in Japanese territory without many
of the things necessary to do their task, let alone to defend themselves.
But Fletcher was unmoved, according to the official report. "In any case,
he would depart at that time."[10]

If Ghormley, the overall commander, had been there he could surely
have overruled Fletcher, but he foolishly chose to sit on his hands at his
headquarters at New Caledonia, hundreds of miles away, sending instead
his chief of staff, who said nothing and only took notes.[11] Be that as it may,
there was no going back now. The invasion had already been set back one
week and Ghormley's headquarters decreed there could be no further
postponements.‡ So on July 31, 1942, the Allied armada of eighty-two ships
began to steam northwestward, toward Guadalcanal.

---

*Among the conferees boarding the *Saratoga* was Admiral John McCain (father of
U.S. senator John McCain), who commanded Fletcher's land-based planes. Just as he began
scaling the precariously swinging Jacob's ladder up the carrier's sides, somebody aboard
Saratoga opened a garbage chute and covered McCain with refuse. As Vandegrift remembered it, "He managed to retain his hold, but a startled officer of the deck soon faced one
mad little admiral."

†*Lexington* at Coral Sea and *Yorktown* at Midway.

‡This was probably a correct decision since if the Japanese completed their air base
on Guadalcanal, which they were close to finishing, they could have bombed the American
fleet and landing force practically with impunity.

*   *   *

It was said by many that you could smell Guadalcanal before you could see it. When the transports and their escorting warships arrived in the dead of night in what would become known as Ironbottom Sound for the number of ships soon to be sunk there, the aroma of fresh ocean breezes soon turned into a fetid, sinister stink of rotting jungle vegetation and scummy, stagnant "rivers" filled with ferocious crocodiles. Guadalcanal was no tropic island paradise like Tahiti or the beaches of Waikiki. It was a mountainous slug-shaped tropical hell ninety miles long and about twenty-five miles wide, roughly the same length as Long Island, only fatter. Actually, it more closely resembled the contour and size of Jamaica, except there was no Montego Bay. Its dark green jungles harbored poisonous snakes and spiders, enormous rats and land crabs, scorpions and leeches, and, worst of all, clouds of the malaria-carrying anopheles mosquito. On the up side, it was also home to beautiful white cockatoos, mynah birds, and macaws and, besides the ubiquitous coconut, wild citrus and other tropical fruits such as papayas and bananas. Most Americans had never heard of Guadalcanal, or knew how to find it on a map, and those who did most likely recollected it from the widely traveled writer Jack London's 1911 short story collection *South Sea Tales,* and here's what he had to say: "The worst punishment I could inflict on my enemies would be to banish them to the Solomons."[12]

All of the day and night before the landings, men sat on the decks of the transports cleaning, oiling, and rechecking their weapons and sharpening their knives and bayonets. Chaplains held services. There were last-minute briefings: "Annex E to General Order No. 3: Paragraph D: Burial: Graves will be suitably marked. All bodies will bear identification tags." Battalion commanders briefed their company commanders ("Goodbye and God bless you and to hell with the Japs!"); company commanders briefed their platoon leaders; platoon leaders briefed their sergeants. Some men played cards or rolled dice and one marine was seen slinging a handful of silver half dollars, one by one, to see how far he could skip them over the ocean waves. "Money don't mean a thing out here anyhow. Even if you stay alive, you can't buy anything." They sang songs, some in harmony: "Down by the Old Mill Stream," "Blues in the Night," "I Want a Girl (Just

Like the Girl that Married Dear Old Dad)." Below, to the boogie-woogie of a beat-up juke box, some marines jitterbugged with each other. The PA system announced that breakfast would be at four-thirty A.M. By ten P.M. the ship was quiet and dark.[13] It was August 6, 1942.

Miraculously the big invasion force had so far gone undetected by Japanese planes, subs, and ships. The convoy had come up along the western side of Guadalcanal, then turned east rounding Cape Esperance with the dark cone of the still active volcano of Savo Island on their port beam, and on into Ironbottom Sound. In the morning darkness they slipped past the exotically named little native villages on Guadalcanal's north shore: Tassafaronga, Kokumbona, Matanikou, Kukum, Lunga, Tenaru, Tenavatu—most destined to become blood-soaked battlegrounds in the months to come. Other transports went farther north before turning east, leaving Savo Island on their starboard, and headed for landings at Tulagi, some twenty miles north of "the Canal."

The night heat from the island blew at the men like a bad breath as they lined the decks, waiting to descend rope ladders to the landing craft. So far there was no indication whatsoever that they had been discovered by the Japanese, but in fact they had. Before the first light of dawn Tulagi radio tapped out "Large Number of Ships, Unknown Number or Types, Entering the Sound. What Can They Be?"

The officer receiving this message at Rabaul, six hundred miles to the north, was Admiral Sadayoshi Yamada, commander of the Imperial Navy air group.

At first he thought it was just a hit-and-run raid and sent out a reconnaissance plane to see what was what. Just about that time practically every big gun in the U.S. Invasion Fleet opened up on the landing beaches. It was 6:14 A.M. and thousands of big six- and eight-inch shells were being hurled toward the Japanese airfield and surrounding areas. Richard Tregaskis was a young correspondent for the International News Service (INS) standing on the deck of one of the transport ships, waiting for word to climb down onto the landing boats.* "It was fascinating to watch the apparent slow-

---

*His account of the battle, *Guadalcanal Diary*, published in 1943, became an instant best seller and is one of the classic works of American war reporting.

ness with which the shells, their paths marked out against the sky in red fire, curved through the air. Distance, of course, caused that apparent slowness. But the concussion of the firing shook the deck of our ship and stirred our trousers legs with sudden gusts of wind, despite the distance."[14]

It did not take long for the Japanese radio operator on Tulagi to send his next and final message to Rabaul: "Enemy Forces Overwhelming. We Will Defend Our Posts to the Death, Praying for Eternal Victory." This news got Admiral Yamada's undivided attention and he immediately began organizing an air raid on the American armada: twenty-seven twin-engine bombers, to be escorted by eighteen Zero fighters. The commander of the Zeros protested that it was suicide to send fighters six hundred miles, fight off the enemy, and expect them to return; they would run out of gas.* Yamada didn't care. He wanted to stop the invasion before it got started.

Here is also where the coast watchers came into play. From his hiding place far up the island chain, an Australian planter turned coast watcher radioed, "Twenty-seven Bombers Heading Yours." That gave Admiral Turner plenty of time to stop his transports from unloading, clear the decks, pull up anchor, and begin fast evasive action: for the cruisers and destroyers to get into position to defend against the incoming Japanese aircraft and for launching fighter planes from Fletcher's carriers, a mere hundred miles away, to flame the bombers and their Zero companions. In a quick and fierce action fourteen of the Japanese planes were shot down and the rest failed to score any hits and flew off back to (or, in any case, toward) Rabaul. Admiral Halsey later assessed it bluntly, as usual, stating, "The intelligence signaled by [the coast watchers] saved Guadalcanal, and Guadalcanal saved the Pacific." Be that as it may, there was still a heap of fighting to do before Guadalcanal was saved, as the marines landing there and at Tulagi would soon find out.

This coast watchers' warnings notwithstanding, Admiral Yamada kept sending down more and more of his bombers as they became available, torpedo bombers, dive-bombers, and so on, so that for the first day of the landing Turner had to stop unloading no less than four times to weigh anchor and

*The maximum range of a Zero fighter at *cruising* speed was 1,150 miles; this did not take into account the dramatically increased fuel consumption during fighter engagements.

run out to sea, maneuvering to keep his transports from becoming sitting ducks. The American carrier-based fighter planes and ship-based anti-aircraft fire disposed of most of the enemy planes, but it took hours off the unloading schedule. This of course was eating gravely into Admiral Fletcher's arbitrary time frame of spending no more than two days in support of the marines who were just now being landed on the unforgiving beaches at Guadalcanal.[15]

To the Americans' grand amazement and relief there was little or no opposition from the 2,000 or so Japanese troops on Guadalcanal, most of whom were laborers working on the airfield.* As the first naval bombardment shells began to burst, they ran off into the jungles, leaving everything behind, including their half-finished breakfasts in their mess tents, still warm in bowls with chopsticks. Naturally, because of Fletcher's severe dictum that he would depart with all his carrier-based fighter protection after forty-eight hours, the scene on the landing beach was a complete mess. Stores and equipment were piled up right out in the open because there was no time to properly move it inland and disperse it among the palm groves where it could not be so easily bombed by Japanese planes.

Absurdly, the Japanese for some reason did not molest this precious cargo, instead turning all their attentions to the navy's ships; if they had, the situation for the marines on Guadalcanal might well have become untenable because Fletcher, going back even on his promise for the meager two days' protection, got cold feet and announced he was pulling out twelve hours early, leaving the marines on shore to their fate. With only half their food, supplies, and weapons unloaded and sitting out in the open, if the Japanese planes had concentrated on this, instead of the ships, the marines probably would have had to be evacuated. Worse, with no fighter cover from Fletcher, Turner apologetically told Vandegrift that he would also have to withdraw his precious transport and supply ships next morning, else they be sunk at their undefended anchorages. Vandegrift reluc-

*U.S. naval intelligence had expected 4,000 to 6,000 Japanese combat troops for the marines to contend with.

tantly had to agree with him, but neither ever forgave Fletcher for his timidity in their time of peril.

With the pleasant surprise that the Japanese would not contest their landing, the marines began exploring their newfound domain and were delighted to find that the Japanese left them many blessings. Wandering among the coconut groves they found some one hundred trucks, a Japanese imitation of the Chevrolet type, gasoline-storage tanks, bulldozers, paving machines, many tons of concrete, and a repair shop, as well as the small narrow-gauge railroad train, which the engineers soon put to good use.* The Japanese had nearly completed the airfield runway; they had been working at it from both ends and only a two-hundred-foot section in the middle was left to finish. There was a gasoline generator–run ice house, an aircraft control structure the marines named "the pagoda," and goodly stores of rice, tinned fish, medical kits, and, best of all, Japanese beer and sake. By nighttime a drenching rain began to fall, but all considered it had been a good day on Guadalcanal, though not so good on Tulagi, and soon not so for the remaining U.S. Navy fleet of surface warships, the only force left to protect the marines who had been left stranded by Fletcher's abrupt departure.

Soon after they learned of the American landings, the Japanese dispatched to Guadalcanal not only air strikes but a powerful surface fleet consisting of seven big cruisers and escorting destroyers under Vice Admiral Gunichi Mikawa. This movement was reported several times to the U.S. Navy but in all cases failed to achieve an appropriate response. An army B-17 radioed a report early on but failed to properly identify the ships or give their speed. An American submarine also spotted the Japanese fleet but it was still too close to Rabaul to determine its destination. An Australian air force pilot saw the fleet next morning as it raced down the Bougainville Strait toward the Slot, but instead of breaking radio silence and immediately filing a report the pilot finished his patrol and headed back to his base on New Guinea, where he stupidly took his "tea" before telling anyone what

---

*The marines quickly named this the Toonerville Trolley after the cartoon image of the day, but it proved invaluable in transporting fill and other landing-strip materials.

he had seen. By now it was almost sunset, too late for Turner to send out any search planes, even if he had them, which he didn't because Fletcher had sailed away, leaving him "bare-assed."[16]

The Allied naval force at Guadalcanal at this time consisted of one battleship (gone off with Fletcher's force), six cruisers, nineteen destroyers, and eighteen transports. It was the transports that Mikawa wanted, and the warships must first be brushed off to get at them. After nightfall, August 8, the Allied cruiser force was patrolling Ironbottom Sound, which is roughly thirty by fifty miles in area; its centerpiece was the volcanic cone of Savo Island. Everyone aboard the patrolling ships was completely exhausted from the repeated Japanese air attacks over the past two days and to a man they were hoping the night would be quiet. This was not to be.

The Allied force was divided into two sections; one, consisting of the Australian cruiser *Hobart,* the American cruiser *San Juan,* and two destroyers, was the Eastern Force, covering the waters between Guadalcanal and its landing beaches and Tulagi. Second was the Northern Force, cruisers *Astoria, Quincy,* and *Vincennes,* with two destroyers, operating north of Savo Island and commanded by Captain Frederick Riefkohl. And finally the Southern Force, the U.S. cruiser *Chicago* and two Australian cruisers, the *Canberra* and *Australia,* patrolled the Guadalcanal coast from the landing site at Lunga Point to Cape Esperance on the far western tip of the island, commanded by the British Rear Admiral V. A. C. Crutchley.

The night was hot, humid, and squally with occasional lightning flashes lighting up the ominous-looking cone of Savo. As an additional precaution the U.S. destroyers *Blue* and *Ralph Talbot,* both equipped with radar, had been sent forward as pickets to guard the approaches to the sound, each cruising a rectangular back-and-forth course. On paper it was a good and solid plan, but soon things began to go very wrong.

For one thing Turner, in the Guadalcanal anchorage, summoned both Crutchley and Vandegrift to a midnight conference aboard his flagship to discuss the unpleasant repercussions of Fletcher's early retirement. This of course pulled *Australia,* Crutchley's flagship, out of the line, and Crutchley, as commander, away from his command. Meantime, a little after eleven P.M., Mikawa steaming at nearly thirty miles per hour, and approaching Ironbottom Sound, launched a number of floatplanes from his cruisers to scout and at the appropriate time to drop illuminating flares on the Allied warships. The Japanese were highly skilled night fighters with superior night glasses, searchlights, and heavy training in night pyrotechnics. Their cruisers and destroyers also were equipped with the deadly two-foot-thick "long lance" torpedo. Near midnight, one of the Japanese floatplanes was sighted and identified by the picket destroyer *Talbot,* which radioed an emergency warning to the fleet but failed to say it was a floatplane, which would have meant that it had probably come from an enemy cruiser. Other Allied ships heard the planes overhead but did not report them. The American commander Riefkohl assumed that the plane reported by the *Talbot* was friendly, since it had fired on no one, and he had not been informed of Fletcher's departure, meaning that it might be one of the planes from the U.S. carrier force. But assumption is often the mother of much grief and it turned out to be so in this instance.

Watching through their powerful nighttime optics as they entered Ironbottom Sound, lookouts aboard the lead Japanese ships were happily flabbergasted to see the crucial picket destroyers *Blue* and *Ralph Talbot* steaming leisurely away from them on their rectangular courses about five miles off to starboard and port. In a line one after the other, the big Japanese cruisers raced into the sound at full speed. Then all hell broke loose. At 1:43 A.M. the radio aboard the U.S. destroyer *Patterson* suddenly came to life: "Warning! Warning! Strange ships entering the harbor!" No sooner had this urgent message been broadcast than the entire night sky over the Guadalcanal landing beaches and anchorage was lit up by flares from the Japanese floatplanes, also silhouetting perfectly the cruisers of the Southern Force.

First to go was the *Canberra,* which was struck almost immediately by two torpedoes, and in the next instant a salvo of twenty-four eight-inch shells exploded on her bridge and in the engine room, killing almost everybody in both places; she immediately caught fire and began drifting away, only to go down the following morning. Next in line was the *Chicago,* which took a torpedo that blew off most of her bow; a number of shells blasted her decks rendering her hors de combat and she wobbled off westward, out of the fight. Worse, in all the confusion *Chicago*'s captain, Howard Bode, forgot to warn Captain Riefkohl commanding the Northern Force that the Japanese were in the sound and headed their way. Thus in a matter of six minutes the Southern Force was put out of action, since its third Allied cruiser, the *Australia,* still had not returned from the conference with Turner.* Now it was Riefkohl's Northern Force's turn.

It wasn't that the Northern Force was unaware that something was happening; they had seen the flares off Guadalcanal and picked up some of the radio traffic from the Southern Force. They just didn't know what exactly it was that was happening, or that the Japanese had quickly turned northward toward them. The first inkling they got of it was when the *Astoria,* last in line of the Northern Force cruisers, was suddenly caught in the powerful searchlights of Mikawa's flagship *Chokai* and immediately afterward a big salvo of shells threw up geysers of water off the port bow. The *Astoria*'s gunnery officer had already asked for permission to fire but, because the exhausted captain was asleep in his cabin, he received none. He took it on his own initiative to commence firing, but this order was quickly countermanded by the now wide-awake captain who, when the big guns roared, rushed out fearful they were firing on their own ships.

The gunnery officer, however, knew he was firing at Japanese and cried out over the telephone to the captain, "Sir, for God's sake give the order to commence firing!" But a crucial two minutes had been lost and another Japanese salvo from about three miles away exploded upon *Astoria* amidships, setting her afire. The Japanese kept bombarding her, killing the navigator, the helmsman, and the signal officer. The *Astoria*'s catapult planes amidships had been hit and flaming gasoline enveloped the ship. She still fought, though, throughout it all, and with her last shot managed to blow off the forward turret of her tormentor, the *Chokai.*[17]

Meantime, the cruiser *Quincy,* next in line ahead of the *Astoria,* was suddenly caught in the searchlights of the Japanese cruiser *Aoba.* Her horrified crew rushed to their battle stations just in time for a Japanese salvo that torched off one of her catapult planes and, like *Astoria,* she became a flaming pyre for the Japanese fleet to aim at. *Quincy*'s captain, Samuel Moore, shouted to his gunners: "We're going down between them! Give

*It is merely a matter of speculation as to whether or not the presence of *Australia* on the scene would have made any difference. Might it have brought its guns to bear decisively on the Japanese fleet, or just become another ship to be sunk? Who can possibly know?

them hell!" An instant later a salvo hit the bridge, killing Captain Moore and everyone else. As salvo after salvo plowed into the proud ship, men died in agony from flames, were scalded to death from ruptured steam pipes, or in many cases were simply obliterated without a trace. The engine room was wiped out and she was sinking fast by the bows; there was no question that the *Quincy* was doomed and going down, but not before she, like the *Astoria,* got off a final salvo that might just have saved Turner's helpless transports at the Guadalcanal anchorage. The salvo crashed into the *Chokai*'s chart room, destroying it and killing thirty-four men. Now without charts, on a rainy night in the hazardous confines of shoal waters, Mikawa had to wonder what his fate would be if he led his fleet aground.[18]

By now Mikawa was steaming to the north around Savo Island, having completed a shockingly destructive three-quarters of a circle from the point at which he entered Ironbottom Sound. But one more prize awaited him; this was the cruiser *Vincennes,* now alone and facing all seven of the Japanese cruisers. Captain Riefkohl was living in a fool's paradise. He and his watch had seen the flashes from the Southern Force group area about ten miles south, but for some reason assumed they must be shooting at planes. The weather and visibility were bad, but even when he was suddenly caught in the searchlights of three enemy cruisers, he thought they must be friendlies from the Southern group and politely sent out a radio request that the lights be shut off. No sooner was this being done than a great salvo crashed into the water just ahead of the *Vincennes* and another immediately afterward hit her amidships. As occurred on both *Astoria* and *Quincy* the catapult planes went up in a great conflagration of gasoline. This illumination of course made *Vincennes* the perfect target. After a continuous blasting for the next few minutes, Riefkohl tried to escape by turning eastward, but as he did so at least two if not three torpedoes exploded on his port side. Communications and power were cut off and the gun turrets would no longer operate. The *Vincennes* took about sixty more hits and another torpedo in these closing moments and was sinking quickly when the Japanese broke off the action.

Mikawa had by now completely rounded Savo Island when his cruisers ran into the destroyer *Ralph Talbot,* whose crewmen had seen and heard the gunfire in the sound but were unaware of the terrible results. Suddenly a searchlight from one of Mikawa's ships singled her out of the gloom, and she quickly came under fire from three enemy cruisers. *Ralph Talbot* returned fire as best she could, launching four torpedoes, which, as usual, failed to score, and let loose with her five-inch guns against the far larger and more heavily armed Japanese ships. She was burning and listing twenty degrees when a dense rain squall intervened and doubtless saved her from utter destruction.

By now Mikawa had decided he had done enough for one night. It was nearly two-thirty in the morning and by the time he would have gotten his force reorganized and accomplished his primary mission of destroying the American transports at the beachhead, and then headed back to sea, dawn would have broken and his fleet become an easy target for the U.S. carrier planes, which he did not know had already departed the area. That coupled with two more minor problems, the loss of his charts and the fact that they had used up all their torpedoes, convinced him that the damage inflicted on the Americans at this point was sufficient to justify his withdrawal, which he soon ordered.

As the sun came up over Ironbottom Sound that Sunday, August 9, a pitiful sight greeted the rescue craft that had been dispatched to the area. Furiously burning ships and thousands of oil-covered sailors, many gravely wounded or burned, huddled in lifeboats or were clinging to any piece of flotsam they could find. They of course were the lucky ones. One thousand and twenty-three U.S. sailors were dead or dying. The channel itself from Cape Esperance to Savo Island was littered with foul oil slicks and any amount of floating refuse from the sunken or sinking ships. *Quincy* and *Vincennes* were already at the bottom; *Canberra,* damaged beyond repair, was scuttled just after sunup, and *Astoria* managed to linger until a little after noon before she heeled over and sank. *Chicago,* the lone survivor, was sent limping back to dry dock in Australia.

It would come to be known as the Battle of Savo Island and was the worst disaster the U.S. Navy has ever suffered in a sea battle. It had taken just thirty-five minutes from beginning to end.[19] It would not, however, be correct to call it a total defeat, since the Japanese had not accomplished their primary mission, which was to forestall the U.S. invasion of Guadalcanal, and this is a very important point to remember.

By the time the sun set on that tragic day, Admiral Turner had sadly and angrily departed with his transports, still only half unloaded. From the landing beaches the marines gaped incredulously as the transport ships sailed away. They had scarcely enough food for three weeks, and no more air or sea protection; none of their large five-inch coast defense guns had made it ashore to repel a Japanese counterinvasion. They had less than a week's ammunition supply and countless items that they desperately needed had sailed away in the transports, from barbed wire to sandbags and shovels to bulldozers and all of the other heavy equipment. They didn't even have a radio that worked well. They were on their own as they stood on the beaches, staring as small boats began arriving with hundreds of oil-blackened, burned, or dead sailors fished from the bloody, tepid waters of Ironbottom Sound.

The Battle of Savo Island stunned U.S. naval leaders, who withheld the news from the American public for two months, in order not to let the Japanese know how badly they had been hurt. How could it have happened? The answer was soon surmised: surprise and lack of communication.* It had all happened so quickly, but four big Allied cruisers were sunk, along with the loss of more than a thousand of their sailors. Clearly, something must be done, and soon it was—orders being issued from Washington and from Nimitz's headquarters to prevent it ever happening again. Unfortunately, these orders could not and did not prevent this, but the precautions probably helped anyway. It was found that the old-school practices had no place in modern warfare. Paint, for instance, which kept the ships looking shipshape, would burn like tinder when exposed to fierce gasoline fires, and so it was decreed that paint would be stripped off of decks and superstructures. The ships might not have looked as good but at least they wouldn't become flaming coffins if hit. The linoleum used to carpet the floors also was identified and removed as a fire hazard, as was all the

---

*This is what the U.S. Navy officially concluded. But the fact was that the Japanese had perfected naval night-fighting techniques beyond anything the U.S. Navy had ever imagined. It would take them a long and agonizing period of time to figure this out themselves.

wood furniture the ships had accumulated over the years. The time-honored navy witch hunt for culprits whenever a ship is sunk was suspended by Nimitz, who found that there was enough blame to go around for everybody. Things were bad enough as it was.

For their part the Japanese proclaimed, correctly this time, a great victory, and mass parades were held from Tokyo to Yokohama. Still, Tokyo newspapers and radio broadcasts screamed with exaggerated and fantastic headlines and bulletins proclaiming that five American cruisers and four destroyers had been sunk, as well as "eleven transports filled to capacity" with U.S. marines.*[20]

The Japanese soon discovered there was no longer U.S. air protection for Guadalcanal and happily began a Rabaul-relay to bomb the helpless marines below. One bomber, a floatplane that appeared at night, was nicknamed "Louie the Louse" and another "Washing Machine Charlie," for the strange clanking of its unsynchronized engines. These two characters soon passed into Marine Corps legend and remain so today, in story and in song. Japanese submarines also found that with the departure of the surface fleet, particularly the destroyers, they could operate with impunity, and so would frequently surface and lob shells onto the marine beachhead at Lunga Point. Frantically the engineers, using the captured Japanese construction equipment, worked to finish the airstrip so at least they could get some cover from these tormentors.

Meantime, the Tulagi operation had not gone nearly so well for the Japanese as things had on Guadalcanal. There were some eight hundred Japanese troops on Tulagi and they were not simply laborers, as the main body on Guadalcanal were; they were combat soldiers and sailors, avowed to die to the last man for their emperor. And this they just about did. Vandegrift had sent over a force of about 5,000 of his marines to secure Tulagi and almost immediately upon moving inland they began running

---

*Frustrated by the U.S. Navy's silence on the results of the Savo Island debacle, Time magazine took it upon itself to announce to the public some two weeks later "a licking for the Japs." Where they got this ridiculous information has never been determined. But the marines on Guadalcanal, listening to Tokyo Rose, knew the truth, which was that they were there and that at least they hadn't been sunk.

into stiff resistance. The Japanese had set themselves up in a series of caves on a ridge overlooking the cricket field, from which they shot at, mortared, and grenaded the Americans. At night they fiercely attacked the marines, who had dug shallow foxholes, but did not break their lines. As the sun came up, Captain Lewis W. Walt (later to become commander of the Marine Corps in Vietnam) found one of his riflemen, Private First Class John Ahrens, in a foxhole, dying from bullet wounds to the chest and literally covered by dead Japanese, fifteen of them in all. As Captain Walt gently "gathered Ahrens into his arms to carry him to the colonial Residency, the dying marine, still clinging to his BAR, said, 'Captain, they tried to come over me last night, but I don't think they made it.'"

"They didn't, Johnny," Captain Walt replied softly. "They didn't."[21]

The only way to get at the Japanese holed up in the caves was to climb on top of the ridge's backside, and using explosives or gasoline cans tied to poles fling them into the openings. This was done time and again; one marine officer early on had his pants blown off by an explosion but merrily continued his work, pantsless, until most of the caves were sealed. By the time the fighting on Tulagi was finished, several days after the landing, more than seven hundred Japanese were dead; only a handful of others escaped into the nearby jungles of Florida Island. Nearly three hundred Americans had been killed or wounded. Now they settled down to the grim business of securing Guadalcanal. No one, not even the most pessimistic, would have believed how long it was going to take or the ordeals they would soon endure.

★ Chapter Fifteen

At the beginning of August, 1942, the Japanese had not yet apprehended American intentions at Guadalcanal; in fact, they would not understand them until much later. Both Imperial General Headquarters in Tokyo and the Japanese army and navy commanders at Rabaul still seemed to believe it was some kind of raid, or "reconnaissance in force," and not a full-scale invasion. Thus they began wishful countermeasures inadequate to the circumstances, and with nauseating results. Yet the U.S. invasion had stopped the Japanese in their tracks, and ultimately it stopped them from further conquests in the Pacific—all of it—because the United States Navy and Marines, and soon the Army, did not give any ground, despite horrific losses; this was the beginning of the end of the Japanese grand design. It had already become apparent to everyone, however, with the heavy casualties at Tulagi and the calamity of the Battle of Savo Island, that it was not going to be without a high cost in lives and treasure.

First there was the Goettge Raid, one of those cowboy sorts of things that occur all too frequently in war when a hotshot ranking officer decides to get into the action instead of staying where he belongs. Four days after the landings, a patrol had gone westward several miles from the marine encampment and run into gunfire from Japanese soldiers situated on the banks of the Matanikau River.* The Matanikau as it emptied into the Lengo Channel was wide, unfordable upstream, and crocodile infested but, like most rivers on Guadalcanal, it had a sandbar at its mouth along the beach that allowed a crossing. It was here that the marine patrol suffered an officer killed and several marines wounded. Those returning, however, reported to the division intelligence officer, Lieutenant Colonel Frank B. Goettge, that they had seen a strange sight at the Matanikau—a white flag from the Japanese side of the river.† No one knew what to make of this, since the ambush of the marine patrol did not sound like the Japanese were eager to surrender. Next day brought a further clarification, when a Japanese prisoner told his marine interrogators that hundreds of his fellow soldiers were starving in the jungles and wanted to give up.

This prompted Lieutenant Colonel Goettge to organize a patrol to investigate, with himself as patrol leader and many of his noncombat intelligence staff acting as combat patrolmen. General Vandegrift was not keen on the notion, and should have stopped it, but he let himself be argued into it by Goettge, who apparently conjured up visions of the remaining Japanese force on the island marching in behind him hands in air, willing and starving prisoners. They got off late, in the wee hours of the morning, in a noisy landing boat, which put them ashore near the mouth of the river. They never had a chance. Goettge was hit first and killed immediately, followed by one of the regimental medical officers and some interpreters; as dawn broke, of the twenty-six men in the patrol only three had survived, and those only by running into the ocean and swimming and crawling several miles along the coast back to the marine encampment. Along the way their knees and hands were terribly cut up by the sharp coral heads. The other marines had tried to dig in for a fight after the first shots but, alas, their entrenching tools were aboard the transport ships headed back south, so they dug frantically with their helmets and with their hands. The Japanese had

---

*Within weeks, because of press reports, the Matanikau became almost as well known to Americans as the Hudson or the Potomac.

†The flag turned out to be just a Rising Sun flag, which, drooping in the tropical heat, concealed the red rising sun and looked white to the marines from across the river.

met them with overwhelming force, however, and the slaughter was quick. One survivor, a twenty-two-year-old sergeant, who was half American Indian, watched the Japanese closing in, hacking up the remaining marines. "I could see swords flashing," he told a reporter afterward.[1] After this, there would be little or no talk of any surrender by the Japanese, and all now realized that the easy landing had been a chimera.

Ten days after the landings the marines received an unusual visitor. Out of the jungle and onto the beach near the perimeter marched a tall and aristocratic-looking young Englishman dressed in a tattered khaki shirt and shorts and wearing a new pair of oxford shoes.* He was Martin Clemens, a famed Oxford University oarsman and newly appointed district commissioner for Guadalcanal. Behind him were two neat columns of very black, bushy-haired, half-naked Solomon Islanders, one wrapped in the British Union Jack, as sort of a shift. These were members of Clemens's Guadalcanal constabulary who had remained with him as scouts and bearers for his coast-watching duties ever since the Japanese first landed. Clemens had seen and reported it all, from the Japanese invasion of Tulagi, to their invasion of Guadalcanal, to the construction of the Japanese air base there, and then the subsequent marine landings and the Battle of Savo Island, which they had watched from high in the hills. Now he was down to his last few cans of food and wanted to speak to the marine commander. Clemens had been looking forward for months to sleeping in a real bed and having a warm bath and hot food; instead, like everyone else, he ate cold tinned beans and Japanese rice and slept dirty in a foxhole as Japanese planes bombed them.[2]

Vandegrift was pleased as punch to receive Clemens because of his firsthand knowledge of the big island, his native scouts, and especially his radio, which was far better than anything the marines had. When Vandegrift asked how he kept his radio working in this wet, humid climate, Clemens responded, "I just wait until morning, open it, dry it out

---

*The shoes were borrowed, and were two sizes too small and squeezed his feet, but Englishmen of his class had a dress code, and proper shoes were deemed essential.

and by afternoon it works."[3] Vandegrift was also impressed by Clemens's ability to communicate in the pidgin English the Solomon Islanders spoke when they talked with white men. Savor the following colloquy between Clemens and one of his native scouts.

"One thousand Jap-an come 'shore 'long Lunga 'long Monday. Altogether come 'shore 'long big fella launch-ich catch'm one hundred man, got'm big fella machinegun."

"Which way you savvy altogether one thousand 'e stop 'long Lunga, Donvu? Which way you take'm long time for come tell'm me?"

"Me fella sit down 'long scrub, catch'm ten fella stone 'long hand, and me count'm altogether come 'shore, got'm tin hat, khaki boot, allsame pigpig got'm two toes and long fella bayonet. Me get'm sore leg, pain, 'long belly b'long me."[4]

Whatever that exactly meant, Vandegrift marveled not only at Clemens's language skills but that he had been able to teach natives how to identify a tank when they had never before seen one and to tell the difference between a destroyer and a cruiser. He immediately offered the Englishman a position on his intelligence staff (which had just been wretchedly depleted).

Meantime, the Japanese were not idle. The Japanese Seventeenth Army was headquartered at Rabaul and preparing to deploy to the north side of New Guinea, where it hoped to cross that island's huge mountain spine and take Port Moresby from the land side. (It will be remembered that a direct invasion of Port Moresby by sea had been foiled as a result of the Battle of the Coral Sea.) But now with the Guadalcanal landings the Japanese recognized the closer threat, though they underestimated its dimensions. When Admiral Mikawa brought his cruisers down for the Battle of Savo Island on August 8 he had also brought a destroyer with several hundred Japanese troops as a sort of stopgap measure. By now many of them had been killed in piecemeal actions by the marines, including some sixty-five in the sharp battle at the Matanikau, where Colonel Goettge's patrol had been wiped out and where Vandegrift had sent further patrols to clean out the Japanese positions.

And so the commander of the Japanese Seventeenth Army now decided to send to Guadalcanal a crack combat infantry outfit that had been languishing on Guam ever since the Battle of Midway forced the Japanese to cancel their invasion of that island. About a thousand of these soldiers under the command of Colonel Kiyono Ichiki were the first to land, in the darkness of August 18, about twenty miles east of the airfield. Another five hundred Japanese "marines" from the Special Naval Landing force had come ashore to the west of the airfield, near the Matanikau River. Even though a much stronger Japanese force was already under way to join them Ichiki, against orders, decided not to wait but to attack the Americans immediately and, so he thought, recapture the airfield.

Vandegrift and his marines knew something was up. In the early morning after the Ichiki force had landed, marines on the beaches heard and spotted the waves from several of the Japanese destroyer transports washing ashore and a marine patrol ambushed and killed a number of Japanese troops wearing fresh uniforms with all the accoutrements of the hardcore Japanese soldier. Convinced he was going to be attacked from both sides by a newly landed force, Vandegrift wisely increased his patrol and sent out a remarkable man to assess the situation.

Sergeant Major Jacob Vouza was one of Clemens's native scouts who had recently retired from the small so-called Solomon Islands Constabulary and been fighting with Clemens as one of the coast-watcher patrolmen. While a battalion of marines moved through the coconut groves toward what they thought was the Tenaru River about two miles from the airfield (it was actually the Ilu, according to some accounts, so bad were the marines' maps)* Vouza, bushy-haired and bandy-legged and somewhat larger than most Solomon Islanders, went deep into the jungle and swung around again, coming up on the coconut groves near the beach. There he saw a large number of Japanese soldiers, well armed and well organized, moving toward the marine positions along the river, and in the process he was seen and captured by the Japanese. When he was taken before one of Ichiki's commanders he refused to answer questions and so

---

*The maps are still bad today. Pick up any book on the battle for Guadalcanal and you are likely to see the Ilu and Tenaru rivers interchanged in the insets. In any case, the marines who fought this battle believed they were fighting on the Tenaru and the Marine Corps got so tired of hearing all the arguing that five years after the war they officially named the action the Battle of the Tenaru. So be it.

was tied to a tree and brutally beaten with rifle butts, then bayoneted several times in the chest; his throat was slashed by a Japanese officer's sword and he was left for dead when Ichiki moved out.

Vouza was still alive, though, and soon as the coast was clear he began gnawing at his ropes, freed himself, and somehow struggled into the marines' lines. He asked for Clemens who, when he heard the news, radioed headquarters, rushed out to the position in a jeep, and translated Vouza's report that a large body of Japanese were moving toward them. Then Vouza said to Clemens and the others surrounding him, "I didn't tell them anything," and collapsed. Clemens put him in the jeep and rushed him back to the hospital, where he was sewn up. Meantime, the lucky marine battalion commander, acting on Vouza's intelligence report, managed to get a large force across the river and onto Ichiki's left flank and rear.[5]

About one-thirty A.M., August 21, a single green flare burst brightly over the coconut groves, signaling the beginning of the Japanese attack. It was a fiasco from the start, because of Vouza's information and the smart and quick use of it by the marine commander. The 870 Japanese troops were trapped between the main marine lines on the river and the new ambush force set up on their left flank and rear. Ichiki's not too imaginative plan had been to march straight alongside the beach using the long coconut grove as cover, then rush the American lines and overpower them by sheer force of will. The sea was on their right, blocking any movement in that direction. The only thing for the Japanese to do now was fling themselves forward in a banzai charge, which they did. It was the perfect trap and they were mowed down by the hundreds, their bodies piled up three and four deep in front of the marine machine-gun pits, especially on the sand spit along the beach that generally blocked the flow of the river into the ocean. American artillery and mortars crashed down on them in the coconut groves. When some tried to escape by running into the ocean and swimming away, the marines aimed at their bobbing heads and pulled the trigger. Some hundred or more were killed in this way and washed up on the beaches with the next high tide, a frightful sight.

At daylight there were still Japanese sporadically firing at marines from the coconut grove. At this point Vandegrift had had enough. He sent forward his little platoon of five light tanks for mopping up. These machines moved back and forth in the groves, uprooting trees and blasting or running over the remaining Japanese. Newsman Richard Tregaskis was on the scene at that point: "We watched these awful machines as they plunged across the spit and into the edge of the grove. It was fascinating to see them bustling amongst the trees, pivoting, turning, spitting sheets of yellow flame. It was like a comedy of toys, something unbelievable, to see them knocking over palm trees which fell slowly, flushing the running figures of men from underneath their treads. We had not realized there were so many Japs in the grove."[6]

Vandegrift himself remembered that, by afternoon's end, the tanks' treads "looked like meat grinders." He was also appalled at the tenacity and treachery of the Japanese, writing in a report to his superior that "I have never heard or read of this kind of fighting. These people refuse to surrender." He went on to say how some Japanese wounded would call out in English for help, then "wait until the men come up to examine them and blow themselves and the other fellow to pieces with a hand grenade. You can readily see the answer to that . . . the answer [is] war without quarter."[7]

Robert Leckie* was an eighteen-year-old private and machine gunner, just a few months out of basic training. He was manning his gun on the banks of the river just before the attack. "The Tenaru River lay green and evil, like a serpent, across the palmy plain. Normally the Tenaru stood stagnant, its surface crested with scum and fungus; if there were river gods, the Tenaru was inhabited by a baleful spirit." As he and his companions watched, "suddenly in the river there appeared a V. It seemed to be moving steadily downstream. . . . To our right came a fusillade of shots. It was from G Company riflemen, shooting at the V. The V disappeared."[8]

When the fighting broke out it quickly became a melee in the dark, red tracer bullets arcing everywhere and the terrific explosions of mortars, artillery, and flares eerily lighting up the hot tropical landscape. One of Leckie's nearby platoon mates was killed by a bullet to the heart while

---

*Leckie became one of America's finest war writers; his book *Helmet for My Pillow* is one of the classic first-person accounts of the marines in the Pacific war.

firing his machine gun, and the assistant gunner Al Schmidt later received the Navy Cross for continuing to fire the gun even after he had been almost completely blinded by fire.*

The fight lasted all night and into the next day but the American shells and machine-gun and rifle fire took a deadly toll. As Japanese fire from the grove dwindled, marines could be seen walking among the wrecked trees. "Dead bodies were strewn about the grove," Leckie wrote. "The tropics had got at them already and they were beginning to spill open. I was horrified at the swarms of flies, black, circling funnels that seemed to emerge from every orifice: from the mouth, the eyes, the ears. The beating of their myriad tiny wings made a dreadful low hum."[9]

Leckie went on, "One of the marines went methodically among the dead armed with a pair of pliers. He had observed that the Japanese have a penchant for gold fillings in their teeth, often for solid gold teeth. He was looting their very mouths. He would kick their jaws agape, peer into the mouth with all the solicitude of a Park Avenue dentist—careful, always careful not to contaminate himself by touch—and yank out all that glittered. He kept the gold teeth in an empty Bull Durham tobacco sack, which he wore around his neck in the manner of an amulet. 'Souvenirs,' we called him."[10]

When Leckie got back to the other side of the river and approached his machine-gun pit he saw a crowd of marines gaping at the opposite bank, where a number of dead Japanese had fallen into the water. What they were gaping at was frightful—a crocodile was eating a Japanese body. "I watched in debased fascination," Leckie said, until the crocodile "began to tug at the intestines." Later that night, he recalled, "the V reappeared in the river. Three smaller V's trailed afterward. They kept us awake, crunching."[11]

Forty-three marines were killed in the action, and twice that number wounded. But practically all of Colonel Ichiki's force was dead, nearly eight hundred of them. Ichiki himself ordered the regimental colors

---

*Schmidt later became one of the principal characters in the blockbuster 1943 movie *Guadalcanal Diary,* based on Richard Tregaskis's book of the same name.

burned, then drew his sword and committed hara-kiri; thus ended the first attempt by the Japanese to retake Guadalcanal.*

The victory had brightened even further the afternoon before the Battle of the Tenaru with the arrival of the first American warplanes on Guadalcanal. Admiral McCain, good to his word, had located a small escort carrier and had it steam to within fly-off distance of Guadalcanal and launch twelve dive-bombers and nineteen Wildcat fighters. When the first plane landed and taxied up the newly finished runway, Vandegrift remembered, "I was close to tears and I was not alone, when this handsome and dashing aviator jumped to the ground.

"Thank God you have come, I told him."

Not only that, but McCain "took a terrible chance" sending in a small convoy of destroyer escorts carrying aviation gasoline, tools, spare parts, bombs, ammunition, plus a good-sized (900-man) Seabee battalion to help the engineers further improve the airfield.[12]

The Seabees were a brand-new animal for the U.S. Navy. After Pearl Harbor it quickly became apparent that global war would require huge construction projects all over the Pacific, and elsewhere, projects that would demand very proficient craftsmen such as welders, iron- and steelworkers, road and airfield building experts, mechanics, shipfitters, pier and dock builders, carpenters, pipe fitters, electricians, and so forth. Most Americans possessing these skills were older—most, in fact, because of their age, were not even subject to the draft—but there was simply no time to train the younger draftees for these highly skilled jobs. Within a few months after the Pearl Harbor attack, more than a hundred thousand accomplished craftsmen had volunteered for new Naval

*Ichiki's behavior, beginning with the ill-advised attack and ending with his suicide, demonstrated the remarkably flawed thinking ("military logic" would not be a term properly applied here) of so many Japanese officers. Once a plan was set to paper, there was no turning back, nor was there any flexibility, no matter the circumstances, and if the plan failed suicide was the only recourse. Before the war's end, Japanese commanders would be killing themselves at a rate far higher than the Americans could kill them.

Construction Battalions, the Seabees, and by war's end they would number a quarter of a million. These were the men who built Boulder Dam, the Lincoln Tunnel, and, for that matter, the Pentagon. Their motto was "Can Do!"

Vandegrift was damned glad to have them, too; the Seabees had gone right to work finishing up his airstrip with the left-behind Japanese equipment and cement. It was then christened Henderson Field, after the marine major Lofton Henderson, who, it might be recalled, had been killed leading his squadron of untrained dive-bomber pilots in the "glide-bombing" attack against the Japanese fleet that first fateful morning of the Battle of Midway. Their arrival was none too soon. By day and by night the Japanese bombed and shelled the airstrip, trying to put it out of commission, and the Seabees' job was to keep it functioning. This entailed almost superhuman effort. The leader of these Seabees, forty-five-year-old navy commander Joseph Blundon, a former civil engineer and World War I veteran, explained, "When the Jap bombers approached, our fighters took off; [then] their bombers blasted the airstrip; and then if we couldn't fill up the holes fast enough before our planes ran out of fuel, they would have to try to land anyway. I saw seven of our fighters crack up on one bitter afternoon."

Blundon continued, "We pitched our camp right on the edge of the field to save time [thereby putting themselves in some of the worst harm's way on Guadalcanal]. We found that a 500-pound bomb would tear up 1,600 square feet of Marston mat, so we placed packages of this quantity of mat along the strip, like extra rails along a railroad. We figured how much sand and gravel was required to fill the average bomb or shell crater, and we loaded these measured amounts on trucks and placed the trucks under cover at strategic points. Then when the Jap bombers approached, every Seabee, including our cooks, manned his repair station. The moment the bombers had passed over, these men boiled out of the holes and raced for the craters. We found that 100 Seabees could repair the damage of a 500-pound bomb in forty minutes, including the replacing of the Marston mat.*

---

*A flexible, perforated, all-weather runway surface placed, on Guadalcanal, on top of a crushed coral base, rolled smooth.

"In other words, forty minutes after that bomb had exploded, you couldn't tell that the airstrip had ever been hit."

Blundon recalled that there weren't enough shovels to go around so some of his men had to use their helmets to scoop up dirt and lug it to the craters. During the first six weeks there were 140 Japanese air raids in which the strip was hit at least once. "Our worst moments were when the Jap bomb or shell failed to explode when it hit. It still tore up our mat, and it had to come out. When you see men choke down their fear and dive in after an unexploded bomb so that our planes can land safely, a lump comes in your throat and you know why America wins wars."[13]

Back at Pearl Harbor Admiral Nimitz and his staff were racking their brains about how to ease the strain on the marines at Guadalcanal. Even before the Battle of Savo Island, they understood there were simply not enough capital ships in the South Pacific to hold at bay the strong Japanese fleet at Rabaul, let alone the fact that there were hardly enough transports and destroyers to keep the marines on Guadalcanal fed and supplied. It was agonizing, but then someone came up with an idea.

In the early days of the war the U.S. Marines had formed three special Raider Battalions, each about a thousand men strong—elite troops whose mission was to go in quickly and destroy an enemy outpost. One of these battalions, Lieutenant Colonel Merritt Edson's First Marine Raiders, had already been used in the fierce battle at Tulagi, but another was still sitting at Pearl Harbor: Lieutenant Colonel Evans Carlson's Second Marine Raider Battalion, and a plan began to emerge to use them to take some of the pressure off Guadalcanal. What was contemplated was a raid on another Japanese-held island, which might lead the Japanese to conclude that America was going to land in a number of places almost simultaneously. This, it was hoped, would keep the Japanese off balance, guessing where the Americans would turn up next, and possibly stop them from reinforcing Guadalcanal until the marines had established a formidable defense there. The island selected for this ruse was called Makin, an atoll in the Gilbert Islands chain, a thousand miles northeast of Guadalcanal and two thousand miles from Hawaii. There were about a hundred Japanese soldiers manning it, and the theory was to have Carlson's people land there, shoot up the place, put the radio station and anything else out of business, capture any documents they could, and then scram as fast as possible.

Accordingly, on August 9, 1942, the day after Vandegrift landed his men on Guadalcanal, and the night of the awful Savo Island disaster, Carlson and 222 of his raiders set off in two U.S. Navy submarines for the eight-day trip to Makin. It was a grueling passage. There wasn't room enough on the submarines for everyone and so the marines, when they were not eating, had to lie in the submariners' bunks just to keep out of the way.

When the submarines surfaced off Makin on August 16, rubber boats propelled by outboard motors were launched and the raiders landed on the atoll just before dawn of the seventeenth. The boats were pulled up into beach brush and hidden and everyone prepared to move stealthily inland toward the Japanese installations. Then some marine accidentally fired off his weapon and Colonel Carlson decided just to rush across the two-mile-wide atoll and make a fight of it. The Japanese met them with their usual ferocity. One of the submarines began to fire salvos from its deck gun into the Japanese positions, killing sixty, and the Japanese commander reported to his superior by radio, "All men are dying serenely in battle." The Japanese had lashed themselves in trees from which they sniped at marines. The fight lasted until late in the afternoon and the Japanese radio station on Makin was destroyed, but when the marines attempted to get back to their submarines the strong surf thwarted them. Rubber boats overturned, outboard motors conked out, and more than half the men were left marooned on the atoll.

After dark Carlson sent his executive officer, Major James Roosevelt, son of the president, ashore with four more boats and they rescued almost all of the stranded marines. Practically all of the hundred or so Japanese on the island had been killed, but thirty marines had died as well. Nine marines, however, had somehow been left behind, though Carlson didn't know it,* and the submarines submerged and departed Makin for Hawaii. What happened to the nine missing marines was yet another example of Japanese consideration for the provisions of the Geneva Convention.

*Carlson declared later that he never would have left if he had known it.

At first the nine were treated fairly well by the Japanese reinforcements who soon arrived and captured them. They were quickly shipped north to the island of Kwajalein, in the Marshalls, where other Japanese troops gave them cigarettes and candy and described the things the marines would see when they were eventually shipped to a POW camp in Japan. The nine prisoners remained on Kwajalein for six weeks, languishing in what they thought was the goodwill of their captors. Then the Japanese naval commander of the islands, Vice Admiral Koso Abe, intervened. (It was he who had commanded the Japanese transport fleet that was foiled from landing at Port Moresby following the Battle of the Coral Sea.) For some grotesque reason Abe sent an order for the Kwajalein commander to execute the nine American prisoners.

The naval commander of Kwajalein, Captain Yoshio Obara, protested Abe's repulsive order, but to no avail. Not only that, Obara couldn't even find volunteers willing to carry it out, so he selected four of his own officers to do the dirty work. On October 16, 1942, the nine marines were taken to a freshly dug gravesite, forced to kneel, and one by one were beheaded by the sword-wielding Japanese officers, with Vice Admiral Abe on hand to watch.

Doubtless it was small consolation for the dead marines, or for their families, but a native Makin Islander had been hiding in nearby weeds and saw the executions. After the war, when an inquiry was made by the U.S. Marines as to where their nine captured men were, the native man testified as an eyewitness before one of the Allied military tribunals. Admiral Abe was convicted of war crimes and hanged, and Captain Obara received ten years' hard labor.*[14]

The destruction of Colonel Ichiki's force by the marines at Guadalcanal did not discourage the Japanese; in fact it propelled them into further action. It was decided between Imperial Army headquarters in Tokyo and the Japanese military authorities at Rabaul to send an even more powerful

*What effect the Makin Island raid had on Japanese intentions to refortify Guadalcanal is uncertain, but it appears it had little.

force to deal with the upstart Americans. This was the so-called Kawaguchi Detachment, named for its commander, Major General Kiyotake Kawaguchi, some 4,000 men strong. This bunch was ferried to Guadalcanal* in an almost nightly "rat run" of fast destroyers and slow "ant run" barges by Admiral Raizo Tanaka, who came to be known as Tanaka the Tenacious, commanding what would become branded infamously as the Tokyo Express, the transport service of Japanese troops to Guadalcanal through the Slot between Rabaul and Guadalcanal.

By this time the Japanese had begun a Monday-through-Sunday nighttime aerial and naval bombing of the marines on the island, but the U.S. Navy, Marine, and Army planes on the "unsinkable aircraft carrier" of Guadalcanal now "owned the daytime," so far as Japanese shipping went, and the Japanese "owned the night," reinforcing their troops on Guadalcanal and bombarding the U.S. troops from warships. Thing about the Japanese bombers was that they had to fly the six hundred miles south from Rabaul, and then back, while the Guadalcanal pilots had only to take off and fight when the enemy entered their own flight range. But this was far easier said than done. The Japanese bombing missions caused damage, misery, and death among the beleaguered marines but it also was beginning to cost the Japanese even more dearly in losses of aircraft and pilots; here are some reports: "August 26: sixteen Japanese bombers shot down and seventeen Zero fighters; August 29: four Japanese bombers shot down, four Zeros; August 30, eighteen Zeros shot down," and so on.[15]

Naturally this was taking a hard toll on the American fighter pilots and their planes as well; of the original nineteen Wildcat fighters flown in by Admiral McCain on August 20, only five were still flyable by August 30; thus 75 percent of U.S. fighter strength on Guadalcanal had been knocked out in only ten days.[16] Indeed, something had to be done, but there wasn't much McCain could do because he was in charge only of land-based aircraft. Then there came a series of dubiously fortunate calamities; in the space of the next few weeks the aircraft carriers *Enterprise, Saratoga,* and *Wasp* were either torpedoed or hit by Japanese bombs

---

*Not all of them made it. U.S. warplanes now stationed at Henderson Field sank several of their barges and transports with great loss of life.

and put out of action (the *Wasp* was actually sunk), but almost all of their planes had managed to get off and were recovered and many eventually wound up at the Guadalcanal airfield.* This prompted one marine general's cynical calculation that "Guadalcanal was saved by the loss of so many carriers."[17]

Among the first marine pilots to land on Guadalcanal were members of the 212th Fighter Squadron, whose planes had taken off from the little escort aircraft carrier that Admiral McCain had sent and inspired Vandegrift's stunningly emotional "Thank God you've come!" Having just arrived from the brand-new training base on the New Hebrides island of Efate, these men, like the vast majority of American pilots at the time, were completely inexperienced, having never before seen combat. But they were a rare breed, trained on Efate by one of the rarest of the rare breed, Lieutenant Colonel Harold W. ("Joe") Bauer, a former standout football player at Annapolis and a widely acclaimed master of the skies. Bauer had personally developed a number of aerial techniques to try to overcome the almost universally conceded superiority of the Japanese Zero against any fighter plane the Allies could put up against it at that point. They all called Bauer the Coach.

The Zero was lighter, could climb and accelerate faster, and was far more maneuverable than the Grumman F4F Wildcat, which the U.S. Navy and Marine Corps at that point considered their top-of-the-line fighter. The Wildcat was a stubby, square-winged little plane whose main advantage was heavy armament and durability (which made it slower and less maneuverable). In other words, it took a lot to bring one down. It had self-sealing gasoline tanks, unlike the Zero, and instead of two 7.7mm machine guns and two 20mm cannons, the Wildcat carried six heavier .50-caliber machine guns. The trick with the Wildcat was to teach the young American pilots how to get the advantage over the much-daunted Zero. Colonel Bauer believed he had come up with a solution, which was the so-called overhead pass, a fearsome and complicated maneuver in which the American pilots

*The damage done by the Japanese to these U.S. aircraft carriers left the U.S. Navy, for several months, with only one carrier, the *Hornet,* in the entire Pacific. But the American production system, which Admiral Yamamoto had so much feared, was gearing up, and before the war's end there would be more than one hundred aircraft carriers, large and small, in the U.S. fleet.

were trained to dive at the Zero head-on at their flat-out max speed of 320 miles per hour, then suddenly swoop, flip the plane over, and, flying upside down so as not to lose sight of the Zero, pass him by overhead, delivering a long burst from all six .50-calibers.

Bauer's overhead pass was not for the faint of heart, but the marine aviators of Fighter Squadron 212 were not fainthearted people. In fact, among military pilots, they were the elite, carefully selected for fighter duty because of their intelligence, mechanical instincts, dexterity, coordination, reaction time, common sense, and, well, just plain fearlessness. And it was a good thing, too, because flying an airplane, especially a high-performance fighter, was not, in those days—any more than these—like operating any earthly vehicle, such as a car or boat or train or even a horse and buggy, propelled by unmanageable beasts. Flying is a multidimensional affair: up, down, forward, sideways, at all angles, at terrific speeds, and factoring in wind speed and direction, altitude, humidity, tremendous cold and stifling heat, which change the flying characteristics of the plane at various heights. Engine oil, for instance, could freeze above 20,000 feet or run too hot at ground level. Even normal weather was a tribulation: rain, fog, clouds, or blinding sun; all of these elements had to be calculated instantly by the fliers and recalculated, and then recalculated again, without the aid of a computer, and put correctly into the constantly changing mix.

These pilots were welcomed as heaven sent by the ground-pounding marines fighting on Guadalcanal and taking a daily beating from Japanese airplanes. "It looked so damn good to see something American circling in the sky of the airfield," one of these grounded marines later recalled. "It was like being all alone, and then the lights come on, and you've got friends from home in the same room with you."[18]

Flying above the Solomon Islands then was an especially tricky and deadly business. The job of the U.S. Wildcat fighters was to shoot down the Japanese bombers, which normally came in well above 20,000 feet to get over the marine positions on and around Henderson Field. But to do that the American fliers first had to tangle with the bombers' escorting Zero fighters. To understand the complexities and sheer scariness of this task it is worth listening at length to Marine Lieutenant Jack Conger, who gave these impressions to the fabled writer Max Brand* during a rare stateside leave from Guadalcanal.

Conger had become separated from the rest of his flight, and knew he was in trouble: "That's very bad. You never should get split up. I was watching the Zeros coming down and not paying enough attention to where the rest of the boys were going. I was too inexperienced. I was too green to remember everything that the Coach [Colonel Bauer] had been hammering into our heads. Pretty soon I found myself scissoring with a Zero. That is to say, he had the altitude to keep diving at me, and I kept turning into him, trying to stay behind and below. We scissored five or six times, and every time I made a sharp, steep bank I lost altitude. Altitude is what pays off in an air fight, and this looked bad. He forced me to keep making those quick turns to keep him off my tail, and with each turn my plane shivered and shook and lost altitude. It was hell.

"He passed above me and did a steep wingover. I dived and started to climb. It wasn't an intelligent thing to do, but I was lucky. He couldn't quite get his guns on me. Then he did the damnedest thing you ever saw. He came down from above and behind, and instead of riding it out on my tail and filling me full of bullets, he let himself go too fast so that he went by me. He should have dodged off to one side and got out of there, but instead the fool rose right up under my nose, and did a roll.

"What was he trying to do? Impress me with his gymnastics? I don't know. Apparently those fellows had been told that they were the best flyers in the world, and so they were like little children with toys; they had to show their tricks when they had an audience. Or maybe he thought I couldn't hit him if he kept his plane tumbling like that. As a matter of fact, he was just making himself a bigger target. I used a three-second burst and he was dead before I stopped firing. We had scissored all the way down to

---

*Max Brand, the pen name of Frederick Faust, was the creator of, among many other works, *Destry Rides Again* and the Dr. Kildare movie series. In 1943 he managed to interview a number of the Guadalcanal Marine Fighter Squadron 212 aviators who were temporarily living at an oceanside cottage near Los Angeles. Brand had intended to turn the interviews into a book but a year later he was shot dead in Italy while serving as a war correspondent and the manuscript, a true gem, languished for more than fifty years until it was discovered and published, thanks to his daughter, by the Naval Institute Press.

eight thousand—to show you how he had been driving me into the ground—
but even eight thousand is a long way when you're looking down. He made
a splash no bigger than a porpoise. Then he was just part of the soup."[19]

Back in the United States, things were chugging along. The Departments of
the Interior and of the Navy had figured out that it was unproductive to keep
transporting gasoline and fuel oil from the rich Texas and Louisiana fields
up to the cold Northeast via tanker ships, which were too frequently blown
up by German submarines. So now railroad tanker trains were being used,
and while they stood no chance of being hit by torpedoes they certainly caused
infuriating tie-ups for the passenger trains, which were already taxed to their
limits with the huge influx of military personnel shuffling from one place to
the next around the country. A convoy system was beginning to come together, but escorting destroyers were hard to come by since they were being
so heavily employed in North Atlantic convoys bringing desperately needed
arms and supplies to England and the Soviet Union.

Subchasers were coming into place too, but presently they consisted
for the most part of a few old World War I converted boats, which quickly
became known as the Donald Duck Navy. As well, the navy recruited a number of large private yachts and converted them, too, often with the white-
flanneled yacht owner remaining aboard as skipper. These included several
famous Bermuda Race sailing yachts and other pleasure craft renowned in
society circles—not unlike the private boats that went out from England in
1940 to help evacuate the British army stranded at Dunkirk. And like the
Donald Duck Navy, this collection of "college boys, adventurous lads of shore
villages, Boy Scouts, beachcombers, ex-bootleggers and rum-runners" was
soon enough characterized as the Hooligan Navy. Blimps were used as well,
and more and more Civil Air Patrol volunteers were coming in.* The army
and navy were also beginning to ratchet up their domestic presence, as Washington authorities both civil and military became more and more alarmed
by the commercial shipping losses. Interlocking airfields were established
along the U.S. coast from Galveston, Texas, to Maine, and for a change it

*There were now about 75,000 members of the Civil Air Patrol.

was starting to work: German subs found that for the first time they were becoming the hunted and not the only hunters.[20]

The "sailor suit" had become one of the most popular items for young children to wear—navy blues with bell-bottom trousers and white-striped collars and the little white cap. Children continued to donate their lead and tin soldiers to scrap-metal war drives, and women were still turning in their aluminum pots and pans. Now that warm weather had arrived, the victory gardens that had been planted in backyards and vacant lots all over America— from slums to mansions—were beginning to thrive. Also thriving was a national black market, which had evolved in practically every town and city to trade and sell things rationed or no longer available in stores.

Try as it might, the federal government was able to do little about this; entrepreneurs to the last gasp, Americans with the cash were simply not going to be denied that which they wanted. Rubber, of course, was in even tighter supply and new (or even used) tires were almost impossible to come by. Somebody thought to start manufacturing wooden tires for cars, but these did not work well, especially on highways, and in any event gasoline was so short that very few could go much of anyplace anyway. As the Roosevelt administration's resident playwright, tall, gaunt Robert Sherwood, observed, "The American people, who were so willing and proud to give whatever was required of them in blood and sweat, were loudly reluctant to cut down on their normal consumption of red meat and gasoline and their use of such essentials as electric toasters and elastic girdles. More than any other people on earth, Americans were addicted to the principle that you can eat your cake and have it too; which was entirely understandable, for Americans have been assured from the cradle that there is always more cake where that came from."[21]

In Washington, the New Dealers in the Roosevelt administration were about gone by mid-1942, replaced by regular politicians and so-called dollar-a-year businessmen who, it was believed, could better get the nation on its war footing. Henry Kaiser, for instance, was now churning out "liberty ships" by the thousands—the ubiquitous cargo transports* that were to become the indispensable backbone of the navy—at the rate of several per week from

---

*One of these ships was made famous in the splendid movie *Mister Roberts* (1955), starring Henry Fonda and James Cagney and featuring Jack Lemmon as Ensign Pulver in his award-winning first movie appearance.

various shipyards on both coasts. As a publicity stunt he even produced one, from keel laying to launching, in the remarkable time of just three days.

Meanwhile, trouble had been boiling up in other parts of the world. With the Japanese military now in control of most of Burma, Japan was threatening to expand its empire into India, and thence westward across that vast subcontinent to Iran, Iraq, and the oil-rich regions of the Persian Gulf. There it was feared the Japanese would link up with their Axis partners, the Germans, who were pushing eastward in the opposite direction. This would have spelled much difficulty for the Allied war effort, and to make matters worse Mohandas Gandhi, the charismatic, popular spiritual leader and advocate for India's independence from Great Britain, had suddenly issued an appeal to all Indians not to resist a Japanese invasion of their country.

This was an irresponsible position for Gandhi to have taken. Great Britain by that time had already promised India its independence but felt it had to postpone the promise when war suddenly broke out, lest the Germans or Japanese invade and occupy the subcontinent.* The rightly suspicious Gandhi apparently based his position on the theory that even if the Japanese conquered India, his country would at least be rid of the British once and for all. He didn't seem to take into account what would happen to his people if and when the Japanese occupied India. To complicate matters further, Roosevelt and his administration kept trying to persuade Churchill to give up India immediately on the (basically prewar) notion that Americans would be more favorably disposed if they did not think the war was about saving the British empire. This was basically nonsense—most Americans at that point did not care a whit about India vis-à-vis Great Britain—but it still caused all sorts of weird finagling and behind-the-scenes diplomacy, which only detracted from the instant issue, which was the winning of the war against the Germans, the Italians, and the Japanese.[22]

---

*A German occupation of India would have been the perfect launching point for invasions of other British colonies in Africa and the Middle East, and even more so for Japan when she entered the war.

Then there was the problem of old Joe Stalin, sitting in the Kremlin in Moscow and refusing to meet with free-world leaders because he was afraid to fly, and ships or trains couldn't get him close enough for a face-to-face meeting. The Americans and British were sending him all the guns and tanks and planes they could spare* but he was fighting a desperate battle on his western front against his erstwhile "ally" Nazi Germany. Now he was demanding that England and America open a second front, on the shores of France, so as to relieve Soviet troops battling ferociously around Stalingrad and Moscow. To open a second front in the summer of 1942 probably would have been suicidal and both the Americans and the British knew it, but they went ahead anyway and drew up plans in case the Russians began to crumble. They had already named it Operation Sledgehammer but, mercifully, it never had to be set into motion.

Stalin then sent to Washington his foreign minister, V. M. Molotov (he of "Molotov cocktail" fame), who arrived at the White House under the curious pseudonym "Mr. Brown." Molotov told the president that if the Americans and British could open a second front it would "draw off 40 German divisions," and then the Russians would win the war before the year was out.[23] But drawing off forty German divisions (about 600,000 men) was a tall order, and Roosevelt wisely declined to commit himself to this improbable scheme. What Roosevelt did do, after the foreign minister's departure, was crank up his plan to invade North Africa and capture or expel the German-Italian forces there.

All of this was going on behind the scenes and the American people knew little or nothing of it from their newspapers and radio and, for that matter, still very little of what was going on at Guadalcanal, and certainly nothing yet about the terrible naval losses at the Battle of Savo Island. In fact, Admiral Ghormley and his staff, in overall charge of the Guadalcanal operation, continued to fear that the American force was not going to succeed.

Thus even if the Americans had scored a great victory at Midway, as the end of summer 1942 rolled around, it was far from clear to the mili-

---

*During April, May, and June of 1942, the United States sent eighty-four cargo ships to the Soviet Union. Half of them ended up at the bottom of the sea, destroyed by German torpedoes.

tary commanders and their bosses in Washington whether that decisive battle was really the turning point of the war or just a fleeting ray of sunshine in the eye of a hurricane that would soon be upon them once again.

Back on Guadalcanal, in addition to the daily air raids, nightly shelling from Japanese warships, and their half-starvation diet, the marines began to suffer terribly from tropical diseases: dengue fever, dysentery, gastroenteritis, and, most especially, malaria. Tropical ulcers caused by a nasty fungus ate holes in their skin big as quarters or even half-dollars, sometimes through to the bone. Usually the ulcers appeared after a man had received a cut of some kind, which could come from a nick by barbed wire or a slash from the razor-sharp kunai grass that abounded in the area. Dysentery, on the other hand, far more serious than normal diarrhea, was pervasive and it caused men to have to visit their crude latrines ten or more times a day. They became dehydrated, lost weight rapidly, and became so weak they frequently could not walk, even to the latrines. There was no remedy; it had to run its course. Then there was the gastroenteritis, which struck a man down suddenly, almost like a bullet, with horrible stomach pains, vomiting, fever, and often delirium.

It was malaria, though, that caused the most trouble and at one point the division surgeon estimated that 70 percent of the marines had it in one form or another. The symptoms could be eased by quinine, but not cured, and the fever would return periodically to again strike the man down. It got to where a marine had to run a temperature above 103 degrees before he would even be placed in sick bay.

They had now been on Guadalcanal for more than a month and everybody was asking, "Where is the army?" Under joint navy-marine-army doctrine, the marines' task was to seize a beachhead by amphibious assault and, once it was secured, the army would relieve them and take over from there. Well, they argued, hadn't they seized the Guadalcanal beachhead and secured it—but still no army? The reasons were severalfold. At that point there were three full U.S. Army divisions in the area, two under MacArthur in Australia (with another on the way) and one on New Caledonia, about fifteen hundred miles south of Guadalcanal. That was the Americal Division (standing for "Americans on New Caledonia"), only recently organized from a number of activated National Guard units. It had been placed there to protect New Caledonia and other islands along the South Pacific supply-and-communications route from the United States.

At present, however, there was little or no notion being entertained in Washington to send any army troops to relieve or even reinforce the beleaguered marines on Guadalcanal. The reasons given by the joint planners changed almost daily, depending on the intelligence that was understood by them. After the calamity at Savo Island, the planners were at first astonished, then relieved, that the Japanese had not immediately sent forward an overwhelming force to retake Guadalcanal. Then in early September they suddenly learned of General Kawaguchi's intentions to assault the marine positions, and at the same time came disturbing reports from MacArthur that on New Guinea the Japanese had undertaken the stupendous task of crawling across the vast Owen Stanley Range and were at that moment only twenty miles from Port Moresby. It seemed as though Washington was simply taking a wait-and-see attitude.

Whatever it was, the Guadalcanal marines remained on their own, still subsisting to some extent on captured Japanese rice, supplemented by what other meager rations and supplies could be shipped in between Japanese air raids from Rabaul.*

General Kawaguchi had arrived on Guadalcanal in the dark of night, August 31, 1942. He and 2,400 of his men had been ferried down the Slot from Rabaul and entered Ironbottom Sound with no opposition from the U.S. Navy, which had abrogated its presence there. They landed on a beach at Taivu Point, about twenty-five miles east of the airstrip at Henderson Field—

*At some point they managed to ship in a fairly large consignment of flour. One of the cooks had been a chef at New York's Waldorf-Astoria and his specialty was making pancakes for breakfast. And so for more than a week the marines' diet at Henderson Field was pancakes, morning, noon, and night, topped with some jelly that had turned up in big five-gallon cans.

the same place where the unfortunate Colonel Ichiki had landed his thousand men less than a month earlier. Another of his regiments, 1,100 troops under Colonel Akinosuka Oka, riding in forty-eight slow barges, would come ashore in a few days at Kukumbona, ten miles east of Henderson Field. Kawaguchi's plan was simple—or so he thought; once Oka's men had landed, and once he had rounded up the remainder of Ichiki's force plus whatever original defenders of Guadalcanal could be dragooned into the fight, they would storm the marine lines from three different directions and retake the airstrip in a single fell swoop. For the occasion Kawaguchi had brought along his brand-new white full-dress uniform, which he intended to wear at a ceremony at Henderson Field to dictate surrender terms to Vandegrift. As an additional bow to posterity he had also brought along a newsreel cameraman and newspaper photographer.

Kawaguchi had been unreliably informed that the Americans had no more than 5,000 men defending Guadalcanal and he reckoned that his force would be at least equal to them. Had this enemy troop strength report been correct, he might easily have pulled off his scheme. Indeed, the Americans had more men than the Japanese suspected, but these had to be strung out over a large perimeter nearly five miles in circumference, while Kawaguchi's force could attack in strength at any point or points along it. The plan called for capture of the airfield no later than September 12. These were his instructions from his boss, Lieutenant General Harukichi Hyakutake, commanding the Japanese Seventeenth Army at Rabaul.

Vandegrift's people gave Kawaguchi a hot reception from day one. Alerted to their landing by Martin Clemens's native scouts, planes from Henderson Field—when they weren't fending off attacks from enemy air raids—strafed and bombed the area daily. Not only that but Vandegrift decided to send two battalions of crack marine raiders and parachutists under Colonel Merritt Edson to raid the suspected Japanese encampment. They arrived only an hour or so after Kawaguchi and his troops had marched off into the dark interior. After a brisk firefight Edson's raiders killed about thirty of the enemy, while another 250 ran off into the jungle. Among the raiders' prizes was the fancy white dress uniform belonging to General Kawaguchi.

For four long and rainy days Kawaguchi's thousands hacked their way through the thick, steaming jungle trying to get around to the south side of Henderson Field, all the time awaiting word from Colonel Oka as to whether he had landed and was in a position to attack. At one point General Kawaguchi stopped to address his officers with a toast of whiskey. "We are obviously facing an unprecedented battle," he told them, "and so gentlemen, we cannot hope to see each other again after the fight. This is the time for us to dedicate our lives to the Emperor," after which there was much shouting and rejoicing.[24]

Meantime, Colonel Edson, back from his raid on Taivu Point, was surveying the situation vis-à-vis the marine perimeter around the airfield. Headquarters knew from intelligence reports received from native scouts that Kawaguchi had disappeared into the jungle and was marching, or struggling, southward in order to come around on the south side of the marine lines. Edson walked the southern positions and decided Kawaguchi's attack would probably come along a large ridge that extended southeast about three-quarters of a mile from the airfield. The ridge itself was about a mile long and bulged out into the jungle in the shape of a diving humpback whale.* Assessing the precipitousness of the various fingers, Edson concluded that the Japanese attack would probably come at the far southern edge of the ridge, because this way afforded the easiest means up, and he ordered his men to dig in.

By this time the marines were becoming more and more attenuated to jungle night fighting. They strung an apron of barbed wire in front of their positions, to which they attached tin cans and shell casings meant to alert them in the dark. They sent out listening posts to warn of an approaching enemy. They even deployed primitive listening devices out into the jungle. They put their machine guns in deep, fortified pits, cleared fields of fire, registered their mortars and big guns from the artillery regiment, and hauled up extra ammunition, grenades, rations, and water. Then they sat down to wait, sharpening their knives and bayonets.

Kawaguchi was not particularly happy with his situation. First, although Colonel Oka had finally shown up, he apparently would not be in position to launch his attack until September 13, a day later than planned. Second, his men were suffering greatly from lack of food and

---

*The Japanese called it "the centipede."

A lone destroyer tends to the stricken *Yorktown* before she sinks at Midway. (*inset*) Admiral Raymond Spruance, credited with the victory at Midway, June 1942, at which four Japanese aircraft carriers were sunk and the war in the Pacific began to turn to the Allies.

Chinese soldiers bring the crew of one of Doolittle's bombers to their village after their plane had wrecked, April 18, 1942. (*left*) Admiral William "Bull" Halsey (center), operational commander of the U.S. Pacific Fleet, aboard the U.S.S. *Saratoga*.

The PURPLE decoding machine that "hissed and sputtered and sometimes threw out a shower of sparks" but managed to break the Japanese code, leading to American victories at Midway and elsewhere.

As the battle raged, there was always office work to be done in the notorious Malinta Tunnel. This photo, taken by someone from the last submarine to stop at Corregidor, shows the finance office and, farther back, the Signal Corps message center.

The "Dog Army" was one of several "win-the-war-quick" schemes, along with the "death ray" and the "bat bombers." Shown here, on top-secret Cat Island off the Mississippi coast in 1942, are some of the thousands of dogs that were proposed to be unleashed on unsuspecting Japanese during the Pacific invasions.

The last few miles of the Bataan Death March in which thousands of Americans perished. Here those too weak to walk are carried by their companions.

(*above*) General Jonathan "Skinny" Wainwright
surrenders to Japanese General Masaharu
Homma (right center) after the fall of
Corregidor. Wainwright spent three years
starving in a Japanese prison camp before being
liberated to be present at the Japanese
surrender ceremony in Tokyo Bay. In 1946
Homma was hanged by an Allied war tribunal
for his role in the Bataan Death March.

(*right*) Japanese General Tomoyuki Yamashita,
the "Tiger of Malaya," who was later put in
charge of the Philippines. An Allied war
commission sent him to the firing squad for the
so-called "rape of Manilla" as the American
army closed in.

(*above*) Claire Phillips (aka "High Pockets"), American spy and owner of the Tsubaki Club in Manila, was a godsend to U.S. prisoners for the medicines and other essential items she managed to smuggle into the POW camps. (*left*) *Banzai!* Japanese soldiers celebrate victory on Bataan in the Philippines on Good Friday, 1942.

American soldiers surrender on Corregidor at the rubble-strewn entrance to the Malinta Tunnel.

The famous B-17 was the workhorse heavy bomber in both the Atlantic and Pacific theaters during the early years of the war. It could take a lot of punishment, yet thousands were shot down.

Sergeant Major Jacob Vouza, a celebrated Solomon Islands coast-watcher scout who, after being beaten, stabbed, and left for dead by the Japanese, managed to make his way to the marine lines and warn U.S. soldiers of an impending attack.

Catholic marines on Guadalcanal receive communion.

Japanese soldiers had a rendezvous with death on the Tenaru River on Guadalcanal. The Ichiki Detachment was the first of several failed Japanese attempts to wrest control of Guadalcanal and its vital airfield from the U.S. Marines.

General Alexander Archer Vandegrift, who led the First Marine Division through its ordeal on Guadalcanal in 1942. He later became commandant of the Marine Corps.

A Solomon Islands coast watcher with some of his scouts at Guadalcanal, August 1942.

Typical day at a marine camp on Guadalcanal, 1942.

Admiral Norman Scott, killed during the naval Battle of Guadalcanal.

Admiral Daniel Callaghan, President Roosevelt's former naval aide, was killed during the disastrous naval Battle of Guadalcanal in November 1942.

Toward the end of 1942, the U.S. Army finally began arriving to replace the marines. Here, troops of the Thirty-fifth Infantry leave the line after twenty-one days of jungle fighting. The expression on the lead man's face tells it all.

The day after the Battle of Bloody Ridge on Guadalcanal, September 13, 1942. Here, a marine looks at the foxholes where Colonel Merritt Edson's raider battalion slew thousands of Japanese banzai chargers.

A Japanese troop shipwrecked by U.S. planes during the naval Battle of Guadalcanal, November 13–15, 1942.

Japanese tanks destroyed on a sand spit at the mouth of the Matanikau River on Guadalcanal, October 1942.

The navy's Dauntless dive-bomber was primarily responsible for the American victory at the Battle of Midway.

There were no true rest areas on Guadalcanal but from time to time marines were allowed to bathe in the rivers. The machine-gun guards are on the lookout not only for Japanese soldiers but for the man-eating crocodiles that inhabit the waters.

U.S. Army landing in Morocco, October 1942.

German Panzer tanks attacking from the desert near El Guettar. The white puffs around them are explosions of U.S. artillery shells. After half a day's fight, the Germans retired, giving the Americans one of their first significant victories in the Battle for North Africa.

General George S. Patton on the Moroccan beaches, October 1942.

U.S. soldiers inspect a wrecked German tank during the Tunisian Campaign, winter 1942.

A funeral for U.S. soldiers killed in action in Algeria in 1942. MP's had to post guards at the cemeteries because Arabs often tried to dig up the dead for their clothing.

the travails of marching in the jungle. But by dusk on the twelfth he was coming, ready or not, and gave his junior officers the same speech about giving their lives for the emperor. Then they, too, sat down to wait for darkness.

Vandegrift, who had moved his command post up to the far end of the ridge, also had reason to be worried. For one thing, the Japanese had dramatically stepped up their air raids and night naval bombardments of Henderson Field, damaging many planes. Worse, Admiral Kelly Turner had shown up a couple of days earlier and relayed to Vandegrift some very bad news from his boss Admiral Ghormley, way back in Nouméa, fifteen hundred miles south. It came in two parts: first, intelligence and aerial photography had determined that the Japanese were massing for "a huge amphibious effort against us in two or three weeks"; and second, that because of the lack of shipping, supplies, airplanes, and the like, the United States Navy "no longer could support the Guadalcanal operation."

Coming as this did in the face of an impending attack by a powerful enemy infantry force, a lesser man might have quavered, but Vandegrift didn't bat an eye. He handed Turner's message from Ghormley to his own operations officer and told him, "Put this in your pocket. I'll talk to you about it later, but I don't want anyone to know about it." Then he took a drink of scotch and prepared to meet the immediate danger.[25]

Kawaguchi's fears were soon realized, and although Vandegrift's were not he had no way of knowing it at the time. On the night of September 12, Kawaguchi launched a heavy probe at the marine position. It was beaten back, but the forward companies decided to withdraw to a more defensible line farther up the ridge. Next day Edson, sitting on a log and eating from a can of cold hash and potatoes, called in his company commanders and told them, "They're testing, just testing. But they'll be back. Maybe not as many of them. Or maybe more. I want all positions improved, all wire lines paralleled, a hot meal for the men. Get some sleep; we'll all need it."[26]

At nine P.M., September 13, "Washing Machine Charlie" clattered in the night sky and dropped a pale green parachute flare over Henderson Field. Moments later seven Japanese warships in Ironbottom Sound opened up on the airstrip with a huge barrage. Simultaneously, Kawaguchi launched his 2,400 men out of the jungle against Edson's 600 marines defending the far end of the ridge. They came on screaming banzai—"Maline you die!" and other things not immediately intelligible to the defenders.

The marines met them not with words but with a curtain of fire and steel unleashed by the American artillery, mortars, rifles, and machine guns. Marine parachute flares illuminated the battlefield. Lieutenants rushed from position to position checking on their men, exhorting them to hold. Artillery blasted many of the attackers into oblivion—more than two thousand rounds were fired that night, until the barrels of the guns were so hot they nearly began to melt; automatic-weapons and rifle fire mowed down others, but still they came on. No sooner had one wave collapsed under the fire than another rushed out from the jungle's edge and some even broke through into the marine positions; then it became a deadly brawl with pistols, rifle butts, shovels, bayonets, knives, fists. A few marines panicked and ran. Colonel Edson stopped two of them and hurled them back into the line, screaming, "Go back where you came from! The only thing the Japs have that you don't is guts!"[27]

More waves of Japanese emerged from the jungle and started up the hill, lit up by the pale flickering light of flares. By now it was evident they were there in overwhelming numbers. The racket was deafening and sur-real; artillery bursts, machine-gun and rifle fire, grenades and mortars boomed and flashed and there was all kinds of hollering and shouting. Edson yelled out an order over his field telephone for the marines to pull back to the next defensive position and called for the artillery to bring its barrage in closer.

Within an hour or so the attack subsided, leaving the slopes of the ridge, soon to be officially known as Bloody Ridge, washed in a sea of dead and dying Japanese. Those who could retired back into the jungles, but only to reorganize for another assault, which was not long in coming. Again at midnight came the screaming banzai charges, again the bursts and din and racket and moans of the battlefield, and again the Japanese were stopped in a hail of bullets and a curtain of steel laid down by the big 105mm howitzers beyond the crest of the ridge, with Edson yelling back into his field phone, "Closer, bring it in closer!"

This went on for most of the night, with Edson's men outnumbered four to one. Some people said there were at least twelve separate assaults, but nobody knows for sure. Each Japanese charge was announced with a flare and frequently the fighting was hand-to-hand. At two-thirty in the morning the Japanese fell back again and Edson contracted his lines too; it was just about the last position he could take before being forced off the ridge. But he said into his field phone, "We can hold," to the great relief of everyone in Vandegrift's command post, which had already begun sending up the last marine reserves.

In between attacks desultory firing was unceasing. The marines would learn that this was the way the Japanese fought: they did not simply attack and, if defeated, run away; those who remained alive were sure to set up a fire of some kind to keep everyone on edge. Japanese who were left on the field, lying under a log or whatever else they could hide behind, also kept up their chorus of "Maline you die," answered by a corresponding chorus of "You'll eat shit first, you bastards!"[28] Somebody shouted out, "Tojo eats shit!" and it echoed back from the enemy lines, "*Roosevet* eat shit!" Then it was, "The emperor eats shit," answered by, "Babe Ruth eat shit." Then it got down to the basics: "Fuck Ereanor Roosevet!," which was answered, "Fuck Tokyo Rose!" and "The emperor's wife eats shit!" Finally, from one or more Japanese, came perhaps the most original of all: "Fuck Roy Acuff!"*

At one point during the battle Edson was talking on his field phone when a voice broke in and said in stilted English: "Our situation here, Colonel Edson, is excellent. Thank you sir."[29] Clearly this was not anyone authorized by the marines to talk on their line. With units spread out all over the place, and all the phone lines connecting them to their commander, and thence to Vandegrift's headquarters, it would not be unusual for Japanese infiltrators to have crawled up and tapped into a phone grid or snatched messages out of the air from a field radio, both to listen in and

---

*Roy Acuff was a popular country music singer on radio, television, and the Grand Ole Opry, from the 1940s until his death in 1992. Accounts of expletives used against him by the Japanese appeared on the jacket cover of at least one of his old record albums. Some years ago the author encountered him in the makeup room of a television program, on which both were appearing, and asked about the truth of the story. "Yep," Acuff replied, "that's what I always heard. And I was really flattered."

to give out phony information. To counter the former, the Marine Corps had devised a truly ingenious plan.

Philip Johnson, a World War I veteran, had grown up the son of a missionary to the Navajo Indian tribes in Arizona, Utah, and New Mexico. He remembered that the U.S. military had once used the Choctaw Indian language to create secret codes and it occurred to him that Navajo was, of all Native American languages, the most difficult to penetrate. For one thing, it was unwritten. There is no alphabet—not even symbols—and it has such unique pronunciations that the only way to become familiar with it was to have lived with the Navajos. Few had.

Shortly after Pearl Harbor, Johnson took an idea to the marines: why not utilize the particular abilities of Navajos to communicate among one another to create an unbreakable field code. For unit commanders in the heat of battle who could not wait the excruciatingly long time it took cryptographic machines to encode, transmit, and decode messages, this truly would be a godsend. The marines were enthusiastic and tests showed that the Navajos could send and decode a short message in thirty seconds when it would have taken an encoding machine a half hour to perform the same task. They quickly set up a special school for members of this small, civilized, and educated tribe at the marine base at Camp Pendleton, California. Four hundred Navajo volunteers were put through a crash course in which they were taught to assign to English words a Navajo meaning that had no English equivalent in their language. Such words as "tank" became *chay-da-gahi* (tortoise) in Navajo, but it could also be several other things as well. Only the Navajos knew—and they weren't telling.

These "code talkers" served in every marine campaign in the Pacific, including Guadalcanal, and the frustrated Japanese never did manage to crack their communications, despite laborious attempts. After the war the secret of the Navajo military code was considered so important that it was strictly classified for nearly forty years. In 2001 the Navajo code talkers were awarded medals by the U.S. Congress for their unique and priceless service.[30]

Meantime, General Kawaguchi's plan had fallen to pieces before his eyes. He idiotically kept ordering assaults on the ridge across ground littered with his own dead, but these became feebler and feebler as the night wore on and dawn approached. He was enraged at one point to learn that, in the confusion, one of his battalions had not even gotten into the battle at all, and he screamed at its commander, when he finally showed up at Kawaguchi's headquarters, "Coward! Commit hara-kiri!"[31] Worse, the battalion-sized force of Colonel Ichiki's remnants, which Kawaguchi had sent to attack across the Tenaru several miles to the north, had gotten off late and was repulsed and practically annihilated by the First Marine Regiment. Worse still for the Japanese, Colonel Oka's battalion, about eight miles west, which was supposed to assault simultaneously near the Matanikau River, presumably to draw off the marine reserves, had failed to do so, and when he finally got around to attacking later that afternoon, Oka's force was blasted back into the jungle.

Kawaguchi's battle plan had been a miserable failure and there was nothing but to organize what was left of the troops and hack a path back through the jungle away from the horrid scene of the ridge. He had gotten to about a thousand yards from the airfield, but no more. Instead of returning to Taivu Point along the trail he had just chopped out he decided, probably wisely, not to return to that place, but instead to hack his way westward, toward Colonel Oka, near the Matanikau, and thence beyond. This became a wretched, excruciating journey lasting six long days, with men trying to drag the more than five hundred wounded on litters through the twisted, fetid jungle.

There was practically nothing for the retreating Japanese to eat, since they had planned on eating the marines' food once they captured the airfield—such had been their hubris. Soldiers drank rain or dew water from jungle vines and ate whatever berries, roots, leaves, or grass they could find. Much of this proved disagreeable; some even fatal. Men were dying at an alarming rate, especially the wounded, and practically all heavy equipment was thrown away or buried along the trail. More than six hundred of Kawaguchi's men lay rotting in the tropic sun in front of the marine positions on Bloody Ridge; out of the 2,400 Kawaguchi had ordered into his main attack, only 800 remained unscathed. Another couple of hundred from the remnants of the Ichiki force lay dead along the crocodile-infested banks of the Tenaru. The marines called them "gator bait."

At last Kawaguchi's pathetic little band emerged into a coconut grove at the edge of Ironbottom Sound, where at least there were coconuts to eat and their milk to drink. The humiliated Kawaguchi, as filthy, tattered, and hungry as the rest, prepared to find transportation to Rabaul to face the medicine.

Admiral Kelly Turner, who had stayed through the initial stages of the fight, departed on his flagship the day of the big battle, but not before informing everybody that "things would get worse before they get better." Nevertheless, Turner promised Vandegrift that, despite Ghormley's pessimistic appraisal of the situation, he would reinforce Guadalcanal with another 4,100-man marine regiment, a promise he kept, to Vandegrift's great relief, astonishment, and gratitude.[32]

A couple of days after the Bloody Ridge action, the venerable *New York Times* military correspondent Hanson Baldwin showed up. He informed Vandegrift that the American people were getting a warped view of the situation on Guadalcanal. The people understood, he told the general, that the marines were holding most of the ninety-mile-long island and were "strongly entrenched."

Vandegrift filled him in on the true situation, which was that they were hanging on to their tiny airstrip only by a MacArthurian eyelash, that the daily Japanese air raids were choking off much of their supply and the nightly, unopposed Japanese naval bombardments were wrecking his warplanes almost as fast as they could be brought in, and also that the Japanese could transport their own troops to Guadalcanal at their own pleasure and were, in fact, planning a far larger invasion in a few weeks. After Vandegrift concluded this litany of agony and grief, reporter Baldwin asked him, "Are you going to hold this beachhead? Are you going to stay here?"

Vandegrift didn't hesitate: "Well hell, yes. Why not?"[33]

Chapter Sixteen

During the dog days of August and September of 1942, while American marines were fighting and dying on Guadalcanal, and the Germans were knocking at the gates of Russian Stalingrad, a kind of near panic had taken hold in Australia. Because of the steady Japanese encroachment across the Owen Stanley Range on nearby New Guinea, those who could in northern Australia began relocating their families and possessions southward for fear of an invasion. There was much talk in political circles of abandoning northern Australia altogether and setting up a defensive line farther south, to protect the heavily populated areas around Sydney, Brisbane, Adelaide, Melbourne, and Canberra.

General MacArthur and, for that matter, the Australian army were having none of this. The army intended to stop the Japanese in their tracks in New Guinea's mountainous jungles or die trying, or at least send troops to the island to die trying, which is what they did. MacArthur by now had more than 100,000 American soldiers on the southern continent, though only one-third of them were combat infantry troops. Still he was loath to send any of them to help out the beleaguered marines on Guadalcanal. He was worried, and rightly so, that the Japanese overland movement from northern to southern New Guinea portended a dangerous and immediate threat to Australia and New Zealand and thus America's shipping lifeline to them. If Australia and New Zealand were taken out of the play, quite literally there would have been no place except Hawaii—which was too small—from which the Allies could launch an effective counterinvasion to get at the Japanese mainland, far away as it was.

New Guinea is the second largest island in the world (after Greenland); about the size of California, it is shaped like a large turkey, or, some say, a peacock. It is mostly a hot, steamy rain forest, punctuated by a spine of mountains known as the Owen Stanley Range, which rise to heights of 15,000 feet or more, and some are actually capped in snow most of the year. Below are swamps, jungles, and inhospitable territory inhabited by malaria-carrying mosquitoes, scorpions, crocodiles, poisonous snakes such as the taipan and death adder, and huge constrictors like the python. As on Guadalcanal, hundreds of miles away, the natives were thought to be both cannibals and headhunters. In short, it was a place where civilization had not made appreciable inroads. Early explorers gave the place a wide berth for centuries. Then, as in the Solomon Islands, in the nineteenth century missionaries and coconut plantation farmers began to arrive, but settled only in the coastal areas.[1]

Frustrated by the Battle of the Coral Sea in their attempt to land an invasion force to take Port Moresby, the Japanese instead tried to take the Allied airstrip town of Milne Bay, at the very southern tip of New Guinea, but they were surprised and frustrated again, in fact flat kicked out, by a determined battalion of Australian troops. Then the Japanese decided to regroup with a much larger army and go back against Port Moresby the hard way—by the land route over the formidable Owen Stanley Range from their new base on the north side of New Guinea near the coastal villages of Buna and Gona. Nobody believed they would even try it, but they did. The stakes were high, because if the Japanese conquered the southern coast of New Guinea they would solidify their air control of the Coral Sea as well as gain the freedom to bomb Australia at their pleasure and even to invade it.

There were only two rough native trails over the Owen Stanleys, and foot trails they were, thousands of feet up and down, amid perhaps the most frightful and disagreeable landscape in the world. The New Guinea natives themselves believed that the trails were haunted. It rained practi-

'cally all the time, up to 300 inches a year, and knee-deep, sometimes waist-deep mud was omnipresent. For soldiers on either side carrying heavy rucksacks that contained all their food and other gear there was a constant danger of toppling over backward with any misstep; men frequently slept in these steeps by hanging or roping themselves onto jungle plants, vines, or trees. Depending on the altitude it was either steaming hot or freezing cold and changes of clothing were out of the question. One man was found, so the story goes, after being attacked while asleep by a large constricting python. His body was said to be completely flattened, like a deflated balloon, as if every bone in it were crushed by the enormous snake.

By September 20, a Japanese force of more than 5,000 had crossed the Owen Stanleys and were perched just twenty miles from Port Moresby when they were suddenly ordered by their army headquarters at Rabaul to halt, and then were called back. The reason for this was the U.S. Marines' resounding defeat of General Kawaguchi's force on Guadalcanal; the Japanese finally woke up and decided to put all their resources into annihilating U.S. forces in the Solomon Islands. Port Moresby would have to wait.

The Japanese at this point had just under 10,000 men in that part of New Guinea, and their new instructions were to retreat to their bases between Buna and Gona on the north coast and fortify and hold them, pending some clarification of the situation at Guadalcanal. But MacArthur and his people were not content to allow this. He had two U.S. infantry divisions and one Australian division, and he decided to try and kick the Japanese out of eastern New Guinea altogether. This, as it turned out, as with so much else, was far more difficult than expected.

First was the problem of just how to get at the Japanese force, now ensconced in positions on New Guinea's north coast, about a hundred miles from Port Moresby. A seaborne invasion was out of the question—there wasn't enough shipping—and so it was decided to send Allied infantry along the same mountainous trail that the Japanese had come across. Actually, there were two trails, the Kokoda and the Kapa Kapa. The Australians were to use the Kokoda and the Americans the Kapa Kapa, which was so remote no white man had been known to climb it since 1917. As at Guadalcanal, things got off to a bad start.

First, the American infantry divisions were woefully undertrained for their task. Both were federalized National Guard units that had been shifted from pillar to post in the wake of Pearl Harbor, at first destined for the European theater, then ordered to garrison Ireland, and then told to head to the South Pacific. Thus they had scant time between all this moving around to establish proper training facilities. This had left them un-"hardened," the military expression for being out of shape, and certainly not up to the rigors of climbing for days on end along the wild leech-infested jungle trail they were soon to endure. So many could not stand up to the constant ascending and descending (with no place to rest since the trail was generally narrowed to only a few feet) that they were left strewn prostrate along the way, and others had to step over them. Such was the exhaustion that officers sent to the rear to push along stragglers were simply not able to move them. At one point along the trail, which "reeks with the stench of death, the remains of an enemy soldier lie on a crude stretcher, abandoned by the Japanese retreat. The flesh is gone from his bones, and a white bony claw sticks out of a ragged uniform sleeve, stretching across the track."[2]

Worse, their food was no good. Most of it consisted of Australian Bully Beef (corned beef in five-pound tins), which had soon rusted out in the hot humid climate and spoiled the beef. They either ate it or starved, and those who ate it often got horrible diarrhea or dysentery so bad that they had to rip out the seats of their trousers in order to quickly take care of their needs. Even considering their woefully shabby circumstances, one thing any combat infantryman, anywhere, anytime, looks forward to every day is the ability to take a good, clean shit, and now even this small dignity was no longer available to them. The rain was such that practically all meals had to be eaten cold and raw since fires were not possible. Matches and all toilet articles were soon soaked, including toilet paper, and antimalaria pills disintegrated within a day or so. They tried parachute airdrops to resupply the troops but most of these drifted off course and were not recoverable.*

*This gave rise to the curious "cargo cults" of New Guinea and elsewhere in the South Pacific. The natives frequently were able to recover for themselves the booty dropped by Allied airplanes and considered it some kind of manna from heaven. For many years after the war some native cultures continued to clear drop zones and landing strips, in the belief that Allied planes would someday return and resume offering these generous gifts.

Look at the photographs taken on New Guinea during this period and you will not see happy or smiling soldiers, as you might see even in photographs of men at Guadalcanal; instead you will be struck by the haunted, hollow, almost frightened look of civilian soldiers being pressed to their utmost limits by strange and gross vicissitudes, with no apparent end in sight. The Japanese, crawling over the mountains first southward, then back to the north coast, did not fare much better. They and their supply lines were relentlessly bombed by Allied planes and their food was not much better, but being smaller people, perhaps only half the weight of an American soldier, they could subsist on much less, mostly rice, though they had already stripped the native villages along their tortured path of any and all garden produce: yams, beans, pumpkins, sugarcane, melons, bananas. And they were battle hardened, having fought in China, Malaya, or the Philippines, but the soldiers on both sides nevertheless gave a name for all these trials: the Green Hell.

When the exhausted Allied army men finally reached the Japanese positions on the New Guinea north coast they were in for another rude surprise. They had been informed, thanks to several intelligence reports, that most of the Japanese had been evacuated and that they would meet only token resistance. This was not at all true, as they would soon enough find out. The 10,000 Japanese had dug themselves into a pocket about ten miles long between the villages of Buna and Gona. The terrain surrounding this pocket was mostly waist-deep sago palm muck and jungle. The lanes of the only practical high-ground approaches had been strongly fortified by the Japanese with registered mortar fire and machine-gun nests and direct-fire artillery concealed in strong coconut-log bunkers, and with snipers everywhere. It was a most obnoxious position from the attackers' point of view; in fact, the U.S. Army official history of the battle describes the Japanese position as "a masterpiece."[3]

This soon became apparent to MacArthur, who had now moved his headquarters to the former New Guinea governor-general's elegant bungalow at Port Moresby, where he paced the veranda dressed in "a pink silk dressing gown with a black dragon painted on the back," and "munched on one of the crisp heads of lettuce specially flown in by the crate."[4] He had already received disturbing reports of unmilitary conduct by members of his Thirty-second Division. They were said to be lackadaisical in performing attacks on the Japanese positions, throwing away their rifles, disobeying their officers, and so forth. In some ways you could hardly blame them; the area has been described as "literally a pesthole." The average daily temperature was 96 degrees F, and in addition to the omnipresent malaria there was jungle rot, ringworm, dengue fever, typhus, and dysentery to contend with. Although the Allies had discovered and improved an airstrip about fifteen miles away, there was still difficulty getting needed supplies to the troops in the field. For this they employed loin-clothed native bearers (known to the Australians, because of their hair styles, as Fuzzy-Wuzzies) who, as they had no concept of money, had to be paid off in such things as pots and pans, utensils, tobacco, cloth, salt, and garden seed.* The problem with this was that all these goods also had to be transported by air through the already taxed facilities of the air force, struggling desperately to supply the men in the field.[5]

In any case, MacArthur was still exceedingly unhappy with the reports of his infantry's performance and so summoned to Port Moresby his newly arrived corps commander, Major General Robert Eichelberger, and told him to go to Buna and relieve the present commander of the Thirty-second Division. He also told him to relieve anybody else who wouldn't fight, and replace him with somebody who would, even if it meant putting sergeants in charge of battalions and corporals in charge of companies. Then he gave the fifty-five-year-old Eichelberger perhaps the most extraordinary order ever issued in modern times by a commanding general to one of his senior officers: "Bob, I want you to take Buna, or not come back alive." And, for added emphasis, MacArthur pointed a bony finger at Eichelberger's startled chief of staff, who was standing there watching, and said, "And that goes for your chief of staff, too." As Eichelberger recalled it later, "Well, that was our send off, and hardly a merry one."[6]

Contretemps between commanders and the long-standing interservice rivalries were of course not unknown, and were not helpful to the war

---

*At one point one thousand Boy Scout knives were ferried in. The garden seed must have been a boon, though; because of the climate, it was said that if a man threw a half-eaten tomato onto the ground in a sunny place, within three weeks there would be an entire vineful of ripe tomatoes to eat.

effort. Admiral Ghormley, as has been seen, was opposed to the entire marine invasion of Guadalcanal, and took a consistently pessimistic (and some say foot-dragging) view of the operation. Good commanders, as history demonstrates, seek to overcome obstacles instead of complaining about why something can't be done. Accordingly, Ghormley was relieved as commander of the South Pacific and in his place was put the irrepressible, fifty-nine-year-old William F. (Bull) Halsey.* Upon assuming his post on October 18, 1942, Halsey immediately called Vandegrift from Guadalcanal for a meeting and asked him if he could hold the island. Vandegrift replied that he could, if he could get better support from the navy. Halsey told him that, yes, he certainly would, beginning right away. This was very good news.

Another unwelcome thorn in the side of the marines had become Admiral Kelly Turner, who was still in charge of the beachhead at Guadalcanal, funneling in men, food, weapons, and supplies. Turner was earnestly trying to be helpful, had defied Ghormley on several occasions, had performed miracles with the meager ships he had, but he also tended to meddle with the dispositions of infantry on Guadalcanal, something an admiral in the navy was not especially trained for. In particular Turner, who was de facto superior to Vandegrift, wanted to create more marine raider battalions out of regular marines, and to put them in locations outside of Henderson Field, out in the bush or in beachfront bivouacs where, presumably, they could intercept Japanese landings or disrupt their operations. At first glance, this was probably not a bad idea and the concept has been adopted in more modern military strategies. But faced with his own situation, Vandegrift was appalled at Turner's persistence in these matters, branding them "dangerous nonsense." His position on the island, Vandegrift asserted, was critical and defense of Henderson Field paramount. After all, without the airfield, what were they doing there anyway? And if they lost it they could not hold the island.

---

*"Bull" was a nickname given Halsey by the press, possibly due to some misspelling or mistranslation. People who knew him well called him Bill, which he had gone by since his Annapolis class of 1906. People who didn't called him "Sir." Nobody actually called him Bull, except the newspapers and radio. But Bull he became to millions of Americans.

His lines were thin enough as it was, and he needed every man available to defend the perimeter against further Japanese attacks.[7]

Another dispute had broken out in MacArthur's headquarters way back in Australia. Major General George Brett was commander of the U.S. Air Force there, such as it was. But MacArthur was in charge of everything, and his chief of staff, Brigadier General Richard Sutherland, presumably spoke for MacArthur, or at least he thought he did. Sutherland did not get along well with Brett or, for that matter, with a lot of people, who thought of him as high-handed, even rude. In Brett's case it may have been a simple case of interservice rivalry, except that at the time the air force was still, technically, the U.S. Army Air Corps, and not a separate service, and Sutherland apparently made certain assumptions on the uses of airpower that rankled the airmen who had to carry out his orders.

Soon (some say at the doings of Sutherland), Brett was replaced by Major General George C. Kenny, a diminutive and feisty two-star pilot-general who set Sutherland straight the first time he met him. Waiting for a meeting with MacArthur, Kenny found himself in Sutherland's office on the receiving end of a lecture about how he should deploy his air force, now that he was under MacArthur's command. Kenny listened for a while, then went over to Sutherland's desk and picked up a sheet of blank paper and a pencil. On the paper he tapped a little dot in the center with the pencil, then handed it to MacArthur's chief of staff: "That dot I just put there represents what *you* know about the use of airpower. All the rest of this sheet of paper represents what *I* know about airpower!" he told the flabbergasted Sutherland. After that he had little trouble from Sutherland, which was probably a good thing, too, for Kenny proceeded to orchestrate an ongoing display of the proper use of an air force throughout the Pacific war, which soon helped save the faltering New Guinea campaign.

Back on Guadalcanal, despite the complete repulse of General Kawaguchi's attack at Bloody Ridge, the situation was not at all a happy one. Nobody put it better than Marine Major Frank Hough, who observed that "no clairvoyant was needed to figure out the shape of things to come."[8] The Japanese strategy was becoming clear to everyone: with the U.S. Navy now seemingly out of the picture, they would come in at night with warships and shell hell out of Henderson Field to keep U.S. planes from taking off after them. At the same time the Japanese could land troops to build up for another attack. This they would do almost every night, and there was little the marines could do about it, as they landed their soldiers anyplace on the island they wanted—except for the tiny marine perimeter—to the east of the marines, to the west, and, if they wished, in the south. From a variety of intelligence reports, including aerial reconnaissance of the ships assembling at Rabaul, it was apparent the next Japanese attack was going to be far larger than those previous. The Japanese also managed to ship in a battery of big 150mm artillery, heavier and with a greater range than anything the Americans had to knock them out with. Moving these from place to place in the jungles and on the ridges, the Japanese now shelled the airfield with impunity, night and day. If nothing else, this kept everyone's nerves even more on edge than they already were, which was considerable.

As we have seen, the Marine Corps had been established as a small amphibious assault force: to take a beachhead and hold it. Then, in a week or two, the much larger U.S. Army would come in and take over from there. The marines were neither trained nor equipped as a defense force, but that is precisely what they had become for more than two long months on Guadalcanal. By now almost everyone on the island was running a high fever from malaria and/or other tropical ailments for which there was little proper treatment or cure. They had been shelled by Japanese naval ships or artillery, bombed from the air, or otherwise attacked night and day, practically since the moment they arrived. Even during World War I, in the grisly trenches of the Western Front, soldiers had to serve only forty-eight hours at a time before being rotated out to the rear, the lesson having been learned early on that any longer would lead to crack-ups. On Guadalcanal this was simply not possible. For one thing, there *was* no rear.

That meant of course that there was no place for R & R or any other kind of amusement or relief, except for dodging bombs, shells, and bullets. Men could go occasionally to the beach or to the Lunga River for bathing, but they took the chance of being strafed, bombed, shelled, machine-gunned, or, for that matter, eaten by crocodiles. Armed guards had to be posted on both banks of the Lunga to prevent Japanese snipers from shooting the bathers, and they kept a sharp lookout for the crocodiles, too. The marines were still down to two meals per day, and nothing much appetizing at that, but eating was about the only pleasure the men had; everything else was either work, illness, or terror. Most men had by now lost between 10 and 15 percent of their body weight during the two months they had been there. Lunch was not an option. There was no mail from home; it was difficult enough just to ship in rations and ammunition. Some units, particularly the raiders, had been riddled with casualties. The pilots and their crews were under an enormous strain, flying mission after mission in beat-up planes, most of which required maintenance that no one could properly perform.

Looking at it now from the standpoint of military science during World War II, the servicemen on Guadalcanal were little better than guinea pigs, or lab rats, whose trials and sufferings would be officially filed under "lessons learned" for future operations. From a standpoint of troop morale, it was pathetic, but there wasn't much anybody could do about it. The marines understood this, as most combat troops eventually do; they simply reached into themselves for their own accommodation.

The late Pulitzer Prize–winning author John Hersey* had been sent to Guadalcanal as a correspondent for *Time* and *Life* magazines. He went into a battle one day with a company of marines trying to clean out a pocket of Japanese along the by then infamous Matanikau River, which had been a painful thorn in the side of those trying to hold Henderson Field. They marched practically all day, using up most of their canteen water in the wretched heat, then plunged into the fetid steaming jungle toward the river. First they were beset by Japanese snipers who had hidden themselves in trees; then they were hit with machine guns, and then blasted by preregistered mortar fire. In the end they ran into what amounted to a serious ambush. The marines fought it out until it became obvious they were getting the worst of it in a well-prepared Japanese position, and would continue to do so unless they withdrew. A dozen marines in that company

---

*Author of *A Bell for Adano* (1944) and *Hiroshima* (1946), among others. He recorded his experiences on Guadalcanal in a wonderful short book called *Into the Valley*, published in 1943.

were killed and many more wounded. All told, more than sixty were killed in the entire two-day, two-battalion operation. The Graves Registration people were called in to carry the bodies out to the blossoming cemetery created around Henderson Field.

Hersey had made friends with the company's commander, a Captain Charles Alfred Rigaud, in his mid-twenties, who was raised in upstate New York and, like so many company-grade officers, was the son of a middle-class family who wanted nothing more than a decent career in some proper job, with a wife and family, far away from the killing and mayhem in the South Pacific. Right after the battle Hersey found Rigaud, muddy, exhausted, and hollow-eyed. Hersey asked if there was anything he could do for the captain when he got back to the States. Captain Rigaud asked if Hersey might at least phone up his parents and tell them he was okay, and then Rigaud asked if Hersey planned to be going to New York City. Of course, Hersey told him, yes, since the Time-Life offices were there. And here is what the captain asked next:

"I want you to take a hot bath. In a bath tub. Long one, about twenty minutes. Then put on a soft white shirt, with a good-looking tie, and a double-breasted blue suit. And then go out and—what's a good bar in New York?"

"Oh," Hersey said, "I don't know, there are lots."

"Well," Captain Rigaud told him, "go to one of them that's good and walk up to the bar and order two Tom Collinses, tall ones. One is for you, and one belongs to Captain Charles Rigaud. I don't care how you drink yours; gulp it for all I care; but Captain Rigaud's drink, sip it, take a half an hour if you got to. And you may as well mumble something formal, like a toast. Drink a toast to Company H. If they aren't on Guadalcanal, they'll be way the hell and gone out to somewhere. Yeah, that's a good idea. Do that."[9]

Today, looking back, when you speak of military morale, you had best take into account the morale of Captain Charles Alfred Rigaud, and all the other marines, sailors, and soldiers who fought the fight around that weird, bitter little island in the middle of the South Pacific, in the doubtful year of 1942. And the situation was getting more uncertain by the day, because the Japanese were now coming down in force, with two full infantry divisions, to attack Vandegrift's men.

✭ Chapter Seventeen

After the resounding defeat of General Kawaguchi's force, the Japanese command at Rabaul, as well as the General Staff in Tokyo, finally realized that the American landings in the Solomons were far more dangerous than they had imagined. Worse, the tactical situation had changed dramatically, and it was at last understood that the U.S. Marines would be formidable to defeat.

Much of the reason for this was the continued American operation of Henderson Field. From it, with new warplanes arriving as fast as they could get there, transport and supply of Japanese troops to Guadalcanal became problematic. The simple math became obvious to Japanese planners. To bring in troops they had to load them on either slow transports traveling at about twenty miles per hour or fast destroyers traveling at more than forty miles an hour. And it was six hundred miles—round-trip—from Rabaul to Guadalcanal, half of this distance in daylight hours when the U.S. planes could get at them. Either way—destroyer or troop transport—it was a risky proposition, because the American Dauntless dive-bombers, so deadly to Japanese ships at Midway, had a range of about eight hundred miles, that is, about four hundred miles each way from takeoff to return. Henderson Field was an aircraft carrier the Japanese could damage but not sink.*

*The expression that an island airfield was "an unsinkable aircraft carrier" is true enough in a sense. But the difference was that island airfields could not sail around like carriers and so the combatants on both sides always knew where they were.

Now the problem for the Japanese was that, once they got to Guadal-canal, by transport or destroyer, there were of necessity many hours of debarking men and unloading of food, artillery, tanks, ammunition, sup-plies: all the equipment needed to keep an army in the field. And because daylight at that latitude lasted from about six A.M. to six P.M., there was simply no way they could get the ships and supplies from Rabaul to Guadal-canal and have them off-loaded without exposing themselves to attacks from the American planes the next morning. This had been strikingly proven during the Kawaguchi buildup when marine dive-bombers blew up a Japanese transport destroyer in the Slot, killing about six hundred soldiers and sailors. Such was their dilemma.

The Japanese pondered the question and came up with a bold plan. They simply had to destroy Henderson Field, or, at a minimum, keep it out of operation when they made their Tokyo Express runs. Since daily bombing and nightly shelling from smaller warships had proved inconclu-sive, they would bring in—battleships! It seemed the only thing that might work, except for one problem: there were no battleships available. They were all under command of Admiral Yamamoto, who was languishing up at the great Japanese naval base on the island of Truk, waiting for his chance to lure the Americans into his fantasy of the Great Sea Battle, in which he would need all his battleships.

There then appeared on the scene a familiar figure, the ubiquitous Colonel Tsuji—instigator of the murders of thousands of Chinese on Singapore and of the Bataan Death March—who had become more ubiq-uitous than ever, if that was possible. He had been sent by officials in Tokyo to find out what was going on and so, risking life and limb, he traveled to Guadalcanal to visit the troops. Here is what he found: "Our troops have been cut off for more than a month. Officers and men have to dig grass roots, scrape moss and pick buds from the trees, and drink seawater to survive." Tsuji managed to get back to Rabaul and then by plane to Truk, where he found Admiral Yamamoto in his cabin aboard the leviathan battle-ship *Yamato* painting pictures, his hobby. Tsuji imparted his information to him, describing the Guadalcanal soldiers as "thinner than Gandhi."[1]

The great admiral was so moved by the end of Tsuji's report that he reversed himself and promised forthwith to send battleships to bombard

Henderson Field. Thus, on the night of October 13, marines and other American troops were treated to something a participant later described this way: "They had lived through [bombardments] before, but they had never lived through anything like that and, praise God, would never have to again."[2]

The fourteen-inch shell of a battleship is almost as tall as a man, weighs 1,400 pounds, and is accurate up to sixteen miles. Its explosion is, exponentially, about ten times as powerful as that of a cruiser's and far more than ten times that of a destroyer's. For an hour and twenty minutes, the Japanese battleships lobbed more than a thousand of these monsters on and around Henderson Field. There was nothing the marines could do but take it. It was dark and they had no night-fighter capabilities; besides, the planes couldn't take off anyway because of runway damage. Many Americans had their eardrums blown out; forty-one were killed, some of them atomized. Hundreds were wounded. Everyone was terrified, including General Vandegrift, who remarked later that "a man comes close to himself in those times."[3]*

Morning brought a horrific sight: Henderson Field was almost a total wreck. Considering that one thousand-pound bomb can sink an aircraft carrier, imagine what a thousand of these things could do. Deep craters and ruptured steel matting pockmarked the field. Seventy percent of the U.S. bombers had been blown up or put out of action. The field was a Dantesque inferno of burning planes and gasoline. Practically all the aviation fuel had been destroyed. Buildings and equipment, including the air control center, were demolished. It was almost as if they would have to start over again; indeed, it was surely a time that tried men's souls.

If October 13 had been a bad day, there was at least one bright spot, and a crucial one, too. That morning thirteen transports had arrived carrying the 164th Infantry Regiment of the U.S Army's Americal Division, 3,000 well-equipped soldiers, and though they had not previously seen combat, they were a most welcome sight, at least to the marines.† The Japanese, too,

---

*To get an idea of what it must have been like, picture yourself in an area of about five square miles where, in the space of two hours, more than a thousand gigantic lightning bolts are cracking down all around you at the rate of about one strike every seven seconds.

†Whenever these American troopships would arrive, marines manning the launches would flock out to them, loaded to the gunwales with souvenirs: Japanese flags, rifles, helmets,

gave them a most spectacular welcome. As Marine Major Hough pointed out, "If ever soldiers were pitchforked abruptly into battle, it was on this island."[4] First, just as the troops were debarking from the ships, the Japanese came over and bombed the army men trying to get ashore. No sooner had they gotten ashore than the big 150mm long-range howitzers, which the Japanese had recently registered from positions in the hills two miles away, opened up on the field. The soldiers were directed to a bivouac in a palm grove, but they hadn't even finished pitching their tents when the Japanese battleships arrived with their screaming rain of hell to turn the whole place into a deafening holocaust. If they could have run off the island at that point, some probably would have, horrified that this was the way it would be every day. Who could have blamed them? But that was not an option; the transports had long since steamed away, and there they were.

Next day, it was more of the same: the Japanese came back first with bombers, then the artillery, which was out of reach for the marines' guns to reply, and again that night with another terrific bombardment by cruisers and destroyers. Vandegrift grimly sent a message to Allied headquarters at Nouméa: "Enemy landed about 10,000 troops yesterday on [Guadalcanal] with considerable equipment and supplies bringing total force on shore to at least 15,000." He went on to "urgently" request a major naval effort, air reinforcements, and a full army division. Everybody in the know understood this was the beginning of the big Japanese counterattack.[5]

Hanson Baldwin, the New York Times correspondent who had visited Vandegrift and told him the American people did not fully understand the situation on Guadalcanal, had gone home to explain it to his readers. He compared it with Long Island. It was, he said, as if the marines were holding Jones Beach, and the Japanese controlled everything else.

Kept up-to-date on the fighting, Roosevelt was extremely troubled by the marines' perilous situation. "My anxiety about the Southwest Pacific,"

---

whatever they could scrounge. Pathetically, they would trade these things to the sailors for food: canned ham, fruit, canned milk, fresh bread—anything to supplant their meager, twice-a-day diet of Japanese rice, powdered eggs, Spam, crackers, and canned vienna sausage.

he told Harry Hopkins privately, "is to make sure that every possible weapon gets into that area to hold Guadalcanal. And that having held it in this crisis, that munitions and planes and crews are on the way to take advantage of our success."* Publicly, however, Roosevelt was less sanguine about success, what with all the glum news coming in. "We must not *over*rate the importance of our successes in the Solomon Islands," he told reporters, "though we may be proud of the skill with which these *local* operations were conducted" (emphasis added). Hopkins's biographer Robert Sherwood interpreted these remarks this way: "Roosevelt spoke thus cautiously of a critical battle because he knew, as the public did not, of the severe naval losses we had sustained and he was seeking to prepare the people for possible news that the Japanese had driven the Marines from the positions so precariously held on Guadalcanal."[6]

Meantime, on Guadalcanal (or just the Canal, as the marines and soldiers had come to call it), all preparations were being made to fend off the next enemy assault, which they had every reason to believe would be powerful indeed. The fortunate thing was that by now they had had ample time to strengthen and fortify their positions. Double and sometimes triple belts of barbed wire had been strung along the entire perimeter; fields of fire had been carefully cut out and artillery preregistered on all likely avenues of approach. Extra supplies of ammunition and other critical items had been brought forward and double communication wires run. Strong entrenchments had been dug and fast reaction reserves placed at critical points. The Seabees and engineers had repaired Henderson Field and, mercifully, new planes were arriving, many of them soon to come from the carrier *Hornet*, which was sunk in the Battle of the Santa Cruz Islands, but not before they'd gotten most of the planes off.

There was delicious irony in this, for the battle of the nearby Santa Cruz Islands was fought by the Japanese to keep the Americans from reinforcing Guadalcanal, but aside from sinking the *Hornet* all it accomplished

---

*Roosevelt also told Hopkins to compose these sentiments into a message for the Joint Chiefs of Staff.

for them was to have the *Hornet's* planes arrive at Guadalcanal, from where they could more closely bomb the Tokyo Express and shoot Japanese bombers out of the sky. In any event, all that could be done by the Americans had been done. There was only now to sit and wait.

The blow began to fall on October 23, with an attack near the mouth of the now infamous Matanikau River. General Hyakutake's battle plan was apparently to divert the Americans' attention with this assault on the far western side of the perimeter, while the main attack would fall just east of Bloody Ridge with about 6,000 troops.* So confident was the Japanese commander that he had prepared an order of instruction as to how the surrender of Henderson Field would be handled: once it had been overrun, Lieutenant General Massao Maruyama, leading the attack, was to march Vandegrift and his staff to the mouth of the Matanikau, where the formalities would take place, after which they would be flown to Japan and paraded in disgrace through the streets of Tokyo.[7]

The attack on the Matanikau began near sundown when nine Japanese tanks rolled out of the jungle toward the sand spit that blocked the mouth of the river and afforded its only crossing. Marines had heard the tanks rumbling in the jungle for the past day or so and were waiting on the other side with 37mm antitank guns. As the tanks emerged the marines blasted them one after the other with armor-piercing phosphorus shells. Eight of them were almost immediately destroyed and the ninth, as it slowly made its way forward, was attacked by a lone marine, who pitched a grenade into its track and ducked: the explosion blew off the track and the tank wobbled off across the sand spit and into the surf, where a big 75mm gun from a marine half-track used it for target practice. Not only that but the marines were savvy enough to understand that tanks do not operate without infantry and, assuming these were not far behind, an enormous preregistered artillery barrage was walked back and forth through the jungle in the direction from which the tanks had come. In between explosions, the marines could actually hear an unearthly chorus

---

*Some historians do not believe the Matanikau attack was intended as a diversion, but was simply another example of an uncoordinated or badly executed plan. After reviewing all points, the author is convinced that it was indeed a diversion gone awry—or, perhaps, a combination of both theories.

of screaming from the jungle. Later, several hundred Japanese bodies were found there. So ended the "diversionary" phase of General Hyakutake's assault.

Next afternoon, from the marine position on Bloody Ridge, a Japanese officer was spied at the edge of the jungle, observing the ridge and surrounding area through binoculars. Understandably this raised suspicions, and the marines were ready, commanded by Lieutenant Colonel Lewis (Chesty) Puller, who had prepared his positions well.

The Japanese attack was to have been led by that old Guadalcanal hand General Kawaguchi, who had already had his fill of the Bloody Ridge and wanted no more of it, but his strident arguments to move the assault farther to the east only got him sacked. At three A.M. the now familiar *Banzai!* was shouted from thousands of throats as the Japanese stormed out of the jungle toward the lower slopes. They were mowed down by the hundreds. Those who were left ran back into the jungle to regroup, work themselves up into another bloodthirsty frenzy, then swarm out again, only to receive another dose of the same medicine. They did this time and again until daybreak, when they gave up and marched back westward through the jungle from whence they came. At places the Japanese had made inroads, and there had been hand-to-hand fighting, but the marine line remained intact. In the part of the line held by the army's newly arrived 164th Infantry Regiment, the Japanese were met with a particularly fierce fire. This was because the soldiers came equipped with the new M-1 Garand, an eight-shot, semiautomatic rifle that replaced the old 1903 bolt-action rifle the marines had been using. It was to remain the standard infantry weapon for another twenty-five-years, until the Vietnam War era.

Sunrise revealed a horrific sight in front of the American positions: thousands of Japanese lay dead on the slopes, sprawled in seemingly every grotesque position imaginable. All day long the air above was filled with fighting planes, and the marines and soldiers, in between sharpening their trench knives and cleaning their weapons, watched in fascination as Japanese plane after Japanese plane was flamed out of the sky. Newly arrived Lieutenant Joe Foss became an ace in one day! That afternoon and into the night there was more fighting to the west, between the Matanikau and the main marine perimeter, led by the Japanese colonel Oka, who must have been a trial to his superiors, as he had done nothing right since he had arrived on the island. He didn't do it right this time, either; he had only to attack a very thin position held by a single marine battalion, which he out-numbered three to one. After several furious assaults he was thrown back with heavy losses, but this was not entirely without its tribulations. At one point Oka's troops succeeded in breaking a part of the line, but they were soon kicked out by an assortment of cooks, bakers, jeep drivers, clerks, band members, and other headquarters personnel, hastily armed and dra-gooned into action by the battalion's executive officer.

The night of October 25 brought renewed attacks around Bloody Ridge, which met the same fate as those previous. In the middle of all this somebody foolishly told General Maruyama that Henderson Field had been conquered. Relishing the thought of marching Vandegrift and his staff down to the mouth of the Matanikau for the prearranged surrender ceremony, Maruyama signaled this news to the powerful Japanese fleet under Admi-ral Nobutake Kondo, which had been steaming restlessly in the Slot north of Guadalcanal, to come and take possession of the airfield and all its Ameri-can prisoners. Dawn, however, told a different story to one of the admiral's floatplanes, which had flown over Henderson Field just to make sure. It received a warm reception from American antiaircraft fire.

In the end, Hyakutake's attack had been a revolting bloodbath, owing to the stubbornness of the Japanese command, which seemed to have learned nothing from the previous lessons and continued with the suicidal tactic of human-wave assaults. The sheer number of dead posed an imme-diate problem since in the tropics bodies begin to decompose within hours, attracting flies that carry all kinds of diseases associated with rotting flesh. By morning, the wrecked Japanese army had slunk off, perhaps to fight another day, while the marines called in bulldozers from Henderson Field to dig trenches for a 3,500-man mass burial. General Vandegrift got his picture on the next cover of *Time* magazine.

With Admiral Halsey now in overall command, the U.S. Navy re-turned to the bloodstained waters around Guadalcanal. It was a good thing, too, because despite the utter defeat of Hyakutake's army, the infuriated Japanese became more determined than ever to eject the Americans from the island. They concluded that in order to do so they needed more men,

ships, planes—everything—and to that end they began shipping in on the
nightly Tokyo Express *two* full divisions, 24,000 strong. Fortunately, the
Americans had received reinforcements too: more army regiments and
a marine regiment, bringing Vandegrift's strength up to about 22,000
effectives. Heavy artillery had also been landed to counter the big 150mm
Japanese guns. Not only that, but U.S. fighter strength at Guadalcanal was
now up to ten full squadrons, marine, navy, and army. This began to put
a serious dent in the bomber groups the Japanese were sending down from
Rabaul to plaster Henderson Field. The fighting continued daily throughout October and into November, though not with the intensity of the big
battle just launched by Hyakutake. Vandegrift now felt confident enough to
go over to the offensive and there were many clashes around that perpetual
hotbed the Matanikau River. At first glance it would seem the Americans
were getting things under control, except for one thing: the Japanese navy.
So long as they could land troops and supplies every night and shell Henderson
Field with impunity, the issue would remain in doubt. The issue was soon
to be resolved, however, though with a terrible price to pay.

The naval Battle of Guadalcanal was actually three separate battles on suc-
ceeding nights, November 13 to 15, 1942. It was one of the most ferocious naval battles in history, involving only surface ships: battleships,
cruisers, and destroyers. It took place where the previous battles had
erupted, in the waters of Ironbottom Sound around the dark cone of Savo
Island.

 Halsey, recognizing the Japanese naval threat, had sent northward
to the Solomons three powerful armadas of ships: two task groups consisting of six cruisers and thirteen destroyers and a full task force with
two modern battleships escorted by four destroyers. The task groups
were under command of rear admirals Daniel Callaghan and Norman
Scott, and the task force of battleships was led by Rear Admiral Willis
Lee. With a force this size, Halsey could have intended only a showdown,
because intelligence indicated that a powerful Japanese fleet, including
two battleships, was now bearing down on Guadalcanal to conduct another bombardment of Henderson Field.

The forces under Callaghan and Scott—five cruisers and eight destroyers would see action—arrived off the island on November 12, escorting a flotilla of transports and supply ships. After unloading, they steamed away southward. The warships, under overall command of Callaghan, then steamed westward into Ironbottom Sound to find the enemy, who at that point had not yet arrived; so, just after nightfall, Callaghan set up his ships in a snakelike line of battle and began to patrol. Professor Morison, the navy historian, sets the scene: "A nine knot easterly breeze scarcely rippled the surface. The stars shone brightly and jagged flashes of lightning over the islands fitfully illuminated low lying clouds. The new moon had vanished below the dark horizon. Sailors peered from darkened bridges, waited in crowded plotting rooms and sweated in stifling engine rooms,* wondering what the score would be."[8] At 1:24 A.M. the cruiser *Helena* reported radar contact with a large group of strange ships steaming fast into the sound from the northwest, straight down the Slot from Rabaul. It was Friday the thirteenth.

Admiral Callaghan, known to his crew as Uncle Dan, was a charismatic figure. He had been Roosevelt's naval aide in the White House before joining Ghormley as his chief of staff. In that capacity it was Callaghan who had sat silently in Ghormley's place in the crucial admirals' meeting before the Guadalcanal landings, in which Admiral Fletcher decreed he would stay for only forty-eight hours after the landings to protect the invasion force.

The radar blip that appeared on the *Helena*'s screen was about sixteen miles northwest, and getting closer by the second, since the two fleets, each steaming at about twenty knots, were closing on each other at nearly fifty miles per hour. Instead of moving off to the flank and launching a torpedo attack, Callaghan decided to pitch right into the Japanese. Perhaps this was because he was aware of the woeful deficiencies of American torpedoes; in any case, the die was cast—the Americans knew the Japanese were coming, and the Japanese were as yet unaware of the American presence. But here Callaghan seemed to have faltered. It was not until 1:45

---

*Because the ships were "buttoned up" for battle, almost all ports and doors and vents were closed, and temperatures in the engine and boiler rooms often exceeded 150 degrees F.

that he gave the order, "Stand by to open fire." By now the Americans were actually within sight range of the Japanese ships, which were steaming in two parallel columns. Callaghan's course pitched him right between them and a melee ensued.

The whole ghastly business took no more than fifteen minutes. At 1:50 Japanese searchlights suddenly flashed on, illuminating the bridge of the cruiser *Atlanta*, Admiral Scott's flagship. *Atlanta* began firing at the offending light, but it had already worked its evil; a salvo from one of the Japanese ships crashed into the *Atlanta*'s bridge, killing Admiral Scott and most of his staff. Then a torpedo exploded amidships, "lifting her bodily out of the sea"; when she settled back, she was dead in the water and sinking. It was then that Callaghan was overcome with confusion, and he gave an order, "Cease firing own ships!" It proved to be a fateful order.* With all the maneuvering and blasting and radio chatter, the admiral obviously believed that his ships were firing on their own—one of the major dangers in a night naval action—but he seems to have been wrong.

In any case, no such order was given by the Japanese commander who, aboard the battleship *Hiei*, spied Callaghan's flagship, *San Francisco*, just about the same time that *San Francisco* spied him. *San Francisco* fired first, but her salvo fell short. When *Hiei* fired, she was short also. Then, traveling parallel to each other at flank speed, the two ships blasted away in a duel that has been compared with naval actions of the seventeenth century. The *San Francisco* definitely made some devastating hits on her three-times-larger antagonist, with Admiral Callaghan shouting into the radios, "We want the big ones! Get the big ones first!" Then, suddenly, the *San Francisco* found herself caught in powerful searchlights, probably from a destroyer, and a stupendous salvo from the *Hiei* crashed into her bridge, killing Admiral Callaghan and all his staff as well as the ship's captain and putting the *San Francisco* temporarily out of the action.

Meantime, the other American ships had resumed fire on their own. The major target for many was the *Hiei*, which began receiving shells from American cruisers and destroyers—eighty hits by one account—and her

---

*Some say this order was intended only for Callaghan's own *San Francisco*, but that does not explain why it was broadcast throughout the fleet, except as a mistake.

rudder was jammed. This was the flagship of the Japanese commander Admiral Hiroaki Abe,* who surveyed the damage and decided he had had enough. He ordered the *Hiei* and her sister battleship *Kirishima* to turn northward, out of the battle. This had the effect of breaking off the action for all intents.

Thus the night action was over, but there were other dramas to be played out as the sun rose over the carnage. Ironbottom Sound was again littered with the debris of war and the bobbing heads of oil-soaked sailors in the shark-infested channel. The scenes aboard ships were frightful; mangled bodies and body parts were strewn over decks awash with blood. Fires raged in many ships helplessly adrift or crippled. One of those cripples was the cruiser *Juneau*, last in the American battle line, which had been fighting the good fight when she was suddenly struck by a torpedo from a destroyer and left nearly dead in the water. As she tried to limp south a Japanese submarine periscope rose above the surface, then fired two torpedoes, one striking *Juneau*. According to Lieutenant Commander Bruce McCandless, watching aboard the *San Francisco*, "*Juneau* didn't sink— she blew up with all the fury of an erupting volcano. There was a terrific thunderclap and a plume of white water that was blotted out by a huge brown hemisphere a thousand yards across, while from within which came the sounds of more explosions." Of the eight hundred sailors aboard *Juneau* only ten survived and among those who perished were the five Sullivan brothers.[†]

The battleship *Hiei*, after making her desperate turn toward Rabaul, managed to get only to the north side of Savo Island, so badly was she

---

*Not to be confused with Admiral Koso Abe, who had ordered the beheadings of the American prisoners—Carlson's marine raiders—on Makin Island.

[†]The Sullivan brothers became nationally celebrated after this horrendous episode. After Pearl Harbor the five brothers had enlisted in the navy on condition that they could serve together. Their wish was granted and they were assigned to the *Juneau*. A popular motion picture was made of their story and their likenesses were placed on a U.S. postage stamp. But the War Department was alarmed at the devastation that could fall upon a single family if siblings were put in the same unit, and decreed it would no longer be official practice. Not only that but the department also decreed that if one sibling was killed in action, the other would be pulled out and assigned noncombatant duty.

mangled. And there, at sunup, the planes from Henderson Field found her. All day the Americans bombed and strafed her, even a squadron from the *Enterprise,* which was in the area to deliver the planes to Guadalcanal. Smoke and flames were visible from her stem to her stern, but still the *Hiei* did not go down. It was beginning to seem that she was unsinkable. She wasn't. Japanese destroyers returned to take off her crew and after dusk she went down by the stern, scuttled—the first Japanese battleship lost in the war.

The final tally for the first day of the naval Battle of Guadalcanal revealed this: one Japanese battleship and two destroyers sunk versus two American cruisers and four destroyers. American casualties had been far greater than those for the Japanese—1,300 sailors perished, including two admirals. But the U.S. Navy had prevented the Japanese from again shelling and wrecking Henderson Field, and that was its great strategic victory.

Even as sporadic fighting and bombing continued over Ironbottom Sound and rescue parties fished American sailors out of the water, another large Japanese fleet was headed south to finish the job. With practically all the American ships that had engaged in the first night of the naval battle having been either sunk or badly damaged, there was little resistence to be offered and on the night of November 13 the Japanese bombarded Henderson Field with a thousand rounds of eight-inch shells from two cruisers, as well as smaller shells from destroyers. Americans on the receiving end "ran the gamut of profanity and prayers."[9]

Help, however, was on the way. It came in the form of Admiral Willis Lee's battleship force, which was already steaming toward Guadalcanal but would not arrive before the night of November 14. Unaware of this, the Japanese had already debarked one of its strongest forces yet. Its first echelon was spotted just after dawn by pilots from Henderson Field: eleven troop transports with more than 13,000 men destined for Guadalcanal escorted by eleven destroyers. The American fliers had a field day, and by nightfall seven enemy troop transports had been sunk in the Slot and the rest badly damaged. Not only that but they sank one of the Japanese cruisers that had shelled Henderson Field the night before. The Japanese, however, managed to transfer about 10,000 of the soldiers off the sinking transports and place them on destroyers for the rest of the ride to Guadalcanal, alongside the remaining four transports. Some 3,000 more Japanese soldiers were killed when their ships sank.

That night Admiral Lee finally entered Ironbottom Sound. His two brand-new battleships, the *Washington* and the *South Dakota,* were screened by four destroyers, which soon clashed with the screen of the Japanese fleet. As Lee entered the sound he tried to establish radio contact with Henderson Field, but as he had not yet been assigned a call sign he was told, "We do not recognize you."

Lee, staring into the darkness from the bridge of the *Washington,* growled out in a plain voice, "You tell your big boss [Vandegrift] that Ching Lee is here and wants information." (Because of his somewhat oriental-looking features, "Ching" had been Lee's nickname from his Naval Academy days and he knew his pal Vandegrift would recognize that!)[10]

At eleven P.M. the *Washington'*s radar made contact with an unidentified ship, which was soon sighted through powerful gunnery telescopes. The ship was the Japanese cruiser *Sendai,* which had also sighted Lee's force and which its captain reported back to fleet command as "two cruisers and four destroyers." The Japanese captain was soon disabused of this notion when the mighty sixteen-inch guns of the *Washington* roared out at him. He immediately turned tail, made a smoke screen, and ran for cover.

Lee's destroyers had less luck, and for a while it seemed this night was going to be a repeat of the brutal action of November 12 and 13. The Japanese destroyers were steaming in the lee of Savo Island, and thus their silhouettes were not clear on the horizon. After a five-minute action three of the four American destroyers were sinking or sunk, with great loss of life.

Worse, as Lee's big ships closed with the Japanese battleship *Kirishima* and her four escorting cruisers, the *South Dakota* suddenly suffered a power outage, which put her in the dark and knocked out her radar. No sooner had this happened than she was caught in the powerful searchlights of two Japanese destroyers and seemingly all ships in the Japanese fleet opened up on her. Fortunally, her modern armament—an eighteen-inch belt of steel around her hull—saved her from catastrophe, but her lighter superstructure was blasted by the many calibers and weights of Japanese shells and more than a hundred men were killed. More fortunately, Admiral Lee,

aboard the *Washington*, had spotted the *South Dakota*'s principal tormentor, the *Kirishima,* which was about five miles distant and happily sending
salvo after roaring salvo at the hapless American ship. Lee suddenly opened
on *Kirishima* with massive salvos of his own and within seven minutes the
big Japanese battlewagon was aflame from stem to stern and staggered off
out of the action, only to sink a few hours later. Ching Lee then turned his
attention to the Japanese cruisers and blasted two of them, as did the *South
Dakota,* whose power had been restored. With that the Japanese had again
had enough and turned northward toward Rabaul.

Admiral Tanaka, perpetually in charge of the Tokyo Express, had
been waiting in the wings while the battle raged, his destroyers and troop
transports crammed with Japanese soldiers destined for Guadalcanal. He
knew that if he waited for them to unload they would all become ideal
targets in the morning for the American planes, so he ordered the four
remaining transports to sacrifice themselves by beaching while the troops
got off. As for himself, he disgustedly sped back toward Rabaul behind
his fellow sailors, his destroyers overflowing with soldiers who would
not reach Guadalcanal that night, if ever.

Even though several thousand Japanese soldiers managed to debark
that night from the transports beached at the western end of Guadalcanal
near Cape Esperance, they were bombed and strafed beginning at sunup
and none of their critical supplies or heavy equipment got ashore. Again,
the U.S. Navy had saved Henderson Field from a major bombardment and,
though the Americans had no way of knowing it at the time, never again
would the Japanese send their major warships down from Rabaul to strut
around Ironbottom Sound, blasting Henderson Field at will.

Now the tables were turning quickly, and Guadalcanal was becoming a
sinkhole for Japanese soldiers, planes, and ships, which they could ill afford
to lose. However, during the coming weeks the Tokyo Express managed
to sneak through again and again in the dark of night so that by the first of
December Japanese troop strength on Guadalcanal totaled about 30,000.
This was a formidable force, except for one thing: the Japanese had not
figured out a way to keep them supplied, and they were beginning to starve.

It is one thing to dash in with troops who can quickly jump off ship and go ashore; it is another to have to wait to unload the tons of supplies and food to keep that many men active in an offensive battle. The Japanese command tried everything they knew, including loading destroyers with thousands of big oil drums filled with food and ammunition, roped together on the decks. The theory was to get close enough to the beaches to heave them over and the men on shore could pick them up and tow them in. It did not work well: ropes sawed loose on sharp coral heads and most of the drums sank or washed out to sea.

By the first of December it was apparent to Japanese authorities back at Rabaul that Guadalcanal must be evacuated, but since they had all made such a big production of it, and so many men and planes and ships had been lost, somebody was going to have to tell the emperor, and nobody wanted to. So the Japanese on Guadalcanal now had to go over to total defense, digging in and making the Americans pay for every yard. It was tough going for the American soldiers and marines, who now got their own taste of what it was like to attack well-fortified positions. Nevertheless, they pressed forward, driving the Japanese slowly west, well beyond the Matanikau and into the jungles and hills well south of Bloody Ridge. By this time Guadalcanal had acquired a name given by the Japanese who fought there: the Island of Death.

In early December the U.S. South Pacific Command decided that the First Marine Division had done enough. It was about time, too. They had been on Guadalcanal four long months and almost everybody was suffering from malaria and any number of other tropical ailments. They had been under almost constant fire during that time, from ground attacks to air bombing and naval shelling, and everyone's nerves were on edge. Combat fatigue had become an increasing problem. By the first week in December they were packing up, headed for Australia, and the rest of the U.S. Army's Americal Division was moving in. Not only that, but the 16,000 soldiers of the Twenty-fifth Infantry division, a regular army outfit that had been stationed at Schofield Barracks, Hawaii, was also alerted for Guadalcanal.*

*This was the outfit made famous by James Jones in *From Here to Eternity* and *The Thin Red Line*.

By the end of the year, Henderson Field had been modernized and permanant buildings were beginning to spring up; air strength now exceeded more than two hundred warplanes. Japanese bombing attacks had slacked off, not just because American aviators were shooting them down at such high rates but because they had already shot down so many there just weren't enough left to send, as in weeks past. American transports could now off-load men and supplies almost with impunity, and they did. Engineers and Seabees had built roads over much of the area, bridging streams and ravines, so that men could now get to the fighting areas in trucks and jeeps and tanks and artillery could move up quickly.

On New Year's Eve, the Japanese emperor was finally told that Guadalcanal had to be evacuated. It was a sour thing, given all that had been lost there, but he gave his assent. Still, it would be another six weeks before a scheme could be put in place to accomplish this vast retreat. Meanwhile, the Japanese hung on, starving and emaciated and suffering from tropical diseases even more so than the Americans, since their medical care was not as efficient.

To call the remaining fighting "desultory" would be a grave disservice to those who had to do so. The army divisions, as well as elements of the Second Marine Division, had to continue cleaning out pockets of well-entrenched Japanese who would not surrender. Weak and sick as they were, they could still fire their machine guns and throw grenades, of which they had plenty, and many Americans died trying to root them out. Using intelligence compiled by the marines, army commander General Alexander Patch began a systematic offensive to rid the island of Japanese. Aerial reconnaissance revealed key terrain features and the army gave them picturesque names such as the Galloping Horse and Sea Horse. These were bombarded relentlessly by planes from Henderson Field and by artillery; then the soldiers went in with flamethrowers and employed methodical fire-and-maneuver tactics practiced by the U.S. military.

The departing marines presented a poignant and disturbing picture to arriving soldiers as they marched down off the ridges toward the beach, past the growing new cemeteries with their neatly arranged white wood crosses and Stars of David. The newly arrived soldiers looked at them askance and almost in embarrassment at their tattered, filthy utility uniforms and worn-out shoes, at their scraggly beards and hollow, haunted, emaciated expressions. Out in the harbor lay one of the old Dollar Line ships, the *President Wilson*. Also known as the President's Line, these former trans-Pacific liners were named for presidents of the United States, but after Pearl Harbor they had been commandeered by the military and turned into troopships. Robert Leckie, whose battalion had been in the line for four months, described the scene.

"We were so weak that many of us could not climb up the cargo nets. Some fell into the water—pack, rifle and all—and had to be fished out. Others clung desperately to the nets, panting, fearful to move lest the last ounce of strength depart them too, and the sea receive them. These had to be rescued by nimble sailors swarming down the nets. I was able to reach the top, but could go no further. I could not muster the strength to swing over the gunwale and I hung there, breathing heavily, the ship's hot side swaying away from me in the swells—until two sailors grabbed me by the armpits and pulled me over. I fell with a clatter among the others who had been so brought aboard, and I lay with my cheek pressed against the warm, grimy deck, my heart beating rapidly, not from this exertion, but from happiness."

Once aboard, Leckie and a friend went below to get a cup of coffee, where they encountered a newly arriving soldier who had not yet debarked. He asked them how it was.

"Guadalcanal? It was rough," they both answered. Then they asked the soldier if he'd ever heard of the place before, since they had gotten no news whatsoever from America during the time they were there.

"Guadalcanal! Hell yes!" the soldier replied. "The First Marines— everybody's heard of it. You guys are famous. You guys are heroes back home."

Leckie and his friend quickly went off in opposite directions, each not wanting the other to see the tears in his eyes.[11]

Rumor had it among the First Marines that they might be going home for Christmas. Like most rumors it was untrue, and they were taken first to the island of Espíritu Santo, where they spent Christmas Eve in close order drill, running through the manual of arms. Several more Christmases would pass before they would see home again.

Meantime, bitter fighting remained for those at Guadalcanal. General Patch now had under his command about 40,000 men of all arms, while the Japanese force under General Hyakutake had dwindled from 30,000 to 25,000 and downward from there as American airpower, artillery, and ground troops as well as disease and starvation took their toll. By the end of January all Japanese frontline troops who were able were ordered to move silently to the rear, and to the beaches near Cape Esperance on the western tip of Guadalcanal. Those too weak to make the move were ordered to hold their positions, put up a good fight, and die for their emperor.

The vast fleet of Japanese warships gathering south of Rabaul had been duly noted by coast watchers and was falsely interpreted by Halsey's headquarters as signaling a new reinforcement of Hyakutake's army. Consequently, General Patch pulled back large numbers of his men from the jungle fighting toward Henderson Field, in preparation for defending it against attack. Nobody expected a Japanese evacuation.[12]

Thus, on two moonless nights beginning February 4, nearly 12,000 Japanese officers and men were secretly loaded aboard twenty destroyers of the Tokyo Express, which had brought them there, and turned full steam back toward Rabaul. They had narrowly escaped an amphibious pincer movement organized by Patch, in which a sizable American force had been loaded into LSTs and sailed around Cape Esperance to land just southwest of it, while others pushed along the northern beaches toward the cape. When the two forces finally met up on February 9, everyone involved realized that the Japanese had gone.

Theirs was a textbook demonstration of withdrawal under fire, perhaps the most difficult military maneuver on the books. While there was a sense of disappointment among the American command at not having bagged the lot of them, all were nevertheless relieved. It was finally over.

The Japanese had left more than 24,000 soldiers dead on Guadalcanal, many of them from disease. At least that many more were killed in the Slot on their way from Rabaul, victims of American airpower, or they had died in battle on sunken warships. Two Japanese battleships, a carrier, four cruisers, and twelve destroyers had been sent to the bottom. As bad if not worse for the Japanese, they had lost 1,827 warplanes and 2,362 pilots and crews during the struggle for Guadalcanal, a testimony to the dogged persistence and ferocity of the American pilots of Henderson Field. The superiority of U.S. fighter tactics against the much-vaunted flying characteristics of the Zero is grimly illustrated by the fact that 909 Zeros were shot out of the skies over the Solomons and nearby waters.

The struggle for Guadalcanal was won by the Americans through tenacity, superior infantry tactics, and almost unimaginable sacrifices by its navy to keep the Japanese fleet at bay. It was lost by the Japanese because of incomprehensible infantry tactics and an almost criminal lack of combat intelligence regarding U.S. troop strength on the island. Thus the Japanese attacked headlong time and again with inferior forces and paid the cost, while Henderson Field became stronger day by day.*

The importance of the Battle of Guadalcanal can hardly be overstated. First it stopped the huge Japanese Pacific offensive in its tracks. It helped make Australia safe from Japanese air attacks on its sea-lanes of communication and supply. It sucked up Japanese troops destined for the New Guinea campaign. It gave the Allies a solid, strategic forward base from which to launch the long and bloody war across the Pacific to Tokyo. It relieved the menace to shipping lanes from the United States to Australia and New Zealand and protected vital U.S. outposts such as Fiji, Samoa, and the Hebrides. And, finally, it confirmed for the American public and its fighting troops that the Japanese army was not the invincible machine they had been led to believe.

From the Japanese perspective all of this at last became painfully clear. Admiral Tanaka, architect of the Tokyo Express, summed it up later:

*British officer Peter Fleming, brother of novelist Ian Fleming, creator of James Bond, concluded after studying Japanese documents following the war that the intelligence section at Imperial General Headquarters was fantastically inept. It would be "a waste of time," he said, "to give them information about battalions or regiments, since, although they were glad to get it, they were unable to make any deductions from it" (Thaddeus Holt, *The Deceivers*, 2003).

"There is no question that Japan's doom was sealed with the closing of the struggle for Guadalcanal." After the war, when he was asked by a U.S. interrogator when he first thought "the balance had swung against you," Vice Admiral Takeo Kurita, one of the most respected of the Imperial Navy's senior commanders, did not hesitate.

"Guadalcanal," he replied.[13]

Chapter Eighteen ★

As the big land battles on Guadalcanal were winding down, General Eichelberger arrived on the northern coast of New Guinea, with MacArthur's admonition, "Take Buna or don't come back alive," still ringing in his ears. What he found was the U.S. Army's Thirty-second Infantry division in deplorable condition and disarray, physically and mentally. It was composed mostly of National Guardsmen from Michigan and Indiana who, not having Navajo code talkers like the marines, often spoke their immigrant parents' Scandanavian or Dutch over field radios to confuse and baffle the Japanese.

Every man in the division was running a malarial fever; they suffered from jungle rot, dengue fever, ringworm, and ulcers. They were subsisting on a third of a ration a day, some less than that. One of the inspecting officers wrote, "They wore long dirty beards. Their clothing was in rags. Their shoes were uncared for, or worn out. There was little discipline or military courtesy. When Martin and I visited a regimental [headquarters] to observe what was supposed to be an attack, we found it four and a half miles behind the front line. The regimental commander and his staff went forward from this location rarely, if ever. The attack had been ordered, and it could be entered on the headquarters diary, but it didn't exist."

Eichelberger visited the front only to find there *was* no front; units were so jumbled up nobody could figure out who was who or what was what. He came across troops lying along trails doing nothing, and when he urged them forward they gaped at him like he was crazy. When Eichelberger got back to his tent camp that night he ordered all fighting stopped for two days in order to straighten out the mess. Then he started firing people, beginning with the division commander. Orderlies had pitched Eichelberger's tent "alongside a small crystal clear creek" and as he finally lay down, exhausted, for a good night's sleep, it began to rain. "Next morning, I found the creek inside my tent," he reported, "and within an inch of the bottom of my cot. Various personal possessions floated around like chips in a millstream. I waded knee-deep to get to my shaving mirror, which hung on a bamboo tree outside. In Buna that year, it rained about a hundred and seventy inches."*[1]

As Eichelberger soon found out, the weather and terrain were as much an enemy as the Japanese. After the two days of military housekeeping were up, he ordered an immediate attack on Buna. "In any stalemate," Eichelberger recalled later, "it was obvious the Japanese would win, for they were living among the coconut palms along the coast on sandy soil, while our men lived in swamps."[2] Eichelberger himself took a personal hand, sending companies forward, coordinating various aspects of the assault.[3] But they were met with murderous fire from the Japanese and, though Eichelberger rightly told MacArthur that the troops had fought well, one of his regimental commanders reported, "We have hit them, and bounced off."

The Japanese were fighting from behind the most formidable bunkers seen since the Western Front of World War I. Trenches, shored up with coconut logs, cement, and sand-filled oil drums, were reinforced on top by more logs—and steel, if they could find it. Earth was then shoveled on top and then camouflaged with palm leaves and grass so as to be almost invisible and mostly impervious to artillery or all but the largest bombs. A dozen or more men would occupy these, firing machine guns and rifles from small slits. It was almost impossible to pick them out from more than a few yards away. The Allied troops were repelled to the point

*Seattle, Washington, which is commonly used as the watershed of excessive rainfall in the United States, gets an average of about thirty-six inches of rain per year.

of nausea by odors from these positions, blown directly at them by a prevailing onshore ocean breeze. What they found when they captured one was revolting.

"Rotting bodies, sometimes weeks old, formed part of the fortifications. The living fired over the bodies of the dead, slept side-by-side with them. Inside one trench was a Japanese who had not been able to stand the strain. His rifle was still pointed at his head, his big toe on the trigger, and the top of his head blown off. . . . Everywhere, pervading everything, was the stench of putrescent flesh." In some of the bunkers, the stench was so bad the Japanese had to put on gas masks.[4] Almost worse, there were obvious signs of cannibalism. The Japanese were even more poorly fed than the Americans and carved-up bodies—many of them Allied soldiers, whom the Japanese preferred to eat before eating their own—were scattered about the rear of many entrenchments. After the war, incidents of Japanese cannibalism were found to have been widespread, shocking the Allied world.*

On one of Eichelberger's visits to the front, as he was attempting to get close enough to Buna to observe the Japanese, a near tragedy occurred. Eichelberger's party consisted of General Albert Waldron, who had just been appointed the new commander of the Thirty-second division, two colonels, and his longtime aide, young Captain Daniel Edwards, of whom Eichelberger said, "My regard for him was akin to that of a father for a son." Moving forward on a jungle trail, the party came on a kind of marshy no-man's-land, which was filled with Japanese snipers. First, Waldron was shot in the shoulder by a sniper, so seriously that it ended his military career.

No sooner had Waldron been carried off than Eichelberger, standing under a tree with Edwards, felt a bullet whiz by, which struck Edwards

*Two types of cannibalism were practiced by the Japanese. The first, and most common, was simply to stay alive when Imperial troops were abandoned by their superiors on far-away islands with no food to speak of. The second, and more disgusting, was the custom of some ranking Japanese officers who, in the spirit of Bushido—the way of the ancient Japanese warrior—deliberately eat the livers and other organs of fallen enemies in the belief that it made them strong and brave. Grotesque but instructive examples of this are given in James Bradley's best-selling book *Flyboys* (2003).

in the side. "It was like a slow-motion picture," Eichelberger recalled. "Slowly his knees began to bend and then he fell forward, calling to me to keep cover." Since the stretcher bearers had just carried out General Waldron, Eichelberger had a hard time finding another. When he did and Edwards was loaded on it, "all hell broke loose." Machine guns from Buna opened up, as well as all the Japanese snipers who had been hiding in trees. The stretcher bearers kept having to drop Captain Edwards on their torturous trip to the rear, where there was a makeshift aid station.

Eichelberger then returned to the front to help direct the action but, as we have seen, to no avail. They had gotten right up against the defenses at Buna but could not break through. That afternoon he went back to the aid station, where he was given bad news. The bullet that had struck Captain Edwards was one of the explosive types, Japanese sniper ammunition designed to do maximum damage. It had entered his abdomen and blown a "gaping hole near his spine." The doctor told Eichelberger that Edwards was going to die; "that there were no facilities that far forward to take care of a man so severely wounded 'and, Edwards,' he said, 'was too ill to be moved.'

"Right then and there I decided to take Edwards back to the field hospital. If he was going to die, he might as well die on the hood of my jeep," Eichelberger recounted. "We carted him out like a sack of meal, lashed him to the hood, and started down the trail. Much of it was corduroy road; coconut logs had been imbedded in the mud to give our jeeps traction. Edwards took a terrific and painful jolting but he offered only one protest. Once he said, 'Could you just stop a minute and let me rest?'" Finally Eichelberger got him to the field hospital, where he was operated on. "The operation," reported the very relieved Eichelberger, "saved his life."[5]

While the Americans had been smashing up against Buna, an Australian division, with great loss of life, had managed to take a similar Japanese redoubt at the village of Gona, about eight miles north along the beach. This was a relief but not for long, for many of the Gona Japanese escaped down the beach and set up another position halfway between Gona and Buna, where a river ran into the sea.

It became unpleasantly obvious to Eichelberger that no amount of artillery or bombing was going to dislodge the Japanese from their bunkers; that the only way to beat them was to go in and root them out hand to hand or with bayonets, rifles, and grenades. And this is what the Americans and Australians finally did. A large roadblock was set up to prevent the Japanese force that had escaped from Gona from linking up with the Buna garrison. Then the soldiers began the bloody process of reducing Buna bunker by bunker. Almost to a man, the Japanese fought to the last, exacting a terrible toll on U.S. troops. This shocked American commanders, who deemed it beyond all reason in the world of military science. General George Kenny, who had put MacArthur's chief of staff Sutherland in his place a few weeks earlier, wrote to his superiors in Washington, "There are hundreds of Buna's ahead of us," and forecast that defeating the Japanese "may run to proportions beyond all conception."[6]

The fighting on the north coast of New Guinea went on for another dreadful month as the Americans and Australians tried to dislodge the 7,000 Japanese who had escaped from Gona and set up along the beach between the two villages. MacArthur, in one of his now famous dispatches, callously classified this as a mopping-up operation, yet it was anything but that to the soldiers on the ground. As they had at Guadalcanal, the Japanese command at Rabaul tried to reinforce and resupply their troops on New Guinea with fast destroyers carrying men and oil drums full of food and other equipment. Three times the U.S. air forces turned them back, leaving a wake of burning ships. Finally, in what came to be known as the Battle of the Bismarck Sea, the Japanese advance was halted for good.

Even as their last remaining troops were being evacuated from Guadalcanal, the Japanese command at Rabaul decided on a major effort to reinforce New Guinea. Six thousand Japanese soldiers were placed aboard eight troop transports, escorted by eight destroyers, with a host of Zero fighters hovering above. Japanese weather forecasters assured senior officers that bad weather would mask the convoy for most of the trip. General Kenny received intelligence of this convoy making up at Rabaul and ordered more than two hundred bombers—mostly heavy, four-engine B-24s from Australia—to New Guinea to make sure it did not arrive safely. In fact, it did not arrive at all.

The Japanese meteorologists were wrong by a day, but that's all it took. As the clouds over the Bismarck Sea began to clear, waves of American planes appeared from the south. Japanese antiaircraft gunners on the destroyers rushed to their weapons, only to be startled by a sight they had never seen before. The big bombers came in at mast-top level, like torpedo bombers, and released their bombs into the sea in an amazing demonstration of skip bombing, which had been tried without success at the Battle of Midway six months earlier but had been perfected by Kenny's air force. The bombs hit the water and "dapped," like stones skipped across the surface of a calm flat pond.

All eight of the troop transports sank, as well as four of the eight destroyers. Not only that, but sixty of the escorting Zeros were shot out of the sky by American fighters. Only 2,000 of the 6,000 Japanese soldiers aboard the transports were rescued by the remaining four destroyers, which then turned tail and sped back toward Rabaul fast as they could. When news of this disaster reached Rabaul, it ended further attempts to reinforce the Japanese army on New Guinea, which sealed its fate. No attempt was made, as at Guadalcanal, to evacuate the troops. And since surrender was not an option they were simply left there, as were the sick and weak on Guadalcanal, to die for the emperor.

Admiral Yamamoto had predicted from the beginning that if Japan made war on the United States he could "run wild" for the first six months, but he had no confidence in what might happen next. Now his worst nightmare was coming true: American industrial might and moral outrage, which was beginning to send planes and ships, guns and men into the Pacific at a rate that presently amounted only to a trickle but had been enough to halt the Japanese advance and, soon enough, as Yamamoto and others well knew, that trickle would become a flood.

In the meantime, the joint American-British Germany First doctrine was about to be tested in the severest way. So many of those troops, ships, tanks, planes, and guns that might have eased the strain on the marines and soldiers fighting on Guadalcanal and New Guinea during the battles of October and November 1942 were now on their way across the Atlantic Ocean in a convoy of hundreds of ships, bound for French Morocco on North Africa's Atlantic coast, and for its neighbor Algeria on the Mediterranean. Soldiers who might have enjoyed the movie *Casablanca** were now about to see the place for themselves.

Thus was operation Torch conceived by the British both as a way to eject the Germans and Italians from North Africa and to allay the chaffing and insistent demands by Stalin for a second front to relieve his beleaguered armies. The U.S. Joint Chiefs of Staff did not at first buy into this idea; they, like Stalin, wanted to prepare immediately to invade France from the English Channel coast and drive the Germans back into Germany at the earliest possible moment. To the chagrin and annoyance of the Roosevelt administration, American communists had begun using their news organs, as well as slogans painted on walls and fences in their strongholds in the Northeast, to demand a "Second Front Now!"

Even though he was also against a North African invasion at first, Roosevelt was slowly brought around by the persuasions of Churchill. Neither America nor Britain, the prime minister told the president, currently had the strength to invade France, while they did have the strength to oppose the Germans and Italians in North Africa. And it was important to do so, because if the Germans managed to push the British out of Egypt, they could pass unmolested into the oil-rich Middle East and thence to India, where they could link up with the Japanese. The Germans and Italians already controlled most of the Mediterranean, blocking British convoys from using the Suez Canal to resupply their armies in Africa, the Middle East, India, and Burma.

Furthermore, in the back of Churchill's devious mind was the notion that after expelling the Germans from North Africa the Allies could then attack through the soft underbelly of Europe—Italy—knocking her out of the war, thereby gaining total control of the Mediterranean and isolating Germany. This would also have the effect of stabilizing Britain's colonial possessions in the region. The British prime minister was also savvy enough to realize he had best not bring this up to the Americans as yet;

---

*Casablanca was released in the United States in November 1942, *after* most of the Torch invasion force had sailed for North Africa.

they had much on their plate for the moment, and it was enough to get them into the fight right now.

The Torch plan was to land an initial force of 100,000 men, most of them Americans, in the French colonies of Morocco and Algeria, now controlled by the German puppet government at Vichy. Through these colonies, the Vichy French were supplying the German North African armies of General Erwin Rommel (whom the press had dubbed the Desert Fox) with everything from food to gasoline. It was hoped that once French Morocco and Algeria were secured, American and British troops would hurry east to capture Tunisia and trap Rommel's army between there and the British army fighting them in Egypt and Libya. It was a bold scheme on a very large scale, complicated by a dogging political issue: What would the Vichy French do?

The Germans had allowed the French to organize and keep a well-supplied army of 120,000—nearly ten divisions—in their North African colonies, just to prevent something like Torch from happening. This freed up German troops to fight the British farther east, but one great fear of the Allies was that the Germans would somehow learn of the invasion plans and begin heavily reinforcing the defenses of western North Africa, which then would have made Torch impossible. That they did not was testimony to the solid planning and strict security imposed by the Allies; it was said that only about eight hundred people out of the hundreds of thousands who would eventually fight there actually knew what the plan entailed and when it was scheduled to come off.* The overall commander of this vast enterprise was General Dwight D. Eisenhower, operating from the British bastion of Gibraltar, which guarded the narrow straits leading into the Mediterranean.

Like so many Allied operations at the beginning of the war, Torch got off to a rocky start. First, there was simply not time enough to train the U.S. Army troops properly for an amphibious landing, since it had been deter-

*Thaddeus Holt, however, in his masterful work *The Deceivers,* points out that the U.S. military feared by sailing time that as many as 5,000 American troops probably knew at least some of the plan and that it had likely been compromised by the Axis. In fact they never found out, and if that is not a miracle it ought to be.

mined by meteorologists that November 8 would be about the last possible date for the invasion. After that the huge surf created by winter Atlantic storms would foreclose landing on the Moroccan coast until the middle of the following year. Marines had been training for amphibious operations for decades but, as we have seen, they were almost completely tied up in the Pacific, in particular at Guadalcanal. The army and navy tried a number of rehearsals, but because of the German U-boat menace along the American Atlantic coast they had to do their practicing inside, within the calm confines of the Chesapeake Bay, which presented none of the problems associated with the large surf and rough weather they would encounter on the Atlantic coast of Morocco.

Be that as it may, the American armada sailed October 24 and 25, 1942, in three separate groups out of Norfolk, Virginia, and Portland, Maine. For days it wove a crazy quilt of courses to confuse and deceive any Nazi submarines that might try to attack or even guess its destination. More troopships sailed from England, all timed as daintily as a minuet to arrive simultaneously near the Atlantic coast ports of Casablanca and Safi in French Morocco and the French Mediterranean ports of Algiers and Oran in Algeria.

Meanwhile, the Americans were using every stratagem they could think of to convince the Vichy French not to oppose the invasions. To the disgust of many of its own citizens, the United States had continued diplomatic relations with the Vichy regime on the theory that it might somehow be useful. In fact, it was. Robert D. Murphy, the American consul general at the Vichy court, had been currying favor with a number of ranking French officers and political figures thought to be opposed to the Vichyites, and who he hoped would cooperate with the Allies once the time came. Being a diplomat from a supposedly friendly country, Murphy was allowed to travel to North Africa, where he not only continued to cultivate important friendships but also gathered critical information on such things as harbor and beach defenses, tide and surf conditions, airfields, roads, and the attitudes of French troops.

Not only that but just as the U.S. troop convoys were steaming out from American ports, U.S. Army General Mark Clark was sent by Eisenhower to cram his lanky form into a British submarine and cross the Mediterranean to Algiers, where he would meet with French commanders believed to favor the Allies. Here the situation became especially tricky.

Most French commanders still detested the British for what they had done to the French navy in the summer of 1940, not long after the fall of France. Then, British high command had realized immediately that if the powerful French naval fleet fell into the hands of the Germans, it would spell catastrophe for the British, who would have to face a German navy suddenly more than doubled in size, in addition to the Italian navy. Consequently, plans were laid for the neutralization of the French navy. Those French warships that were in England at the time were seized before they could sail back to France, but that still left four strong French fleets in the Mediterranean and in Africa. One, at the French Mediterranean port of Toulon, was untouchable, but there were other forces at Dakar, French West Africa, in Alexandria, Egypt, and at Oran, in Algeria. The British attacked the French fleet at Dakar without success, but in Alexandria an agreement was reached with the French commanding admiral, who would disarm his ships and not try and sail out of the harbor. It was in Oran that the trouble occurred.

On July 3, 1940, a British admiral had appeared off the French fleet anchorage near Oran with three battleships, two cruisers, eleven destroyers, and an aircraft carrier. He presented the French admiral with an ultimatum: 1) Come fight with us, 2) Sail your ships to England, America, or some other neutral port, 3) Sink your ships yourselves, or 4) We will sink them for you. Being bottled up in harbor put the French at a decided disadvantage, but the French admiral was having none of the British ultimatum. He radioed for reinforcements from the French fleet at Toulon, then began stalling for time. The British were soon on to this and, just before sunset, they reluctantly opened fire, "the first shots fired by the British against the French since Waterloo."[7]

In the ensuing brief and unequal fight, three French battleships were sunk, as well as many destroyers and support ships, with the loss of more than 1,200 French sailors. The French, from Vichy on up, were enraged at their former ally for taking what they saw as a brutal and unnecessary action.*

---

*As things later turned out, it might not have been so unnecessary after all. During the North Africa invasions the Germans did indeed march into Toulon and demand that the French hand over to them their remaining fleet. Instead, the French scuttled their ships right there and then, much to the dismay of the flabbergasted and irate Germans.

In any case, two years later, by the autumn of 1942, the French had still not forgiven the British for this perceived treachery and their animosity remained such that even though General Clark arrived at Algiers in a British submarine, the sailors who rowed him ashore were prudently dressed in American uniforms. Clark's secret talks with the French leaders, held at a farmhouse not far from the coast, were encouraging but inconclusive. For reasons of secrecy, Clark did not divulge the date of the invasion, and so it became difficult for the French leaders, even if they wished, to pass along advance orders to their troops not to resist. There was simply too much risk of a leak.

Two hours before dawn on November 8, 1942, the U.S. invasion force appeared off Casablanca and also Safi, well to the south. Meteorologists in Washington and elsewhere had gloomily forecast fifteen-foot breakers crashing onto the Atlantic coast, but the American admiral commanding decided to rely on his own weather forecaster, who thought the storm that would bring such dangerous surf was still a few days away. Turned out he was right. Six thousand soldiers, the first wave of the invasion force, began climbing down cargo nets into waiting Higgins boats and navy launches and heading for the beach. Tanks and artillery were loaded into larger landing vessels. The lights of Casablanca twinkled in the distance.

Noise from the surf rolling onto the beaches masked the sound of the American landing boats for most of the trip, but as they neared shore searchlights began to flash on, first up in the air to look for aircraft, then onto the water where they discovered the invasion force. Almost immediately guns from U.S. destroyers put the lights out, and most of the troops were landed safely on the beaches near the town of Fedala, about twelve miles northeast of Casablanca. Just as a soggy gray dawn began to break over the Atlantic coast, the question of whether or not the French would oppose the invasion was answered by a roar from shore batteries located on either side of the landing beaches. American destroyers, cruisers, and a battleship immediately returned fire and a half day gun battle ensued. Powerful batteries at Casablanca, as well as the large guns of an unfinished French battleship lying in the harbor, entered into the fray. Seven French destroyers and a cruiser sortied from the harbor and joined the sea battle, as well as eight submarines.

By noon, all of the French destroyers had been wrecked; five of the submarines were sunk and the rest were chased off. The French cruiser was badly damaged by the American cruisers *Augusta* and *Brooklyn* and turned tail for the harbor. Aboard the U.S. destroyer *Wilkes,* which had been screening for the *Augusta* and *Brooklyn* during their fight with the French cruiser, the following colloquy was reported between an engine-room officer and a man on the bridge who was sending down orders on the telephone concerning speed. The officer in the engine room felt great shuddering blasts from the *Wilkes*'s guns and the bridge called for more speed. When he asked, "What's going on up there?" he was told, "Enemy cruiser is chasing us!" Suddenly he was nearly knocked down by an abrupt swerve as the ship changed directions and an order came down for more speed. "What's going on now?" the engine-room officer shouted back. "We're chasing the enemy cruiser!" came the reply.[8]

Meantime, Major General George S. Patton sent two colonels and a major bearing an American flag and a white flag of truce to see the French admiral about a cease-fire, but he would not see them and instead sent an aide to tell them to go away. As one of the American officers demanded, "in his best Harvard French," a personal response from the admiral, a blast from one of the shore batteries firing at the American forces rattled the windows of the Admiralty building, rendering everyone momentarily silent. Then the French aide said haughtily, *"Voilà, votre réponse!"*[9]

By afternoon of D-day the town of Fedala had been secured by American troops, but only about 7,500 of the 19,500 soldiers destined to capture Casablanca had been able to disembark, due to the naval battles, lack of landing craft, and other reasons.* The French continued whatever resistance they could manage, but over the next two days they were worn down by planes from American carriers and the big shells from U.S. battleships, whose fingers of death ranged eight to ten miles inland to break up

---

*More than half of the American landing craft had been smashed up on the beaches because of heavy surf and the inexperience of their drivers, and thus could not return for more troops.

truck convoys of reinforcements. By November 10 Casablanca was sur-rounded and French *honneur* at last had been satisfied. At a hastily called peace conference, the French admiral François Michelier, who had caused all the trouble, finally shook hands with the American admiral Kent Hewitt. "I had my orders and did my duty," he told Hewitt. "You had yours and did your duty; now that is over, and we are ready to cooperate."[10]

The landings at the other invasion points in Morocco and Algeria had gone off, if not smoothly at least sufficiently well to convince most French troops to stop fighting. More than a hundred thousand American and British soldiers were pouring in, but diplomatically and politically the affair was still a mess. French admirals and generals had been running about arrest-ing fellow admirals and generals whom they suspected of being disloyal on behalf of the Allies, and all this needed to be straightened out. Further, some weeks before the invasion the Allies had buttonholed a French gen-eral named Henri Giraud, who had been hiding in southern France after having escaped from the notorious German prison at Konigstein. Giraud, a nationally known figure who had also escaped from the Germans during World War I, was considered by the Allies a good choice to lead and rally French Vichy forces in North Africa, a man of stature and loyalty, or so they had been told. Accordingly, Giraud was loaded into a British sub-marine and taken to Gibraltar on the eve of the invasion and led into Eisen-hower's underground headquarters, where he made himself unbearable.

Giraud's story warrants amplification. The sixty-three-year-old general was, among other things, a master of disguises. When he had escaped from the Germans in 1914, he made his way across half of Europe posing as "a butcher, a stable boy, a coal merchant and a magician in a traveling circus." In his more recent escape from the Konigstein dungeon, he "shaved his mustache, darkened his hair with brick dust," and, using a homemade rope, which he had plaited himself, lowered himself down 150 feet to the Elbe, after which he billed himself as an engineer from Alsace and made it back to France "with a 100,000 mark reward on his head."[11]

After the formalities were concluded, the first thing Giraud an-nounced to Eisenhower—through an interpreter, since he spoke no En-glish—was that he expected to be in supreme command of all Allied forces in North Africa. He had even brought with him detailed plans for defeating the Germans completely, as well as for the liberation of France. The startled Eisenhower offered Giraud command of all the French forces in North Africa, but was not about to offer him his own job, especially not since the invasion was set for the following morning. For his part, Giraud persisted, grandstanded, sulked, and threatened not to help the Allies at all.

Meanwhile, Eisenhower had found bigger fish to fry. It turned out that on D-day, November 8, the five-star French admiral François Darlan, the current supreme commander of all Vichy affairs in North Africa, had gone to Algiers to visit his sick son, arriving as it turned out just in time for the Allied invasion. He was promptly captured and put under the screws of the American high command. If nothing else, Darlan was a superb waffler. He at first agreed to order all French sailors and troops to lay down their arms; then he changed his mind and said he would first have to ask Pétain at Vichy. When, as expected, Pétain told him to fight on, Darlan caved again to Allied pressure, but then lied and insisted he had no legal authority outside the city of Algiers.

As the invasion progressed, Darlan—then jailed by the Allies—began to see the magnitude of it, and the handwriting on the wall, if he refused to help. Finally he began issuing orders in the name of the Vichy government, which slowly brought the French military and civil units around. For the present, this was a good thing; French North Africa was populated with more than twenty million dependent Arabs, all of whom required at least the facade of civilization: the administration of railroads, electric power, water, roads and bridges, hospitals and other civil services, and infrastructure, which would have been almost impossible for the Allies to have taken over and still fight a war against the Germans. Over time, however, Darlan proved to be, in the words of one American commander, "a needle-nosed, sharp-chinned little weasel," and thus there was little or no regret in the Allied high command when he was assassinated in his own office by an Algerian lunatic whose goal seemed to be the restoration of the monarchy in France.[12]

In the midst of this *opéra bouffée* came excellent news from a thousand miles to the east. There, after defeating the army of General Rommel on November 5, and (once again) driving it out of Egypt, the British Eighth Army, under General Bernard Montgomery, was pressing the Germans westward across the great Libyan Desert, hoping to deliver it into the waiting embrace of the Americans who, according to plan, should have occupied Tunisia within a few weeks. As it turned out, the road to Tunisia was a hard road to travel, harder than anyone would have expected. Not long after Casablanca was taken, an American lieutenant wrote to his mother, "This is a land of strange ways, just like the old Bible pictures. Camels and donkeys plow together, the Arabs pray and the women do all the work."[13]

★ Chapter Nineteen

While encouraging events were coming to pass in North Africa, in the South Pacific, and for the Russian armies around Stalingrad, an ordeal of fiendish cruelty was in progress in the Philippines, where thousands of American prisoners languished in Japanese prison camps.

After the horrid Bataan Death March and the misery and death at Camp O'Donnell, in June 1942 the Japanese decided to move the American soldiers to a more permanent POW camp: Cabanatuan, about forty miles northeast of O'Donnell. Cabanatuan, which means "place of rocks," had been a half-finished training camp for a newly created Philippine army division. It was located in flat, arid country about ten miles outside the city of Cabanatuan, a bustling town of about fifty thousand. About seventy rickety, palm-thatched barracks had been constructed there to hold forty men each; when the POWs arrived, they were crammed in as many as a hundred and twenty to a building.

Fewer than 9,000 Americans out of the original 12,000 who had been captured on Bataan ever got to Cabanatuan; the rest had died or been murdered on the way. Most of those who did arrive were in terrible health and not much could be done for them. They had diphtheria, chronic dysentery, beriberi, pellagra, edema, scurvy, malaria. Although there were a number of American doctors in the compound, lifesaving supplies such as sulfa, quinine, bandages, antiseptics, and anesthesia were unavailable. There wasn't even soap or toilet paper. Food was at the starvation level, and most of the men had become scarecrows or, as one man expressed it, "the living dead." If only because it was larger, and there was more water (though most of it was disgustingly polluted), Cabanatuan was at least a slight improvement over the hellhole of O'Donnell.

Cabanatuan was surrounded by barbed wire, with guards manning machine guns posted in towers at each corner. Still, the Japanese were fearful about possible escapes and to discourage this they divided all the prisoners into ten-man "shooting squads." In other words, if any man in the squad escaped, the rest would be lined up and shot. Once, the Japanese roster showed that a man was missing and the other nine were sent to the guardhouse to await the firing squad. At the last moment good news arrived: "the tenth man's body was discovered under one of the buildings where he had crawled to die. He was clutching the uneaten portion of a dead rat."[1]

Occasionally, sympathetic Filipinos from the city would try to get a little food to the prisoners, but this was dangerous business. One night three officers were caught dragging sacks of food and a Japanese court was convened. The three were given a choice of being executed immediately or enduring three days of torture. The officers elected for the torture, hoping to make it through. They were taken just outside the fence, in plain view of the entire camp, and forced to dig their own graves. Then the torture began. The three Americans were tied to poles in the baking sun and the Japanese took turns beating them. They cried pitifully throughout the day as they were beaten by each change of the guard. An old colonel was the first to crack, begging to be shot. The Japanese obliged him; a firing squad was hastily assembled and he soon toppled into his grave. Next day a second of the officers, whose eye had been gouged out and hung from its socket, could stand it no more and also asked to be shot, and was. The third man, a lieutenant, "toughed it out until nearly the third day. Beaten until an ear hung by a thread down to his shoulder, and unrecognizable," he too asked for death. Army Captain Ralph E. Hibbs, a doctor, who saw it all, remarked, "He was a brave man. He gave it all he had. They killed him with a three-man execution squad as he knelt at his grave staring at them."[2] Atrocity stories such as this are so common they soon become depressingly repetitive and so I have tried not to relate too many of them in this narrative.

The American prisoners continued to die at a horrific rate: in June, 503; in July, 786. A crude hospital was quickly set up by American POW medical officers, but there wasn't much that could be done; soldiers who were clearly dying got sent to a lice-, rat-, and maggot-infested barracks known as St. Peter's, or in one case the Zero Ward. Few got out alive. Disposing of the bodies was a particularly hideous chore. The men had blocked out ground for crude cemeteries, which were given such names as the Pearly Gates and Boot Hill—this passed for humor among those tormented souls.

"All that could be done was to bury the dead each day in mass graves, over which dirt was shoveled, and when it rained the dirt would often wash away and the bodies float to the surface in various stages of decomposition. Once an old toothless sergeant appeared at the hospital and asked to speak with the colonel:

" 'Colonel, we're uh . . .'

" 'Speak up, sergeant.'

" 'We want a doctor to go to Pearly Gates with us. Uh, we're afraid.' "

The colonel, who was witnessing death by the hour, became flushed and angry.

" 'Afraid? *Afraid!*'

" 'Not like that, colonel. The other day we laid one out and were getting ready to cover him up, you see, and, well, I looked down and he was still breathing, and, well . . .'

" 'I see,' the colonel said, softening. 'Yeah, okay. I'll send a doctor in each morning.' "[3]

The poet-lieutenant Henry Lee, soon himself to die, looked out on the foulness of the burial grounds and composed a heartbreaking epitaph to his fellow prisoners, living and deceased.

Group Four
(Cabanatuan Concentration Camp Cemetery)

We'll have our small white crosses by and by
Our cool, green lawns, our well-spaced, well-cared trees

Our antique cannons, muzzles to the sky,
Our statues and our flowers and our wreaths.
We'll have our bold-faced bronze and copper plaques
To tell in stirring words of what we saved
And who we were, with names and dates; our stacks
Of silent rifles, spaced between the graves.

We'll have our dedications by and by
With orators and bands to set us free—
And shining, well-fed troops. Above will fly
The planes with stars we never lived to see.
We'll have our country's praises, here below
They'll make a shrine of this small bit of Hell
For wide-eyed tourists; and so few will know

And those who know will be the last to tell
The wordless suffering of our lives as slaves
Our squalid deaths beneath this dripping sky
The stinking tangle of our common graves,
We'll have our small white crosses by and by.[4]

Everyone knew that if it kept up this way they would, all of them, be dead in a year or so. Yet through some unfathomable mercy it did not. By the autumn of 1942 the death rate began to level off, first to fifty a week, then to ten. The ones who were so sick and weak from the death march and Camp O'Donnell had pretty much already died off. The deadly epidemic of diphtheria had subsided. Finally, too, they had begun to get some medicines, clothing, and food—much of it through a very unlikely source.

She called herself High Pockets but her real name was Claire Phillips, and she became, over time, a true angel of mercy to the men in the POW camp. Her remarkable story is worth telling here, at least in brief.

Claire Phillips was a young, pretty actress and dancer who had toured the Philippines in the late 1930s with an American musical stock company and while there met and married a man by whom she had a child. The marriage did not last and she returned to the United States only to sail back to the Philippines, bringing her infant daughter with her, at the end of September 1941, barely two months before war broke out.

She quickly got a job singing at several of Manila's fancy clubs and hotels and lived a fairly comfortable life, with a nice apartment and servants. One night during a performance she met a handsome sergeant named John Phillips, from the Thirty-first Infantry, fell in love, and was soon married. When the Japanese began bombing Manila, Sergeant Phillips rushed from his post and told Claire to take all their money in the bank and exchange it for U.S. currency, then go to town and buy all the canned food she could, as well as medicines and anything else that might be needed for an extended trip, and pack it into the car. Then, as the Japanese bombing reached unbearable proportions, she loaded up her baby girl and took to the hills.

There she stayed, hiding out in the jungles north of Bataan, eating monkey meat with rural families, until the Japanese conquest was complete. At one point a Catholic priest told her that her husband John Phillips was alive and a prisoner of war in Cabanatuan. With few other options, Claire sneaked back into Manila and, with her dark good looks, managed to get phony papers from a Philippine authority she knew, stating that she was an Italian citizen. As she later wrote, "I spoke no Italian, but neither did the Japanese." She reinstated herself in her old apartment building and collected her former nurse to watch her baby while she found a job singing in a nightclub "owned by a German Jewess," which was presently being patronized almost exclusively by ranking Japanese officers. Then, using her remaining money, plus her jewelry, she managed to borrow enough from a Chinese merchant and moneylender to open her own nightclub, the Club Tsubaki, which, in Japanese, means "camellia."

Club Tsubaki was an instant hit; several of the best singers from her old music company joined her. She made it "as high hat and snobbish as possible," complete with a five-piece orchestra playing Hawaiian music. Before long it became Manila's hot spot of the moment for Japanese military elite. Soon she made contact with a German priest who often visited Cabanatuan and he agreed to take with him a few articles of clothing for her husband. But because there were so many prisoners, the priest could only leave the package and hope it arrived at its destination. Then one day, while walking her daughter in a Manila park, Claire saw several American POWs on a work detail being guarded by Japanese soldiers. She quietly approached one and told him who she was and asked about her husband.

"You are Mrs. Phillips?" he asked. "I'm sorry. Phillips died last July in Cabanatuan." It turned out the soldier had been in Phillips's outfit. Claire staggered away in tears, which, after a period of grief, soon turned to anger, then to rage, and she vented her fury by organizing a spy-and-supply ring both to get desperately needed items into the POW camp and to probe Japanese officers for any interesting intelligence information. Soon Claire's ring, operating out of her office at the Club Tsubaki, became the center of Manila espionage, with operatives who had code names such as Looter, Sassy Suzie, Zig-Zag, Boots, Rocky, Morning Glory, and Sparkplug. In addition to the hostesses of her club, some of the members of this remarkable organization were among the elite of Manila prewar society, among them wealthy Europeans who had operated utilities and shipping companies in the Philippines, as well as a network of Catholic priests, some of them in fact German. They assumed identities like Fancy-Pants and Swiss, and so long as they weren't American or British the Japanese usually left these people alone.

High-ranking Japanese officers who patronized the Tsubaki, such as naval captains or army generals and some colonels, were plied into a jovial mood with booze and flattery by the hostesses, then pried for information about shipping or troop movements. This news was vital, since Manila had become one of the great staging and stop-off areas for the Japanese army and navy, funneling troops and supplies en route to the many conquered islands in the Southern Area. One Japanese aircraft carrier captain divulged that in a few days his ship was sailing for Singapore, then to Rabaul, in the Solomons, where the Guadalcanal fight was at its hottest. Another, an army man, revealed that he was taking a force of 30,000 men north to the shores of Lingayen Gulf to strengthen defenses there. These crucial pieces of information were immediately passed on to MacArthur's headquarters in Australia via a shortwave radio located in the mountains.

Claire Phillips—High Pockets—remembered her encounters with these Japanese with undisguised contempt. She recalled Japanese officers telling her, "I rove you. You rove me? You very pretty girr. You rike me?" She found these advances "nauseating." The Japanese called her Madam Tsubaki, and the reason she had chosen "High Pockets" as her code name was because of her long-standing habit of hiding her money and other important items in her bra.

Valuable as High Pockets's contributions were to military intelligence, her aid to the American prisoners at Camp Cabanatuan was priceless. Her spy ring had managed to establish contact with several operatives there—mainly American chaplains (known to the men as "sky pilots")—who managed to send out notes describing their needs. By this time the lowly Japanese guards, who received practically no pay at all, were clamoring for cash money while Claire's Club Tsubaki was making a mint off their high-ranking officers. Also, a new and more lenient Japanese commander had replaced the brute who had originally run the camp. It turned out that this man, a major, had owned a popular bicycle shop in Manila before the war and, according to POW accounts, he seemed uninterested in strict discipline.

Thus a new kind of black market came into being, with Japanese guards bribed to look the other way when food, medicine, and clothing were smuggled in—but only as long as they got their cut. The urgent problems were quickly identified. "We knew that the principal cause of the deaths among the prisoners was disease chiefly brought about by malnutrition," High Pockets said. Quinine, sulfa, antiseptics, and other desperately needed medicines were smuggled in, as well as staples such as rice, beans, peanuts, fruits, and vegetables. She would have tried to smuggle in precious canned goods as well, but these had virtually disappeared from Manila's foodstore shelves. What had also nearly disappeared was liquor, the life's blood of the Tsubaki, and without which she'd have to close it. But this problem was solved when a wealthy Filipino collaborator who owned a distillery began supplying her with enough stock to keep the club in business.

High Pockets managed to smuggle in clothing for the neediest of the prisoners as well as money for bribing the guards but, of course, not nearly enough to supply all the thousands of prisoners. In addition, Red Cross packages were beginning to reach the prisoners, but not before all had been rifled by Japanese guards for prized items such as cigarettes, candy, and the tastiest canned goods. The guards, having stolen the items from the prisoners in the first place, then tried to sell these things back to their pathetic charges at exorbitant prices. In the meantime, the Japanese had begun to terrorize the citizens of Manila. The homes of wealthy Filipinos and other Europeans were entered at will by Japanese soldiers who stole anything that caught their fancy. High Pockets remembered seeing Japanese convoys of old U.S. Army trucks lining the streets leading to the piers, "loaded with every conceivable cargo . . . food, electric refrigerators, bath tubs, radios," all on their way to the soldiers' homes in Japan. "And what they did not like," she said, "they wantonly destroyed." Frequently they would barge in and demand food and drink and "even made us mend and wash their clothes for them. We dared not refuse them." Anyone remotely suspected of undesirable activity was arrested by the Japanese secret police and would simply disappear. "It was not an uncommon sight," High Pockets recalled, "to glimpse bloated, headless cadavers floating in the Pasig River."

Despite the hardships, High Pockets and her little band were a godsend to the thousands of pitiful Americans imprisoned in Cabanatuan. For many, even years later, it brought tears to their eyes when they spoke of her. Through the shortwave radio in the mountains, she was able to smuggle in news sheets compiled from broadcasts by San Francisco radio stations and give uplifting news to the prisoners, who were constantly being propagandized by the Japanese, who naturally insisted that America was losing the war.

As her spy ring grew, there was always danger of betrayal or detection. High Pockets had several close calls, one in particular when a Japanese officer who was quite familiar with Italy appeared in the club and insisted she sing "O Solo Mio," which every Italian singer presumably knew. High Pockets was familiar with the tune, but the only Italian lyrics to the song she knew were the words of the title itself. Nevertheless she whispered to the band to play loud and mumbled and faked the verses in pidgin Italian, belting out a big "O Solo Mio" at the end of each chorus. The Japanese officer never caught on and kept shouting "Viva! Viva!" over and over again. It was almost inevitable that sooner or later she would be caught.

One morning as she was feeding her daughter breakfast there were loud raps at the door and four members of the *Kemptei,* the Japanese secret police, burst in with drawn pistols. One of them said, "You are Madam Tsubaki?"

"Yes."

"Take us to your office, High Pockets!"*⁵

Though life in the prison camps had improved somewhat, it remained a hell on earth. Beatings at random by the guards continued unabated and the men were forced to work long and arduous hours at details ranging from cutting wood and gardening to building roads and airfields. The gardening was performed at a cobra-infested location known as the Farm, where the men grew vegetables, ostensibly to feed themselves, but the Japanese always took the lion's share. Dentistry, such as it was, became a trial for both the patients and the dentists. The multitude of tropical diseases—especially scurvy, caused by lack of vegetable vitamins—resulted in unpleasant shrinking of the gums and attendant loss of tooth fillings. Since there was no dental-filling material available, and certainly no painkillers, the dentists began collecting silver coins—dimes, quarters—from anyone who had them and using the metal obtained from these employed a hammer to fill the men's teeth.†

Meanwhile, the camp leaders had organized engineers to build some better kind of sanitary system, which they did, and it contributed much to stem the death rate. The prisoners continued to be assailed by great swarms of flies, and everyone developed the so-called Cabanatuan Flip, a dexterous maneuver in which one continuously swats with one hand while lifting food to mouth with the other—akin to trying to rub your tummy and pat your head at the same time. After a while the camp hierarchy came upon a novel plan to reduce the population of flies. They fabricated thousands of flyswatters out of palm leaves and men were rewarded for killing

*The fascinating tale of Claire Phillips, from which this condensation is taken, is told in its entirety in her autobiography, *Manila Espionage*, published in 1947.

†Heaven knows what they would do in the same situation today, since American coins now contain little or no silver.

the insects. For instance, a man who turned in a sixteen-ounce can filled with flies was given the equivalent of twenty-five cents in Philippine pesos.

Entertainment groups were also organized, since it was realized that the morale of the prisoners had a direct correlation to their health. From out of the thousands of POWs they turned up a few musical instruments: some old trumpets, trombones, a beat-up banjo, a harmonica or two. Concerts were held at night, with the men singing along to familiar tunes, such as "The Tennessee Waltz," "Stardust," and "A Pretty Girl Is Like a Melody," as well as others that had been composed in camp. A theater ensemble was formed, known as the Cabanatuan Mighty Arts Players, comprised of soldiers who'd had some kind of acting experience before the war. Many of them could still remember lines from productions they had been in, or movies they had seen, but sometimes they just made them up. Over the years the group staged no less than fifty-four different productions, beginning with *Our Town* and followed by *In Old Mexico, Gone With the Wind, Journey's End, Queen for a Day, Othello, A Christmas Carol, Uncle Tom's Cabin,* and *The Bride of Frankenstein,* among others.[6]

Some of the more entertaining moments came from behind the barred windows of the shack that served as the psychiatric ward. A number of American prisoners had snapped under the pressure and torture and the camp doctors had them locked up for their own good. One of these cases, with a voice like a radio announcer, had a kind of genius for remembering all the baseball games he had ever seen or heard on the radio, and when he was in the mood he could recite them chapter and verse from the first inning onward, complete with players' names, runs, hits, errors, double plays, stolen bases, and pop-up flys. On those frequent occasions when he felt the call, this man began broadcasting from behind his window and the word would quickly spread that a baseball game was on. Prisoners from all over the camp would rush over to gather around for a couple of hours of live sports entertainment. "It was so realistic," recalled one of prisoners, "that late-comers would ask, 'What inning is it?'"[7]

So life in the camps went on, and then the Japanese came up with another horror. It was decided back in Tokyo that all those Americans who were simply languishing in the Philippine compounds could be put to better use by His Majesty's Imperial government. Accordingly, those not too ill to be moved were marched from the camps in large groups to the docks at Manila, where they were shipped out for slave labor in the iron mines or steel mills of Manchuria or in Japan itself. In thousands of cases, it proved to be their death warrant.[8]

The ever spreading global conflict in 1942 continued unabated on other fronts, some more obscure than others. In both Burma and China there was bitter and savage fighting in what became known as the "forgotten war."

When war broke out in the Pacific a year earlier, Japan had moved to consolidate her supremacy in Southeast Asia and, after easy victories in Malaya and Siam (now Thailand), quickly proceeded to conquer Burma. Burma was a British colony defended by a single division of Indian troops commanded by British officers. The British at first did not expect that Japan could extend itself so far, but they were wrong. The Japanese high command sent to southern Burma an entire army, which began gobbling its way northward toward the Indian border. Rangoon was bombed mercilessly, creating a refugee problem of enormous proportions, as the British fought a rearguard action.

Burma was important to the Japanese and the Allies alike, for two reasons. First, it was the gateway into India, a huge country that, as we have seen, was critical to hold because if it, too, fell there would be little to stop the Japanese from pressing on into the Middle East and linking up with their German counterparts. This became a very real danger after Gandhi ordered all Indians to offer only "passive resistance" to the Japanese, as if that would have done them any good. To further this cause, Gandhi led a mass demonstration urging the four hundred million inhabitants of India to protest continued British rule in their country. Though the British government had already promised Indian independence after the war, Gandhi had brushed aside the offer as "a post-dated check," and the so-called peaceful protest ignited weeks of deadly rioting, arson, bombings, and sabotage. At the end of it more than a thousand people were dead and it took sixty battalions of Allied soldiers to restore order. The British threw Gandhi in jail, along with some hundred thousand of his followers, but there remained a lingering fear that the Indian people would not help in defending themselves, and the Allies simply did not have enough manpower to stop a determined Japanese invasion.[9]

The second reason Burma was now so important had to do with the famous Burma Road. This had been set up in early 1940 to carry supplies from the Allies to the Chinese army under Chiang Kai-shek, headquartered at Chungking, deep in China's interior. Until the Japanese occupied Indochina (Vietnam, Cambodia, Laos) just before war broke out, there was another, shorter, and easier road to supply Chiang's army that began at Hanoi, but with the Japanese arrival in 1941 this route was closed off. Thus the Burma Road, cut through a thousand miles of some of the most inhospitable territory in the world, remained the single lifeline for the Chinese, carrying hundreds of millions of dollars of military supplies and equipment (most of it American Lend-Lease) to keep the Chinese in the war.

From the Allied point of view it was critical to keep the Chinese fighting because it tied up a million Japanese soldiers and their support services, which could—and would—have been better used elsewhere, particularly in 1942, at places such as Guadalcanal and New Guinea. Although the Chinese armies did not initiate any major operations against the Japanese, they were still a threat because of their hit-and-run tactics, employed against any Japanese force with a perceived weakness. If the Japanese had been smarter, they might have pulled their large units out of China altogether, and let the Chinese have it, and used them instead in the big Pacific battles against the Americans. But this they did not, and apparently could not, bring themselves to do for fear of losing face. After all, the whole war in the Far East began in the first place over the Japanese invasion of China. For the Allies, particularly the Americans, this Oriental face-saving was a good thing, because it doesn't take a military genius to figure out what would have happened if the Japanese army had arrived at Guadalcanal early on with four or five infantry divisions to the marines' one.

In any case they did not, and the Chinese kept on fighting their subdued, stubborn, guerrilla-type war, while at the same time performing such services as rescuing the fliers from Doolittle's raid. That the Japanese remained in force in that vast country with their hands tied must have been a strain on Imperial General Headquarters in Tokyo.

After Japan had taken Burma and shut down the Burma Road, it became obvious to the Allies that some alternative method must be found to supply Chiang Kai-shek's armies. The solution arrived at was a vast airlift

flown out of bases in India with American air transports and pilots crossing the Hump, an extremely trying experience for crews and aircraft alike.
This involved a flight of thousand or so miles, much of it above the wild,
15,000-foot-high Himalayan foothills,* which was close to the altitude
ceiling for the planes, and encountering weather that was simply atrocious.
As it turned out, this American airlift actually managed to move to China
more supplies than had been done so along the Burma Road, but nevertheless a new road directly from India to Chungking was begun by American engineers, using coolie labor and American money. It would be paved
with gravel and wind high across the misty mountainsides and, when completed, would handle convoys of hundreds of trucks around-the-clock—
a stupendous undertaking more than twenty times as long as Virginia's
Skyline Drive.

For his part, Chiang Kai-shek demanded that the Americans send him
fifty infantry divisions and five hundred planes, which was not only ridiculous but a practical impossibility since the North African invasion was just
getting under way. Instead, to keep Chiang on the hook, Roosevelt offered
him $500 million more in Lend-Lease supplies, which that wily and ruth-
less old general mostly hoarded away to prepare for the inevitable postwar conflict he envisioned between himself and Mao Tse-tung's army of
communists. In fact, from Chiang's point of view, China's most important role was merely to come through the war intact, so that afterward he
could get at his old nemesis.

While on the subject of China, it is appropriate to revisit the travails of Commander Columbus Darwin Smith, the first U.S. prisoner of the Japanese,
and who did not intend to be the last. We left Commander Smith in a Japanese prison in Shanghai, following his first unsuccessful escape attempt.
The Ward Road, where he was kept, was actually a huge old jail, with all
the accoutrements associated with jails that made escape problematic—
iron bars on the windows, walls, and moats. And most of the prisoners
housed there were not POWs but all manner of murderers, thieves, forg-

*The "big" mountains of the Himalayas include the 29,000-foot Mount Everest.

ers, gamblers, and rapists. Compared with most Japanese prison camps, however, Ward Road was almost luxurious. Commander Smith's private cell had a flush toilet and the food, while monotonous, was at least tolerable and there was enough to sustain life. There was even a prison library, where Smith settled in to a copy of *War and Peace* and began to formulate renewed plans for escape.

The cell across from his housed his old partner in flight, Commander John B. Woolley, of the British navy. The two of them, being of upper middle age, knew they would need a young and strong man to help them through and they soon singled out Marine Corporal Jerold B. Storey, who had been a guard at the U.S. embassy at Peking. The first hurdle would be to break out of Ward Road prison; the second was how to get through seven hundred miles of Japanese-held territory to friendly lines.

During his many years in Shanghai, Smith had made good friends and he would now have to count on them for help. First the prisoners would need hacksaw blades to cut their way through the cell bars. Then they would need clothing, money, and forged papers to get past the ever present Japanese guards and patrols. To facilitate this, Smith buddied up with a convicted murderer, a man named Jenkins, whose ten-year sentence was soon due to expire. He offered Jenkins a large sum of money if, when he was released, he would visit a friend of Commander Smith's in Shanghai and request of him to provide the necessary items. Jenkins agreed, and after he was let out he procured a package of hacksaw blades and pitched them over the prison wall at a specified place where Corporal Storey was tending a garden of beans.

The escape plan was right out of a gangster movie. They would saw through the steel bars in Smith's cell and using bedsheets climb down into the prison yard; then, arriving at the tall outside brick wall, they would scale this, too, using the sheets with a piece of bamboo tied to the end as a grappling hook. All went well but for one thing: Smith, to accomplish his sawing, had to stand on the only piece of furniture in his cell, a three-legged stool, then strain to reach up to the high cell window and saw through the bars. One day as he was reaching to his limit, he "felt something snap" and then a terrible pain in his abdomen. The loss of sixty pounds since becoming a prisoner had caused the tissue holding the muscles of his abdomen to rupture. Now he was the victim of a double hernia. Painful as it was, Smith soon discovered that by holding the rupture in with his hand he could manage, although he was uncertain how it might hold up on a seven-hundred-mile hike. In any event he went ahead, sawing by night and covering his handiwork with dry soap molded to the shape of the bars and disguised with black shoe polish.

When the night for escape came, Woolley and Storey arrived at Smith's cell. They had each sawed through the bars of their own cell doors, and Woolley had knotted the sheets. Down they went through the cell window, across the yard, and up over the main prison wall. Had it not been for Storey, Smith would never have made it. When they dropped down onto one of Shanghai's busiest roads, it looked like they might have a chance. They immediately raced to a prearranged spot where Jenkins was to meet them with the clothing, money, and forged passes. But Jenkins was not there. They waited, then decided to go directly to the house of Smith's friend. He was not there either. Knowing that at any moment the Japanese could discover their escape and sound the alarm, Smith decided they must press on anyway, using only his detailed knowledge of Shanghai's streets and of the Chinese language, and the courage and fortitude within each of them. As it turned out, they would need this last most of all.

Smith somehow got them to the edge of the city, past Japanese bridge and rail crossing guards, and into the countryside, which was swampy and crisscrossed by myriad streams, creeks, and canals. By the end of the first day they noticed Japanese planes patrolling overhead and were forced to lie flat in mucky ground. They knew then their escape had been discovered, and that all Japanese patrols would have been warned to look for them. For the Japanese, losing a prisoner to escape became a severe loss of face.* Smith and his fellow escapees' first encounter with Chinese peasants was fearful. All Chinese were well aware of the reign of terror visited upon them by the Japanese after the Doolittle raid. And the three prisoners

---

*Losing prisoners to murder, starvation, or disease did not seem to have the same effect on the Japanese authorities of Tojo's regime.

had already resigned themselves to the notion that if they were captured they would be beheaded.

The second night out they came across a Chinese peasant and Smith told him they were trying to get away from the Japanese and needed food and somewhere to stay. He immediately took them to his hut, cooked up a supper of chicken, rice, and vegetables, and gave them straw mats to sleep on. To the escapees' astonishment and relief, this treatment was repeated over and again during the weeks they trekked southeastward toward Chungking and friendly lines. The Chinese villagers provided them with sampan transportation over wide streams and directions on how to avoid Japanese-held villages and patrols as well as the Chinese puppet soldiers, who were in the pay of the Japanese army.

They had many close calls, some of them only perceived. Once they encountered a Chinese puppet patrol who demanded their papers. Smith was able to bluff his way through, saying they were French priests. Most of the way they could not use roads or trails for fear they were being guarded and so had to move across country through malarial swamps and sometimes unbearable terrain. It rained almost every day. Storey contracted malaria and was in a bad way. Woolley's feet were in terrible shape and he was having to pull his toenails off one by one. Smith slipped and fell on a rock and cut a nasty gash in his knee, plus he had to keep holding in the painful hernia all the while. At one point he was able to pawn his expensive watch for some local money, which amounted to five U.S. dollars. Each time they met Chinese, which was practically every day, they had no idea whether they would be helped or turned over to the Japanese. In many parts of the provinces the Chinese had never before seen a white man, and the Japanese had persuasive methods.

Most of the time it was the peasants who took them in. Never once, Smith marveled, had he had to use any of the five dollars he'd gotten for his watch to repay them for their kindnesses. "The more I traveled through this back country," he remembered, "the more convinced I became that Japan could never subdue China. I never heard of a single instance where the Japanese secured the whole-hearted cooperation of the Chinese." In this he was correct. Even though it was mostly peasants who helped them, occasionally it was well-heeled Chinese too. "This flight of ours," Smith recalled, "was beginning to have too many characteristics of a bad movie melodrama." Once they were feted at the elegant home of an old, white-bearded mandarin dressed in silks, who greeted them formally, speaking French, and offered them a sumptuous meal complemented by a fine white wine. It reminded Smith of the scene from the movie of James Hilton's *Lost Horizon,* the part when the travelers arrive at Shangri-la and are told to their astonishment by the old Tibetan lama, "I've been expecting you."

Little could be done for their ailments, however; there were almost no Chinese doctors and, if there were, they had no medicines. And they still had a long way to go. The best they could expect was some food, an occasional bath in a hot washtub from Chinese friends, and a few meager clothes to replace their own rags. After weeks of walking the trio finally began to give out. Storey's malaria had left him very weakened, Woolley's feet became nearly useless, and Smith's hernia and the knee injury, which had caused his whole lower leg to turn black, forbade him to go any farther on foot. The Chinese accommodated this by rounding up some "grand-mother's chairs" and stringing them from bamboo poles. Coolies were instructed to carry the party toward friendly lines. This involved trekking over steep mountain trails when even the jerry-rigged sedan chairs were of no use, and so they had to get out and walk again.

Time and again they dodged Japanese patrols. Most conversation was limited to either how to evade the Japanese or where they would sleep at night, and any such casual conversation as arose usually revolved around the food they would eat when they were finally free. After intense discussions of this pressing subject it was unanimously agreed that they would have a steak and lobster champagne dinner. With french fries. That is, of course, if they made it.

On the other side of the world, just about the time the marines were invading Guadalcanal, there had broken out a great sea battle frought with danger for the Allies. This became known as the Battle of the Atlantic.

As we have already seen, shortly after the declaration of war on the United States, Germany set submarines onto the U.S. Atlantic and Gulf coasts, which wreaked havoc on coastwise shipping. At first the losses were horrendous but land-based aircraft, convoys with armed escorts, and sub-chasers began to solve the problem. There was, however, another target the Germans sought even more, which was the U.S. "lifeline" to England and Russia. The Russians, then locked in deadly battle with the Nazi invasion of their country, desperately needed American-made tanks, planes, guns, ammunition, clothing, and just about everything else for their large but as yet poorly equipped army. These were sent over on a steady shipment of Lend-Lease convoys from U.S. ports via Halifax, Nova Scotia, to Reykjavík, Iceland, then on to Murmansk or Archangel in northern Russia. More important, for the contemplated Allied invasion of France enormous trans-oceanic shipments of those same armaments had to be built up in England, as well as hundreds of thousands of American troops.

Admiral Dönitz, Hitler's submarine force commander, was quick to recognize the importance of this lifeline and by mid-1942 had shifted much of his U-boat fleet to prey on the vast convoys of Allied transports crossing the northern reaches of the ocean. During the autumn and winter months, when darkness fell early along the ice packs at the top of the world and daylight lasted only a few hours, the Germans had little success. But as the days grew longer and the sun began to shine nearly twenty-four hours a day, the peril from German U-boat "wolfpacks," surface warships, and aircraft based on the Norwegian coast became acute.

A tragic example of this is illustrated by the fate of convoy PQ-17, which departed Halifax, refueled in Iceland, and set out from Reykjavík on June 27, 1942. The convoy, composed of thirty-three merchant ships, was well protected at first, escorted or supported by a combined American-British force of no less than forty-two warships, including two battleships, an aircraft carrier, seven cruisers, and seventeen destroyers. This should certainly have been enough to fend off any German attack but then, on the Fourth of July, things began to unravel.

At about seven P.M. on July 4, the convoy recieved word that a power-ful German force consisting of the battleships *Tirpitz* and *Scheer* and the battle cruiser *Hipper* with an escort of seven destroyers had broken out of their sanctuary in a Norwegian fjord and were headed toward PQ-17. The order came down for the Allied warships protecting convoy PQ-17 to abandon it and go after these prized German targets. The thirty-three ships of PQ-17 were then ordered to scatter and make their separate ways to the north Russian ports.

What followed was a massacre. As the ships of the Allied convoy entered the Barents Sea they came within range of German fighters and bombers based at airfields in northern Norway. There was no hiding in darkness because there was no darkness, and the arctic ice pack blocked them from steaming farther north and out of harm's way. German planes picked off the lightly armed merchantmen at their leisure, and when it was finished twenty-two of the thirty-three ships of PQ-17 lay on the cold bottom of the northern seas.

The German high command was delighted, but not for long. Plainly, the Allies could see that something further had to be done. First of all, they had been taught a stern lesson about leaving an unarmed convoy to the mercy of German planes and warships. Second, they had begun to realize that two things must be accomplished in order to keep the Atlantic lifeline open. One was to produce more transport ships than the Germans could sink;* the second was to organize more effective antisubmarine and antiaircraft defenses. This they did in the time-honored American way: producing more of *everything*—warships, antisubmarine aircraft, transports. To add to this orgy of construction, they were receiving priceless information from the British as to the plans and location of the German "wolfpacks." This was courtesy of Ultra, England's code-breaking counterpart to the U.S. code-breaking MAGIC, with which the Allies, following the capture of one of the German U-boat's decoding machines, were able to read the Germans' mail. By the end of 1942 the number of German submarines sunk had doubled from the first half of the year, and by war's end there were practically no U-boats left at all.

At about the time that convoy PQ-17 was meeting its fate another great American military institution was being formed in England. This was the

*Which they did. Beginning in 1942 the shipbuilding industry began turning out "liberty ships" at the rate of approximately one every two weeks.

famed U.S. Eighth Air Force, which was to lay waste not only to innu-
merable German industries but to entire German cities.

The workhorse of the Eighth Air Force was the B-17 Flying Fortress,
the big four-engine bomber so toughly constructed it was immensely difficult to shoot down and so well armed, with up to fourteen .50-caliber
machine guns, that it became a formidable foe to any enemy pilot who ventured anywhere near it.

Take, for example, the celebrated *Memphis Belle,* which flew her first
combat mission for the Eighth Air Force on November 7, 1942. Over the
next seven months she flew her required twenty-five combat missions,
bombing German installations in France and Germany and shooting down
at least eight German fighters (and probably more), remarkably without a
single loss of life to the crew.*

While the B-17 was a tough customer, it was certainly not invulner-
able to enemy attack. Initially the Eighth Air Force had concluded that the
best way to get at the heart of German industry was to hit them in daylight
when the targets could be clearly seen. The British had already tried this,
with terrible losses, and they now struck only at night. The brash Americans, however, stuck to their daylight bombing strategy, which cost them
a frightful 80 percent loss in planes from July to September 1942. A major problem was that in order to hit Germany proper the bombers had to
fly without fighter escorts to fend off the German fighters for hundreds of
miles over enemy territory. This difficulty was not solved until new American fighters with much greater fuel capacity came on line in 1943 and afterward. Consider the chilling irony and shocking conclusion of Randall
Jarrell's "The Death of the Ball Turret Gunner," one of the best-known
American poems to come out of the war.

> From my mother's sleep I fell into the State,
> And I hunched in its belly till my wet fur froze.

*In May 1943, the *Memphis Belle* was retired and she and her crew were sent back to
the States for a bond-raising tour. After the war, instead of being scrapped like thousands
of other B-17s, the *Belle* was enshrined in a special viewing hangar on Mud Island, in the
Mississippi River at Memphis, where it can be seen today.

Six miles from earth, loosed from its dream of life,
I woke to black flak and the nightmare fighters.
When I died they washed me out of the turret with a hose.

Another airplane in the U.S. arsenal was the B-24 Liberator, a heavy bomber flown mostly in the North African and the Italian campaigns. Once the Allies secured Italy, Liberators were able to bomb Germany from the south, in addition to the B-17s in England flying from the west. This forced the German armaments minister Albert Speer to disburse his industrial plants to the far reaches of the countryside, or move them underground, seriously disrupting the German war machine.

The Eighth Air Force was by far the most well known of the American air forces of its day and its last commander was none other than the famed Jimmy Doolittle. Books were published and movies were made about the Eighth Air Force, including the classic *Twelve O'Clock High,* starring Gregory Peck. Hundreds of thousands of Americans fought with the Eighth Air Force, and tens of thousands died, high in the skies, destroyed by German bullets and flak, tumbling back down the interminable miles to crash upon the earth.

Except for the ferocious clashes against German fighter planes, the U.S. Army Air Force fought primarily a sterile, almost impersonal battle, dropping its bombs from heights of 30,000 feet or more, unlike the grubby marines at Guadalcanal or the army soldiers on New Guinea, who often saw their foes face to face on a daily basis. Yet the fliers' impersonality was not felt by everyone. Listen again to the terrible irony of poet Randall Jarrell, who was there.

In bombers named for girls, we burned
The cities we had learned about in school.

Chapter Twenty ★

In North Africa the situation was boiling up to its critical mass. By mid-November 1942, all American and British troops and their equipment were ashore, the French had been subdued, and a fresh Allied buildup was under way. Now the problem was to race into Tunisia and occupy it before the Germans could reinforce it from their bases in Sicily and Italy, the Allies' utmost fear. Tunisia was already held by the Germans, and there were a number of Luftwaffe airfields there, but the German garrison was light and there appeared a good chance to overcome it quickly. Thus the Allied forces began their long eastward trek across the rugged heights of the Atlas Mountains and through the vast reaches of Morocco and Algeria: tanks and trucks and artillery and, by now, 180,000 soldiers, with more arriving each week. And yet, to say the least, it did not go well.

Before we go to Tunisia, let us visit for a moment a desolate spot of land in the Libyan Desert just across the Egyptian border where, just as the Allied armada was landing in North Africa, the British were winning a superlative victory against General Erwin Rommel's Afrika Korps. In the summer of 1942 Rommel had pushed the British Eighth Army all the way across the Libyan Desert and into Egypt with brilliant armored tactics that left the British reeling. For a time it appeared the British would lose not only their army but Egypt itself, as well as the Suez Canal, which were the keys to all of North Africa and the Middle East and which, if lost to the Axis, would have upset the entire Allied scheme of the war. The "desolate spot of land" referred to above lay near an obscure Arab town called El Alamein, which became the name given to perhaps the most famous tank battle of all time.

After the German and Italian forces took the Allied fortress of Tobruk and shoved the British back into Egypt, the British commander General Sir Bernard Montgomery stiffened up and pushed the Germans back out again. By then he was in dire straits, and for the moment the Germans had the advantage. Rommel, the foxy general who had gained a reputation for outwitting the British at almost every turn, now prepared for his final annihilation of the Allied forces. The only thing he awaited were critical shipments of fuel and ammunition for his tanks and for the Luftwaffe to knock the Royal Air Force out of the sky. For supplies, Rommel depended on shipping from the Italians; what he got from them instead were platitudes. And for German superiority in the air, what he got were bromides from Der Führer. These were not enough and Rommel had put up with them far too long.

For more than a year the Axis had controlled most of the Mediterranean, and convoys from Britain—Montgomery's only supply line—had to be routed all the way down the African Atlantic coast, around the Cape of Good Hope at South Africa, then back up the Indian Ocean and through the southern end of the Suez Canal, a detour of several thousand miles. But the British were relentless in their determination to supply Montgomery's army. Braving German submarines and air attacks, they managed to stockpile in Egypt vast numbers of the new American Sherman and Grant tanks, and artillery and fuel, so that by September, when Rommel realized his only choice was to attack or retreat, it was too late. He attacked anyway.

The first battle began in the darkness of the last day of August, at a rocky ridge in the desert called Alam Halfa, and it went completely wrong for the German and Italian armies. The British in fact had hoped for such an attack and had prepared well to meet it. First, they had placed hundreds of thousands of antitank mines before their positions and were well dug in. Second, they made excellent use of their airpower with a new tactic: as the German tanks and troops moved forward, a continuous relay of RAF bombers began. They were each led by a single plane that circled above the Germans, relentlessly dropping magnesium parachute flares, which were impossible to put out, "bathing the whole of the desert in a brilliant light." Hundreds of German and Italian tanks and trucks were blown to bits and soldiers were atomized by the high-explosive bombs as well as by British artillery that had registered in on them.

Just as Rommel was sourly ordering another withdrawal, a New Zealand brigadier, one General George H. Clifton, was brought to his tent as prisoner. "He said that he was ashamed to have to admit being taken prisoner by the Italians," Rommel remembered. "He had been in the act of persuading them to surrender and they had, in fact, already started taking the bolts out of their rifles, when to his disgust a German officer came along and ruined the whole affair." Rommel grilled the New Zealander on "various acts contrary to international law, for which the New Zealanders had been responsible." In particular Rommel was referring to "repeated massacres of German prisoners and wounded by this particular division." Clifton explained to the German commander that this was due to the large number of Maoris the division contained."*

Rommel found General Clifton a likable character and the two were having a nice chat while they waited for the military police to escort Clifton to the POW compound. At one point, Rommel recalled, "Clifton asked to be taken to the lavatory, where he climbed out of the window and vanished without a trace." A few days later, however, "several members of my staff were out hunting gazelles when they suddenly spotted a weary figure plodding across the desert carrying what looked like a jerry-can of water with him." It was Clifton, and the German officers promptly gathered him up and brought him to Rommel again. "I had a talk with him," Rommel said, "and expressed my appreciation of his exploit. Such a trek through the desert is not everybody's meat, and not surprisingly, he looked exhausted."[1]

By October 23, 1942, Rommel had gathered his army at El Alamein, about twenty miles from the Alam Halfa Ridge battle, and prepared for

*The Maoris were a fierce tribe of natives who had inhabited New Zealand before the British came. Even after 250 years of "civilization," they were known to revert to tribal savagery during the rigors of war.

the worst. Despite repeated pleas to Berlin and Rome, few if any supplies ever reached him, and the British maintained control of the skies. On October 23 the British attacked with ten divisions—120,000 men—along a front of forty miles, advancing with a thousand tanks, to Rommel's five hundred. Noting the disgraceful unreliability of the Italians, Rommel arranged that they would be interspersed among the Germans, "so that every Italian Army battalion would have a German neighbor."

Just hours before battle began, the British soldiers were read a message from Montgomery: "When I assumed command of the Eighth Army I said that the mandate was to destroy ROMMEL and his army, and that it would be done as soon as we were ready. We are ready NOW." The British attack progressed applying the same tactics it had used in the defense of Alam Halfa—a tremendous artillery barrage, followed by planes dropping parachute flares to light the desert landscape for the bombers. The fighting was fierce and bloody but the British forces soon began to close in on the Afrika Korps. The desert around Rommel's position soon became a sea of burning tanks, smashed artillery, and the bodies of dead German soldiers strewn about like chaff in the wind. With Rommel hanging on by a thread and pleading with authorities to send him critical supplies and fuel, he received instead a congratulatory note from Mussolini conveying his "deep appreciation for the successful counter-attack led personally by you," as well as his "complete confidence that the battle now in progress will be brought to a successful conclusion."[2]

Rommel must have wondered at this point just what kind of lunatic Mussolini really was. He was already becoming aware of Hitler's lunacy, which was reinforced during the height of the battle—with the only question left being whether his army could be saved by retreat—when he received the following message from Der Führer:

"In the situation in which you find yourself there can be no other thought than to stand fast and throw every gun and every man into the battle. The utmost efforts are being made to help you. Your enemy, despite his superiority, must be also at the end of his strength. It would not be the first time in history that a strong will has triumphed over the bigger battalions. As to our troops, you can show them no other road than that to victory or death." To this, Rommel remarked acerbically, "Arms, gas and aircraft could have helped us, but not orders."[3]

With the German army now down to about eighty tanks—against some eight hundred for the British—Rommel was forced to begin a retreat toward Tunisia, more than fifteen hundred miles to the west where, unbeknownst to him at the time, the strong Allied force of Americans and British were preparing to greet him. His withdrawal, however, was a military classic. Instead of conducting a slow retrograde movement, fighting to keep Montgomery's Eighth Army at bay across the vast Libyan Desert, with his last remaining fuel Rommel made it literally a race, using the only road, the one that ran along the Mediterranean coast, to speed his army along so fast that the British could not even catch the retreating tanks and troops, let alone outflank them. From time to time, he stopped the Afrika Korps at good defensive positions and put up a brisk fight to keep his enemy off balance. But even as they eluded the rapacious British, Rommel and his army had to wonder if in the end it would all come to naught.

Thus, both sides were rushing toward Tunisia from opposite directions: the Americans and British from the west and Rommel's Afrika Korps, for different reasons, from the east. By late November 1942, the spearhead of the Torch army that landed in French North Africa had made its way east into Tunisia. These first were only 12,000 strong and received a hot reception from units of the 56,000 Germans who now occupied Tunisia, with more arriving every day. Terrain was a major obstacle. Tunisia is slightly larger than the state of Florida and much of the eastern part is mountainous, with steep valleys and few roads and bridges, and the Germans had thoughtfully covered them all with powerful, well-dug-in and camouflaged defensive positions, bristling with artillery, armor, land mines, and antitank guns. These would soon prove to be a disaster for the Allied forces.

Not only that but unlike the German predicament in the far eastern Libyan Desert, the Luftwaffe now could bring to bear in Tunisia overwhelming airpower from its bases in Sicily just a hundred miles across the

Mediterranean. Worse, the American armored troops who had landed with Torch were equipped for the most part with outdated and pathetically armed and armored General Lee and General Stuart tanks, the newer and more powerful Grants and Shermans having been sent to Montgomery's army. This generous Lend-Lease donation may have helped save the British Eighth Army from defeat at the hands of Rommel, but to the Americans involved in Torch their obsolete vehicles—run on gasoline instead of diesel oil—became "flaming coffins," and one old soldier seeing a column of the high-profile Lees clanking down the road described the tank as looking "like a damn moving cathedral."

Everything seemed to go against the Allies as they pushed into Tunisia—including the weather. Winter in North Africa is the rainy season, and tanks and trucks could scarcely move even when not confronted with German strong points. Furthermore, the temperature hovered around freezing and they were unprepared for it. As they crossed the higher elevations, there was even snow and ice. Heat, such as in the Guadalcanal and New Guinea jungles, is unpleasant, but for troops having to fight and live in frigid weather it can be disastrous without proper clothing. Brigadier General Theodore (Ted) Roosevelt Jr., the spitting image of his Rough Rider father, and a cousin to FDR, was assistant commander of the First Infantry division and a jovial wit and raconteur under normal conditions. But in a letter to his wife, he complained, "It is still bitter cold and as our military with its customary dumbness did not envisage this and considered Africa a tropical country; we are not well prepared. I have not changed my underclothes for twelve days," he told her, and described his dress as a "wool union suit, then my wool trousers and shirt, then a sweater, then a lined field jacket, then my lined combat overalls, then a muffler, then my heavy short coat." And still he was cold.[4]

Meanwhile, taking advantage of the Allied holdup at the bridges and passes leading into Tunisia, the Germans began to rush across by sea and air huge numbers of troops and hordes of munitions from their Italian and Sicilian bases. One arrival was the Mark IV Tiger tank, whose main 88mm cannon outgunned the Allied U.S. Stuart's 37mm, somewhat as a rifle compares with a peashooter or, in the words of one officer who had to fight one, "popcorn balls thrown by Little Bo Peep would have been just as effective."[5] Furthermore, by Christmas 1942, the vanguard of Rommel's remaining 80,000 troops had begun to arrive in Tunisia after their grueling retreat across the western desert. Hitler, for his part, had finally decided to do what he should have done in the first place, which was to provide all the arms, men, fuel, and supplies available to make a stand against the Allied armies in an all-or-nothing gamble for North Africa and control of the Mediterranean.

There were other issues, too. For one thing, the North African Muslims had been propagandized by the Germans to believe that the American and British presence was a prelude to establishing a Jewish state in their countries, as had been done in Palestine. Not all Arabs believed this, but enough did so that sniping, sabotage, and espionage—principally as to Allied troop movements—became a constant threat.* After the fall of France, courtesy of the Vichy regime, Jews in French North Africa had been stripped of most of their rights, including voting, and were banned from working in occupations such as law, medicine, education, and banking. When the Americans arrived in Morocco and Algeria they pressed the French to restore Jewish rights, but the French demurred, claiming it might ignite an Arab uprising, and that they had trouble enough ahead as it was.

In Tunisia, the plight of the Jews became far worse as the Germans poured in and took over the country completely. Jews were rounded up by the thousands and forced to work for the German army, building defensive fortifications and airfields and set to other labor-intensive drudgery. To add insult to injury, they were ordered to bring their own tools and food. Not only did the Germans begin to loot the Jews' bank accounts, gold, and jewelry but they accused them of supporting the Allies and levied the equivalent of a $25 million fine on them, which had to be paid through usurious bank loans, with Jewish land, farms, and houses as collateral.[6]

Through November and December the Americans and British pressed forward along the main road leading from Algeria through northern Tunisia

*On several occasions during battles American troops noticed Arabs lighting fires, "sending smoke signals" to warn Germans of approaching Allied forces. These people were ordered taken under fire, and the practice diminished.

to its capital, Tunis. Once, on a clear day, from a rise of hills, the Allied columns even got a glimpse of the famed ancient city gleaming white against the cobalt blue of the Mediterranean Sea. Tantalizing as that vista was, it was also "to remain a haunting memory through many tough days ahead," since the Germans were now coming in great strength. By the end of December the Americans and British had arrived in the valley of the Medjerda River.[7]

Here was the land of the Carthaginians of antiquity, who had built a great Mediterranean empire and fought the Punic Wars against Rome and lost their civilization because of it. The Romans then occupied the place and turned it into a prosperous and abundant province until their hour finally came round at the hands of the Vandals, plunging Western culture into more than a thousand years of darkness. Ruins of Roman houses, temples, and baths still stood among the fertile hills and fields where Arabs now cultivated their crops: oranges, lemons, and other citrus, almonds, grapes, olives, apricots, and wheat. One American officer observed, almost wistfully, that "the citrus fruit was almost ripe."[8] And it was upon this bountiful land, amid the groves and vineyards, that some of the fiercest tank battles of the war took place.

"Tunisian mud had the consistency of chewing gum," wrote Brigadier General Paul M. Robinett, commander of a tank regiment of the U.S. First Armored Division.[9] The incessant rainfall reduced the roads and countryside to almost unimaginable traveling conditions. Trucks and artillery sank axle-deep in the muck. Even tanks often could not operate properly. Oxen, commandeered from local Arabs by the exasperated Allies, managed to haul a few guns forward and get some trucks unstuck, but all in all it was beginning to seem as futile as had the mud-bound attacks on the Western Front during World War I. Worse, this spirit of futility seemed to be spreading into the rank and file of the American army. Unlike the Germans, who had been fighting for two years, the Americans were not yet "battle-hardened," and the combination of cold, wet, and mud and constant German air attacks was badly affecting their morale. There were few hot meals and the men were filthy from living in the open or in watery holes in the ground; anyone who was clean became immediately conspicuous.

In the midst of all this, the diminutive Ernie Pyle, beloved Scripps-Howard newspaper correspondent, made one of his many insightful observations: "The battlefield was an incongruous thing. Always there was some ridiculous impingement of normalcy on a field of battle. There on that day it was the Arabs. They were herding their camels, just as usual. Some of them continued to plow their fields. Children walked along, driving their little sack-ladened burros, as tanks and guns clanked past them. The sky was filled with planes and smoke burst from screaming shells."[10]

The Americans, fighting in the Medjerda River valley, and the British, who had proposed taking from the Germans an eminence they named Longstop Hill,* soon began to run into fierce opposition. Not only was the superiority of the German Mark II and Mark IV Panzer tanks quickly apparent, but the Germans were now bringing in their new Mark VI Tiger, the most powerful tank in the world. The slaughter was both pitiless and pitiful; Allied tank shells simply bounced off the German armor. Hideous scenes were offered up: crews roasted alive in a field of flaming tanks, decapitated or blown to atoms by German guns. Despite mounting casualties the Americans and British fought bravely and with much painful sacrifice while surgeons did their grim work round-the-clock in crude field hospitals. There was little quarter given, and little asked for, most notably by members of certain ethnic groups fighting for the Allies. A mercenary tribe known as the Goums from the deserts of Morocco and Algeria were infamous for entering Allied camps carrying the severed heads of Germans, for each of which they were paid a bounty. A similar terror tactic practiced by the British Gurkhas, learned presumably in their native Nepal, was to sneak up on a sleeping patrol of Germans and slit the throats of all but one, leaving him, when he awakened, to spread the news.[11]

For more than a month the battle seesawed as the Allies inched stubbornly forward, only to withdraw in the face of German counterattacks. Time and again orders would come down from some headquarters far behind the lines to do this or that, or thus and so, when the men actually fighting on the ground, from privates to senior commanders, could plainly

*Dj El Ahmer was the Arabic name for the hill but, just as the Americans have the shortstop in the game of baseball, the British named it after a cricket term.

see it was either impossible or foolhardy. This prompted one GI to declare, "Never were so few commanded by so many from so far away."[12] At last the Americans and British were forced to draw back to regroup and refit at a position about twenty miles inside the Tunisian border and sixty miles from their farthest point of advance. General Robinett's corps alone had lost nearly 75 percent of its equipment and 22 percent of its men.

Finally, on Christmas Eve 1942, Eisenhower himself reached the fighting front. He had been so harassed by political concerns—who would lead the French North African army; how was the British army to be deployed?— that General Marshall himself had to personally order his North African commander in chief to drop these matters entirely and concentrate on beating the Germans. When Eisenhower's big armored Cadillac staff car pulled up to a camouflaged little farmhouse just inside Tunisia, where Allied headquarters was located, the general had already become depressed. During the entire fifteen-hour trip from Algiers he had witnessed firsthand the effects of the rain and mud on troop movement. From the window of his car he had seen men straining and struggling to free vehicles hopelessly mired and knew deep down that no army could conduct an offensive battle in such conditions. After a few cheerless and uninspiring remarks to American and British senior officers, including General Robinett, Eisenhower was briefed on the tactical situation. It was even more agonizing than he had imagined; because of terrain, the lone road into Tunis, along which the Allies had been fighting so bitterly during all these weeks, had become an unmanageable bottleneck.

Eisenhower asked questions but said little else until the briefing was over, then made his pronouncement: the battle would have to be called off until spring, when the ground had dried out. It was a terrific disappointment, all the wasted lives, all the lost time, but what he had seen and heard made the decision inevitable. That done, at eleven P.M. he went in to Christmas Eve dinner with the British and French senior commanders. As a student of the Punic Wars from his West Point days, it might have crossed Eisenhower's mind that in the time of Hannibal, the Carthaginians often crucified generals who failed. And fail Eisenhower had; the race for Tunisia had been lost and now he was faced with stalemate, which might easily degenerate into the appalling static warfare experienced in the First World War.

Uninvited to any Christmas supper of their own, the troops outside the farmhouse headquarters huddled beneath haystacks or in tents and vehicles, listening to the rain drum down. Lonely, homesick, and frightened, whether they knew it or not, or even cared, the blood of soldiers on both sides was now being mixed in the same rich dirt as those who had died two thousand years earlier under Hannibal, or Caesar or Scipio. One of their number had composed a piece of verse:

> Twas the night before Christmas, in Africa's plain,
> The men were all drenched in a deep drizzling rain.
> Tomorrow our folks will eat turkey and duck,
> We'll probably have C-rations down by the truck.[13]

No sooner had Eisenhower returned to his headquarters in Algiers than he received an alarming message. In under three weeks' time the president of the United States and the prime minister of Great Britain, and their top staffs and aides, were coming to Casablanca for a meeting—as if Eisenhower didn't have enough on his plate already.

The Casablanca Conference was convened because, assuming they took North Africa from the Germans, the Allies had no agreed-upon plan whatsoever for what they would do next. Casablanca had been decided as the site for a variety of interesting reasons. Churchill had visited the United States twice since the war broke out, and Roosevelt, ever the politician, was champing to take a trip himself. At first it was suggested that the conference should be held in England, but this was vetoed when someone pointed out it might anger the powerful British-hating American Irish vote. Roosevelt himself wanted to convene somewhere close to the war itself, and Churchill agreed. They tried to persuade old Joe Stalin to join them but he begged off on grounds that the fighting around Stalingrad had reached critical proportions and he was needed in Moscow. (This did not square with the reports stating that Stalin didn't like to fly, which would have been the only way he could have gotten to Casablanca.)[14]

Roosevelt left Washington under a cloak of utmost secrecy. In the middle of the night he was spirited out of the White House by Secret Service agents and taken to the Bureau of Printing and Engraving, an imposing redbrick building a few blocks away. There, in an underground tunnel, waited his private train cars. To preserve security, the regular porters and dining car waiters had been replaced by Filipino staff servants from his mountain retreat at Shangri-la. After a few fake maneuvers to discourage possible espionage agents from divining where the train was headed, the entourage took off southward for Miami. Aboard with the president were General Marshall and Admiral King, and their staffs, representatives from the Department of State, and Roosevelt's close aide Harry Hopkins.

At Miami Roosevelt boarded a big flying boat and took off for Trinidad, then to Belém on South America's Brazilian coast, and from there an exhausting eighteen-hour flight across the South Atlantic to the West African nation of Gambia, arriving at an old slave port on the Gambia River. An army transport plane then carried them north, above the Atlas Mountains to Casablanca.

Vast preparations had been under way since Eisenhower first got the word, and the man he appointed to receive this great assembly of free world leaders was none other than General George Patton. Pomp and circumstance was Patton's specialty but there was little of it here because of the secrecy imposed. Patton, who was chafing to get into the battle, found himself scouring army units to find a band that could play "Hail to the Chief," quietly.* Outside of Casablanca Patton's staff had located a comfortable and secure compound where everyone could stay, and as they arrived at the airport Roosevelt, Churchill, and their people were hustled into waiting cars whose windows had been plastered with mud by a GI detail in order to conceal the identities of those inside. One thing that incurred Patton's displeasure was Roosevelt's accompanying guard of Secret Service agents, who rode in a open jeep behind his limousine brandishing pistols. Patton felt that with his 50,000-man Western Army Corps he had provided adequate security and described the Secret Service men as "a bunch of cheap detectives always smelling of drink."[15]

*Fortunately, they settled on the Third Division Artillery Band, which not only played "Hail to the Chief" but entertained the distinguished conferees with such selections as "Missouri Waltz," "Deep in the Heart of Texas," "Alexander's Ragtime Band," and "The Naughty Marietta Waltz."

When the luminaries arrived at their elegant villas it was like Old Home Week. Roosevelt's sons Elliott and FDR Jr. were there in their army and navy uniforms, respectively. (Another son, James, was still off in the Pacific with the marines.) So was Churchill's son, Randolph, who was serving with the British commandos near the front. As well, Sergeant Robert Hopkins, Harry's son, whom Eisenhower had dug up out of his foxhole in Tunisia, arrived to complete the party.[16]

The principal agenda of the conference had been set by both the British and the Americans—on opposing sides. The Americans wanted to attack the Germans in France the following year (1943) and the British still wanted to attack someplace in the Mediterranean so as to get at Italy: Sicily, Sardinia, Crete, Rhodes, or even the mainland of Greece were all on the table as potential points of invasion. This was Churchill's pet theory of invading Europe's "soft underbelly," until they were strong enough to attack across the English Channel, and it had much to recommend it. British staff officers estimated that there were eighty German divisions in France, but only forty Allied divisions would be capable of invading in 1943. Yet there were troops enough to knock out Italy beginning as soon as North Africa was conquered—assuming that it was; so far things had not been looking up along those lines.

To bolster their argument the British pointed to their disastrous raid on the French port town of Dieppe only five months earlier. The raid had been planned partly in response to Stalin's continued insistence on an immediate second front in France and partly to see just how hard or easy it would be to breach the German defenses.* They might as well not have bothered. Some 6,000 soldiers, most of them Canadians,† had landed on the beaches of Dieppe, August 19, 1942, a few days after the U.S. Marines landed on Guadalcanal. The Germans were ready for them. Machine

---

*Sir Roy Jenkins, in his brilliant biography of Churchill, suggests that "The main result—maybe the main purpose—of the action was to take the edge off the mounting obstreperousness among idle Canadian troops in the South of England and to demonstrate how difficult was a landing on a fortified coast." If that is so, it was indeed a cynical mind that conceived it.

†With a few U.S. Army rangers and British commandos thrown in.

guns blasted many of the invaders before they could even get out of their landing barges. Tanks that had been sent with them foundered on German obstacles set along the beaches. After nine hours of fighting nearly a thousand of the raiding force were killed and twice that taken prisoner. The rest managed somehow to escape into waiting barges and returned dejectedly to England. With all these arguments on their side, in the end the British Mediterranean attack plan was persuasive and it was decided that Sicily would be the best invasion point once the German armies were captured or driven out of Tunisia.

That out of the way, Churchill and Roosevelt left the details to be bickered about among their various staffs and turned to the ever vexing problem of what to do about France. Roosevelt was enduring vitriolic attacks at home over his administration's decision to continue dealing with the discredited Vichy French regime. Operating from London and a base in the former Belgian Congo, Brigadier General Charles de Gaulle, a borderline renegade, had assembled and taken command of a force he called the Free French and refused to have anything to do with Vichy at all. Like General Giraud, de Gaulle proclaimed himself the only true French leader, which the State Department suspected was done so primarily to gain future political advantage, after the war. (They of course suspected the same of Giraud.) But to ease the political strain back in the United States as well as to get these two vain Frenchmen to cooperate in the common cause, it was considered necessary to present to the public at least a perceived reconciliation of their bitter antagonisms.

This was accomplished, superficially, only with the greatest of difficulties. At first de Gaulle refused to leave his London office and go to Casablanca and did so only after Churchill threatened to cut off his funding. When Giraud and de Gaulle arrived at the conference they said as little as possible to each other and were barely civil, but the propaganda purpose of having them there was brilliantly accomplished when Roosevelt paraded them out onto the lawn with himself and Churchill and had them shake hands for the waiting photographers (after which they were hustled off before any reporters could talk to them). The picture, however, was flashed around the world as proof that Roosevelt and

Churchill had patched up all French dissension when, in fact, it was merely a shrewd photo op.

At one point Churchill, who had wonderful memories of North Africa, took Roosevelt on a sightseeing tour, their limousine followed as always by the pistol-waving Secret Service men. They rode through miles of countryside, past bazaars, veiled dancing girls, snake charmers, and Arabs riding camels, ending up at a six-story observation tower near Marrakech. With Churchill leading the way as Roosevelt, seated in a garden chair, was lugged up the stairs by his Secret Service detail, the two world leaders were treated to a sight to behold: the snowcapped Atlas Mountains in the distance, illuminated by a setting sun reflecting purplish hues upon their magnificent slopes.[17]

On the final day of the conference, with a gaggle of newsmen and photographers standing or sitting cross-legged on the lush grass before them, Roosevelt and Churchill sat in little white chairs amid African palms and fruit trees and gave a brief recitation of what had been decided at the meetings, leaving out of course the part about invading Italy through Sicily. Then at one point, seemingly off the cuff, Roosevelt made one of the most controversial statements of the war.

He and Churchill, the president suddenly announced, had determined that the only way to end the war was by demanding the "unconditional surrender" of Germany, Italy, and Japan. There were to be no "deals," or armistices, such as there were in 1918. The only way out for the Axis, Roosevelt said, was total capitulation. Among the people shocked by this declaration was Churchill himself, who had no inkling that it was coming; for so many years of their illustrious military history the British had always tried to leave themselves a little wiggle room, but here there was none. Roosevelt later told the press that the idea "just popped into my mind," but this was not entirely so; Harry Hopkins revealed that Roosevelt had thought it out the night before and had put it into his notes.[18]

Whatever the case, it created an uproar at the time, and has among historians ever since. "There were many experts," wrote Hopkins's biographer Robert Sherwood, "who believed that the utterance of these words would put the iron of desperate resistance into the Germans, Japanese and Italians and needlessly prolong the war and increase its cost; there are some who still believe it did so. There were others who were violently opposed to the principle itself, and still [attribute] the world's postwar troubles to the enforcement of unconditional surrender."[19]

In any event, the die was now cast, with the end of the game yet to be played out in the years 1943, 1944, and 1945.

Chapter Twenty-one ★

The fateful year of 1942, which began in a cataract of defeat and humilia-tion—in Europe, North Africa, and the Soviet Union, and in the Mediter-ranean, the Atlantic, and the Pacific—would end with the complete and abrupt halt of Axis expansion everywhere—German, Italian, and Japanese.* The Casablanca Conference of January 1943 pronounced its eventual doom. Having said this, it would be not only profoundly wrong but insulting as well to imply that everything coming afterward was somehow anticlimax, for terrible battles remained to be fought and millions of people were yet to suffer and die before the beast was run to ground. Still, it *would not* be wrong to say that a year that began in shock and anxiety for the Allies had ended on a note of high confidence, and with the smell of victory in the air.†

---

*Even the Soviets, who were fighting the battle of their lives at Stalingrad, recog-nized by the end of 1942 that the vast armies they were gathering behind that beleaguered city were capable of extinguishing the German threat.

†As readers will have discerned, massive events such as World War II do not lend themselves to precise pigeonholing calendar dates. Thus for the purposes of this story the import of the year 1942 actually began earlier, on December 7, 1941, with the attack on Pearl Harbor, and ended a month afterward, in January 1943, with the defeat of the Japa-nese at Guadalcanal and New Guinea, and with the Allies overpowering the Germans in North Africa by mid-March.

The stalemate in Tunisia continued until mid-March, when Allied armies began to break out. It was ugly at first. There were frightful American losses at Sidi bou Zid and during the Battle of the Kasserine Pass in mid-February, as the U.S. First Armored Division, the U.S. First Infantry Division, and British units went up against Rommel's veterans of the Afrika Korps. These were among the greatest defeats in American history, some 10,000 men and hundreds of tanks lost. The U.S. forces, it seemed, were simply not performing. As well as verified reports of undaunted courage, there was also evidence of incompetence, shirking, even cowardice. The American army was green and in many cases poorly led. If any good thing came of the Kasserine tragedy it was the replacement of the II Corps commanding officer by General George S. Patton, who would finally get his chance to lead great numbers of men in battle. Rommel had gone back to Germany on sick leave and Patton now faced General Hans-Jurgen von Arnim, but it probably wouldn't have mattered who he faced. By the end of the campaign the Allies had built more than a hundred airfields near the battle area and simply overwhelmed the Germans in every aspect.

As the American soldiers became battle-hardened at last, they also began to harden their souls, and this would haunt some of them for the rest of their lives. Increasingly, incidents were reported of U.S. soldiers raping Arab women and outright murdering Arab men, all of whom they suspected of working for the Nazis, true or not. But murder was something they had now become good at and, like it or no, this is one thing that makes a man into a true combat soldier—absolute hate and desire to kill his enemy. At least it did in World War II, and General Patton, perhaps the greatest German hater of them all, managed to instill in his men precisely that emotion.

Scripps-Howard News Service war correspondent Ernie Pyle detected this new attitude. "The most vivid change was the casual and workshop manner in which they talked about killing," he wrote. "They had made the psychological transition from their normal belief that taking a human life was sinful, over to a new professional outlook where killing was a craft. No longer was there anything morally wrong about killing. In fact, it was an admirable thing. He wanted to kill individually and in vast numbers. He spoke excitedly of seeing great heaps of dead . . . of

Germans by the thousands dying miserably in a final Tunisian holocaust of their own creation."[1]

By mid-May 1943 it was all over and the Axis in North Africa completely smashed. Much of the credit goes to Allied airpower, which cut off the German supply line by sea from Italy and then, when the Germans and Italians tried to resupply the Axis troops by air, shot their transports out of the skies by the hundreds, at a ratio of ten to one. As well, Montgomery's Eighth Army, which had defeated Rommel's Afrika Korps in Libya and chased it back into Tunisia, then proceeded to smash it again and again as the Germans set up rearguard lines, only to have them overrun by Allied tanks and infantry. The Americans had become a formidable battle force by now, too, and the Axis was being hammered on both sides in the unforgiving, mountainous terrain. The fighting was bitter and costly but the the steady stream of American tanks, artillery pieces, and warplanes ferried across the Atlantic supply line from U.S. ports was taking its toll. On May 7 Allied troops entered the major cities of Tunis and Bizerte to a riotous welcome of cheering, kisses, and flowers flung by the liberated French population. The Mediterranean was now open to Allied shipping; there was no more Axis threat to Egypt, Iran, Iraq, Libya, and the Suez Canal and the Germans had been handed their first major defeat. It would not be the last; in fact, it was only the beginning.

Nearly 300,000 Axis troops were taken prisoner, and very few escaped to fight another day—a remarkable achievement, and even more ignominious for the Axis since the newsreel cameras were churning, recording the events. What the Allies had assumed, wishfully, would take a mere month or so had taken seven, with dreadful loss of life. But now they were poised to invade Sicily, and then on into the Italian homeland, with the now hardened American GI sharpening his trench knife or bayonet with bloodthirsty vigor.

Things were going no better for the Germans in their attack on the Soviet Union. They had failed to overrun Stalingrad the previous year but in the late summer and autumn of 1942 they attacked with renewed vehemence, reducing most of the city of half a million to rubble. Still the Soviets held them on the banks of the Volga and, with the harsh Russian winter again coming on, the reinforced Red Army attacked in a pincers maneuver, trapping the Germans in the snow and biting cold. After their last airfield was captured, the German commander, Field Marshal Friedrich Paulus, asked Hitler for permission to withdraw, since his troops were starving, but this was met with the same directive Der Führer had delivered to Rommel at El Alamein: "fight to the last man." This they almost did. By mid-January nearly 120,000 German soldiers had been killed and Paulus surrendered the rest, about 100,000, to the tender mercies of Joseph Stalin's people. Of these, only 5,000 ever came back after the war. Not only that, but the hundreds of thousands of Russian prisoners who were repatriated by the Germans after the war were immediately sent off by Stalin to hard labor in the gulags, branded as traitors.

The Russian affair sealed Hitler's fate. If he had held off declaring war on the Soviet Union until the situation in North Africa had been settled—or not even attacked Russia at all—then the course of the war might have changed in his favor, at least for a while. But Hitler foolishly spread himself too thin and in the end he and his nation paid the price.

The price was high; when it was over Germany was for all practical intents destroyed.* Rather than stand trial for his crimes Hitler shot himself in the final days as Soviet tanks and troops pulverized Berlin. Here was where the argument against Roosevelt's "unconditional surrender" edict came into play. Some believed that high German officials (provided their own lives were spared) would willingly have surrendered Germany to the Allies instead of resigning themselves to being conquered by the Soviets, who they knew would have long memories of atrocities visited upon their country by the Germans. But Roosevelt's unconditional surrender did not include any deals about sparing any high officials' lives and so they fought

*Some people wanted to keep it that way. The most vociferous was Roosevelt's secretary of the treasury, Henry Morgenthau, who was Jewish. It was his incensed conviction that Germany should henceforth "be turned into a sheep pasture," so as never to threaten the world again. This was not to be. When U.S. Army chief of staff George Marshall became secretary of state in the next administration he devised the Marshall Plan, which poured billions of American dollars into the restoration of wrecked Europe and certainly helped stem the spread of communism, which the Soviets were peddling with alarming efficiency among the destitute Europeans.

on to the bitter end. As it turned out, Stalin and the Soviet communists confiscated more than half of Germany and all of Eastern Europe for themselves and stayed put for more than forty years until it was discovered by the Europeans—and the Russians too—that the practice of communism was no bed of roses.

Erwin Rommel, who had lost North Africa for the Third Reich, was rewarded for his efforts by being put in charge of the English Channel defenses for the Allied invasion of France that everyone knew was coming. In 1944 he was seriously injured when a U.S. plane attacked his staff car and, while recuperating, was sucked into the abortive plot to assassinate Hitler, hatched by a number of high-ranking German officers. When it failed Rommel, who had become a German national hero, was found out by Hitler's Gestapo but allowed by the Nazis to commit suicide by poison rather than submit to the dishonor of standing public trial.

The Japanese, after resounding defeats at Midway, Guadalcanal, and New Guinea, unadvisedly hunkered down for a long fight. The spirit of their armies was then necessarily reversed from the offensive to the defensive, at which they excelled if only because of their soldiers' unwavering disposition to die for their emperor. During the long bloody slog across the Pacific there were many harsh battles for Japanese-held islands because, unlike the Germans, when the Japanese said they were going to fight to the last man they actually meant it.

It was this same tenacity that caused the Japanese to pay the price, too. By November 1942, American nuclear physicists, using facilities at the University of Chicago and working under General Leslie Groves, set off the first sustained atomic chain reaction. This demonstrated at least in theory that an atomic bomb could be created. The science was still so new that two different and conflicting methods were used to create the material to build the thing. One was through the production of specially enriched uranium (the same uranium that at the breakout of war had been secretly shipped from the Belgian Congo and stored on Staten Island), processed at an enormous plant built in Oak Ridge, Tennessee, near Knoxville. The other was through use of plutonium, produced at an even more enormous facility near Hanford, Washington.* At their peak these plants occupied thousands of acres and employed tens of thousands of workers, all cleared for the utmost security. Another facility was set up in the desert near Los Alamos, New Mexico, to produce the actual bombs themselves, one igniting uranium, the other plutonium.

Having been driven all the way across the Pacific by the U.S. armed forces and watching their homeland cities bombed to rubble every day, if the Japanese even at that late date had understood the handwriting on the wall and surrendered unconditionally, they surely would have spared themselves the agony of nuclear holocaust. But that would have meant loss of face and thus their misery became palpable. One still has to wonder, though, how much Roosevelt's unconditional surrender proclamation at Casablanca had to do with it.

When the war finally ended General Tojo was convicted by an Allied military tribunal and sentenced to death but not before he attempted suicide by trying to shoot himself in the heart with a pistol. He missed. By then the American and British POWs had been freed and their stories of Japanese atrocities inflamed the Allied world. As Japan's highest commander, Tojo was held ultimately responsible for all of this and, for that matter, for starting the war in the first place. Just past midnight on December 22, 1948, along with six other high-ranking Japanese generals and admirals, Tojo was marched to the gallows in a Tokyo prison and hanged. In a final act of defiance, just before the trap was sprung, each of the seven condemned shouted *"Banzai!"* Among Tojo's final words was a haiku he himself had composed.

> It is time for farewell.
> I shall wait beneath the moss,
> until the flowers are fragrant again
> in the islands of Yamato.[2]

---

*Hanford was chosen not only because of the availability of hydroelectric power but for its remoteness in case something went wrong. The scientists were dealing with a power they had never encountered and if a chain reaction was started they were still not certain they would be able to shut it down.

Nearly a thousand Japanese officials shared Tojo's fate, from high-ranking officers to prison guards identified by former POWs bent on revenge, resolution, and what has now come to be called "closure." Among these were General Tomoyuki Yamashita, the Tiger of Malaya, and General Masaharu Homma, who had led the invasion of the Philippines.

Yamashita, who had replaced Homma as high commander of the Philippines, was convicted on accusations that he allowed the destruction and rape of Manila in 1944 as the Allies closed in. It was not a particularly strong case, and Yamashita, who was several hundred miles away at the time, insisted he knew nothing of the event. But he was convicted anyway and hanged in a prison yard near Manila on February 23, 1946. General Homma was blamed for the Bataan Death March and related atrocities, which he also denied knowing anything about, but he was allowed the more honorable death by an American firing squad a week later.* The executions of these two men created a bit of a stir in the Western press because, unlike the war-crimes tribunals in Tokyo and Nuremberg, their convictions and sentences seemed by some to have come as a result of a kangaroo court ultimately responsible to General MacArthur himself. Perhaps this was so; by that point MacArthur truly considered himself "supreme," and these were the men who had run him out of his beloved Philippines.

The emperor, however, was not punished. This decision was also made by MacArthur who, as commander of Allied forces in the Pacific, wished to use His Majesty as a pawn to bring about harmony between the Japanese people and the Americans who now occupied their country.

The Japanese-American woman known as Tokyo Rose got a six-year prison sentence, but Colonel Masanobu Tsuji, who many later came to believe was responsible for the mistreatment of so many prisoners, was not accused or tried, and lived out his life in Japan, even writing a book and becoming an elected member of the rejuvenated Japanese Diet, or parliament. Commander Mitsuo Fuchida also escaped prosecution, converted to

---

*There is a stirring verse in the Irish ballad "Kevin Barry," about a sixteen-year-old boy who was sentenced to death for his role in the 1916 Easter Uprising: "Oh, shoot me like an Irish soldier/Do not hang me like a dog."

Protestantism, and wrote a book about his experience in leading the attack on Pearl Harbor and the fighting at Midway, published, interestingly enough, by the U.S. Naval Institute Press in Annapolis.

It was nearly two years into the war before the American torpedo fiasco was finally straightened out by the U.S. Navy's Bureau of Ordnance. Until then the bureau insisted on blaming the lack of Japanese ship sinkings on bad marksmanship by U.S. submarines and destroyers. Finally one U.S. Navy sub skipper turned in a report that got the attention of somebody in navy headquarters. He recorded that in July 1943 he had fired four torpedoes at a Japanese tanker at a range of 1,000 yards—sitting-duck range. None exploded. In frustration, he then fired the remainder of his entire arsenal at the enemy tanker—twelve more torpedoes—and found that all were duds.

When the ordnance people finally began looking into the problem they discovered two things. First, the American torpedo firing mechanisms were oversensitive and, if the missile hit an enemy ship head on, it most often would mash into itself and not explode. Second, many other American torpedoes had been equipped with a state-of-the-art magnetic field detonator, which was supposed to make the thing blow up whenever it entered the magnetic field of a ship. Unfortunately, what nobody at the Bureau of Ordnance thought to consider was that near the equator—where so much of the Japanese shipping was concentrated—the magnetic field of ships is quite different than it would be in, say, the North Atlantic or deep in the South Pacific—or even the Caribbean—and thus most American torpedoes were running harmlessly about eleven feet beneath the enemy ships.[3]

At last the torpedo problems were resolved and U.S. sinkings of enemy vessels increased dramatically. But in fact Japan, in particular, had so neglected its merchant marine in favor of building warships that it could not even take advantage of all the bounty of its southern conquests, even without the interference from American subs.

Admiral Yamamoto did not live to see the destruction of his navy and his homeland, and one imagines that this was probably a good thing for him, since he likely would have found himself after the war in some Allied prison, if not swinging from an Allied rope. Two months after the Japanese evacuation of Guadalcanal Yamamoto decided to fly down from Truk and take a tour of the installations on Rabaul to inspect his troops. The message revealing this plan—including date and time—was plucked out of the air by American code breakers in Honolulu and sent straight up to Admiral Nimitz. After a brief consultation with Navy Secretary Knox, it was decided to try to assassinate the Japanese commander by aerial ambush. Sixteen of the new American P-38 fighters were dispatched from Henderson Field and, at precisely the time indicated, Yamamoto's plane appeared over the skies of Bougainville, where it was shot down and crashed into the jungle, killing all aboard. The navy did not reveal this stunning news story to the media for fear of alerting the Japanese that their most secret code might be compromised, and up until the end of the war Imperial General Headquaraters believed it was just plain dumb luck on the part of the Americans. For his part, Nimitz appeared uncharitably disappointed in Yamamoto's somewhat clinical assassination, informing his fellow officers that, instead, he'd "hoped to lead that scoundrel up Pennsylvania Avenue in chains, with the rest of you kicking him in the ass."

Just before the war ended a far more solemn procession was led up Pennsylvania Avenue. After serving the longest term of any U.S. president, Franklin Delano Roosevelt died of a stroke at his retreat in Warm Springs, Georgia, in April 1945. Though he didn't live to see the surrenders, by early 1945 it was clear that the end was near and that the democracies (excepting the Soviet Union) would win. From his first election as president in 1932 Roosevelt had become a lightning rod, loved and hated with as much passion as any U.S. president ever has. But he had been a splendid wartime leader and even his many enemies could not begrudge him that. His faithful aide Harry Hopkins, who was chronically ill all during the war years but had shuttled back and forth to England to carry out Roosevelt's wishes, died the following year.

In England, even before the war ended, the British electorate turned Churchill out of office, owing mainly to the labor union vote. After he had led them so magnificently for seven long and perilous years, it seemed a noteworthy act of ingratitude. Also because of the war, the vast British empire, which in 1939 had encompassed nearly a quarter of the earth, was slowly dismantled. It just wasn't worth it anymore. The process went on for nearly twenty years, but by the late 1960s there remained outside the isles of Great Britain itself no vestiges of Rule Britannia save for a few isolated outposts. For better or worse, her once subject peoples were now free to do of their own choosing, but soon many of these former colonies—particularly in Africa and the Middle East—perhaps inevitably, degenerated into chaos and bloody turmoil, and remain so today.

In France the imperious Charles de Gaulle got his wish and became the leader of the French people (while his old antagonist Giraud had faded into obscurity). But de Gaulle, too, was plagued with colonial unrest, including bloodthirsty revolutions in the French colonies of Algeria and Indochina (Vietnam). Henri-Philippe Pétain, now the eighty-nine-year-old former leader of the Vichy puppet government, was found guilty of treason and sentenced to death by firing squad. The sentence was later commuted to life in prison, where he died in 1951.

Of the other individuals included in this drama: The spy "Cynthia" who had unclothed herself in the French embassy in Washington eventually married the French naval captain who aided her in obtaining the Vichy naval codes that had so assisted the North Africa invasion. According to her biographer, H. Montgomery Hyde, the two were still living happily together twenty years afterward.

Commander Columbus Darwin Smith and his companions Woolley and Storey made it through to Chinese-American positions after a nearly two-month, seven-hundred-mile trek through Japanese-held territory. From there they were flown to India on one of the Hump transport planes, where they finally sat down to the supper they'd been dreaming about: lobster, steak, and french fries, washed down with iced champagne.

Immediately after the Japanese surrender, General Chiang Kai-shek and his Chinese Nationalist Army predictably went to war with Mao Tse-tung's communist forces. After several years Chiang was defeated, whereupon he took the remainder of his troops and their families and supporters to the island of Formosa (now Taiwan), where their multitudinous descendants reside today, much to the irritation and displeasure of China's communist regime.

Of the American military men, Eisenhower of course went on to lead the Allied forces in the D-day landings at Normandy in June 1944 and the ultimate conquest of Germany and, afterward, become the thirty-fourth president of the United States. George Patton, after a tempestuous but successful career as commander of the famed Third Army, which spearheaded the American attack on Germany, died of injuries suffered in a traffic accident just after the war ended. He is buried in the American military cemetery in Luxembourg, where a life-sized bronze statue commemorates his career.

When the First Marine Division was relieved on Guadalcanal General Alexander Vandegrift was made commandant of the Marine Corps, from which position he fought a long but ultimately successful battle after the war to keep Congress from folding the corps into the army and navy.

After fulfilling his promise to the Filipinos that "I shall return," Douglas MacArthur as supreme commander of U.S. forces in the Far East, presided over the surrender and reconstruction of Japan and, in 1950, over the Korean War. Sacked for defying instructions from President Truman, MacArthur finally retired to the United States, a country he had not set foot in since his first commission to the Philippines in 1935.

James Doolittle, after the celebrated Tokyo raid, was named commander of the U.S. Twelfth Air Force during the North Africa landings and later, in Europe, of the Fifteenth and Eighth Air Forces, respectively. At one point when Patton was in the doghouse with Eisenhower for the notorious incident of slapping an enlisted man who had said he had "battle fatigue," Doolittle made a special trip to see his old friend, then in exile in Sicily. "When I landed," Doolittle said, "there was Georgie in his famous jeep with the three-star flags flying, his helmet reflecting the sun gloriously and his ivory-handled revolvers at his side. He rushed forward, threw his arms around me and, with great tears streaming down his face, said, 'Jimmy, I'm glad to see you. I didn't think anyone would ever call on a mean old son of a bitch like me.'"

After the war Doolittle, one of the most decorated officers in the U.S. military, was made a full general and later retired with Joe, his wife of forty years, to build their dream home in Pebble Beach, California, where he spent his days hunting and fly-fishing. Just before he died in 1993 at the age of ninety-six, Doolittle told a newsman, "There has never been a time when I've been completely satisfied with myself."[4]

After nearly a year of Soviet internment in the freezing wilds of Siberia, the B-24 crew of Doolittle's Tokyo bombers that had landed in Russia finally got a response to their letter of complaint to old Joe Stalin. It was not a direct response (but neither was it a firing squad or the gulags, which some feared); instead the eight fliers were bundled up one night and herded onto a rickety train that started south to parts unknown. After days on this train, the crew finally arrived at a filthy and dust-choked town called Ashkhabad and were thrown into a squalid compound surrounded by dirt walls and containing a number of shacks of the outhouse variety. And almost as bad as the cold of Siberia, Ashkhabad, on the edge of the Great Persian Desert, was searing hot.

The men were set to work at dull and tedious labor in an old aircraft factory that made small trainer planes. Soon they all contracted horrible dysentery and, as historian Craig Nelson tells us, "For toilet paper they used *Pravda*." The prospect of sitting out the rest of the war in this hellhole was unacceptable—more so since their condition was being inflicted by our so-called ally, the Soviet Union—and so they contrived to escape.

They managed to make contact with a character of dubious trustworthiness, but who seemed to know the territory. Of course he demanded money. Luckily, one of the crew had several hundred dollars in cash from a poker game their last night on the *Hornet,* and this was offered up to help get them across the heavily mined and guarded Russian border with British-occupied Persia (now Iran).

Like Commander Smith and his party trying to escape from Shanghai, the B-25 crew had to place their lives in the hands of strange and shady natives who spoke no English. After tanking up on vodka, the men began a harrowing odyssey to freedom in May 1943 that involved, at various times, riding in a truck, walking, running, hiding, and finally crawling on their hands and knees until they were finally safe on the Persian side of the border.*

The legendary pilot Charles Lindbergh was never forgiven by Roosevelt for siding with the isolationists and before Pearl Harbor had resigned his

*It was indeed harrowing because in the Russia of the time it was quite customary to shoot first and ask questions later—and that included the native tribes they encountered.

commission as a colonel in the U.S. Army Air Corps, not wanting to embarrass his commander in chief by continuing as one of his officers while publicly opposing him. After war broke out Lindbergh asked friends to intercede in getting his rank back and placing him on active duty, but Roosevelt refused. So Lindbergh, then a high-ranking official with an aircraft manufacturer, went out on his own as an adviser, and soon found himself in the Solomon Islands where, among other things, he designed unique disposable beneath-the-wings fuel tanks that increased the range of fighter planes by several hundred miles. It was said that he even shot down a Japanese plane while on a "training mission."

The youthful marine private Robert Leckie, who had witnessed the crocodiles eating the bodies of dead Japanese on Guadalcanal, went on to become one of America's leading military historians. Admiral William "Bull" Halsey continued commanding the U.S. fleet that fought its way across the Pacific for three more years, virtually annihilating the Japanese navy. From his base at Pearl Harbor Admiral Chester Nimitz made the plans and called the shots, and when the war was over these two overaged seadogs were retired and so passed into legend, long linked with their names.

During the Battle of Okinawa in 1945, little Ernie Pyle, perhaps the most widely read of the war correspondents because he was a "soldiers'" newspaperman, was shot dead by a Japanese sniper.

After the Americans carried the fighting northwestward across the Pacific, Guadalcanal returned to being something of a backwater, but not for long. The Solomon Islanders had seen too much of civilization. For a while after the war various groups began agitating for independance, but Britain had already decided to liquidate its empire and Guadalcanal soon became an active member of the new Solomon Islands nation. Henderson Field is still extant, now an international airport, and cruise ships from Australia sometimes call at the port where the U.S. Marines landed. Housing projects dot the hills, and eminences such as Bloody Ridge, where the fiercest fighting took place, and the Matanikau River, crocodiles and all, have become tourist attractions.[5]

In August 1962, surviving members of the First Marine Division held a twentieth reunion of the Guadalcanal invasion, to which they invited Sergeant Major Jacob Vouza, the native Solomon Island scout who had been stabbed, beaten, and left for dead by the Japanese, but then collected himself and crawled back to marine lines to report the Japanese movement. Vouza sent them the following telegram in reply: "Tell them I love them all. Me old now, and me no look good no more. But me never forget."[6]

Claire "High Pockets" Phillips, after her arrest by the Japanese police, was thrown into a filthy prison and tortured and beaten for months on end. She admitted to sending letters, medicine, and food to the American POWs in the Cabanatuan camp, but her interrogators remained convinced that she had been aiding the guerrillas in the mountains. They gave her the usual Japanese treatment: beatings, burnings by cigarettes, starvation, and when she asked for water they gave her the "water treatment." But High Pockets stuck to her guns and denied knowing any of the guerrillas or anybody else in her spy ring. After enduring more than eight months of this she and her fellow prisoners began to hear bombs exploding, which came increasingly nearer each day, and then there was shelling from artillery. Word got out that the Americans had landed.

Then one day she looked out into the prison courtyard and "There stood ten of the tallest Yanks I had ever seen!" Phillips noted that she had dropped from her normal weight of 145 pounds to 95, her legs were covered with scars from cigarette burns, all of her teeth were loose, and when she tried to brush her hair it came out in great chunks. When she was finally reunited with her daughter, who had been taken by her nurse for safekeeping with an American guerrilla band, the child did not recognize her, and "refused to have anything to do with me." The next day, "when I took her with me to select dresses and shoes from the discarded clothing left with the Red Cross, Dian thawed a little," Phillips recalled. "'Are you my mummy?' she asked and when I replied she trustingly placed her thin little hand in mine." In a few days Claire Phillips and her daughter Dian were standing at the rail of a military transport ship bound for San Francisco, watching the smoking ruins of Manila fade into a distant tropic twilight.*

*Claire Phillips returned with her daughter to her birthplace of Portland, Oregon. In 1951 she received the Medal of Freedom; she died in 1959.

*   *   *

By now, all but 514 of the original 10,000 American prisoners from the fighting on Bataan and Corregidor had either died of disease or maltreatment, been murdered by the Japanese, or been shipped off as slave labor to Manchuria or Japan. Of those sent across the sea thousands died en route, since the Japanese refused to mark their transports as prisoner-of-war ships and were thus fair game for U.S. planes and submarines. They became known as the Death Ships, where living conditions were far harsher than even the prison camps had been. Men were crammed into filthy holds with little food and no water; many became insane, had heart attacks, suffocated, died of heat stroke or thirst, or were trampled to death by their claustrophobic companions.

Once in Japan or Manchuria, those who survived fared little better. They simply got to be beaten by a new set of sadistic guards and what food there was remained rotten. The American generals, from Wainwright on down, had been incarcerated since their capture, and who can forget the newsreel photographs of Wainwright's emaciated figure in 1945 when, during the Japanese surrender on the deck of the battleship *Missouri* in Tokyo Bay, MacArthur called him forward and presented him with one of the ink pens the Japanese had been given to sign the surrender document. Not only that but Wainwright, who had believed he was probably going to be court-martialed for surrendering the Philippines, was pleasantly shocked to find that he had been awarded the Medal of Honor.

It was the 514 Americans remaining behind at Cabanatuan that had the U.S. Army worried. Most had been left because they were too sick or weak to work in Japan. U.S. intelligence had already learned of one ghastly incident in another part of the Philippines where a hundred and fifty American prisoners were thrown into pits and roasted alive by gasoline-throwing Japanese in the face of the oncoming U.S. invasion. U.S. officials were fairly certain that the Japanese were executing prisoners as the Americans advanced and determined to do something about it.*

*This was all too true. After the war the Americans uncovered a document sent from Japanese Imperial Headquarters that instructed Japanese POW camp commanders to kill the prisoners as soon as they appeared to be in danger of being overrun by Allied forces.

What they did was order a special mission for a select detachment of the Sixth Army's Sixth Ranger Battalion: march twenty-five miles through enemy territory held by up to 8,000 Japanese troops and rescue the helpless American prisoners. This they did in a harrowing raid at the end of January 1945, when all 514 were snatched from the jaws of death by the brave and daring rangers.*

The American soldiers who returned from the war were affected by it in many different ways. Those who had seen heavy combat or spent years in prison camps, particularly Japanese prison camps, were profoundly affected.†

Private Robert Brown had survived the fighting on Bataan, the Death March, Camp O'Donnell, and the horror of Cabanatuan before being sent to Manchuria on one of the Japanese Death Ships. When he was finally freed in 1945, Brown was both physically and emotionally unstable. He had endured it all: the constant hunger, beatings, murders, deprivation, and humiliation that not even the poorest American citizen had ever known. By his own admission, Brown was not an educated man; like so many other GIs he'd been raised in a small town, in his case one in northern California. When the troopship bringing him home docked in San Francisco there were few people waiting to greet them, and Brown was ordered into the base hospital for observation and quarantine. When he had left home to join the army in 1939 his parents didn't even have a telephone but now, seven years later, he looked in the phone book and, sure enough, their number was listed. He called and asked if they would come and get him and they arrived next day. Brown had not ridden in a car for nearly four years and the experience of driving home on the California expressways with cars whizzing by "petrified" him.

During his leave he rediscovered whiskey and began to drink. At night after his parents saw him off to bed he found he could not sleep on a mat-

---

*For an excellent account of this raid, see Hampton Sides's book *Ghost Soldiers*.

†Statistics collected after the war revealed that the death rate for U.S. prisoners of war in German and Italian POW camps was about 4 percent. In Japanese camps it was closer to 30 percent.

tress and morning would find him curled up on the hard floor in the living room. He became a bundle of nerves and "couldn't talk to anyone." With all the servicemen now returning from Europe and the Pacific, "there were no jobs," Brown remembered. "I was uneducated, for all purposes, I knew I could survive in the prisoner-of-war camp, but what else could I do?" All the previously valued things in his life had become reduced to basics: adequate food, his health, and clothing, especially clothing, for when he was in the POW camp at Mukden, in northern Manchuria, it had been so bitterly cold, and his clothes had been only rags.

Finally Private Brown went back up to San Francisco to get his discharge from the army. When he got into the discharge line he was told to turn in his uniform. "I didn't have any civilian clothing," Brown remembered, "all I had was the uniform that was on my back." When it came his turn, "I saw all these discarded uniforms piled up and having been a prisoner I just automatically thought, 'Well, Jesus Christ, I'd like to have some of those.' So I asked this guy, 'What do you do with all those clothes?' and he said 'You want something?' and I said 'God Yeah!'"

Brown almost frantically began to gather up everything he could, uniform blouses, pants, socks, jackets, when some fool second lieutenant came up. "What are you doing?" the lieutenant demanded, and when Brown told him the officer made him put the clothes back and then began to bawl him out. Brown remembered that he "about fell to pieces." Standing at attention his knees began to shake and he felt tears beginning to come— just some old clothes they were going to throw away anyhow. He took the bawling out as long as he could, then just did a smart about-face and marched across the parade ground to the office of General Albert M. Jones. Jones had been a corps commander under Wainwright on Bataan and in the same Manchurian POW camp as Private Brown.

"I went straight up to General Jones' headquarters. I steamed in and here's an old bald-headed major sitting there. He looked at me like 'What the hell are you?' I said 'I'm Brown and I want to see General Jones.'

"He says, 'What for?' and I said I was in prison camp with him at Mukden and I have to see him."

Jones had overheard the conversation through the door and came out and ushered Brown into his office. As Brown locked himself at attention he was still shaking and red-faced and the general could see he had been crying.

"What's the trouble?" Jones asked. Brown tried to explain about taking the clothes and about the lieutenant "jumping all over me," and the words just tumbled out, along with the tears, until he finally said, "I didn't know what to do, Sir, so I came to see you."

General Jones stood looking at him. He understood; if anyone could ever have truly understood it would be General Jones because he, too, had known being nearly frozen and starved to death in Manchuria with rags for clothes during those long bitter years, and he must have felt his own anger rising.

"Okay," the general said with an even smile, "you go back down there and you take whatever you want, I'll see to it." Then he told Private Brown to sit for a few minutes and they had "a nice chat about our days at Mukden."[7]

Today on Guadalcanal and New Guinea there are rusted relics of the battles: tanks, wrecked parts of planes, trucks, artillery pieces, and other accoutrements of war. In the depths beneath Ironbottom Sound still lie the hulks of the big ships, dozens of them, in a wavy, algae-covered perpetual silence. Not long ago the famed underwater explorer Robert Ballard, who found the wreck of the *Titanic,* took one of his deepwater submersibles to the Solomons and photographed some of these wrecks. One almost wishes he hadn't; they seem so pitiful there on the seafloor, reduced from their dignity as once great fighting ships. At Pearl Harbor a shrine has been made out of the wreck of the battleship *Arizona,* seen by thousands of tourists every year, who can peer down at it from a glass-bottomed observation platform.

Out on the North African deserts there are relics, too, much better preserved in the rarefied desert air, but most of them long since stripped by Arabs for sale as scrap. For more than twenty years the British had been in the process of clearing the hundreds of thousands of land mines from the battles in Libya when, in the 1970s, Libya's new dictator Colonel Muammar Gadhafi seized power and closed the borders.

It is almost a military axiom that wars are generally fought in unpleasant places, and this certainly went for the year 1942: scorching
deserts, pestilent jungles, endless mud fields, freezing mountain terrain,
or the brutal cold landscapes of Russia, and in those days most of the
men who died were buried near to where they'd fallen. Today on both
sides of the oceans remain the military cemeteries with their neat white
"crosses, row on row" that mark the places, cared for in perpetuity by
the Allies' graves commissions.

The great admirals and generals are all gone now, and the youthful
soldiers, sailors, and marines who fought this long-ago war are going fast
themselves. It had taken a full seven years of war to corner Hitler, who
shot himself, and Mussolini, who was finally killed by his own people and
strung up on a meat hook, and Tojo, who swung at the end of an American rope. But the world at last became rid of these misguided creatures
and their cronies and henchmen, and this was accomplished, in some fine
measure, because of the extraordinary sacrifices of those raw, untried, and
wondering men who served and fought, and died, in 1942.

Afterword

Of course the Allied successes were not due alone simply to the men on the fighting fronts. All of America, the Soviet Union, and Great Britain and her commonwealth and colonies pitched in, men, women, and children. Later, other countries joined the fray, but in 1942 it was basically these two great powers that fought the war on the razor's edge against the Axis cabal.* The older men who served as air-raid wardens or in the beach patrols, the women who worked midnight shifts in the armanents factories—the Rosie the Riveters—the "dollar-a-year" businessmen who volunteered to go to Washington or elsewhere and lend their expertise to the war effort, the millions of families who grew victory gardens, the children who donated their metal toys to be melted down or purchased ten- and twenty-five-cent war bond stamps from their allowances—all these people contributed what they could.

The Allied successes at Midway, Guadalcanal, and New Guinea had halted Japanese expansion and, beyond relieving the Japanese threat to

*Many other nations declared war on the Axis before it was all over, but most waited until they could clearly see which way the wind was blowing. Thus, it was not until 1945, the last year of the war, that such countries as Equador, Paraguay, Peru, Chile, Venezuela, Turkey, Uruguay, Egypt, Syria, Lebanon, Saudi Arabia, Finland, and Argentina finally saw their way clear to enter the fight on the side of the Allies. The so-called neutrals—Spain, Sweden, and Switzerland, among others—remained so throughout the whole nightmare.

Australia, Hawaii, and the U.S. lifeline to the Pacific, had the additional effect of confirming to the American public that the Japanese could indeed be defeated, a notion that had remained in question for much of the year. Soon after Guadalcanal had been conquered, the Americans began to move northward, sweeping the emperor's armies and navies from the Pacific Ocean. In the Solomons Americans invaded New Georgia and Bougainville, and were about to launch a great invasion of Rabaul itself, with its tens of thousands of Japanese troops, when somebody sensibly figured out that by building airfields on these two newly conquered islands they could simply bottle up the huge Japanese garrison with U.S. air- and seapower and leave Rabaul to wither on the vine. Thus the navy forces sailed on, with Rabaul behind them, remaining in effect a large POW camp. This new strategy was employed time and again throughout the long march across the Pacific during 1943, '44, and '45, saving countless American lives. It became famously known as General MacArthur's island-hopping strategy, and though he did not think it up himself, MacArthur embraced it whole-heartedly and, typically, took credit for it in the end.

Wise as the strategy was, there was still a long and bloody road ahead, and everybody knew it. Tiny islands that most people had never heard of, such as Tarawa, Peleliu, Iwo Jima, and Saipan became charnal houses for the U.S. Marine Corps, as did big islands such as the Philippines and Okinawa for the U.S. Army. These places also became graveyards for hundreds of thousands of Japanese soldiers who fought it out, as they usually did, to the end. The last remaining Japanese soldier on Guadalcanal was apprehended several years after the war ended when he was caught stealing vegetables from the garden of the Solomon Islands constabulary, but it was not until the 1970s that the few surviving Japanese on other Pacific islands were persuaded to give themselves up. Suggestions have been made that there might even be a remaining Japanese soldier or two still out there in the remotest jungles, wondering to this day if the war was over and, if so, who won?[1]

After the defeat of the Axis in Tunisia, the Allies quickly moved to invade Sicily, which they did successfully, and from which they invaded Italy itself in 1943. When that happened, the Italians just as quickly surrendered almost within the year, and the Axis was contracted even further. For a time it looked as though it might be a smooth ride through

Italy up into Churchill's soft underbelly of Europe, through the Balkans, and on into southern Austria-Germany. But this was not to be. When the Italians caved in, Hitler dispatched a fierce army into northern Italy, which stalled the American push forward through the rough and mountainous terrain, and they were still fighting it out there as the war ended. It took the massive Allied invasion of France at Normandy in 1944 to finally throw the Germans back in the west, and the great Soviet onslaught coming from the east brought down the final curtain on the Nazis.

For the first six months of 1942, as we have seen, the Allies, and America itself, were in real danger. Our Pacific fleet and Pacific air force had been nearly destroyed at Pearl Harbor and in the Philippines, and our Atlantic fleet wasn't much to begin with. Our vital coastwise shipping was being sunk at an alarming rate by German U-boats and Russia was on the verge of collapse, which would have given the Nazis control of one of the world's most vast areas of food, natural resources, and manpower. This would have thwarted any advantage gained by the British naval blockade of German ports and released millions of German soldiers and their tanks and planes to fight against the Allies in North Africa and elsewhere. Likewise, the Japanese dragon's tongue was lapping toward Australia and India. If any of these immense countries fell, who can say how much longer the war might have lasted or, for that matter, how it might have turned out?

Of course it didn't happen that way, for which everyone on earth should yet be eternally thankful; still the various scenarios remain chilling. It is a noteworthy tribute and a testimony to all Americans and to citizens of the British empire that, from beginning to end, most of them contributed and sacrificed in their own ways, great and small, so that the menace finally could be crushed.

Profound social and economic changes swept through America beginning in 1942. Multitudes of people who had never been out of their own states or even counties now traveled hundreds or even thousands of miles to settle into war work. Women from Appalachia found themselves in places like Pittsburgh or Richmond or Indianapolis working on assembly lines; blacks from southern farmlands migrated to New Orleans, Houston, Mobile, Chicago, and Detroit to build warships, tanks, and airplanes. New and complex skills were learned, to be capitalized on later. Millions of soldiers and sailors finally got to the see the world, and so formed a broader, more enlightened world picture for themselves. Many never returned to their home places afterward, thus resulting in a significant shift in the U.S. population.

For years, even until they were aged, they spoke passionately, as my parents' generation did, in terms of "before the war," "during the war," and "after the war," as they began to forge their own brave new world.

Notes ★

Chapter One

1. Donald Kagan, *On the Origins of War,* p. 282.
2. Adolf Hitler, *Mein Kampf,* p. xv.
3. Francis Trevelyan Miller (ed.), *The Complete History of World War II,* p. 51.
4. Hitler, *Mein Kampf,* p. xix.
5. Margaret MacMillan, *Paris 1919,* p. 294.
6. Kagan, *On the Origins of War,* p. 337.
7. Ibid., p. 341.
8. Hitler, *Mein Kampf,* p. 359.
9. Roy Jenkins, *Churchill,* p. 528.

Chapter Two

1. John Costello, *The Pacific War,* p. 14.
2. Shigenori Togo, *The Cause of Japan,* p. 4.
3. Costello, *The Pacifc War,* p. 16.
4. Author conversation with Arthur Stanton, Stanton's nephew.
5. Togo, *The Cause of Japan,* p. 4.
6. Edmund Morris, *Theodore Rex,* p. 396.

7. Fleet Admiral William F. Halsey and Lt. Commander J. Bryan III, *Admiral Halsey's Story,* p. 12.

8. Togo, *The Cause of Japan,* p. 16.

9. John Toland, *The Rising Sun,* p. 63.

10. Togo, *The Cause of Japan,* p. 17.

11. Lionel Wigmore, *The Japanese Thrust,* p. 3.

12. Haruko Taya Cook and Theodore F. Cook, *Japan at War,* pp. 155–56.

13. Craig Nelson, *The First Heroes,* p. 73.

Chapter Three

1. H. Montgomery Hyde, *Room 3603,* p. 148.

2. John Toland, *The Rising Sun,* p. 53.

3. Robert E. Sherwood, *Roosevelt and Hopkins,* p. 123.

4. Cabell Phillips, *The 1940s: Decade of Triumph and Trouble,* p. 163.

5. General Leslie M. Groves, *Now It Can Be Told,* p. 33.

6. Louis Morton, *The War in the Pacific,* p. 56.

7. Geoffrey Perrett, *Days of Sadness, Years of Triumph,* p. 61.

8. Sherwood, *Roosevelt and Hopkins,* p. 167.

9. Ibid., p. 166.

10. Hyde, *Room 3603,* p. 125.

11. David Kahn, *The Code Breakders,* p. 486.

12. Ibid., p. 487.

13. David Lowman, *Magic,* pp. 123–51.

14. Kahn, *The Code Breakers,* p. 29.

15. Ibid., p. 23.

16. Ibid., passim; Lowman, *Magic,* passim; Ronald Clark, *The Man Who Broke Purple,* passim.

17. Colonel Carlos P. Romulo, *I Saw the Fall of the Philippines,* pp. 3–24.

18. John Costello, *The Pacific War,* p. 81.

19. Samuel Eliot Morison, *The Rising Sun in the Pacific,* p. 46.

20. Toland, *The Rising Sun,* p. 172.

21. Gordon Prange, *At Dawn We Slept,* p. 21.

22. Ibid., p. 278.

23. Toland, *The Rising Sun,* pp. 24–26.

24. Francis Trevelyan Miller (ed.), *The Complete History of World War II*, p. 314.

Chapter Four

1. Richard R. Lingeman, *Don't You Know There's a War On?*, p. 18.
2. Cabell Phillips, *The 1940s: Decade of Triumph and Trouble*, p. 104.
3. Ibid., pp. 3–15; Lingeman, *Don't You Know There's a War On?*, pp. 13–24.
4. John Toland, *The Rising Sun*, p. 66.
5. Ogden Nash, *The Face Is Familiar*, pp. 233–34; Robert J. C. Butow, *Tojo and the Coming of the War*, p. 41.
6. Gordon Prange, *At Dawn We Slept*, p. 22.
7. Samuel Eliot Morison, *The Rising Sun in the Pacific*, p. 85; Toland, *The Rising Sun*, p. 180.
8. Prange, *At Dawn We Slept*, p. 27.
9. Robert B. Stinnett, *Days of Deceit*, pp. 84–97.
10. Prange, *At Dawn We Slept*, pp. 73–75; 254–55; Toland, *The Rising Sun*, pp. 174–77; 190–93.
11. David Kahn, *The Code Breakers*, pp. 7–8.
12. Prange, *At Dawn We Slept*, p. 440.
13. Toland, *The Rising Sun*, pp. 153–55.
14. Ibid., pp. 220–24.
15. Robert E. Sherwood, *Roosevelt and Hopkins*, p. 427.
16. Butow, *Tojo and the Coming of the War*, p. 374.
17. Prange, *At Dawn We Slept*, p. 494.

Chapter Five

1. Gordon Prange, *At Dawn We Slept*, p. 487; Mitsuo Fuchida and Masatake Okumiya, *Midway*, p. 49; Walter Lord, *Day of Infamy*, pp. 19–20.
2. Lord, *Day of Infamy*, p. 37.
3. Ibid., p. 59.
4. Prange, *At Dawn We Slept*, p. 500.
5. Samuel Eliot Morison, *The Two-Ocean War*, p. 63.
6. Lord, *Day of Infamy*, p. 67.
7. Prange, *At Dawn We Slept*, p. 507.

8. Lord, *Day of Infamy*, p. 73.
9. Ibid., p. 93.
10. Prange, *At Dawn We Slept*, p. 516.
11. Ibid., p. 515.
12. Ibid., p. 526.
13. Lord, *Day of Infamy*, p. 165.
14. John Toland, *The Rising Sun*, p. 209.
15. Robert E. Sherwood, *Roosevelt and Hopkins*, p. 431.
16. Toland, *The Rising Sun*, p. 257.
17. Ibid., p. 262.
18. Fuchida and Okumiya, *Midway*, pp. 56–60.

Chapter Six

1. Roy Hoopes, *Americans Remember the Home Front*, pp. 18–28.
2. *Reporting World War II*, pp. 94–98.
3. Walter Lord, *Day of Infamy*, p. 183.
4. Roberta Wohlstetter, *Pearl Harbor*, p. 130.
5. Ibid., p. 369.
6. Ibid., p. 13.
7. Gordon Prange, *At Dawn We Slept*, p. 96.
8. Wohlstetter, *Pearl Harbor*, p. 258.
9. Robert Leckie, *Helmet for My Pillow*, p. 2.
10. Samuel Eliot Morison, *The Rising Sun in the Pacific*, p. 256.

Chapter Seven

1. J. C. Beaglehole, *The Exploration of the Pacific*, p. 54.
2. Samuel Eliot Morison, *The Rising Sun in the Pacific*, pp. 224–25.
3. Brigadier General James P. S. Devereux, *The Story of Wake Island*, pp. 1–17.
4. Ibid., p. 12.
5. Morison, *The Rising Sun in the Pacific*, p. 230.
6. Devereux, *The Story of Wake Island*, p. 34.
7. Ibid., p. 51.
8. Ibid., pp. 53–79; Morison, *The Rising Sun in the Pacific*, pp. 231–35.
9. Devereux, *The Story of Wake Island*, p. 116.

10. Morison, *The Rising Sun in the Pacific,* pp. 151–52.

11. Devereux, *The Story of Wake Island,* pp. 130–32.

Chapter Eight

1. John Toland, *The Rising Sun,* pp. 188–89; 263–64.

2. Samuel Eliot Morison, *The Rising Sun in the Pacific,* p. 157.

3. Toland, *The Rising Sun,* p. 266.

4. Lionel Wigmore, *The Japanese Thrust,* p. 144.

5. *Reporting World War II,* pp. 109–14.

6. Wigmore, *The Japanese Thrust,* p. 144.

7. Toland, *The Rising Sun,* p. 277; John Costello, *The Pacific War,* p. 159.

8. Winston Churchill, *The Second World War,* p. 522.

9. Douglas L. Oliver, *The Pacific Islands,* p. 335; Costello, *The Pacific War,* p. 143.

10. Basil Collier, *The War in the Far East,* pp. 148–55; John Toland, *But Not in Shame,* pp. 130–32.

11. Roy Jenkins, *Churchill,* pp. 668–70.

12. Ibid., p. 678.

13. Costello, *The Pacific War,* p. 129.

14. Ibid., pp. 192, 198.

15. Jenkins, *Churchill,* p. 677.

16. Toland, *The Rising Sun,* p. 133.

17. Costello, *The Pacific War,* p. 201.

Chapter Nine

1. William Manchester, *American Caesar,* p. 229.

2. Ibid., p. 236.

3. General Jonathan M. Wainwright, *General Wainwright's Story,* pp. 19–20.

4. Lewis H. Brereton, *The Brereton Diaries,* pp. 38–47; Louis Morton, *The Fall of the Philippines,* p. 86.

5. Brereton, *The Brereton Diaries,* p. 50.

6. Samuel Eliot Morison, *The Rising Sun in the Pacific,* p. 171; Brereton, *The Brereton Diaries,* p. 55.

7. Brereton, *The Brereton Diaries,* p. 55.

8. Morton, *The Fall of the Philippines,* p. 64.

9.   Colonel Carlos P. Romulo, *I Saw the Fall of the Philippines*, p. 81.

10. Ibid., pp. 78–79.

11. Morton, *The Fall of the Philippines*, p. 116; Manchester, *American Caesar*, p. 240.

12. Wainwright, *General Wainwright's Story*, pp. 29–30.

13. Major General Courtney Whitney, *MacArthur*, p. 21.

14. Colonel E. B. Miller, *Bataan Uncensored*, pp. 73–74.

15. Manchester, *American Caesar*, pp. 239–43.

16. Whitney, *MacArthur*, p. 19; Manchester, *American Caesar*, p. 244.

17. James H. Belote and William M. Belote, *Corregidor*, p. 50.

18. Manchester, *American Caesar*, p. 245.

19. Wainwright, *General Wainwright's Story*, pp. 37–40.

20. Belote and Belote, *Corregidor*, p. 53.

21. Morton, *The Fall of the Philippines*, p. 234; John Toland, *But Not in Shame*, p. 137–39.

22. Morton, *The Fall of the Philippines*, pp. 245–47.

23. Ibid., p. 268.

24. Wainwright, *General Wainwright's Story*, p. 43; Morton, *The Fall of the Philippines*, pp. 268–69.

25. Morton, *The Fall of the Philippines*, p. 270.

26. Wainwright, *General Wainwright's Story*, p. 45; Morton, *The Fall of the Philippines*, p. 258.

27. Brigadier General Steve Mellnik, *Philippine Diary*, p. 97.

28. Morton, *The Fall of the Philippines*, pp. 394–97.

29. Romulo, *I Saw the Fall of the Philippines*, pp. 118–27.

30. Ibid., p. 129; Wainwright, *General Wainwright's Story*, pp. 48–49.

31. Wainwright, *General Wainwright's Story*, p. 48.

32. Toland, *The Rising Sun*, pp. 336–37.

33. Whitney, *MacArthur*, p. 51.

34. Wainwright, *General Wainwright's Story*, p. 5–6.

35. Nigel Fountain (ed.), *World War II: The People's Story*, pp. 132–33.

Chapter Ten

1.   David Lowman, *Magic*, p. 19.

2.   *Reporting World War II*, p. 146.

3. Ibid., p. 148.

4. Rick Atkinson, *An Army at Dawn*, p. 39.

5. Richard R. Lingeman, *Don't You Know There's A War On?*, p. 340.

6. *Reporting World War II*, p. 216.

7. John Hammond Moore, *Wacko War*, pp. 117–126; 149–61.

8. Duane Schultz, *The Doolittle Raid*, p. 18.

9. General James H. "Jimmy" Doolittle, *I Could Never Be So Lucky Again*, passim.

10. Ibid., p. 245.

11. Ibid., p. 249.

12. Ibid., p. 232.

Chapter Eleven

1. Samuel Eliot Morison, *The Rising Sun in the Pacific*, pp. 368–70.

2. Brigadier General Steve Mellnik, *Philippine Diary*, p. 99.

3. Louis Morton, *The Fall of the Philippines*, p. 455.

4. Mellnik, *Philippine Diary*, p. 101.

5. Ibid., p. 103.

6. General Jonathan M. Wainwright, *General Wainwright's Story*, p. 68.

7. R. W. Robson, *The Pacific Island Handbook*, p. 107.

8. Donald Knox, *Death March*, p. 119.

9. Ibid., p. 120.

10. Abie Abraham, *Oh God, Where Are You?*, p. 49.

11. Henry G. Lee, *Nothing But Praise*, p. 36.

12. Donald Knox, *Death March*, p. 121.

13. Wainwright, *General Wainwright's Story*, p. 81; Knox, *Death March*, p. 139.

14. Colonel E. B. Miller, *Bataan Uncensored*, p. 239; Knox, *Death March*, p. 151.

15. Knox, *Death March*, p. 158.

16. Ibid., p. 157.

17. Ibid., p. 159.

18. Alfred A. Weinstein, *Barbed-Wire Surgeon*, p. 72.

19. Ibid., p. 74.

20. John Toland, *The Rising Sun*, p. 337.

21. Lee, *Nothing But Praise,* p. 46.

22. General James H. "Jimmy" Doolittle, *I Could Never Be So Lucky Again,* pp. 273–74.

23. Craig Nelson, *The First Heroes,* pp. 120–21.

24. Doolittle, *I Could Never Be So Lucky Again,* p. 4; Nelson, *The First Heroes,* p. 130.

25. Captain Ted W. Lawson, *Thirty Seconds Over Tokyo,* p. 55.

26. Duane Schultz, *The Doolittle Raid* p. 186.

27. Joseph C. Grew, *Ten Years in Japan,* p. 527.

28. Schultz, *The Doolittle Raid,* p. 191.

29. Nelson, *The First Heroes,* pp. 69–70.

30. Lawson, *Thirty Seconds Over Tokyo,* pp. 74–79.

31. Doolittle, *I Could Never Be So Lucky Again,* pp. 10–11.

32. Schultz, *The Doolittle Raid,* pp. 311–12; Nelson, *The First Heroes,* p. 297.

33. Schultz, *The Doolittle Raid,* pp. 317–18.

34. Ibid., pp. 282–85.

35. Doolittle, *I Could Never Be So Lucky Again,* pp. 286–87.

Chapter Twelve

1. Francis Trevelyan Miller (ed.), *The Complete History of World War II,* pp. 372–73.

2. Samuel Eliot Morison, *Coral Sea, Midway, and Submarine Actions,* p. 7.

3. Ibid., pp. 32–40.

4. John Costello, *The Pacific War,* p. 258.

5. Edwin P. Hoyte, *The Battle of the Coral Sea,* p. 150.

6. Morison, *Coral Sea, Midway, and Submarine Actions,* p. 57.

7. Louis Morton, *The Fall of the Philippines,* p. 495.

8. General Jonathan M. Wainwright, *General Wainwright's Story,* p. 78.

9. Morton, *The Fall of the Philippines,* p. 546.

10. Ibid., pp. 547–50.

11. James H. Belote and William M. Belote, *Corregidor,* pp. 169–71.

12. Ibid., pp. 107–9.

Chapter Thirteen

1. David Kahn, *The Code Breakers,* p. 570.

2. Thaddeus Tulega, *Climax at Midway,* pp. 62–64.

3. Mitsuo Fuchida and Masatake Okumiya, *Midway*, pp. 147–48.

4. John Toland, *But Not in Shame*, p. 416.

5. Ibid., p. 406.

6. Fuchida and Okumiya, *Midway*, pp. 183–84.

7. Toland, *But Not in Shame*, p. 410.

8. Samuel Eliot Morison, *Coral Sea, Midway, and Submarine Actions*, p. 110.

9. Tuleja, *Climax at Midway*, p. 105.

10. Fuchida and Okumiya, *Midway*, p. 196.

11. Tuleja, *Climax at Midway*, p. 124.

12. Fuchida and Okumiya, *Midway*, p. 208.

13. Ibid., pp. 208–9.

14. Nigel Fountain (ed.), *World War II: The People's Story*, p. 158.

15. Fuchida and Okumiya, *Midway*, pp. 211–12.

16. Morison, *Coral Sea, Midway, and Submarine Actions*, p. 125.

17. Ibid., p. 128; Toland, *But Not in Shame*, p. 422.

18. Fuchida and Okumiya, *Midway*, p. 215.

19. Fountain, *World War II: The People's Story*, p. 160.

20. Morison, *Coral Sea, Midway, and Submarine Actions*, p. 136.

21. Fuchida and Okymiya, *Midway*, pp. 233–34.

22. Tuleja, *Climax at Midway*, p. 175.

23. John Toland, *The Rising Sun*, p. 386.

24. Robert E. Sherwood, *Roosevelt and Hopkins*, p. 579.

25. Toland, *The Rising Sun*, pp. 392–581.

Chapter Fourteen

1. David Kahn, *The Code Breakers*. p. 488; H. Montgomery Hyde, *Room 3603*, pp. 115–20.

2. Quentin Reynolds, *Officially Dead*, passim.

3. Geoffrey Perrett, *Days of Sadness, Years of Triumph*, p. 195.

4. Richard R. Lingeman, *Don't You Know There's War On?*, p. 185.

5. R. W. Robson, *The Pacific Island Handbook*, pp. 280–85; Samuel Eliot Morison, *The Struggle for Guadalcanal*, pp. 5–10; J. C. Beaglehole, *The Exploration of the Pacific*, pp. 48–49.

6. John Toland, *The Rising Sun*, p. 398.

7. Ibid., p. 395.

8. Samuel B. Griffith II, *The Battle for Guadalcanal*, p. 24.

9. General A. A. Vandegrift, *Once a Marine*, p. 117.

10. Griffith, *The Battle for Guadalcanal*, p. 35.

11. Vandegrift, *Once a Marine*, p. 120; Griffith, *The Battle for Guadalcanal*, p. 36.

12. Toland, *The Rising Sun*, p. 397.

13. Richard Tregaskis, *Guadalcanal Diary*, pp. 13–30.

14. Ibid., p. 33.

15. Jack Coggins, *The Campaign for Guadalcanal*, p. 38; Toland, *The Rising Sun*, pp. 402.

16. Coggins, *The Campaign for Guadalcanal*, p. 42.

17. Morison, *The Struggle for Guadalcanal*, pp. 43–44.

18. Ibid., pp. 44–45; Coggins, *The Campaign for Guadalcanal*, pp. 48–49.

19. Coggins, *The Campaign for Guadalcanal*, p. 51.

20. Griffith, *The Battle for Guadalcanal*, p. 63.

21. Ibid., p. 47.

Chapter Fifteen

1. Richard Tregaskis, *Guadalcanal Diary*, pp. 85–86.

2. Walter Lord, Walter. *Lonely Vigil*, pp. 44–46.

3. General A. A. Vandegrift, *Once a Marine*, p. 136.

4. Samuel B. Griffith II, *The Battle for Guadalcanal*, p. 20.

5. Lord, *Lonely Vigil*, pp. 49–51.

6. Tregaskis, *Guadalcanal Diary*, p. 124.

7. Vandegrift, *Once a Marine*, p. 142.

8. Robert Leckie, *Helmet for My Pillow*, pp. 51, 53.

9. Ibid., p. 60.

10. Ibid., p. 59.

11. Ibid., pp. 60–61.

12. Vandegrift, *Once a Marine*, p. 138.

13. William Bradford Huie, *Can Do*, pp. 41–42.

14. Samuel Eliot Morison, *Coral Sea, Midway, and Submarine Actions*, pp. 235–41.

15. John Vader, *New Guinea*, p. 114.

16. Ibid., pp. 113–14.

17. Ibid., p. 109.
18. Max Brand, *Fighter Squadron at Guadalcanal,* p. 64.
19. Ibid., p. 92.
20. Mine Okubo, *Citizen 13660,* pp. 271–73.
21. Robert E. Sherwood, *Roosevelt and Hopkins,* p. 547.
22. Ibid., pp. 530–31.
23. Ibid., p. 563.
24. John Toland, *The Rising Sun,* p. 428.
25. Vandegrift, *Once a Marine,* p. 152.
26. Griffith, *The Battle for Guadalcanal,* pp. 116–17.
27. Ibid., p. 119.
28. Ibid., p. 118.
29. Toland, *The Rising Sun,* p. 434.
30. Nigel Fountain (ed.), *World War II: The People's Story,* pp. 168–69.
31. Griffith, *The Battle for Guadalcanal,* p. 132.
32. Herbert C. Merillat, *Guadalcanal Remembered,* p. 133.
33. Vandegrift, *Once a Marine,* p. 163.

Chapter Sixteen

1. Douglas Oliver, *The Pacific Islands,* pp. 235–44.
2. John Costello, *The Pacific War,* p. 376.
3. Samuel Milner, *Victory in Papua,* p. 143.
4. Costello, *The Pacific War,* p. 378.
5. Milner, *Victory in Papua,* pp. 116, 126.
6. Robert L. Eichelberger, *Our Jungle Road to Tokyo,* p. 20.
7. General A. A. Vandegrift, *Once a Marine,* p. 169.
8. Frank O. Hough, *The Island War,* p. 64.
9. John Hersey, *Into the Valley,* pp. 78–79.

Chapter Seventeen

1. John Toland, *The Rising Sun,* pp. 440–41.
2. Frank O. Hough, *The Island War,* p. 65.
3. General A. A. Vandegrift, *Once a Marine,* p. 174.
4. Hough, *The Island War,* p. 66.
5. Vandegrift, *Once a Marine,* p. 107.

6. Robert E. Sherwood, *Roosevelt and Hopkins,* pp. 622, 632.

7. Vandegrift, *Once a Marine,* p. 187.

8. Samuel Eliot Morison, *The Struggle for Guadalcanal,* p. 236.

9. Ibid., pp. 262–63.

10. Jack Coggins, *The Campaign for Guadalcanal,* p. 148.

11. Robert Leckie, *Helmet for My Pillow,* pp. 98–99.

12. Samuel B. Griffith II, *The Battle for Guadalcanal,* p. 243.

13. Coggins, *The Campaign for Guadalcanal,* p. 190.

Chapter Eighteen

1. Robert L. Eichelberger, *Our Jungle Road to Tokyo,* p. 37.

2. John Costello, *The Pacific War,* p. 379.

3. Samuel Milner, *Victory in Papua,* p. 244.

4. Ibid., p. 217.

5. Eichelberger, *Our Jungle Road to Tokyo,* pp. 29–31.

6. Costello, *The Pacific War,* p. 381.

7. E. B. Potter and Fleet Admiral Chester W. Nimitz (eds.), *The Great Sea War,* p. 44.

8. Samuel Eliot Morison, *Operations in North African Waters,* pp. 113–14.

9. Potter and Nimitz, *The Great Sea War,* p. 118.

10. Ibid., p. 122.

11. Rick Atkinson, *An Army at Dawn,* p. 65.

12. Ibid., p. 123.

13. Annette Tapert (ed.), *Lines of Battle,* p. 40.

Chapter Nineteen

1. Billy Keith, *Days of Anguish, Days of Hope,* p. 110.

2. Ralph Emerson Hibbs, M.D., *Tell MacArthur to Wait,* p. 147.

3. Keith, *Days of Anguish, Days of Hope,* p. 101.

4. Henry G. Lee, *Nothing But Praise,* p. 67.

5. Claire Phillips and Myron B. Goldsmith, *Manila Espionage,* pp. 1–226.

6. Major Calvin Ellsworth Chunn, *Of Rice and Men,* pp. 71–73.

7. Ed "Tommie" Thomas, *As I Remember,* p. 221.

8. Colonel E. B. Miller, *Bataan Uncensored,* pp. 364–65.

9. Ronald H. Spector, *Eagle Against the Sun,* p. 337.

Chapter Twenty

1. B. H. Liddell-Hart (ed.), *The Rommel Papers,* pp. 281–82
2. Ibid., p. 317.
3. Ibid., p. 321.
4. Rick Atkinson, *An Army at Dawn,* p. 277.
5. Brigadier General Paul McDonald Robinett, *Armor Command,* p. 66.
6. Atkinson, *An Army at Dawn,* p. 240.
7. Robinett, *Armor Command,* p. 74.
8. Ibid., p. 87.
9. Ibid., p. 95.
10. Ernie Pyle, *Here Is Your War,* p. 170.
11. Gerald F. Linderman, *The World Within War,* p. 97.
12. Carlo D'este, *Patton: A Genius for War,* p. 457.
13. Robinett, *Armor Command,* p. 113.
14. Robert E. Sherwood, *Roosevelt and Hopkins,* p. 669.
15. Ibid., p. 673; Atkinson, *An Army at Dawn,* p. 290.
16. Sherwood, *Roosevelt and Hopkins,* p. 674.
17. Roy Jenkins, *Churchill,* pp. 705–6; Atkinson, *An Army at Dawn,* p. 296; Sherwood, *Roosevelt and Hopkins,* p. 694.
18. Sherwood, *Roosevelt and Hopkins,* p. 696.
19. Ibid., p. 695.

Chapter Twenty-one

1. Ernie Pyle, *Here Is Your War,* pp. 241–42.
2. Robert J. C. Butow, *Tojo and the Coming of the War,* p. 536.
3. Charles A. Lockwood, *Sink 'Em All,* pp. 98–102.
4. General James H. "Jimmy" Doolittle, *I Could Never Be So Lucky Again,* p. 363; Craig Nelson, *The First Heroes,* p. 363.
5. Herbert C. Merillat, *Guadalcanal Remembered,* pp. 283–84.
6. Samuel B. Griffith II, *The Battle for Guadalcanal,* p. 246.
7. Donald Knox, *Death March,* pp. 462–63.

Afterword

1. Herbert C. Merillat, *Guadalcanal Remembered,* p. 285.

Bibliography ★

Abraham, Abie. *Oh God, Where Are You?* New York, 1997.

Adler, Selig. *The Isolationist Impulse, Its Twentieth Century Reaction.* New York, 1957.

Atkinson, Rick. *An Army at Dawn: The War in N. Africa 1942–43.* New York, 2002.

Baldwin, Hanson W. *Battles Lost and Won: Great Campaigns of World War II.* New York, 1966.

———. *Great Mistakes of the War.* New York, 1949.

Ballard, Robert D., with Rich Archbold. *The Lost Ships of Guadalcanal.* New York, 1993.

———, with Michael Hamilton Morgan. *Graveyards of the Pacific.* Washington, D.C., 2001.

Beach, Edward L. *Scapegoats: A Defense of Kimmel and Short at Pearl Harbor.* Annapolis, 1995.

Beaglehole, J. C. *The Exploration of the Pacific.* Stanford, California, 1934.

Belote, James H., and William M. Belote. *Corregidor.* New York, 1967.

Blair, Clay. *Hitler's U-Boat War: The Hunted, 1942–1945.* New York, 1998.

Bradley, James. *Flyboys: A True Story of Courage.* Boston, 2003.

Brand, Max. *Fighter Squadron at Guadalcanal.* Annapolis, 1996.

Brereton, Lewis H. (Lt. Gen., USA). *The Brereton Diaries: The War in the Air in the Pacific, Middle East and Europe 30 October 1941–8 May 1945.* New York, 1946.

Butow, Robert J. C. *Tojo and the Coming of the War*. Stanford, California, 1961.

Carmichael, Thomas N. *The Ninety Days*. New York, 1971.

Chunn, Major Calvin Ellsworth. *Of Rice and Men: The Story of Americans Under the Rising Sun*. Los Angeles, 1946.

Churchill, Winston S. *The Grand Alliance*. Boston, 1950.

————. *The Hinge of Fate*. Boston, 1950.

————. *The Second World War*. Vol. II. Boston, 1948–53.

————. *The World Crisis*. New York, 1923.

Clark, Ronald. *The Man Who Broke Purple*. Boston, 1977.

Clayton, Tim, and Phil Craig. *The End of the Beginning: From the Siege of Malta to the Allied Victory at El Alamein*. New York, 2002.

Coggins, Jack. *The Campaign for Guadalcanal: A Battle that Made History*. New York, 1972.

Collier, Basil. *The War in the Far East 1941–1945: A Military History*. New York, 1969.

Cook, Haruko Taya, and Theodore F. Cook. *Japan at War: An Oral History*. New York, 1982.

Costello, John. *The Pacific War, 1941–1945*. New York, 1981.

Cronin, Captain Francis D. *Under the Southern Cross: The Saga of the Americal Division*. Washington, D.C., 1951.

D'este, Carlo. *Patton: A Genius for War*. New York, 1995.

Devereux, Brigadier General James P. S. *The Story of Wake Island*. New York, 1949.

Doolittle, General James H. "Jimmy," with Carroll V. Glines. *I Could Never Be So Lucky Again*. Atglen, Pennsylvania, 1991.

Drea, Edward J. *MacArthur's Ultra Codebreaking and the War Against Japan 1942–1945*. Lawrence, Kansas, 1992.

Dyess, Lieutenant Colonel William E. *Bataan Death March: A Survivor's Account*. Lincoln, Nebraska, 1944.

Eichelberger, Robert L. *Our Jungle Road to Tokyo*. New York, 1950.

Esposito, Brigadier General Vincent J. (ed.). *The West Point Atlas of American Wars* (vol. II). New York, 1959.

Farago, Ladislas. *The Game of the Foxes*. New York, 1971.

Fountain, Nigel (ed.). *World War II: The People's Story*. Pleasantville, New York, 2003.

Freeman, Roger A. *B-17: Fortress at War.* New York, 1977.

Frelinghuysen, Joseph S. *Passages to Freedom: A Story of Capture and Escape.* Manhattan, Kansas, 1990.

Friend, Theodore. *Between Two Empires: The Ordeal of the Philippines 1929–1946.* New Haven, Connecticut, 1965.

Fuchida, Mitsuo, and Masatake Okumiya. *Midway: The Battle that Doomed Japan: The Japanese Navy's Story.* Annapolis, 1955.

Fussell, Paul. *Wartime: Understanding and Behavior in the Second World War.* New York, 1989.

Gluck, Sherna Berger. *Rosie, The Riveter Revisited,: Women, the War, and Social Changes.* New York, 1987.

Grew, Joseph C. *Ten Years in Japan.* New York, 1944.

Griffith, Samuel B., II. *The Battle for Guadalcanal.* Philadelphia,1963.

Groves, General Leslie M. *Now It Can Be Told: The Story of the Manhatton Project.* New York, 1962.

Halsey, Fleet Admiral William F., and Lieutenant Commander J. Bryan III. *Admiral Halsey's Story.* New York, 1947.

Heinl, Robert Debs, Jr. *Dictionary of Military and Naval Operations.* Annapolis, 1966.

Hersey, John. *Into the Valley: Marines at Guadalcanal.* Lincoln, Nebraska, 1943.

Hibbs, Ralph Emerson, M. D. *Tell MacArthur to Wait.* Carsborg, Washington, 1988.

Higham, Charles. *Trading with the Enemy: An Expose of the Nazi-American Money Plot 1933–1949.* New York, 1983.

Hitler, Adolf. *Mein Kampf.* Germany, 1925.

Hoopes, Roy. *Americans Remember the Home Front: An Oral Narrative of the World War II Years in America.* New York, 1977.

Hough, Frank O. *The Island War: The United States Marine Corps in the Pacific.* Philadelphia, 1947.

Hoyte, Edwin P. *The Battle of the Coral Sea.* New York, 1975.

Huie, William Bradford. *Can Do: The Story of the Seabees.* New York, 1944.

Hyde, H. Montgomery. *Room 3603: The Incredible True Story of Secret Intelligence Operations during World War II.* New York, 1962.

Ind, Allison. *Bataan: The Judgment Seat.* New York, 1944.

Jablonski, Edward. *Air War.* New York, 1971.

Jenkins, Roy. *Churchill: A Biography*. New York, 2001.

Kagan, Donald. *On the Origins of War*. New York, 1995.

Kahn, David. *The Code Breakers: The Story of Secret Writing*. New York, 1967.

Kato, Masuo. *The Lost War*. New York, 1946.

Keith, Billy. *Days of Anguish, Days of Hope*. New York, 1972.

Kennan, George F. *Memoirs, 1925–1950*. Boston, 1967.

Knox, Donald. *Death March: The Survivors of Bataan*. New York, 1981.

Lawson, Captain Ted W. (ed. Robert Considine). *Thirty Seconds Over Tokyo*. New York, 1943.

Leckie, Robert. *Helmet for My Pillow*. New York, 1957.

Lee, Henry G. *Nothing But Praise*. Culver City, California, 1948.

Liddell-Hart, B. H. (ed.) *The Rommel Papers*. New York, 1953.

Linderman, Gerald F. *The World Within War*. New York, 1997.

Lingeman, Richard R. *Don't You Know There's a War On? The American Home Front 1941–1945*. New York, 1970.

Lockwood, Charles A. *Sink 'Em All*. New York, 1951.

Lord, Walter. *Day of Infamy*. New York, 1957.

———. *Lonely Vigil: Coast Watchers of the Solomons*. New York, 1977.

Lowman, David. *Magic: The Untold Story of U.S. Intelligence and the Evacuation of Japanese Residents from the West Coast during WWII*. Stanford, California, 2000.

MacMillan, Margaret. *Paris 1919: Six Months that Changed the World*. New York, 2001.

Manchester, William. *American Caesar: Douglas MacArthur 1880–1964*. New York, 1978.

———. *The Last Lion: Winston Spencer Churchill: Visions of Glory 1874–1932*. New York, 1983.

Martin, Ralph G. *The GI War 1941–1945*. Boston, 1967.

McCartney, William F. *The Jungleers: A History of the 41st Infantry Division*. Washington, D.C., 1948.

McManus, John C. *The Deadly Brotherhood: The American Combat Soldier in World War II*. Novato, California, 1998.

McMillan, George. *The Old Breed: A History of the First Marine Division in World War II*. Washington, D.C., 1949.

Mellnik, Brigadier General Steve. *Philippine Diary 1939–1945*. New York, 1969.

Merillat, Herbert C. *Guadalcanal Remembered*. New York, 1982.

Miller, David. *Battle Winning*. London, 2000.

Miller, Colonel E. B. *Bataan Uncensored*. Long Prairie, Minnesota, 1949.

Miller, Francis Trevelyan (ed.). *The Complete History of World War II*. Chicago, 1945.

Miller, John Jr. *Guadalcanal: The First Offensive*. New York, 1949.

Milner, Samuel. *Victory in Papua*. Washington, D.C., 1989.

Moore, John Hammond. *Wacko War: Strange Tales from America 1941–1945*. Raleigh, North Carolina, 2001.

Morison, Samuel Eliot. *The Battle of the Atlantic, 1939–1943, Vol. I*. Boston, 1947.

———. *Coral Sea, Midway, and Submarine Actions, May 1942–August 1942, Vol. IV*. Boston, 1949.

———. *Operations in North African Waters, October 1942–June 1943, Vol. II*. Boston, 1947.

———. *The Rising Sun in the Pacific, April 1931–April 1942, Vol. III*. Boston, 1948.

———. *The Struggle for Guadalcanal, August 1942–February 1943, Vol. V*. Boston, 1949.

———. *The Two-Ocean War: A Short History of the United States Navy in the Second World War*. Boston, 1963.

Morris, Edmund. *Theodore Rex*. New York, 2001.

Morton, Louis. *U.S. Army in World War II: The War in the Pacific: The Fall of the Philippines*. Washington, D.C., 1953.

———. *U.S. Army in World War II. The War in the Pacific: Strategy and Command: The First Two Years*. Washington, D.C., 1962.

Nash, Ogden. *The Face Is Familiar*. New York, 1940.

Nelson, Craig. *The First Heroes*. New York, 2002.

New Yorker Book of War Pieces. New York, 1947.

Nicolson, Harold. *Peacemaking 1919*. London, 1933.

———. *The War Years: Diaries and Letters 1939–1945*. New York, 1967.

Okubo, Mine. *Citizen 13660*. New York, 1946.

Oliver, Douglas L. *The Pacific Islands*. Cambridge, Massachusetts, 1951.

Olson, John E. *O'Donnell: Andersonville of the Pacific*. Typed manuscript, 1985.

Perrett, Geoffrey. *Days of Sadness, Years of Triumph: The American People 1939–1945*. New York, 1973.

Phillips, Cabell. *The 1940s: Decade of Triumph and Trouble*. New York, 1975.

Phillips, Claire, and Myron B. Goldsmith. *Manila Espionage*. Portland, Oregon, 1947.

Potter, E. B., and Fleet Admiral Chester W. Nimitz (eds.). *The Great Sea War*. Englewood Cliffs, New Jersey, 1960.

Prange, Gordon W. *At Dawn We Slept: The Untold Story of Pearl Harbor*. New York, 1982.

————, with Donald M. Goldstein and Katherine V. Dillon. *Pearl Harbor: The Verdict of History*. New York, 1986.

Pyle, Ernie. *Here Is Your War*. New York, 1943.

Reel, A. Frank. *The Case of General Yamashita*. Chicago, 1949.

Reporting World War II: American Journalism 1938–1946. New York, 1995.

Reynolds, Clark G. *America at War 1941–1945: The Home Front*. New York, 1990.

Reynolds, Quentin. *The Curtain Rises*. New York, 1944.

————. *Officially Dead*. New York, 1945.

Rhodes, Richard. *Dark Sun: The Making of the Hydrogen Bomb*. New York, 1995.

Robinett, Brigadier General Paul McDonald. *Armor Command*. Washington, D.C., 1958.

Robson, R. W. *The Pacific Island Handbook 1944*. New York, 1945.

Romulo, Colonel Carlos P. *I Saw the Fall of the Philippines*. New York, 1942.

Schultz, Duane. *The Doolittle Raid: America's First Strike Against the Heart of Imperial Japan*. New York, 1988.

Sherwood, Robert E. *Roosevelt and Hopkins: An Intimate History*. New York, 1948.

Sides, Hampton. *Ghost Soldiers: The Forgotten Epic Story of World War II's Most Dramatic Mission*. New York, 2001.

Smith, Michael S. *Bloody Ridge: The Battle that Saved Guadalcanal*. New York, 2000.

Spector, Ronald H. *Eagle Against the Sun: The American War with Japan*. New York, 1985.

Stamps, T. Dodson, and Vincent J. Esposito. *A Military History of World War II. Vol. II: Operations in the Mediterranean and Pacific Theaters*. U.S. Military Academy at West Point, New York, 1953.

Stinnett, Robert B. *Day of Deceit: The Truth About FDR and Pearl Harbor*. New York, 2000.

Swinson, Arthur. *Four Samurai: A Quartet of Japanese Army Commanders in the Second World War*. London, 1968.

Tapert, Annette (ed.). *Lines of Battle: Letters from American Servicemen 1941–1945.* New York, 1987.

Terkel, Studs. *The Good War: An Oral History of World War Two.* New York, 1984.

Theobald, Robert A. *The Final Secret of Pearl Harbor.* New York, 1954.

Thomas, Ed "Tommie." *As I Remember.* Sonoita, Arizona, 1990.

Thompson, Robert Smith. *Empires on the Pacific: World War II and the Struggle for the Mastery of Asia.* New York, 2001.

Togo, Shigenori. *The Cause of Japan.* New York, 1956.

Toland, John. *But Not in Shame: The Six Months After Pearl Harbor.* New York, 1961.

———. *The Rising Sun: The Decline and Fall of the Japanese Empire 1936–1945.* New York, 1970.

Tolley, Kemp. *Yangtze Patrol.* Annapolis, 1971.

Tregaskis, Richard. *Guadalcanal Diary.* New York, 1943.

Tuleja, Thaddeus V. *Climax at Midway.* New York, 1960.

Uno, Kazumaro. *Corregidor: Isle of Delusion.* Shanghai, China, 1942.

Vader, John. *New Guinea—The Tide Is Stemmed.* New York, 1971.

Vandegrift, General A. A. *Once a Marine: The Memoirs of General A. A. Vandegrift, U.S. Marines.* New York, 1964.

Wainwright, General Jonathan M. *General Wainwright's Story.* New York, 1945.

Weigley, Russell F. *The American Way of War: A History of United States Military Strategy and Policy.* New York, 1973.

Weinstein, Alfred A. *Barbed-Wire Surgeon.* New York, 1956.

Whitney, Major General Courtney. *MacArthur: His Rendezvous with History.* New York, 1956.

Wigmore, Lionel. *Australia in the War of 1939–1945.* Series One: Army, vol. IV: *The Japanese Thrust.* Adelaide, Australia, 1957.

Wohlstetter, Roberta. *Pearl Harbor: Warning and Decision.* Stanford, California, 1962.

Index ★

www.ingramcontent.com/pod-product-compliance
Lightning Source LLC
Jackson TN
JSHW081323130125
77033JS00014B/420